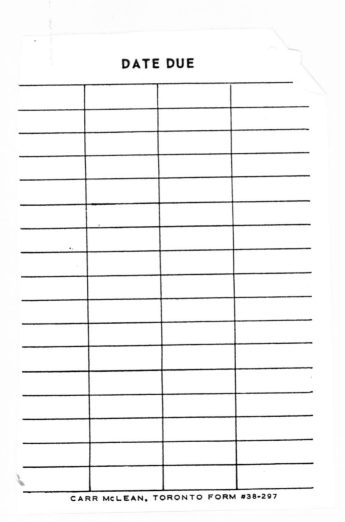

**DATE DUE**

CARR McLEAN, TORONTO FORM #38-297

# OUTSPOKEN

The publisher gratefully acknowledges the generous contribution to this book provided by the General Endowment Fund of the University of California Press Associates.

# OUTSPOKEN
## free speech stories

*160209*

**NAN LEVINSON**

UNIVERSITY OF CALIFORNIA PRESS
*Berkeley · Los Angeles · London*

University of California Press
Berkeley and Los Angeles, California

University of California Press, Ltd.
London, England

Library of Congress Cataloging-in-Publication Data

Levinson, Nan, 1949–
    Outspoken : free speech stories / Nan Levinson.
        p. cm.
Includes bibliographical references and index.
    ISBN 0–520–22370–5 (cloth : alk. paper)
    1. Freedom of speech—United States—History.
2. Censorship—United States—History. I. Title.
    KF4772.L48 2003
    342.73'0853—dc21                    2003000597

Manufactured in the United States of America
11   10   09   08   07   06   05   04   03
10   9   8   7   6   5   4   3   2   1

The paper used in this publication is both acid-free
and totally chlorine-free (TCF). It meets the minimum
requirements of ANSI/NISO Z39.48–1992 (R 1997)
(*Permanence of Paper*). ∞

*In memory of Bertram Levinson, my father*

Congress shall make no law respecting an establishment of religion, or prohibiting the free exercise thereof; or abridging the freedom of speech, or of the press, or the right of the people peaceably to assemble, and to petition the Government for a redress of grievances.

*The First Amendment to the United States Constitution*

# CONTENTS

# AUTHOR'S NOTE

Most of this book was written before September 11, 2001, a day when time seemed to split in two. Then, as uncertainty came to be the measure of our days, pieces of the stories presented here kept pushing their way in to remind me that the tension between freedom and safety has always been part of our national life. "People who believe they are surrounded by enemies will accept strict defensive measures," I had written. "Self-protection is innate, tolerance an acquired taste." But I also wrote, "At a minimum, a society owes its members safety."

Early on, the vice president insisted that we lift our ban on doing intelligence business with known abusers of human rights, a policy that came directly from events in the first story in this book. Another story, which covers the hours after the Oklahoma City bombing, implies that naming our enemies is not always simple. In other chapters, a journalist is accused of encouraging terrorists, and a writer is accused of voicing un-Americanisms, both denunciations that sounded particularly damning in the changed political climate. Then there are those remarkable firefighters who, like the one included here, selflessly assumed the risks of their job.

In contrast, I marveled over the pettiness that swirled around the curriculum of the teacher or the titillation of the performance artist whose stories follow. Such squabbles seem almost embarrassing now, but the fury unleashed against these women stands as a caution about the hazards of fanatical belief anywhere. And for all our hand-wringing about kids and popular culture, it seems clear that violent movies and TV programs hadn't desensitized anyone very much when real horror struck.

After the 9/11 nightmare, when every interpretation felt raw and every response seemed wrong, we found comfort in stories. Speaking plainly of our grief, we clung to tales of bravery, compassion, and grace, confirmation of America at its best. Part of our anxiety still is finding ourselves in the middle of the story we tell about being Americans in the world and not knowing how it will turn out. (One effect of terrorism, and surely one of its intents, is to make its targets doubt what they have trusted in.)

Then reports of other, disturbing, and equally American responses, ranging from the draconian to the silly, began to creep in. The Attorney General scolded Congress that differing with the administration "gives ammunition to America's enemies." A media company issued a list of 150 "questionable" songs to its radio stations with the suggestion that they be avoided. An evangelical leader blamed the catastrophe on gays, feminists, abortionists, and the ACLU—proof, alas, that some things don't change. As the government claimed for itself sweeping new surveillance and prosecutorial powers of dubious constitutionality and with few of the safeguards that had been enacted in response to past abuses, the overarching message became clear: civil liberties, especially free speech, are niceties we can no longer afford.

We lost our innocence, we're told; it's not just our buildings that are more fragile than they seem. But we weren't innocent to begin with, only lucky. More likely, we lost our sense of guilt, which is worrisome because every country needs some of that. As of this writing, the portents of a lockdown state have been worse than the reality for most Americans, but there is a lot about that reality that we don't know, and, as the people in this book learned, not knowing is a danger to those who feel protected, as well as to the targets of the repressive measures.

The stories here might be different if they happened after 9/11, but I doubt their essence would be. They remind us that restrictive laws and policies tend to outlive their purpose. They demonstrate the ability of words to enlighten, bind, comfort, and perhaps even save us, all the things we long for now as a nation. Most important, they are testimony that one of the best reasons to keep our civil liberties intact is that we miss them when they are gone.

*Fall 2002*

# ACKNOWLEDGMENTS

I don't know about raising a child, but it definitely takes a village to write a book. First, I thank the people whose stories appear here for their generosity and their time; my appreciation is surpassed only by my admiration for their smarts, guts, and spirit. Thanks to Barbara Goldoftis for her sagacity and companionship in the writing task; to my keen and helpful readers, Donna Demac, Lanie Zera, Mary Susan DeLaura, and Karen Rosenberg; to my translators, Emilio Vilella, Maria Skufka, Cheryl Smith, and Eduardo Berinstein; and to Jim D'Entremont and Bob Chatelle for their help and their enduring example of commitment to the hard parts of freedom. I thank my excellent editor, Naomi Schneider, who always made me feel that I was in good hands. Thanks also to David Cole, Burt Joseph, Arch Gillies, Linda Backiel, Judy Baca, Dana Moser, the artists at Mobius, Ann Beeson, Declan McCullagh, Philip Mattera, Patricia Goudvis, Paul Cohen, Andrew Graham-Yooll, Philip Spender, and my old pals from *Index on Censorship*. I am grateful to the Andy Warhol Foundation for the Visual Arts, the Fund for Investigative Journalism, the Playboy Foundation, the Somerville Arts Council, and the Puffin Foundation for their support of my work. Finally, I thank my parents, Phyllis Levinson and the late Bertram Levinson, who taught me to speak my mind, and my husband, Alan Lebowitz, who puts up with it. More, I thank him for his wisdom, encouragement, and love, all gifts without measure.

# INTRODUCTION

*A Democracy of Voices*

Americans used to like the First Amendment. Sometimes we added "but" at the end of our declaration of faith, but we had a real soft spot for the idea that speech should be safe from interference by those in power. The first of our rights, freedom of expression, was almost a civil religion, fundamental to how we defined ourselves as a nation and as individuals.

Not any more. Sometime in the mid-1980s, we began to hear angry citizens announce that they would accept this or that outrage no longer; something had to be done, and that something was shutting people up. Throughout the following decade and spilling into the present, we learned of more and more targets: teachers who assigned books with profanity, Web sites that mentioned sex, artists who got grants, movies that provoked, songs that challenged, books that acknowledged ambiguity, anything that encouraged independent thought, and nearly everything on TV. How commonplace it has all become.

The First Amendment used to be the province of lawyers, civics teachers, the ACLU, and the occasional politician in need of a tidy stump speech. Now, a student in my college journalism class declares, "Censorship is cool," which I take to mean that the topic is hot. We do indeed live in a time of talk: rap, memoir, news headlines that read like experimental fiction, conversations that erupt into blame mongering and moral certitude. When this logorrhea spills over into the public arena, we turn ourselves into a nation of buttonholers, all insisting that attention be paid to *our* story, *our* beliefs, *our* gripe. This, we tell ourselves, is democracy: one big call-in show where fervor is a guarantee of truth and having an opinion is practically a civic duty. Through it all, we stalk words, making numerous and noisy claims for their ill effects: dirty ones cause licentiousness, sexy ones cause rape, rabble-rousing ones cause, well, roused rabble.

In this riot of word blame, not all motives are political, nor are all speech disputes played out on the political stage. Other countries kill their dissidents. We frustrate ours into silence, trivializing deeply held convictions and turning their advocates into cranks, or bribing discontent with stardom and spots on talk shows and the covers of glossy magazines. Offending Artist of the Week. Teacher Who Can't Teach That of the Month. All the easier to dismiss their complaints. Still, the bulk of free speech controversies arises from political convictions or political opportunism. Those with political ambitions know well that lewd pictures and loutish talk leave few people dispassionate.

The urge to cover other people's eyes and ears is as ancient and robust as the urge to shock, defy, or annoy, and words and symbols matter deeply to most people, even when language or art is peripheral to their lives. Which ones we get riled up over may vary, as will the manner, intensity, and sophistication of our response. But words cut close to the bone, and the umbrage taken at offending speech may be one of the few things that unites across race, gender, class, and all the other categories we're not supposed to speak disparagingly about.

There are costs to this culture of liberty that we claim for ourselves. At times, putting up with expression that is ugly, crass, wrongheaded, bad manners, bad taste, or just plain dumb is one of them. Some objects of the censor's wrath are meant to be in-your-face challenges: rock 'n' roll is all about rebellion, dissent courts the heterodox, profanity aims to belittle, and pornography is supposed to turn us on. That's their appeal and their usefulness. Defending expression that oversteps some line by asking what all the fuss is about misses the point. The necessary question is what kind of fuss we will have. Will we meet speech that unsettles with the catharsis of response—discussing, debating, debunking, deflating—or will we impose ever more elaborate limits on the speech we don't want to hear?

## GOVERNING THE TONGUE

There are many ways to shut people up: bans on words, images, or discussions; decency campaigns; conditions placed on employment, funding, or publication; control of information media and other restrictions of the marketplace; destruction of books or art; ostracizing of those who don't toe the line; lawsuits; spying; threats; violence; imprisonment. Not every negative response to speech is censorship, however. Censorship is the restricting or suppressing of words, images, or ideas by someone in a position to enforce the ban. It stems from a perception of threat and sets penalties severe enough to make silence worth contemplating. Yet nowhere does the First Amendment say that people cannot be held accountable for their words, so while it is unpleasant to be mocked or made self-conscious because of some utterance, presumably the shamed can reply as effectively as wit, grit, or righteousness allows. In contrast, censorship aims to stop discussion and disagreement by punishing those who have the nerve to answer back to authority or fashion.

The classic censors are the state and the church, which claim censorial powers official or divine. Other censors depend on their ability to dictate the rules, so struggles over what words or symbols will be allowed are almost always about who is in control, even when they appear to be about something else. Their resolution too is a matter of politics more often than justice. As John Stuart Mill tartly observed, about the only reason people don't act more frequently on the natural inclination to impose their beliefs on others is that they lack the power to do so.[1]

The most successful censors, however, are those who have nothing to do because their work is being done for them. Nearly 150 years ago, Frederick Douglass warned, "Find out just what any people will quietly submit to and you have found out the exact measure of injustice and wrong that will be imposed upon them." In many ways, the First Amendment's embrace is more expansive now than ever before, but that easing of legal sanctions has run parallel with mounting social sanctions. The result is that we, as individuals and as a nation, have come to fear language, not just for what it can do, but for how it will be used against us. We have colluded remarkably with those who would muzzle our mouths and our minds and have allowed free expression to be recast as one of many competing rights—civil rights, commercial rights, the right to unruffled feathers—until determining what will and will not be tolerated in its name has become America's defining controversy.

## FIRST RIGHTS

At the legal and rhetorical center of these arguments lies the First Amendment, a forty-five-word addendum to the U.S. Constitution that prohibits the government from either compelling or proscribing any religion, controlling what the press publishes, or restricting individual beliefs or speech, peaceful gatherings, or public protests. As a prerequisite for justice, the right from which others spring and on which others depend, this is an uncommonly broad protection of expression and conscience. It is meant to keep in check the tendency of those in power to try to thwart those who disagree with them.

The First Amendment is a product of the liberal, constitutional state that evolved in the late eighteenth century. Perhaps reflecting ambivalence on the part of its framers, it is a law that says no law should be made and so sets up the paradox of enforced liberty. While its words are stirring, they are also vague, and it was not until after World War I that the courts began to wrestle with the question of just how this guarantee should play out in day-to-day interactions.

First Amendment law developed, as the legal scholar Harry Kalven noted, through a dialogue between the courts and society, and it responded inevitably to the tensions inherent in balancing freedom and order.[2] Because the law has been defined in response to specific cases, our understanding of free speech is haphazard and partial—extensive on government censorship but sparse on commercial speech, for instance. Other significant areas of conflict, such as the regulation of political donations or the speech rights of students, are yet to be resolved.

Historically, the courts have permitted few general exceptions to the rule of free expression: defamation, when presented with careless disregard for truth; "true threats"; "fighting words," defined narrowly since 1969 to include only speech that promotes "imminent lawless action";[3] and obscenity, currently judged by a three-part test known as the Miller Standard.[4] (Though ill-defined, obscenity is a legal category, in contrast to pornography, whose definition is anybody's guess and whose legal status is the subject of continuing controversy.) Despite a fair amount of disagreement over what expression should be safeguarded, the First Amendment has been interpreted quite consistently to mean that the government may not try to control action by controlling speech, that ideas themselves cannot be regulated, and that bad taste, for better or worse, is not a crime. The law covers more than just political speech, also tucking under its mantle artistic expression, satire, and parody, even parody "calculated to injure."[5] Perhaps most important, it has long been a cornerstone of First Amendment law that the state must remain neutral on the content of speech, even when this ends up sheltering what is abhorrent to minority or majority—the latter being the real test, since what is acceptable to most people doesn't need as much protecting.

Yet for all the First Amendment's inclusiveness, the right of free expression remains tenuous and is regularly put to the test. In the late twentieth century, as the Enlightenment optimism that long underpinned our political culture foundered on the rock-hard debate over what constitutes a just society, the First Amendment increasingly came under attack because of the limits of the law itself. It does not guarantee that all voices will be heard equally or at all, or that all ideas will win acceptance, or that protected speech will not clash with other important rights, including the most basic right to be left alone. It is here, where the value of tolerance comes under question, that the First Amendment has been particularly vulnerable to recent challenges. The right charges that it undermines authority, the left that it is a weapon of authority, but the First Amendment is, in fact, antiauthority, and sooner or later it ticks off nearly everyone who pays attention to such things.

## THE GAG REFLEX

Arguments over speech are not all the same—the politics and issues involved matter—but they arrive at the same place. Whatever their political or moral inclinations, people who call for censorship share the conviction that some ideas are so dangerous, subversive, or incendiary that they must not see the light of day. The variety comes in the arguments used to justify this premise. Governments tend to censor in the name of security and religions to quell heresy, while current populist censorship arises primarily from three ways of thinking about speech.

The classic objection to "bad" words is that they are embarrassing or rude. Nice people don't say them, small children shouldn't hear them, and adolescents must be stopped from shouting them loudly and often. The problem is the word itself, not what it conveys, though letting it pass unpunished is often said to "send the wrong message," particularly to kids, who are presumed to be perennially at risk. Advocates of this kind of restraint acknowledge the significance of context. In the I'm-not-in-favor-of-censorship-but tradition, they claim not to want the offending material quashed, only to want it restricted to a more "appropriate" setting. Compromise is often advised: banning a book with vulgarity from the sixth grade but allowing it in the ninth, or moving sexy magazines behind the counter at stores. In a typical instance of this desire to smooth over, when a line of soft drinks with names such as Fukola and Love Potion No. 69 hit convenience stores in Boston, the mayor objected, saying, "I'm embarrassed by this stuff. My concern is that the wrong message is being sent to young people. Yes there's a First Amendment issue here, but this beverage is too readily available to young people."[6]

This objection also applies to timing, as when exceptional circumstances are said to put dissenting views off limits. In the aftermath of the September 11 massacres, when unity of thought seemed a prerequisite for sharing in the national mourning, the White House press secretary responded to a television host's comment that cast aspersions on American military policy by saying, "They're reminders to all Americans that they need to watch what they say, watch what they do, and this is not a time for remarks like that; there never is."[7] People frequently assess their words for appropriateness, but the assessment changes when it is the government telling us to watch our mouths.

A second rationale for limiting expression is a kind of "broken windows" theory of speech. The original theory, which addressed how police maintain order in a community, posited that when a broken window is left unrepaired, people tend to feel freer to break more windows because they assume no one cares.[8] Social disorder is seen as an epidemic, or, as a government official put it when he cited the theory in prepared testimony to Congress, "If we tolerate the small degradations of life, we slowly begin to accept the major erosion of our social values and conditions."[9] When this kind of thinking—that once a threshold is crossed, bad behavior follows—is applied to speech, the conclusion is that offending words and pictures lead not only to more "bad" speech but also to antisocial or dangerous actions. It then becomes necessary to restrict expression to save society from itself.

This idea is popular because it sounds as if it should be true. An influential 1996 poll found that 92 percent of respondents thought TV contributed to violence,[10] and a 2001 survey found 59 percent of fifteen- to twenty-four-year-olds agreeing that "seeing pornography on the Internet encourages young people to have sex before they're ready."[11] In a similar spirit, William Bennett, then of Empower America, and DeLores Tucker, of the National Political Congress of Black Women, called on record companies to stop promoting rap and rock records because, said Bennett at a press conference, the sex- and violence-laden lyrics were "leading society down the wrong road." Amended Tucker, "These companies have the blood of our children on their hands."[12]

Add to this concerns about the sheer mass of stuff coming at us online. The argument over what material should be permitted there purports to be about the material itself, though few words or pictures show up on computer screens that can't be found elsewhere. What is new is the availability of the material, its openness to manipulation, and the head-spinning ease with which we can put messages together and send them out to the world unmediated. The apprehension, bordering on panic, that our new communication technologies engender was captured in the preface to a proposal circulated at a 1997 White House meeting about creating "a Family Friendly Internet." Despite a plethora of filtering software, say the proposal's authors, parents continue to feel insecure "because negligent publishing of data eventually allows material that can harm the child to enter the home. Once this material is experienced by the child, its damage is done. There is no 'oops' factor, no way to undo the unwanted intrusion into a child's innocence."[13] Censorship "reflects a society's lack of confidence in itself," Supreme Court Justice Potter Stewart wrote;[14] it apparently reflects a lack of confidence in our technology too.

The Internet would seem a form of pure speech, but the line between speech and action in many realms is far from definitive. The courts have protected acts such as flag and cross burning as expressive speech but have also upheld some bans on sexual expression in the workplace as redress against sexual harassment. The third framework for reining in expression dispenses with this problematic distinction by claiming that speech *is* action. By this belief, we become what we see and hear: the word turned into offending flesh and impossible to ignore. Though, like Herman Melville's Bartleby, we'd prefer not to—see it, hear it, read it—in this way of thinking, the obvious solution of turning away from an image that bothers us doesn't work because we are stained by its very existence. The only possible solution is to wipe it out.

This idea has been elaborated primarily by antipornography feminists, who have charged that sex talk is aggression and erotic images are rape. Since the government can punish those actions, they contend, it should also be allowed to regulate those kinds of expression. As Catharine MacKinnon, a leader of this movement, wrote in a statement typical of her argument against sexual speech, "Only words, but because they are sex, the speaker as well as the spoken-about is transformed into sex. This is a dynamic common to sexual harassment and pornography."[15]

These feminists have been joined in their word denouncing by a group of legal scholars known as critical race theorists, who argue that racially hostile speech is a form of discrimination and is therefore qualitatively different from other expression. Prominent among these theorists is Mari Matsuda, who maintained that "racist speech is best treated as a sui generis category, presenting an idea so historically untenable, so dangerous, and so tied to perpetuation of violence and degradation of the very classes of human beings who are least equipped to respond that it is properly treated as outside the realm of protected discourse."[16] For both these schools of thought, the inequality and psychic harm they believe stem from expression are greater evils than censorship. This leads them to advocate censorship when it comes to a face-off with other harms, as, by their definitions, it inevitably will.

## OUTRAGE DU JOUR

In the modern-day morality tales we tell ourselves about how we talk, we fall back on two favorite metaphors: war and shopping. The language of censorship has long been that of battle and fighting faiths. In the 1990s, everything from what we listened to on our Walkmans to how we zoned our cities got slugged out in a "culture war," with victors, victims, body counts, and a siege mentality that brooked no ambiguity and dismissed free speech as a peacetime luxury.

Equally popular is the "marketplace of ideas," that vaunted supermarket of the mind, in which concepts and beliefs compete for buyers.[17] The best will triumph, we are assured, never mind that the market is hardly a guarantor of quality in other realms. The utility of the metaphor is that we are accustomed to market discrimination in content as well as quality. We can try to fill a gap or protest an imbalance or send a letter to the editor, but, at base, we accept that money buys visibility for ideas as well as for things. One idea that has sold particularly well is that everything has its price, so that we now find it difficult to imagine a thinker who can't be bought or an idea that exists for a reason other than to make us want things. This explains in part why depiction is often mistaken for advocacy and denounced as such.

When this confusion of word and deed, information and factoid, meaning and marketing, bumps into the question of what expression will be permitted, we are expected to choose sides quickly (controversies over speech are seldom presented as having more than two sides), but often the sides can't even agree on what language to use in discussing the dispute. Many fights over language contain a good dose of disingenuousness, and censors habitually dress up what they're doing in Sunday go-to-meetin' clothes, and so words redefined become thought reconstructed and politics realigned.

The past two decades have seen moralists of all political stripes vying to cut out competing views, as if free speech were a finite quantity that one group can have only when it is denied another. The moralist right has gotten the most press in the censorship game, in part because it is better organized than the moralist left, which tends toward guerrilla censorship. (In one of the odd twists that typify First Amendment arguments, its advocates are assumed to be on the left, as if the Bill of Rights were Marxist doctrine.) Expression that incurs the wrath of the right most often involves dirty words, challenges to religious faith, divergence from conventional relationships (i.e., homosexuality and feminism), and sex. For the left, it is racism, "hate speech" (running the gamut from tasteless jokes to blazing crosses), and sex. It is because everyone is in a snit over sex that we get such unlikely alliances as in the antiporn wars, where one group of feminists cozies up to the religious right and another locks arms with *Playboy* and *Penthouse*.

At the extremes, both right and left, tolerance has come to be seen as liberal whitewash and compromise as capitulation to evil. Even at the center, debate is regularly vilified as an attack on unassailable principles, opponents who aren't wrong enough must be demonized, and unregulated speech is used as a bargaining chip in cultural upheaval. How these tensions played themselves out through word-blame is the story of the past two decades.

## SECRETS, CUNNING, SILENCE

Censorship has two main thrusts: efforts to keep people from saying things deemed dangerous or disturbing, and efforts to keep information secret. The philosopher Sissela Bok has written that secrecy inevitably leads to greater concealment than was originally planned. Censorship, secrecy's sister, also tends toward excess, as we have seen in such repressive measures as the Alien and Sedition Acts of 1798, the Comstock Laws of 1873 and beyond, the sedition trials of World War I, the internment of Japanese Americans during World War II, and the McCarthy witch-hunt of the 1950s. These policies were instituted in response to extreme circumstances, but we came to regret them all long before we managed to get rid of them. As legal theorist Thomas Emerson pointed out, there is consistency in how expression was restricted during these and other dark times: a tendency to overestimate the need for censorship; a penchant for pushing regulation to extremes; overzealousness on the part of enforcers; restrictions that are vague, unenforceable, and easily abused; and minimal social gains paired with heavy social losses.[18]

Throughout our history, our government has fluctuated between se-

crecy and openness. A round of transparency was ushered in with a patriotic flourish on the Fourth of July in 1966, when the Freedom of Information Act (FOIA) became law. It was followed ten years later by the
Sunshine Act, meant to make information about federal decision making more readily available. Together, these laws codified a presumption
toward openness, which prevailed, more or less, until the advent of the
Reagan administration in 1980.

Then, a series of executive orders made the FOIA harder to use, government policies restricted the dissemination and sharing of research,
and spending cuts truncated the government's collection, publication,
and distribution of information. The government justified its strangle-
hold on information by way of a concept known as an "information mosaic," a theory positing that bits of apparently benign information have
the potential to be pieced together into a harmful whole and therefore
need to be restricted. A favorite example of the peril inherent in an information mosaic was an article published in the *Progressive* in 1979
that gave the recipe for a hydrogen bomb, based on data culled from various unclassified journals.

Control of the flow of information became the order of the day, a pro-
clivity apparent in military-media relations. Since the end of the Vietnam
War, the military had been planning how to control journalists in
wartime, and when the United States invaded Grenada in 1983, the press
was not allowed to accompany invading forces. The media squawked,
prompting the Pentagon to allow a limited number of journalists to tour
part of the island under escort and the Defense Department to appoint a
panel to study the issue. One of the panel's recommendations was the
formation of temporary press pools, in which a small group of journalists accompanied by military officials would be allowed near the front to
report back to other journalists. This too proved problematic; when the
United States invaded Panama in 1989, the press pool didn't even leave
Washington until near the time the invasion began, and reporters who
followed were confined to a military base.

The Defense Department again reassessed its relationship with the
press and again proposed new rules, which were instituted for the 1991
Gulf War. Then, a limited number of reporters were herded into press
pools and mostly kept away from the fighting, while the rest of the large
press corps cooling its heels in Saudi Arabia reported out of daily military briefings so uninformative that they became fodder for TV parodies.
The military determined which reporters were permitted to visit which
units and, to a degree, what soldiers were permitted to tell them. It also

reviewed stories, delayed those it disliked, and made it difficult for reporters who asked tough questions to schedule interviews with senior officers.[19] The military has good reasons for secrecy in wartime, and journalists for honoring military discretion, but not all secrets are kept for strategic purposes. In both Panama and the Persian Gulf, one effect of restricting reporters was to cloud forever the question of how many people died there.

During the Reagan era, the fondness for concealment quickly leaked beyond national defense considerations to include spying, gag orders, and other pressures on scholars, teachers, artists, journalists, doctors, and researchers to control what they said and wrote in exchange for employment, funding, or dissemination of their work. The limiting of expression was not confined to the scribbling classes. Federal government workers—three hundred thousand of them—were required to sign lifelong secrecy pledges; the FBI instructed librarians to keep tabs on the reading habits of people who looked as if they were from countries the government didn't like;[20] the Federal Communications Commission expanded its restrictions on "indecent" programming; the president pocket-vetoed legislation meant to protect whistleblowers; and the Department of Health and Human Services barred organizations receiving federal dollars from mentioning abortion to their clients, a principle of control that would eventually be applied as far afield as funding for artists.

Governments everywhere keep secrets and dislike protest, and reformers' zeal has been a part of America longer than there have been laws to protect us from it. It shows up regularly as patriotism, prudery, sex panics, and a deep suspicion of intellectual activity and artistic endeavors. (In 1842, when a group called the American Art Union was charged with promoting bad art, it responded huffily, "No one fears mediocrity in religion or learning, why should we fear it in Art?") But a particularly destructive and far-reaching consequence of these policies was to recast history so that questioning and dissent came to be seen as un-American.

## EXTREMELY MORAL

It was in this climate that the religious right came to prominence. Conservative politicians and fundamentalist religious leaders had been working since the 1960s to organize groups with names using the same unimpeachable words—American, family, morality, freedom—in varying order. (Liberal anticensorship groups later named themselves similarly, making it hard to tell the players even with a scorecard.) Declaring themselves newly awakened to the evil that words do, these groups promoted political and social policies based on their version of virtue as a kind of penal code for pleasure. Though not monolithic, the organizations constituting this moralist right have much in common. Nearly all describe themselves as "profamily" and dedicated to upholding "Judeo-Christian" or "traditional" values. These they define to include the Father Knows Best family, church, and country (which appears to include corporate interests). Closely related is the protection of children, who are always described as "innocent," though it's unclear of what. Originally, these groups argued that whatever challenged their values was immoral; later, they drew on social science and, ironically, radical feminist theory, to call such divergences harmful.

For a while, the purity police on the right concentrated their attacks on public education, independent women, and commercial culture (movies, TV, pop music, video games), but in time, their condemnation spilled over, as these things do, to include "high culture." They were not alone in their uneasiness. Culture doesn't come by fiat and is usually agreed on only once it is entrenched, which creates its own paradox, since received opinion tends to ossify. In many ways, then, a vibrant culture is one that is ever at odds with itself. In our modern world, it is also frequently a seductive culture, since, like it or not, transgression entices, sex and violence sell, and the border between the sanctioned and the taboo is porous at best. In fact, what is condoned often relies on what is not to define and reinforce it, so we tolerate some language and images that flout conventional morality because we've agreed that their context—fashion magazine, poetry reading, one's living room—removes them from the fray or because, at some level, we accept that it is the nature of desire to want what is off limits.

This tension between stability and change is particularly apparent in popular culture, with its appetite for novelty (which it then repeats ad nauseam), and in contemporary art, with its penchant for undercutting expectations and manipulating the familiar to make it seem strange. (When Robert Mapplethorpe photographed himself with a bullwhip, it's a good bet he wasn't trying to make a nice little picture to hang over the sofa.) Art, when it succeeds, touches a nerve, inviting its audience to look or listen in a way different from ordinary attention. Sometimes, as Robert Frost said of poetry, art begins in delight and ends in wisdom. But when it begins with an image or idea we prefer to avoid, being called to engage with it can be troubling, and we may end up feeling that it is less the art than the audience—ourselves—that is being manipulated.

Anything is possible when you're making it up, so the imagination is an appealing target for those who prefer clear boundaries. At the end of the 1980s, the National Endowment for the Arts (NEA), as the federal representative of the imagination, became the bull's-eye. Though the attacks on the NEA were characterized as a taxpayers' revolt, in the realm of unintended consequences, the subsequent efforts to limit what artists were allowed to create or display focused more attention on art than all the grants and good intentions of the preceding thirty years. The language these right-wing groups used was that of moral certainty, conversion experiences, martyrdom, and apocalypse, but their strategies mirrored those of successful political operations. When they embarked on what they portrayed as a holy war against those who would trample the sensibilities of the American public, they adopted the tactics of the anticommunists of the 1950s,[21] then added a few of their own.

A favorite was to take words and images out of context and interpret them as literally and humorlessly as possible so that they sounded really stupid. A related trick was to condemn material sight unseen, then parade the juicy parts before a claque of tongue clickers. Both strategies were particularly effective with words that had acquired a luster of taboo through repeated attacks. Sex words were an obvious target, but others got coyly reduced to a letter, such as "the N word"—as if euphemism snuffed out racism. The purpose of these ploys—presenting opinion as fact, misconstruing cause and effect, lying—was to scare people. Other techniques included framing issues divisively to pit groups or goals against each other—gays against blacks, AIDS research against cancer research—in a kind of misery sweepstakes that made compromise an insult. Perhaps most effective was the stratagem of surprising opponents. Again and again, the objects of morality campaigns didn't see them coming and by the time they were ready to defend themselves, the terms of the debate had been set, seldom to rise above the level of did-not, did-too.

As these quarrels became routine, discussion of the art or the offense it gave rarely moved beyond bluster and ridicule. In an early exchange that presaged arguments to come, a police chief in Providence, Rhode Island, who had yet to see the art exhibit he was condemning, announced to the press that the artists and organizers "think they can do whatever they want to, and I don't agree. If it's obscene, it's obscene. There's no two ways about it."[22] To which an art reviewer replied with equal predictability, "It's about as erotic as a ham sandwich (without mayo) and only slightly pornographic around the edges."[23]

The strategies of censorship have worked, sometimes directly, as when challenges to educational and creative material mounted through the mid-1990s.[24] Other times, the chipping away at protected speech is subtler. In a 2002 survey by the First Amendment Center, 49 percent of those asked if the First Amendment "goes too far in the rights it guarantees" agreed.[25]

## THE SPEECH WE HATE

Inevitably, this emphasis on measuring our words generated a backlash, which took its most vehement form in controversies over the regulation of language labeled "hate speech," "verbal harassment," "assaultive speech," or "discursive violence"—terms more loaded than enlightening. In the late 1980s and early 1990s, cities, states, and universities responded to a spate of nasty confrontations by creating speech codes that set punishment for insult, cloddishness, and belligerence aimed at a notably thorough list of targets. A 1988 policy at the University of Michigan, one of the first, was typical in outlawing any act, "verbal or physical, that stigmatizes or victimizes an individual on the basis of race, ethnicity, religion, sex, sexual orientation, creed, national origin, ancestry, age, marital status, handicap or Vietnam-era veteran status." (Presumably, it was okay to offend the few people who didn't make the list.) A year later, two-thirds of the colleges and universities contacted by the Carnegie Foundation for the Advancement of Teaching had speech codes, and another 11 percent were developing them. Speech codes were ruled unconstitutional all the way up to the Supreme Court, which, in 1992, struck down a citywide hate crime law outlawing certain expressive conduct,[26] but such codes remain on the books at many private universities. Unenforceable though speech codes have proved to be, they trained the spotlight on the controversies surrounding them, in part because they brought questions about free expression into the realms of opinion makers, such as classrooms and newsrooms, and in part because they pulled the political left into the fray.

Antibias speech codes arise from a mixed bag of impulses. Some are classic censorship, such as the desire to clean up the world or irritation because opponents think the principle of free speech applies to them too. Other arguments are newer: that speech is a form of action, that racial slurs are discrimination, that the government is justified in regulating speech to promote communal values, or that a community must make it clear that it will not tolerate such treatment of its members. These contentions arise from the belief that desirable behavior can be legislated and appeal to the hope that by making something unsayable, it will eventually become unthinkable. And so, censors from the left joined the tradition of Americans who treasure the First Amendment—until it becomes difficult, as, bless its little heart, it always eventually does.

These efforts to banish the discouraging word took place as the academy itself was changing. It is stylish to contrast today's academic institutions with some mythical enclave of the past, where overarching civility and shared common purpose made explicit proscriptions unnecessary. There was no orthodoxy then, we imply, because we automatically knew what was right and did it. We were all endlessly tolerant of each other, and everyone understood what we meant, even when what we said was foolish or unfeeling. Americans grow nostalgic for that kind of empathic community (its corporeal form is a pretty little New England town with leafy trees and no parking problems), but they forget how limiting such a place can be.

While the academic harmony of yore may be a fantasy, the essential homogeneity of university campuses was very real. In 1960, 94 percent of American college students were white, and 63 percent were male, as were almost 80 percent of faculty.[27] By the late 1990s, 27 percent of students were classified as "minority," and 56 percent of students[28] and 36 percent of faculty were female (faculty remained overwhelmingly white, at 92 percent).[29] If hate speech is one response to those who are different, it's not surprising that it appeared less prominent before. When everyone is alike, tolerance (or intolerance) is easy.

As campuses diversified, everything came up for grabs—what knowledge is, who possesses it, how it is acquired or passed on. When this reassessment turned its attention to hate speech, civil liberties were pitted against civil rights, and the primacy of the First Amendment was attacked in the name of equality, safety, dignity, and empowerment. In academic circles, the means of dealing with upheaval is talk and lots of it. As censorship showed itself to be an equal opportunity employer, traditional allies turned into enemies, who exhibited all the bitterness of lovers scorned. By this time, the liberal antidotes to antisocial behavior—education, affirmative action, democratic participation—were falling out of favor politically and intellectually. Taking up arms against a perceived evil, be it drugs, poor women, terrorists, or hateful ideas, was in. Still, the distance between criticizing speech and criminalizing it is great, and it is this gulf that made the hate speech issue so unsettling to contemplate.

Why, for instance, the eagerness to believe that threat is everywhere, particularly on the part of people whose lives are not routinely threatened? It is a question Daphne Patai, a professor at the University of Massachusetts at Amherst, raised as she examined the apparent willingness of her colleagues and students to let their speech be curtailed by a typically gung-ho speech code proposed in 1995. Patai writes, "On one of the stalls in the bathroom right outside the classroom in which I was teaching, I read that one out of every two women will be raped in her lifetime. The young women in my course do not seem to question such statistics, and are willing to give away much in exchange for the security they feel they lack."[30] Statistics on rape are notoriously inaccurate, but even so, the sense of danger here is out of proportion. Yet these young people of relative privilege did feel threatened, confident only of their fragility and of the perils of speech.

The stories in this book cover years in which the U.S. economy sagged, soared remarkably, then soured again, and, not surprisingly, our national optimism followed a similar trajectory. In the boom years, our word anxiety abated somewhat and turned its focus inward, so that at the turn of the century, the bulk of our free speech arguments concerned technology, privacy, public protest, and those perennials, sexual imagery and children—or better yet, sexual imagery in combination with children. Then, in the heavy-hearted days after September 11, when our real vulnerability seemed to provide good reason to rein in speech, attention switched to governmental controls, bringing us back to where this cycle began.

## TOO BAD FOR WORDS

Oscar Wilde claimed that whenever people talked about the weather, he felt sure they were really talking about something else. I share that suspicion when it comes to censorship and suspect too that we fight over words and pictures because it is easier to make rules than to make changes. It is also safer, which is why speech battles are usually about problems and resentments we don't know how, or are afraid, to talk about.

Though a good portion of recent attempts to censor have been stopped by the courts, community pressure, or good sense, these fights leave a bad taste in everyone's mouth, and treating lawsuits as a kind of twelve-step recovery program is not a particularly good use of anyone's resources. Moreover, to understand or account for something is not to render it harmless. Measures to control speech confuse a policing action with a political one, and it is not a giant step from policing words to policing people. "Chilling effects" and "slippery slopes," those icy threats brandished in the face of bad laws and policies, are cause for genuine concern, as we are reminded whenever we stop our bickering long enough to listen for those voices that have been stifled in countries around the globe and throughout history.

Many would-be censors are cynics, fanatics, or spoilsports, but those bent on doing good can present as great a threat to free speech and thought. Blaming words is a way to whittle stubborn social dilemmas down to a manageable size. It lets us feel as if we're doing something, even if that something is investing symbols with the power to make the improvements that we can't. And feeling right and righteous among the like-minded is comforting and exciting, as anyone who has ever advocated a cause knows. So for all their virulence, there is something poignant in campaigns to control TV programs because we can't control our kids' behavior, in attempts to remove books from libraries because we can't make sex less powerful in life, in bans on ethnic slurs because we haven't resolved the question that plagues us from our first foray onto the playground of what to do when someone says something rotten to us and it hurts.

Even for those who don't take up morality as a hobby, what we are asked to stomach in the name of free speech can seem like too much: a culture that assaults the senses and talk that is so cheap it might as well be free because no one in his right mind would pay for it. The temptation to squash vexing speech comes in the specific instance too. When someone says something that upsets us, making him or her stop offers more immediate and tangible satisfaction than the idea of free speech. Self-protection is innate, tolerance an acquired taste.

Then too, words have weight and consequences. If we didn't believe that, why all the fuss over what we can and can't say? Separate from any action it may bring about, language contributes to an atmosphere, and contrary to the children's rhyme, names can hurt or scare or disgust us. We may know that words and pictures are representations, not the thing itself, know that tolerating a message is not the same as agreeing with it, know too that should we come across something unbidden and unappealing on TV or a computer, we can turn it off or turn away. And still, words haunt. Underlying the intolerance of words is the fear, justified or manufactured, that our society is coming apart at the seams. Speech codes, cyberfilters, stamp-out-smut drives, curriculum restrictions, and other attempts to hobble expression are a direct response to that fear, as if all our talk about talk will keep the lid on an explosive situation.

## WHY FIGHT IT?

I confess to a little envy here. Being able to speak without official sanction has always seemed such a basic and glorious need to me that I would like to be as certain as the speech blamers appear to be, but what I am, more often, is baffled. For instance, it seems clear that mean, ugly epithets are a form of racism that interferes with people's freedom. But humankind has spent millennia figuring out ways to discriminate against some of its members, and most of those ways undermine much more effectively than invective. So while I don't know how to end racism, I suspect that it won't be by rewriting the dictionary.

Or this: I can make a long list of things I really don't want to see or hear, but I still don't understand how anyone can believe that getting rid of pornography or off-color jokes will improve her life in any significant way. (On the other hand, equal pay for women, adequate health care, and universal literacy, to name just three concrete goals, would get us much closer to the feminist aims of fairness and groceries, and if we put the same effort into achieving these as we have into arguing over pictures, they might just come to pass.) Still, a lot of people do believe passionately that antiporn campaigns will help them, so I'm left to figure that they believe it because they want to. It is a leap of faith, then, which is why I've come to understand that repeating arguments against censorship will not eradicate it any more than censorship will eradicate the evils it is said to fight.

Yet arguments for free speech must be made. Otherwise, it all comes down to who hollers loudest. Free speech gets defended on two fronts: for the principle and for the expression itself. When I can't bring myself to do the latter, I take refuge in the former; hence, my arguments with censorship are both philosophical and practical.

First, being able to speak our minds makes us feel good. True, we tailor our words to civility, persuasion, kindness, or other purposes, but that is our choice. Censors claim the right to purge other people's talk—all the while insisting that it is for our own good.

Second, much censorship appears irrational and alarmist in retrospect because the reasons people choose and use words are vastly more interesting than the systems designed to limit them. It's not hard to make a list of absurdities—I'm particularly fond of a rash of state laws that forbid the disparagement of agricultural products—but simplistic explanations and simple-minded responses are as dangerous as they are ditzy. In one of the few places that postmodern theory and common sense intersect, it is obvious that the meaning and perception of words regularly depend on such variables as speaker and spoken to, individual experience and shared history, and the setting, company, and spirit in which something is said. To give courts or other authorities the power to determine all this is, to put it mildly, mind-boggling.

Third, censorship is inimical to democracy. Cloaking ideas and information in secrecy encourages ignorance, corruption, demagoguery, a corrosive distrust of authority, and a historical memory resembling Swiss cheese. Open discussion, on the other hand, allows verities to be examined, errors to be corrected, disagreement to be expressed, and anxieties to be put in perspective. It also forces communities to confront their problems directly, which is more likely to lead to real solutions than covering them up.

Fourth, censorship backfires. Opinions, tastes, social values, and mores change over time and vary among people. Truth can be a protean thing. The earth's rotation, its shape, the origins of humankind, and the nature of matter were all once widely understood to be something different from what we know today, yet those who challenged the prevailing faith were mocked and punished for their apostasy. Banning ideas in an attempt to make the world safe from doubt, disaffection, or disorder is limiting, especially for people whose lives are routinely limited, since the poor and politically weak are the censor's first targets.

Finally, censorship doesn't work. It doesn't get rid of bad ideas or bad behavior. It usually doesn't even get rid of bad words,[31] and history has shown repeatedly that banning the unpalatable merely drives it underground. It could be argued that that's just fine, that vitriolic or subversive speech, for example, shouldn't dare to speak its name. But hateful ideas by another name—disguised as disinterested intellectual inquiry, or given a nose job like Ku Klux Klansman David Duke before he ran for governor of Louisiana—are probably more insidious than those that are clearly marginal.

The problem is that it is just not practically possible to outlaw only the bad words and leave the good ones unscathed. We may be able to make a list of words or phrases that could be dropped from the language with no significant loss of expressiveness or communication. Profanity, epithets, and adolescent nasties don't contribute much to debate, the pursuit of truth, self-knowledge, or the practice of democracy, the things the framers of the Constitution appeared to have in mind when they sought to safeguard expression. But banned words get replaced by equally offensive ones with a speed that makes our heads whirl. People who want to affront and wound will find a way to do so, no matter how they are constrained, and people who offend inadvertently (probably all of us at one time or another) can be corrected in other, less drastic and more constructive ways.

The alternative to spelling out what is not allowed is to fashion a vague statement of intent and then determine what speech is forbidden on a case-by-case basis. But, with the possible exception of an antinudity ordinance in Florida that took 346 words to define *buttocks,* these statements are inevitably too narrow or too broad. More important, the decisions will always be made by people in positions of control, and those who hope sanitized speech will bring about greater justice are well advised not to trust the powerful to help them out. History is fickle, and nowhere does power give itself up willingly.

There may be much the founding fathers didn't anticipate about America two centuries later, but they were prescient and self-interested enough to craft the First Amendment, which is still admirable for its elegant simplicity, for its defiance of pettiness, and for what it tries to do. What the First Amendment tries to do is support the shut up, the shoved aside, the left out, and the picked on. An anomaly in the mythology of our American selves, it allows us, on occasion, to win arguments with words and expressiveness instead of bank accounts and bullets. It doesn't set up an official truth, but it offers our best hope for getting to some public truth over time. The First Amendment is integral to forging the common awareness that is key to the functioning of democracy, and it suggests a way to bridge the growing gap between the autonomy we cherish and the community we need if we're to live in any sort of harmony. (It certainly illuminates that gap like a sound and light show over the Grand Canyon.) Finally, in its own roundabout way, the First Amendment gives muscle to the idea that what is best about America needs not just praise but also protection, and scrutiny, and honest appraisal.

A character in a story by Grace Paley rails against dumbness, which she defines as "silence and stupidity." "By silence," Paley writes, "she meant the refusal to speak; by stupidity she meant the refusal to hear."[32] The First Amendment may be a whistle in the dark of dumbness, but it is where we begin.

## ABOUT THIS BOOK

As a principle and an aspiration, free expression is fundamental to a society that treats its members decently, but censorship is ultimately a transaction between people. When I reviewed a book several years ago, I found myself lamenting the shortage of stories about the people who had fought the free speech battles reported there. "Imagine the wonderful array of reasons!" I wrote, and then I began to imagine and to recall the stories I had heard, stories that added the human struggle to the theoretical one.

So I began to talk with people who had refused to let someone whittle away at their right to speak, think, create, or demur as they pleased. For this book, I chose the stories of twenty people, hoping they would be both emblematic and individually revealing. They tell of conflicts that were alarming, confusing, mean, or just plain silly, of fights that were never as straightforward as they seemed, of arguments in which many sides had a point and no one had a particularly good solution. While several of the controversies resulted in legal challenges, others make it clear that contemporary disputes over acceptable expression are broader than just what the law allows.

I approached these people wanting to know what they had learned and lost, what it felt like to be at the center of such a controversy, and why their words mattered enough to fight over. I wanted to find out at what point principles trump self-preservation and what happens when people stop being afraid. (When your politics and your self-interest coincide, a friend advised, it's a good idea to look at your politics. To which I might add, beware the man who is convinced he's right.)

The result is a series of portraits told primarily from the subject's perspective, though I sought to verify facts and acknowledge differences of opinion when significant. Taken together, the stories also form a larger picture of the United States and its laws, politics, and culture at a particular moment. I make no claim to speak for other countries, though I think the desire to express oneself unimpeded is widely shared. I'm leery of making sweeping declarations for this country too, since, if nothing else, these accounts illustrate how various Americans are in their thought and expression. I began this book with the working title "A Democracy of Voices" because I liked the way the phrase sounded, but that turned out to be exactly what I found. The voices don't always agree, among themselves or with me, which is as it should be. Democracy is messy, and these stories are meant to make room for the necessary contradictions.

In my talks with these people, I asked if they regretted the roles they had played, and over and over, the answer came back, no. Despite bureaucratic callousness, despite the expense (neither free speech nor censorship comes cheap), despite repercussions ranging from lost jobs to jail time to disrupted families and friendships, each person found relief, joy even, in fighting what felt like the right fight. At the risk of grandiosity, I would claim that they were fighting for democracy, not just in form, but also in practice, making their tales part of our long national conversation about what we mean when we talk about free speech.

part one

# THE POWERS THAT BE

INFORMATION, WE'RE REMINDED FREQUENTLY, is power, so who has it and what it is used for are critical questions for a government and its citizens. In the United States, the pendulum has swung back and forth between secrecy and openness as a governmental predisposition, but beginning in the 1980s, concealment became the norm. Then in the name of national security—always a favorite on the censorship menu—information of all kinds was locked up, and all kinds of people were caught up in what became a comfortable habit of suppression. Governments frequently keep secrets and resist dissent, and openness is not a guarantee against misuse of power. Official misbehavior is more complex than that. But by weakening accountability and allowing individuals to avoid confronting the consequences of their actions, secrecy and censorship become handmaidens to corruption.

What follows are the stories of five Americans whom the government sought to silence or punish for their words and thoughts. Rick Nuccio, a diplomat, fell out with his bosses over the morality of disclosing secret information about government misconduct in Guatemala. Daisy Sánchez, a Puerto Rican journalist, also differed with the government about what to reveal, but here she was the secret keeper, refusing to compromise her professional independence by discussing her sources with the FBI.

For Kwame Mensah, a young Marine reservist, doing his job meant going against how he had come to define himself, so when he was called up during the Gulf War, he went to prison rather than fight what he saw as an unjust war. Questions of what it is to be American also plagued writer Margaret Randall, who was caught in a complicated immigration battle and threatened with exile when the government decided that what she had written made her a danger to the country.

Sometimes the government tries to squash ideas not so much because it finds them menacing as because it finds them politically inconvenient. That is what Susanna Styron came up against when her documentary film was denied a government benefit because the agency in charge disagreed with the film's perspective.

These are quintessential yes-but cases, and the people at the heart of them were not naifs. They did complex work, lived in a world of acts and consequences, and understood that words have power. Still, when they were told that their words and work endangered their fellow citizens, they didn't buy it, and they were unready for the government's heavy-handed response. All, save Susanna Styron, entered the fray reluctantly and then only when it became clear that they had to defend themselves. Quickly, though, the thrust and parry of that defense took over their lives.

Trying to regain their footing as they became "news," some sought publicity to tell their version of events or to protect themselves from re-taliation. Others enlisted influential supporters and organized defense groups. Everyone learned the limitations of journalism by sound bite and the influence of the press in framing and conducting public discussions. Journalists were largely sympathetic, if not necessarily accurate. (Only some people can count on the privilege of being able to speak for them-selves.) It is probably no coincidence that the exceptions to the press's support—Kwame Mensah and the other soldiers who applied for con-scientious objector status and were ignored or portrayed as cowards and ingrates—were punished most harshly.

In most of the controversies presented here, the government justified its efforts to control speech as a security need. To anyone who follows censorship battles, the conviction that some things are too perilous for the uninitiated to know has a familiar ring: books on the *Index Libro-rum Prohibitorum* were limited to church leaders and a few sanctioned scholars, pornography was limited to Victorian gentlemen, and govern-ment secrets are limited to those with security clearances and the "need to know."

Secrecy is seductive, bringing with it a sense of power, real or imag-ined. It feeds on itself and spirals out of control, especially when it is used to hide mistakes. The result is the political crime of our era: the cover-up. By the time the cover is blown, as it inevitably is, those involved have become so invested in keeping the secret that they are unable to recog-nize where the danger came from in the first place.

For all that, at a minimum, a society owes its members safety, so some of the hardest free expression questions arise from the classic American tension between security and autonomy. Does that mean that some words or images or ideas are dangerous enough that they should be re-stricted? It is a dilemma I struggle with, so I wasn't surprised when al-most everyone here stumbled in answering. In 1977, a group of Amer-ican Nazis planned a march in Skokie, Illinois, home to some three thousand Holocaust survivors. When the local government deemed the demonstration too incendiary and blocked it, the ACLU went to court and succeeded in getting the ban overturned. We all have our Skokie, it seems, the idea that stirs a basic terror, the word that chokes in our throat. What did surprise me was that even these people who had been attacked for what they said or believed weren't sure of their authority to answer, as if acknowledging psychologist Alfred Adler's observation that it's easier to fight for one's principles than to live up to them.

Democracy is messy and noisy and not particularly nice, despite our romance with the lines of people who walk for days from remote villages to vote in some other country's election. We don't vote, or at least half of us don't, and democracy eventually disappoints even its most ardent fans. Still we pride ourselves on being the country that did what couldn't be done and says what shouldn't be said. Entangled in this contradiction, the five people whose stories appear here found themselves in the perplexing position of defending core American principles while apparently offending official American doctrine, and they were punished as much for their good old American antiauthoritarian impulses as for their speech.

Political conflicts—which is what everyone here faced, rhetoric about national security to the contrary—are resolved by force, compromise, or law. Liberal democracy is defined by its preference for the rule of law and by its protections against arbitrary accusation—though its practitioners are not above bullying on occasion. (Capricious authority can't be appeased for long because its goal is not a solution or reconciliation but power, and power perpetuates itself by being implacable.) For those whom the system is set up to benefit, justice tends to prevail, which is part of why governmental censorship seems like a particular affront to people who expect to be safe, at least in their words and ideas. When Rick, Kwame, Margaret, Daisy, and Susanna faced the powers that be, they sought not only justice but also fairness. Calling on principles of free expression, they landed directly in the middle of the First Amendment's central paradox: trust in the rule of law but not in the rule of government.

# I PLEDGE ALLEGIANCE

Rick Nuccio

*Cambridge, Massachusetts, Summer 1998*

As Rick Nuccio, a special advisor to the Clinton administration for Central America, finished a meeting with his boss at the State Department in October 1994, he decided to bring up what was on his mind. *60 Minutes* was preparing a segment about Jennifer Harbury, a North American lawyer campaigning to find out what had happened to her husband, the Guatemalan insurgent leader Efrain Bámaca Velásquez, who went by the nom de guerre of Commandante Everardo. She was deep into her second hunger strike in Guatemala City, and questions were inevitable. As the U.S. representative at the Guatemalan peace talks, Rick had been front man on the case, but now he urged his boss, Alex Watson, to prepare to respond himself. A memo compiling all the information the State Department had on Bámaca would be a good idea, Rick suggested, adding that he didn't expect it to be more than a page.

Two days later, the desk officer for Guatemala showed Rick a memo, dated May 1993, in which the CIA in Guatemala reported corroboration of a story about Bámaca being held at a clandestine Guatemalan military prison. The original story, Rick knew, came from a Guatemalan guerrilla who had been captured and held at the prison before escaping to Mexico. He had testified to the United Nations in March 1993 that he had seen Bámaca being tortured the previous July, but U.S. officials had dismissed his story,[1] and Rick too had found it "rather improbable." Now, here was a U.S. government report indicating that it was true and that the CIA had known Bámaca's fate at the very time that Rick and others in the State Department were insisting publicly that the government had no information. The moment he saw the report was, he says, the beginning of the end.

Rick was not surprised to find that the government had secrets. "National security" is a time-honored, if overused, reason for keeping knowledge from the public. Rick had invoked it himself, and secrecy does have its purposes. It allows for free debate in deliberative processes, it is crucial for surprise in strategic situations, and it protects confidential relationships and individual privacy. But the central purpose of secrecy, as with censorship, is control, and secrecy aligned with power invites abuse. Over the next year, Rick would find himself in the conflicting roles of secret keeper and secret sharer, injustice dispenser and injustice collector, betrayer and betrayed. But what alarmed him most now, as he read the CIA report, was that this key secret had been kept from him, and that made him a liar.

---

Rick and I first talk five years later. He has resigned from the government and is in Cambridge on a fellowship at Harvard's Program on International Conflict Analysis and Resolution, while his wife studies at the Kennedy School of Government. (He has since become director of a center for international relations at a small university in New England.) We meet at the Harvard Faculty Club, where the waiters wear tuxedos and the customers wear jeans and everyone appears offhandedly important. Arriving early, I scan the lounge for someone who matches the newspaper photo I've seen. Coming up empty, I sit down to wait.

"You wouldn't be Nan, would you?" asks the man in the chair opposite. He is in his fifties, tall and broad-shouldered, with a trim beard, gray hair growing longish at the collar, wire-rim glasses, and an intelligent face. Rick.

This is a get-acquainted meeting—he has yet to agree to an interview—and he is leery. His words have been misquoted by journalists and used against him by the FBI, and he has rejected the idea of writing his own book, certain it would ensure that he'd never work in government again. And yet, somewhere between salad and coffee, it seems decided: he'll talk.

Interviewing is a strange transaction. I ask questions and someone answers, sometimes telling me things that are none of my business, so each time I approach a person for this book, I wonder why he or she chooses to take part. When the government went after Rick, he tells me later, "I deliberately coordinated a series of public appearances and interviews, so that I would go from sort of obscurity to prominence very quickly, not to give anybody a thought that maybe they could get rid of this guy before he could do more damage. I don't know if I needed to do that, but I do know that the press gave me that opportunity." Now, with not even a job to lose, he's in no danger, so I decide that he agrees to talk because, like most people, he wants to tell his version of the story.

We meet two more times in his office, a small, white room with an air of impermanence. Outside, the occasional siren wails by, breaking the city's summer quiet. Rick is scrupulous in his narration, speaking with the easy authority and occasional impatience of a man accustomed to being listened to. He has spent his professional life studying, teaching about, and advising on Latin America, but he first got involved with Guatemala about fifteen years ago, when his son played soccer with the son of Guatemalan expatriates. This acquaintance eventually brought him to Washington to work at the Roosevelt Center for American Policy Studies, a now-defunct think tank that aimed to educate citizens on policy issues.

He had never been to Guatemala, but the country seems to get under the skin of anyone who spends any time there. "It's a disturbing juxtaposition of this incredible physical beauty," he says, "the beauty of the people, the culture, their traditional crafts, and this determination they have to preserve this culture through all the centuries—with the incredible violence and ugliness of what goes on in politics and between people."

What was going on was a civil war, begun in 1962, but rooted in a 1954 CIA-sponsored coup that overthrew the democratically elected, leftist government of Jacobo Arbenz. The United States had a special relationship with Guatemala, acting as its protector and largest market, while Guatemala provided U.S. businesses with oil, coffee, and the bananas that made the United Fruit Company a powerful political force. Conveniently, U.S. administrations had paid scant attention to how Guatemala governed itself, but with the overthrow of Arbenz, we began overt alliances with a series of military dictatorships that were interrupted only by an occasional coup. Through repression laced with terror, the Guatemalan military protected the class and economic interests it shared with the landowning and business elite. The result was a country divided between a very poor and vulnerable majority and a very rich minority determined to keep its power.[2] The corporeal form of the threat was a ragtag group of insurgents made up, at various times, of disaffected army officers, students, and peasants; by the late 1980s, the major guerrilla group was the United Guatemalan National Revolutionaries, or URNG.

It is hard to know what North American security interest was served by the slaughter of Mayan peasants in the Guatemala highlands, but the United States, with its special relationship and anticommunist faith, was a ready source of training, weapons, and money for the Guatemalan military. In 1988 and 1989, military assistance reached a high of $9.4 million each year.[3] Rick believes, however, that a special relationship also meant special responsibility. "The U.S. created that monster," he says dryly of the Guatemala military. "Who else to slay it when the time came?"

In 1991, Rick went to work with the Western Hemisphere Subcommittee of the House Foreign Affairs Committee, which was chaired by then-Congressman Robert Torricelli, a Democrat from New Jersey. The Cold War had wound down, Nicaragua and El Salvador were approaching peace, but the Guatemalan war had reached an impasse. Though the army had eliminated the guerrillas as a serious military threat, the guerrillas could deny victory to the military simply by refusing to disappear. As tentative negotiations began, Rick used his contacts to arrange meetings for Torricelli with both Guatemala's president and a senior commander of the URNG. From then on, both sides of the conflict tried to keep Torricelli—and, by extension, Rick—actively involved.

His credibility with Guatemalan groups was an asset when he moved to the State Department two years later. Soon he became the U.S. representative to the Group of Friends, a loose association of six countries that had assisted in the Salvadoran peace process. The guerrillas had asked the United States to join the group because, Rick speculates, they hoped it could influence the Guatemalan military, but also because of their relationship with Torricelli.

From the beginning, the United States as peacemaker struck many as a dubious proposition. Guatemala's appalling record on human rights had brought the occasional suspension of aid: Carter cut off all assistance, Reagan restored and increased it, Bush restricted military aid, Clinton reinstated it, then suspended it again. In 1990, when the Bush administration made a show of halting aid, the Guatemalan army made a show of severing ties with Washington, but apparently not everyone got the message. One American journalist later documented authorization of 144 separate sales of guns from U.S. sources after the cutoff,[4] and another found that CIA payments—$5 to $7 million annually—actually went up.[5]

By the time of the peace talks, this combination of largesse and ambivalence had bought the United States mostly mistrust. The guerrillas and the civil groups who sympathized with them—human rights monitors, relatives of the disappeared, labor unions, peasant associations—saw the United States as a source of repression, while the Guatemala army saw no reason to tolerate a rebuke from a country that had lost its own guerrilla war in Vietnam. But even soldiers can grow weary of war—Rick quotes a Guatemalan army officer as telling him, "We don't want to train any more young people to die"—and the Guatemalan public, sick of violence and corruption, was pushing for a resolution.

At first, Rick shared the prevailing skepticism about the peace talks, but when the United Nations became involved, things started moving. Believing the United States had something to contribute, he set himself a goal: to create an "honest broker role" for the United States government. "There's a confidence game here too," Rick notes of the negotiations. "Everyone who had some serious role in the peace process knew that the most important thing was to keep the peace process moving because at some point, Guatemalan society or the Guatemalan government or the international community or some combination would become more committed to the peace process than they were to the status quo. At that point, a kind of a momentum shift would take place."

As Rick talks about the early peace negotiations, it is apparent that he was having a very good time. "All of my professional life, I've been a student of Latin America. One of the first things that every Latin Americanist learns about is the CIA-engineered coup of 1954. And here I had a chance forty years after the United States helped to overthrow an elected government and start forty years of civil war; I was going to help end it. From a position in the U.S. government. It was almost poetic in its symmetry."

Though the United States wasn't directly involved in the negotiations, as its representative in the group of "friends"—Mexico, Spain, Norway, Colombia, Venezuela, and the United States—Rick shared meals with the participants, jogged, chatted, and made himself available as a go-between. Like any good bureaucrat, he worked through channels, but he was perceived as the point man for the United States. "And since only good things were happening at this time, and since nobody particularly cared," he says, "I had tremendous freedom."

North Americans may not have cared, but, I point out, Guatemalans probably did. What did it feel like to have such power?

"Totally exhilarating. The bad part of it—which I never really had direct responsibility for in Guatemala. . . . Sometimes you're exercising power that can end lives." Rick has been talking animatedly, but now there is a long pause. "So where were we?" he says at last.

In June 1994, a series of agreements were hammered out in Oslo, including the creation of a U.N. mission, eventually over one thousand strong, to protect human rights in Guatemala. It came to be called MINUGUA, from its Spanish name. Says Rick, "This was a society where unspeakable things were done behind closed doors and in the countryside where no one knew about it. And now, Guatemala was being forced to open itself up to international scrutiny." But MINUGUA took a long time to get organized, the army was not about to cede power willingly, and the civil sector felt that the guerrillas, on whom they had pinned their hopes, had accomplished too little and given up too much. Against this backdrop of wariness and disappointment, Jennifer Harbury stepped into the spotlight.

Rick's involvement with Harbury and her campaign began shortly after he joined the State Department. The Guatemalan army had informed her that Bámaca had died in an ambush on March 12, 1992, but she too had talked to the guerrilla who had seen her husband at the prison months later, so she had reason to believe that he had survived. About a year after Bámaca's disappearance, Harbury began her campaign to find out the truth and, she hoped, to bring about his release. By the time she got to Rick in the summer of 1994, she had filed a suit with the Organization of American States, presented her case to the U.N. Human Rights Commission, enlisted the support of politicians and human rights groups, attempted (unsuccessfully) to have the grave where Bámaca was purportedly buried exhumed, undertaken a seven-day hunger strike, met with Guatemalan officials, and requested help from the State Department and U.S. ambassador to Guatemala. So when she met Rick, Harbury was frustrated, angry, suspicious, and determined not to be brushed aside. (*Searching for Everardo,* Harbury's book about her campaign, and *Dirty Secrets,* a film about the case, by Patricia Goudvis, are the sources for my observations about her activities. I have tried not to impute thoughts or motives to her that are not recorded there.)

Rick was not unprepared for a dramatic human rights case to emerge and influence the peace process; he had predicted as much. Forensic teams were being trained in Guatemala, and after years of search-and-destroy missions in the countryside, it was likely that mass graves would be discovered. Nor did he find the prospect wholly unwelcome, since he figured it would bring needed attention to the peace process. He had seen that happen in El Salvador, where, he argues, U.S. public support for the war was undermined by the high-profile murders of three American nuns in 1980 and of six Jesuits priests, their housekeeper, and her daughter in 1989. "You remember those in part because they make absolutely no sense," Rick says. "They're innocents. They're nuns, for goodness sakes!"

Guatemala was rife with such cases. In 1989, Dianna Ortiz, an Ursuline nun from the United States, was kidnapped in Guatemala and, after escaping, told of being tortured and gang-raped. She believed one of her torturers had CIA connections and pressed for an investigation, but with little success.[6] The next year, a young Guatemalan anthropologist named Myrna Mack Chang was stabbed repeatedly in broad daylight outside her research institute in Guatemala City, her offense apparently that she was collecting information about displaced Guatemalans.[7] Then in June 1990, the nearly decapitated body of Michael DeVine, a U.S. citizen who ran an inn, was found by the side of the road in the northern part of the country. All signs pointed to the Guatemala military, which had a base nearby, but when the U.S. ambassador tried to investigate, he was stonewalled. The Bush administration suspended military aid, and several soldiers were eventually convicted of the murder, as was an army captain—a first, as far as anyone could remember—but he escaped immediately with notable ease.

A year after DeVine's murder, the CIA got a report implicating a Colonel Julio Roberto Alpírez, who ran the neighboring base. The CIA knew Alpírez well—he had been trained at the infamous School of the Americas,[8] and he was one of their "assets," or paid informers—but when the U.S. ambassador asked the CIA about a connection to the killing, he was told there was none.[9]

Rick maintains that Bámaca's killing was different from these. "Jennifer's case is about a man of war who was in the field of battle, captured by the Guatemalan army, and executed, presumably. Were his human rights violated? Absolutely. Did he suffer unspeakable, inhuman, illegal, and immoral torture before he was executed? Absolutely. Was his murder a violation of every law: Guatemalan? international? Absolutely. The nature of a civil war is that people on both sides shed innocent life."

Long before he joined the government, Rick wrote a short book called *What's Wrong, Who's Right in Central America?* in which he offers his readers a test to see if they are a "national security analyst" (NSA) or a "human rights activist" (HRA). In his equation, the moral dilemmas of realpolitik, which make HRAs queasy, are pitted against the moralism of human rights, which NSAs dismiss as naive. Rick appears to see himself as straddling the two camps, but he is primarily a pragmatist, and his pragmatism served him well until it bumped into Harbury, who refused to be placated or derailed.

Soon it became clear that hers was the case that would put Guatemala on the human rights outrage map and, like it or not, Rick was going to have to deal with it. For one thing, Harbury was adept at capturing public attention. She came from the educated middle class the U.S. media like to report on (articles never failed to identify her as "a Harvard-trained lawyer"). Also, by framing her case as the test of human rights in Latin America, she garnered the support of the human rights groups Rick was counting on as allies.

"Who cares about Guatemala?" he asks rhetorically. "Do mainstream, well-informed, middle-of-the-road kind of people care about Guatemala? Or do people who care about the CIA and conspiracy and so on, are they the ones who are liable to be following Guatemala? Well, mostly the latter, I think."

Governments don't need conspiracy to act shamefully, and critics of U.S. policy in Central America had cause for suspicion, since the FBI had spied on their activities from 1981 to at least 1985, but more to the point, activities carried out in the shadows draw suspicion. Says Rick, "Jennifer's case sort of made everything fit into place: Guatemala is a place where things are black and white, there are the good guerrillas and there's the bad army. Now along comes this guy, Nuccio, and he says, no, actually, Guatemala is a place of grays. And the way you judge who's good and who's bad is by whether they're for peace. It doesn't matter what slogans they mouth; it matters how they behave. That was much too complicated a worldview."

The tension between Rick and Harbury was also a matter of temperament, as evidenced by their books. Hers—romantic, passionate, polemical—is a narrative of her relationship with Bámaca and her fight to get some answers and some justice. His is a primer for understanding U.S. policy in Central America. It is spare, factual, dry, and even-handed to a fault. Yet they meet in odd ways. Harbury's loyalties are more unitary—this was her husband, her cause, and she changed a country's history in pursuit of it—but Rick cares about human rights too, and both inevitably view Guatemala's politics through a North American lens.

For a long time, Rick tried to win Harbury to his side. How? "I guess the best way I can say it is, unlike many people in the State Department, I took her seriously," he explains, then lists all the elements of the case he had trouble taking seriously. Harbury had met with Guatemala's defense minister, General Mario Enriquez Morales, whom she thought had offered to release her husband if she dropped her campaign. In the cruelest irony of the case, it is almost certain that by the time Harbury began her efforts to save Bámaca, he was already dead, but since neither she nor Rick would know that for some time, when they met and he asked what she wanted him to do, she urged him to pursue Enriquez's offer. Rick didn't believe Enriquez had any intention of negotiating with Harbury, but he nonetheless pressed him to pay attention to her demands. Enriquez, he says, found a hundred different ways to say no. More than an exercise in futility, though, their meeting turned out to be a "fatal error" for Rick, because from that point on, he was no longer perceived as impartial.

"About a month ago," he says, "I had a lunch with the Guatemalan ambassador in Washington, someone I got to know pretty well through the course of the peace process. The purpose of the lunch was to start my own process of reconciliation, and I asked him, where were my problems with the Guatemalan government? He said, 'Your meeting with Jennifer on the plaza, because that confirmed to all of us that your sympathies really lay with the guerrillas.' " Rick tells me this story shortly after it happened and again, almost word for word, a couple of months later. Both times, he is incredulous. "I said, 'Have you ever read what Jennifer thought of my meeting with her?' From her point of view, [it] was the confirmation that I was really a tool of the Guatemalan army!"

The meeting took place as Harbury was conducting her second hunger strike on the plaza in front of Guatemala's National Palace. Rick visited her there on October 27, 1994, her forty-third birthday and a week after he saw the first CIA memo. The ambassador, Marilyn MacAfee, sent flowers, along with embassy police to guard her at night. "They don't get it," Harbury says in Goudvis's film, "I don't need the protection. Everardo does." Her protestation to the contrary, Guatemala was a dangerous place, and prolonged fasting—the strike lasted thirty-two days—takes a toll on the body. A hunger strike is as much symbol as flesh; Harbury staged hers as a very public event, attracting international news coverage, including the *60 Minutes* investigation that had concerned Rick. She writes that she thought he knew "all along," but he insists that they were both just beginning to move toward the truth.

———————

Even now, with Guatemala's civil war over, the enormity of its impact is hard to fathom. In a country of just under twelve million people, some two hundred thousand were killed or "disappeared" (the usage originated here), two hundred thousand children were orphaned, and over 440 villages were destroyed. One million people were displaced internally; hundreds of thousands took refuge abroad, and those who remained lived in a culture soaked in blood and shot through with fear.[10] Some of these numbers were compiled only recently, but *la violencia* was never a secret, and unlike other Central American countries, Guatemala made no pretense about its disregard for the most basic rights of its people.

At the time of Harbury's hunger strike, the extent of U.S. involvement in this destruction may have been hard to gauge because so much information was secret, but some indicators were available. Rick reports in his book that between 1978 and 1985, political deaths averaged about six hundred a month.[11] During that time, the Commerce Department issued licenses for over $100 million in "military or dual-use supplies."[12] In 1989, the year Congress approved over $9 million in military aid on the condition that the Guatemalan army respect human rights,[13] forty thousand Guatemalans were disappeared or unaccounted for.[14] If U.S. officials had few answers for Harbury, it seems that they were asking the wrong questions.

In late 1994, when Rick finally got around to asking those questions, no one was eager to respond. After he saw the first incriminating memo, he "raised holy hell" with his superiors at State, but their only concession was to ask the CIA if it had other reports. Indeed it did. It circulated to Congress a list of all the reports it had filed about Bámaca but found numerous reasons not to make the reports themselves available. Slowly, though, details began to dribble out.

In a report dated March 18, 1992, the CIA had informed the State Department and White House that the Guatemalan army had captured Bámaca, who was lightly wounded. The heavily blacked-out cable that Harbury eventually obtained under the Freedom of Information Act (FOIA) also states, " 'Everardo' continues to cooperate with the army, which will probably keep news of his capture secret, or even claim that he was killed, to maximize his intelligence value." A September 1993 report adds, "Efrain (Bamaca) [sic] was not killed during a firefight with army troops, but was captured, interrogated and killed."

Politicians, soldiers, and bullies have argued that torture, or interrogation, as it is euphemistically called, is necessary to ensure national security, but information gained under such duress is unreliable and seldom new, and, according to international law, prisoners of war are not supposed to be tortured.[15] So once the U.S. government knew Bámaca was being brutalized, what was its responsibility? Rick insists the United States was limited in what it could make Guatemala do, even as he admits that pressure had probably been brought to bear in other instances. Ultimately, though, his answer is that a government is responsible not to lie to its citizens.

Not lying to Harbury proved to be hard for the State Department, perhaps because secrecy was so ingrained. "Good brief . . . I mean good grief!" begins an in-house State Department memo the week before the *60 Minutes* program aired. After advising that they continue to insist that they do not know if Bámaca is dead or alive, the memo concludes: "If pressed on what we knew and when, the answer is that this is an intelligence matter that we cannot discuss. If pushed harder on this, about all we can say is that we have consistently done everything we can to assist Ms. Harbury in her search for her husband. . . . We have not tried to conceal anything from her."[16]

This less-than-forthcoming strategy wasn't confined to the State Department. Earlier that month, Harbury had met at the White House with then–National Security Adviser Anthony Lake and other top human rights and intelligence officials. According to a White House account of the meeting, Harbury was told more of the same. According to Rick, he was told to have nothing further to do with her because he upset her.

Meanwhile, more damning information was being uncovered. The May 1993 report had been initialed by Alexander F. Watson, Rick's boss, indicating that he had read it sometime that month as he awaited confirmation as Assistant Secretary for Latin American Affairs. "But," says Rick, "if you asked him on October 19th [in 1994, when the report reappeared], do you remember ever seeing it, the answer would be no, because that day, he probably read a stack of papers this high. He'd never served in Guatemala. He'd never heard of a guy named Bámaca, or of Jennifer Harbury, and the significance of this report was lost on him. Frankly, probably in that month of that year, it would have been lost on me as well.

"Now, one might ask, you mean you get reports about the Guatemalan army about to assassinate people all the time and you don't do anything about it? The answer is yes." He sighs deeply, though it's not clear if from the weight of that knowledge or from frustration that others don't see it the same way. "If you don't like that, change your government"—which is what Harbury was trying to do.

Rick continued to ask questions that he assumes the CIA found "inconvenient" up to February 1995, when he learned that the source of the reports was none other than Roberto Alpírez, the Guatemalan colonel and CIA informant who had been connected to the murder of Michael DeVine. Rick is careful not to mention Alpírez's name, though everyone else discussing the case does. When I do, he says only, "That's what's been reported." But with this revelation, his difficulty in getting the information and the CIA's interest in burying the story fell into place. He pauses dramatically to let this sink in.

"What did you think?" I ask.

"I thought, shit! There's not a single person who's dealt with me who's going to believe that I'm just now finding it out."

---

On March 10, 1995, President Clinton suspended military aid to Guatemala, which is where things stood as Harbury began another hunger strike to mark the third anniversary of Bámaca's disappearance. "Everyone felt very comfortable, except me," Rick reports. "As far as they were concerned, the matter was resolved. There was this minor matter of a woman on a hunger strike. Who was as much my enemy as a person could be politically. About whose husband we still had information we had not given her."

The official justification for withholding the information was that it was classified. Basically a bureaucratic phenomenon, classification has been invoked with varying degrees of zeal since 1951 when the system was established by presidential order.[17] FOIA made government documents more available to the public, but its first exemption was for national defense or foreign policy, and CIA "operation files" were exempted in 1984. Today, the CIA is second only to the Defense Department in secret keeping.[18]

In 1995, when President Clinton issued the current directive, there were 21,871 "original" and 374,244 "derivative" Top Secrets, a significant decrease from a decade earlier. Numbers this big slide into meaninglessness, but the consequences of extensive government secrecy are clear: in addition to breeding mistrust between the governing and the governed, as in the Harbury case, secrecy hobbles scientific and techno-logical development, hampers honest historical appraisal, and fosters all the dangers of an electorate with a political awareness full of holes. It is also expensive: according to one reckoning, the federal government pays over $6 billion a year just to maintain its classified documents.[19]

In a 1997 congressional report on government secrecy, Daniel Patrick Moynihan writes of an elaborate "culture of secrecy" and asks, "Can there really have been some 400,000 secrets created in 1995, the disclo-sure of any one of which would cause 'exceptionally grave damage to the national security'?"[20] Rick, who had the highest clearance, Sensitive Compartmented Information, or SCI, adds, "A lot of classification is done to cover up mistakes. Wouldn't you like to have all your relations with your loved ones, your employer, conducted in secret so that no one would ever have to know about them?"

I answer that I do my best to make that happen, as I assume most people do, to which he replies, "Most of us don't have a stamp."

As for keeping information from Harbury, Rick points out that the president has the power to declassify any document and that, as his ad-visor, Anthony Lake could have urged him to do so in this instance. But White House officials "decided that that would be too confrontational with the CIA. They preferred to let Jennifer twist." He lets this hang in the air. "It was very nice for them."

———

As Rick describes his growing sense of dread, his voice goes quieter and slower, and as I replay the tape of our conversation, certain words etch themselves in my mind: peace, human rights, fear, trying. By mid-March, he sums up, "Every fear I had and every argument I made checked out to be right, but nobody acted on them. There was this accumulation of information which had gone from a single report, unconfirmed, sug-gesting Jennifer's husband had indeed been alive at some point to docu-mentation that a CIA asset had been directly involved with Jennifer's husband *and* in covering up the murder of an American citizen. In legal terms and moral terms, that's a very long journey."

Loyalty in politics may be honored largely in the breach, but the re-sponsibility of someone who knows of wrongdoing has always been less straightforward than we would like to think. We shun the stoolie who turns on his buddies, yet despise equally the collaborator or the good sol-dier who just follows orders. People seldom thank you for exposing their shortcomings, and punishment for breaking rank is often harsh; those who blow the whistle are routinely ostracized, silenced, and stripped of power. Protective of our liberties and anxious that there might be such a thing as too much freedom, we struggle to pin down the point at which responsibility trumps loyalty. Or is it the other way around? All this makes keeping quiet—self-censorship—an appealing option.

Rick did keep quiet about the secrets he now knew, even as he continued to argue for disclosure, but when his bosses didn't respond, he consulted the Bureau of Legislative Affairs, the office at the State Department that authorizes contacts with Congress. There, someone advised him to find an ally in Congress who would understand that he had not intended to mislead when he had testified that the State Department knew nothing about what had happened to Bámaca.

Abba Eban said, "History teaches us that men and nations behave wisely once they have exhausted all alternatives." On March 17, Rick ran into Robert Torricelli at a congressional hearing, and all the vectors—his concern that he was acting wrongly, his anxiety over his career and Harbury's health, the advice from the Bureau of Legislative Affairs—came together. He walked up to Torricelli and said, "Bob, there's something that's bothering me. Do you have a moment?"

"Fate," Rick pronounces. "He could have said, I'm very busy right now. He could have said, come back and see me tomorrow, and I would have gone back to the State Department and told my bosses, who would have said, like hell you're talking to Bob Torricelli! But instead, he said, yeah, sure, why not just walk back to my office with me?" And so Rick related what he had learned about the CIA's connection to the Bámaca and DeVine murders.

He characterizes it as a political conversation as much as an exposé; the murders had occurred under the Bush administration, but the cover-up could become a serious scandal for the Clinton administration then in office. Assuming that Torricelli shared his interest in protecting a Democratic presidency, Rick advised caution, but apparently Torricelli had something else in mind. Several times over the next week, he urged Rick to resign and criticize the CIA with him. By then, Rick had told his bosses what he had done, and they seemed to take it in stride. He had also been told by lawyers not to worry about Torricelli's charge that, in covering up illegal activity, he had acted illegally. Confident that he had the backing of his superiors and the law, he refused Torricelli's requests. Torricelli told Rick that he was going to act but didn't spell out how; nor did Rick ask, since he wasn't eager to help. Besides, he says, "Only someone who doesn't know Robert Torricelli would think anyone would be capable of dissuading him from something."

Torricelli settled on writing a letter to the president based on what Rick had told him but not naming his source. To ensure that it wouldn't get buried, he copied the *New York Times*—at which point, everything speeds up like film slithering through a projector at the wrong setting. On March 23, a week after Rick had unburdened himself, the *Times* ran a front-page story linking Alpírez with the murders and the CIA with Alpírez and quoting Torricelli as saying, "The direct involvement of the Central Intelligence Agency in the murder of these individuals leads me to the extraordinary conclusion that the agency is simply out of control."[21] Follow-up stories began to document just how out of control it was: from 1988 to 1991, the CIA in Guatemala had a budget of at least $10 million a year for operations and "liaison" programs, which apparently functioned with little congressional or presidential oversight.[22]

In the meantime, Torricelli had met with Harbury to tell her that the government knew her husband was dead and had known for some time. According to Torricelli, she wept.[23]

---

Guatemala had finally captured the public's imagination, though hardly in the way Rick had hoped. The president asked the Intelligence Oversight Board, a presidential advisory panel, to investigate CIA activities in Guatemala. The Departments of Justice, Defense, and State, the CIA, and the House Intelligence Oversight Committee also launched investigations. The president's and CIA's investigations, completed the summer of 1996, found that the agency had continued to pay Guatemalan operatives whom it knew to abuse human rights and had been remiss in not telling Congress about these relationships, but both reports agreed that it had not acted illegally. The findings could not be ignored, however, and in an unusual shake-up, the CIA dismissed two high-placed officers and disciplined nine agents.[24] The House report, issued in March 1997, came essentially to the same conclusions as the presidential panel. Torricelli's allegations notwithstanding, it found insufficient evidence that the CIA knew of human rights crimes in Guatemala, but Congress nonetheless imposed stricter informant-recruitment measures, which would become particularly controversial after September 11, 2001.

The State Department conducted its own low-level investigation, and then, says Rick, "Seemingly, that all went away." But the Bámaca scandal had badly undermined the U.S. role in the peace process and Rick's standing in Guatemala. Unable to complete his work there, he moved to the White House to serve as a special advisor for Cuba.

A few months later, he got a call from the State Department's Inspector General asking if he would mind stopping by to answer a few more questions for their investigation. He arrived just before lunchtime a day or two later and was greeted by the Inspector General, who ushered him into a conference room and introduced him to the FBI liaison for the U.S. Attorney's office and the Assistant Attorney General for Transnational Crimes in the District of Columbia, a man named Daniel Seikaly. "We're here to talk about your involvement in the disclosure of classified information and the murder of CIA assets in Guatemala," the Inspector General announced.

Rick narrates this nightmare moment with a mixture of deadpan and disbelief. "I said, 'What!' And this guy, Seikaly, plops down these books about four or five inches high and opens them and says, 'Your conduct is responsible for the loss of people's lives, the disclosure of highly sensitive national security secrets, and potentially the disclosure of national security information to foreign nationals. You are not yet the target of my investigation, but I will be empaneling a grand jury and what you say here may potentially . . .' "

Rick interrupted, asking if he was not entitled to a lawyer. Not from the State Department, he was told. And if he wanted his own lawyer? That was his right, of course, but the record would indicate that he had failed to cooperate with the investigation. When he declined to answer any more questions without legal counsel, Seikaly ordered his office locked and everything inside impounded and catalogued.

Rick continues, his voice loud and firm imitating Seikaly, soft and tentative for his replies.

*Seikaly:* Are you prepared to go through those files with us?

*Nuccio:* Sure, I have nothing to hide in my files.

*Seikaly:* Well, let's do that right now.

*Nuccio:* I'm sorry, I didn't know this was what I was coming here for. I have other things to do today and I'm not interrupting them for you to go search files that I haven't seen for six months.

*Seikaly:* Well, we'll have to indicate that that's also a failure to cooperate.

As Rick's lawyers negotiated terms in the weeks that followed, Seikaly made clear his disdain for political appointees like Rick, whom he disparaged as an academic dilettante and, worse, an abuser of his security clearance. His job was to investigate leaks, but the fervor with which he pursued the case seems to Rick to reflect the CIA's anger at being found out and punished for its conduct in Guatemala. "Someone had to pay for that," he says. "Their preference, frankly, would have been Torricelli, but because of his congressional position, they couldn't get him, and so I was the next best thing." To Rick, blaming him is a classic case of missing the point. "The problem was the CIA's misconduct," he points out, "but that's the way these guys think about these things: it's not that they did something wrong; it's that they did something wrong and somebody found out about it."

Among Seikaly's charges was that Rick had confirmed to the *Times* Alpírez's role in Bámaca's murder, but Rick never spoke with the reporter until after the story was published.[25] Seikaly also claimed Rick had identified a CIA source. A rumor was circulating about killings in Guatemala because of Rick's disclosure, though it was never confirmed. Besides, he says, with notable sangfroid, "People in Guatemala die all the time. People in the intelligence world get bumped off all the time."

Under the Agents Identity Protection Act of 1982, it is illegal to identify anyone as a covert agent, even if that information is publicly available. Obviously, to name intelligence sources is to put them in jeopardy, but why shouldn't Alpírez have been accountable for his murderous actions? The extent of his responsibility for the deaths of DeVine and Bámaca may be unclear—truth being another casualty of secrecy—but his involvement wasn't. In a cable sent to the National Security Council in January 1995, well before Rick or Torricelli spilled the beans, the U.S. embassy in Guatemala wrote, "By all reports, Alpírez is a bad egg. He is corrupt, a liar and has been negatively involved in matters involving human rights."[26] Yet between DeVine's murder in June 1990 and the summer of 1992, when he was seen torturing Bámaca, the CIA paid him at least $60,000, and his severance package when he was finally let go later in 1992 was $44,000.[27]

---

The villain of the piece, for Rick, is the CIA, deceitful even to the State Department, with whom it was supposedly working. Yet fair-minded to the core, he says, "Why I should try to be sympathetic to them, I have no idea, but there is a part of this that is right, which is that they were following rules that other people set down for them. The CIA is not a rogue operation, out doing things that nobody knows about. It's out doing things that people know about and don't want to stop them from doing. These guys felt that somebody had changed the rules on them, and they never made that transition."

The CIA's learning curve aside, it is hard to switch loyalties abruptly. In fact, that switch can look a lot like betrayal as, overnight, allies are turned into enemies and vice versa. Where the CIA errs, Rick says, is in thinking that there is something unfair about that. Wars begin and end, politicians go in and out of office, alliances shift, rules change. "I don't mean to portray them as dumb," he observes of the agents who continued to play by the old rules, "But I do mean to portray them as arrogant."

CIA agents, like all government employees, are supposed to carry out the policies of whatever administration is in office. Rick's assessment of what this entails sounds simple enough: "I believe that if you're getting lawful, ethical orders, and you're a government employee, you follow them or you get out of government." What is legal isn't necessarily ethical or wise, however. Some policies should be changed or at least challenged, and the best way to do that may be from inside the government. Then there is Rick's dilemma of how to respond when you're ordered to do something that is neither legal nor ethical.

There is also the question of how much citizens need to know. Governments routinely come down on the side of too little, and when hidden information is finally released, much of it is laughably tame.[28] The flip side is burying controversy by drowning the public in minutiae until no one gives a damn. But only by having information available can we judge if we need to know it. The distinction between being able to decide for ourselves and having the decision made for us is not a trivial one.

When Rick got his clearance, he agreed not to tell the secrets he learned, and, as intelligence officials were fond of pointing out when his case became public, you can't run a government with everyone second-guessing policy decisions. It's hardly surprising that the CIA and State Department resented Rick for breaking rank; communities usually circle the wagons when threatened, and all institutions have secrets they don't tell outsiders willingly. The difference here was that the intelligence community wouldn't exist without its secrets.

The CIA, for much of its history, has existed more or less outside the reach of the Constitution and beyond political scrutiny. In the two decades after its creation in 1947, the agency reported on its activities through a kind of gentlemen's agreement, whereby Congress was told what it wanted to know as long as it didn't want to know much. (There appear to have been no briefings on CIA involvement in covert actions in the early 1950s, for instance, when the Guatemala coup took place.)[29]

Then, in the wake of Watergate and scandals over the CIA's role in Chile and domestic spying on antiwar activists, Congress set up permanent intelligence oversight committees. By law, these committees are to be kept "fully and currently informed" of CIA activities,[30] though subsequent legislation cut the requirement back to informing "where appropriate."[31] Congress was vastly better informed by the time of the DeVine and Bámaca murders, but apparently the CIA found it inappropriate—not to mention inconvenient and embarrassing—to fill in the grim details. The issue then became not just secrecy but secrecy without accountability.

Despite his problems with government secrecy, Rick still staunchly defends its use, particularly as a decision is being deliberated. "But," he says, "the decisions that are made belong to the American people, and there has to be total openness about those decisions. Hiding mistakes or decisions of government that may make you uncomfortable or unpopular, I don't believe in that kind of secrecy. That's why we have whistle-blower statutes." Unfortunately for Rick, whistle-blower protection laws provide little cover for executive branch employees who reveal classified information, even if they do it to expose illegal or fraudulent activity.

Through the fall of 1995, as the government pursued its investigation, Rick kept a low profile, believing "that I had done the right thing, that my administration would support me, and that this was some sort of crazy vendetta by spooks and creepy guys at Justice and the CIA." So certain was he of exoneration that he failed to see that his actions had pleased no one: not his bosses, for whom he had become an inconvenience; not people in Congress, who found the whole story unsavory; not human rights groups, who suspected his motives; not his Guatemalan contacts, who no longer trusted him; not even Jennifer Harbury, whose gratitude appeared less than fulsome. He had been warned not to mess with the CIA before, but he thought that, as a political appointee, he was supposed to shake things up. Now he hears a deeper message: rhetoric and good intentions aside, the White House wasn't about to take on the CIA. Rick thinks no administration will.

While all this was going on, Rick was back at the State Department, where he ran into colleagues with whom he had worked before the Harbury story broke. Some supported him, but others refused to help or made sure that he, and not they, got the blame. Some even crossed the hall to avoid facing him. He likens it to the Quaker practice of shunning. So perhaps what surprised him most was that, in the end, he had so few friends.

By April 1996, he had been working on Cuban issues for about a year, but Guatemalan issues followed him: Sister Dianna Ortiz was staging a hunger strike to press for information about her abduction,[32] and Jennifer Harbury had filed a $28 million suit against the U.S. government. (In June 2002, the Supreme Court ruled unanimously that Harbury could not sue government officials for deceiving her but did not address whether government officials are permitted to deceive the public.)[33] Then Rick's boss announced that the CIA was going to revoke his clearance if he didn't leave the White House. "I agreed voluntarily, if there is such a thing," he says. The same day, Seikaly announced he was dropping his criminal investigation.

Furious at all that implied, Rick decided to fight back. It felt good to do that at last. He appealed the revocation of his clearance, talked to the press, and, in two days, got twenty-two members of Congress to sign a letter to President Clinton asking that Rick's clearance be reinstated. Despite this flurry of activity, John Deutsch, then director of the CIA, ruled against him, and on December 5, Rick's security clearance was revoked for good, making it impossible for him to continue his work.[34] Three weeks later, the Guatemalan peace accords were signed.

For four months, Rick tried to reposition himself within the government; then, finally, he understood that it was time to leave. Though Torricelli had repeatedly offered him a job on his staff, Rick had been reluctant to take it, in part because Seikaly had predicted that he would do just that. Now it was his only option.

On February 25, 1997, he resigned, writing to President Clinton: "Despite the conclusions of the Star Chamber proceedings to which I have been subjected, I faced no easy choices in March 1995. . . . I made a choice that was consistent with the values of your Administration and the law, and gave Congress the ability to provide real oversight of intelligence activities. For that act of conscience the CIA is being allowed to end my service in your Administration."

———————

In our first conversation, Rick and I had talked about the need to get the truth out, especially after a prolonged period of secrecy and repression. As the bloody twentieth century wound down, fact-finding commissions around the world were issuing reports with such lovely, hopeful names: *Truth and Reconciliation* in South Africa, *We Will Remember Them* in Northern Ireland, *Never Again* in Argentina, Brazil, Uruguay, Paraguay. Meanwhile, civil and religious groups were demanding official apologies;

recovered memories were invoked to illuminate a host of traumas; memoirs, primarily in the confessional mode, were heralded as the literary event of our time; and a psychologist would sum up his research about "online sex addiction" by saying, "If it's a secret, that's a problem."[35] Eighteenth-century Enlightenment philosophy, it seemed, had converged with modern psychological therapy in the nearly sacred conviction that freedom, personal or political, is won only when truth is made to emerge.

Guatemala too was undertaking investigations into its decades of atrocities, but to me, Rick's story demonstrated that truth alone is insufficient to restore justice. People also long for fairness, which can be quite a different matter, and though secrets can fester, so can public airings when the consequences are unclear. Rick's assessment is multilayered. "It wasn't important to me to reveal classified information to Jennifer or to the *New York Times*. That's not what I meant by getting the truth out. On the issue of the truth commissions, we in the United States give lectures to people in Central America saying that there has to be a process of acknowledging the past, asking for forgiveness for the violations, and reconciling. I believe that's right. Each country has to decide how to strike the balance. Some people believe it's an absolute: absolute truth, absolute accountability, and then you move on to reconciliation. I don't think it is possible in any of the Central or Latin American countries."

In February 1999, the U.N. Commission for Historical Clarification issued a surprisingly frank report about Guatemala's civil war entitled *Memory of Silence*. The report held the government responsible for 93 percent of the 42,275 human rights violations it investigated, the guerrillas for 3 percent, a disproportion so great as to render pointless the oft-cited excuse that everyone was doing it. The report also denounced the United States government for funding and training Guatemala's military in counterinsurgency and in reinforcing the intelligence apparatus, "key factors which had significant bearing on human rights violations."[36]

The Clinton administration had declassified over one thousand documents and provided them to the commission, along with $1.5 million in funding. On a visit to Guatemala just after the report was delivered, the president said that the United States was wrong to have supported "violent and widespread repression of this kind" and "must not repeat that mistake."[37] A few days later, a former URNG leader also apologized.

Public remorse and symbolic punishment matter, but they are not the same as contrition, and if events leading up to the report are any indication, the odds for reform are not promising. The year before, when pre-

senting a similarly critical report on behalf of the Archdiocese Office of
Human Rights, Bishop Juan Gerardi said, "We want to contribute to the
building of a country different than the one we have now. For that reason we are recovering the memory of our people." Two days later, Gerardi was murdered. The military was widely suspected of committing the
murder, though it took three years to get convictions in the case, and in
2002, the three military officers and one priest found guilty of the murder were granted a new trial.[38]

Still, Rick says, "There has to be some process. Guatemala's may fall
short of what it should be. It's very much a political question. It's not just
a question of human rights and justice." He continues, "We have our
own process to go through. We owe it to ourselves as a people to recognize the truth about what our policies were in these countries. We need
to ask forgiveness for the wrongs that we committed. And I don't mean
we, them, the CIA. I mean we, the citizens of the United States. We need
to acknowledge that this went on. Then we need to engage in a process
of reconciliation with these countries and with the people who lost loved
ones, at times because of our policies, because of our participation,
sometimes with our direct involvement. It's only through a recognition
of the past that you move toward ensuring that it doesn't happen again."

A way to do that is by declassifying information and allowing it to be
put in context. "Ninety percent of what you get through intelligence
channels is worthless, but it doesn't matter whether it's valuable to us or
not. We should provide this information because we have it and because
it's a part of acknowledging the past. It may be embarrassing, it may not
help people solve human rights cases, but that's why we should do it."

As for his part in this process, he says, "I had a great deal of investment in what was happening in Guatemala, and the idea that I would be
in the U.S. government covering up a CIA murder in Guatemala was not
acceptable. If I had made a different choice, I wouldn't be the person I
thought I was. I would have lost myself in some profound way."

He sounds surprised to know this and laughs when I point that out.
Then he grows ruminative. "I'm not a very good person. I'm capable of
being a bad husband and bad father, a bad friend, but I wasn't capable
of being a bad U.S. government official. Maybe I'm lucky that I was at
once naive and arrogant in thinking that my administration would back
me. I guess it's good that I didn't know how easy it would be for other
people to squirm out of it. Yeah," he says, "I guess I did surprise myself."

chapter two

# A MATTER OF CONSCIENCE

Kwame Mensah

*St. Louis, Missouri, June 1998*

I don't remember exactly why I called Kwame Mensah the first time. It was 1991 and I was researching an article on resistance within the military during the Gulf War. I had compiled a list of over one hundred people trying for discharge as conscientious objectors (COs) and had read dozens of applications, but why I chose Kwame out of all the possibilities, I can't say. I do recall my phone answering machine beeping every thirteen seconds as I taped our conversation. Graciously ignoring the noise, he explained that the previous October, he had been a twenty-four-year-old student at Southern Illinois University at Edwardsville (SIU-E), when he announced that he would not join his Marine reserve unit as it mobilized for active duty in Operation Desert Storm, otherwise known as the Gulf War. Though Kwame was a Lance Corporal in the 24th Marine Reserve Division, he had known for some time that what he had come to believe about himself and his country made it impossible for him to fight a war. So as the United States prepared for its largest military action since the end of the draft, he had applied for an exemption as a CO, an option under the rubric of the First Amendment's religious freedom clause.

Conscience is perhaps the slipperiest of the First Amendment rights, and for members of the military who refused to fight in the Gulf War, competing ideas of duty—to one's country or to one's conscience—collided with particular ferocity. Two weeks later, Kwame was arrested for going AWOL and flown to Camp Lejeune in Jacksonville, North Carolina, to face court-martial. Over the next six months, twenty-seven other Marine resisters from around the country would also be tried there. They would be called simply "the COs," and none would be acquitted.

According to a survey by the New York–based War Resisters League, some 2,500 enlistees in all four branches of the military completed CO applications between August 1990, when Iraq invaded Kuwait, and mid-June 1991, when most U.S. troops had returned home. The Pentagon puts the figure much lower, counting only the 352 applications that had made their way through the review process to Washington between October 1990 and August 1991. In that time, 192 CO exemptions were granted.[1] By any reckoning, those seeking CO status accounted for a fraction of the troops involved in Desert Storm, and most were processed out of the military quickly and quietly. But disciplinary charges were brought against about 150 servicepeople who filed claims and then didn't join their units when they were activated or who then refused orders related to the war. In their defense, they claimed that the military dragged its feet on their applications, leaving them no choice but to disobey commands that went against their beliefs. Kwame is black, as were nearly half of the CO applicants, and faced with preconceptions about what a CO is, he and others had a particularly hard time convincing their mostly white superior officers of the sincerity of their convictions.

It is seldom simple to "prove" that you believe what you profess to believe, as CO claimants are required to do, and in this instance, making a public statement only complicated the issue. Political speech has limited protection in the armed forces, dissent is viewed as a special threat in times of war, and the military clearly wanted to hush up antiwar sentiment within its ranks. (An Army sergeant who went AWOL after his efforts to apply for CO were thwarted told me that he had learned through the grapevine that his was labeled a "national embarrassment case.") Those who, like Kwame, went public with their refusal to go to war were treated much more harshly than those who quietly avoided fighting, putting the country in the contradictory position of claiming to fight for democratic ideals abroad while stifling dissent at home.

It is easier to laud dissidents somewhere else, harder to champion those who challenge home truths, but protection of unpopular beliefs is what the First Amendment is all about. "Struggles to coerce uniformity of sentiment in support of some end thought essential to their time and country have been waged by many good as well as by evil men," Justice Robert Jackson wrote in his elegant defense of a Jehovah's Witness's refusal to salute the flag in school. But "those who begin coercive elimination of dissent soon find themselves exterminating dissenters. Compulsory unification of opinion achieves only the unanimity of the graveyard."[2]

Kwame too was caught in contradictions. We nurture the belief that education encourages intellectual growth and social usefulness, that our young people and ultimately our country will benefit. By this standard, he was impressive: he studied psychology, read hungrily about the world beyond his native St. Louis, became a leader in campus politics, volunteered to counsel poor kids away from violence. But when his education led him to rethink his ideas about patriotism, duty, and race, no one wanted to hear about it. "Our children are asked to get out of organized gangs into unorganized gangs with M-16s instead of Uzis," he said when we first talked. I remembered that.

I had been at Lejeune earlier that year for another court-martial held on a late September day so hot that the schools were closed. Yet in the military courtroom, the pleats in the uniforms were knife-sharp, the postures erect, and the responses crisp. In a culture where politeness seems almost a fetish, it didn't surprise me that Kwame's blunt challenge to military order, tradition, and cohesion would draw attention, or that he had received an uncommonly stiff sentence.

In that first phone call, he said, "White males are able to grow and mature, read, enhance their minds. When black males mature [and change], they're asked, 'Who put you up to this?' " Of all the rhetoric I heard about conscientious objection at that time, this comment stuck in my mind as the sharpest summation of what was at stake. So I do know why I got back in touch with Kwame six years later.

———

I hadn't thought I had formed a picture of him from our phone conversations, but I must have—attenuated as a basketball player, maybe—because I'm surprised when he stands up to shake my hand in the hotel lobby in suburban St. Louis where we meet in the summer of 1998. Kwame, now thirty-two, is a big man: big hands, thighs, ears, teeth. He is dressed casually in sandals and navy shorts and T-shirt, appropriate to the humid weather and apparently to work as well, since we're fitting in our talk around a last-minute change in his work schedule at a center for mentally disabled adults.

Kwame used to be Eric Hayes. His mother had called him Eric for its Nordic sound, but he didn't feel Nordic, so a few years ago, he renamed himself: Kwame for "he who has the cure" in Ghanaian, Mensah for "third son," though he has only one brother. Sprawled in a chair, his fingers laced in his lap, he gives me a sweet, open smile, and says, "I tell you, Nan. . . ." He uses my name often and engagingly as he talks, eliding words, leaving sentences unfinished, rambling on some topics, leaning forward to pounce on others. He says he has been perceived as angry and hostile, but what I see is someone scratching at the world to get at something that will sustain him over time.

Kwame became a Marine in 1986 when he was twenty. His father had fought in World War II, an uncle in Korea, so "halfway buying" that he had a duty to enlist, he joined the Marines. "And halfway buying it," he adds "is the reserves, rather than active duty." He chose the Marines for the swashbuckling challenge of it. "I was really green about social consciousness, about where I fit in," he says, amazed and amused at his younger self. "I believed there were bad people out there who wanted to occupy this country. It was a joke. Not to say that people don't want to do that, but I think people love this lifestyle so much they don't want to destroy it."

Kwame spent twelve weeks at boot camp in San Diego. "Basic training"—he grins—"I loved it. I knew that it was a head game and once I got past that, I really did excel in it. Boot camp is basically just breaking you down and making you into a killing machine." He heard talk about "ragheads" and "camel jockeys," that sort of casual racism, but he shrugged it off, especially since boot camp looked like a manual for diversity. One drill instructor was African American, another Native American, a third Chicano. "Wherever we went, there was that color ratio. They put their best foot forward in boot camp."

Boot camp was followed by eight weeks at a duty station in Southern California, which is where Kwame realized how tame basic training had been. "I'm really starting to see some things almost immediately. I had no idea—I was just *green!* The Marines, they really attract some unstable people," he says, following up with a story about a white Marine spouting anti-Semitic vitriol one night. At first, Kwame was frightened, then he started to argue, then just listened. "And I'm like, damn! He's so far gone, there's no bringing him back." He shakes his head. "After that, one veil went up and I started looking more closely." What he found was that most of the racism was subtler.

Race hadn't been a big issue in his life before then. Class was what first challenged his ideas about how the world worked. He grew up in North St. Louis, then largely a black, middle- and working-class neighborhood.

"Street lights came on, kids went in, neighborhood store, policeman patrolling. My dad played sports with me and my brother in the front yard. We had a dog, two-car garage. We actually had a white picket fence. The whole nine. I thought I was in heaven." His parents made a decent living, his father as a contractor, his mother as a teacher.

In 1976, when Kwame was ten, the infamous Pruitt Igoe public housing development was demolished and its inhabitants were moved to other parts of the city, including North St. Louis. "Those black people who didn't know what a knife and fork is," he says of the changing population of his old neighborhood. "The first time I found out what a pimp was. . . . There were no more block meetings. They didn't understand about taking care of your own stuff, teaching the children not to curse. That was the biggest culture shock that I've ever seen in my life."

A few years later, his family moved. His parents had divorced, and Kwame moved with his mother to University City, which he calls UC, a pleasant neighborhood near Washington University, which he calls Wash U. Though Kwame's mother taught at a public school, she sent him to Catholic schools, where questioning was not encouraged. "We had a few teachers who taught more contemporary views on Catholicism and bringing up issues that the church opposes and looking at them and saying, why is that? And they were ostracized as being hippies."

So joining the Marines was an eye-opener on several fronts. "Middle-class blacks are not promilitary at all," he insists. "They will, if anything, become an officer, but it is really talked down. Lower-class blacks, it is absolutely one of the options out of high school." He thinks it's an over-rated option across the board, but the disenchantment may be greatest for young, poor blacks and Latinos with few alternatives. Recruited straight out of high school, many of the reservists who resisted fighting in the Gulf complained that they were enticed by promises of job training and stipends for education, which in the end didn't amount to much. "Realistically on a national level, when it comes to military service, all of us who sign up are expendable," Kwame says philosophically. "In peacetime, when it comes to promotion and who's in charge of a job, it's just as racist as any other facet of society."

Striving to be different, the military has turned itself into one of the most racially integrated institutions in the country, but according to an extensive survey of racial experiences and attitudes within the military, completed in 1997 but not released until late 1999, a majority of black servicepeople share Kwame's dimmer view.[3] Enlistment figures point up another disproportion: in 1990, when Kwame was a corporal, black men accounted for 20.2 percent of enlisted Marines but only 4.5 percent of commissioned officers.[4] By September 1999, black men and women made up 16.5 percent of enlisted Marines but only 6.5 percent of officers.[5] In 2002, they accounted for less than 4 percent of elite special forces throughout the military.[6]

It's hard to gauge how much all this bothered Kwame at the time, since what came afterward changed his perception so radically. He's clearer about his acceptance of the militarism he encountered: Marines, after all, are supposed to be gung-ho. In their applications and interviews, some CO claimants cited bloodthirsty chants they were taught as evidence of what they found repugnant about the military, and the press was fond of quoting them, probably because they're jaw-dropping. Another Marine CO had offered me the refrain, "Kill the town / Rape the people / That is what we like to do."

"Did I tell you that?" Kwame asks. "I was just thinking about it when you called the other day." He begins to recite as if recalling a nursery rhyme: "See the little children / Watch them as they gather round / Slap a mag in your M-16 / Blow the little somethings down."

"You can say the something," I tell him.

Sheepishly, he amends, " 'Blow the little fuckers down.' That was a cadence you sang when you ran. Something is very, very wrong with that."

After his five months of training, Kwame returned to St. Louis, and, in the fall of 1987, enrolled full time at Southern Illinois University at Edwardsville, a state university across the Mississippi River. He went there, he says, because it was close, it was a university, and it was cheap. He estimates that a third of the eleven thousand students were black, mostly from big cities, and didn't mix much with the white students from nearby rural areas. At the urging of his uncle, a vice president at San Francisco State University, he majored in psychology, then added a minor in anthropology. As a reservist, he got $140 a month toward tuition.

At college, Kwame's world opened up. He roomed with students from other countries and traveled abroad for the first time—to Ghana in 1987, Egypt the following year. "You really don't see the United States until you leave the United States, and the presence of the United States in another country is staggering," he says. "Richard Pryor said the first time he went to Africa, 'All these black people and there's no niggers!' I felt like that absolutely." By his sophomore year, he was elected the first American president of the African Student Association, giving him a platform for his evolving political views and making him a presence on campus.

Kwame is a quester by nature, and in his early twenties, he set out to learn about his race and his role in American society. He says that as he learned, "I became angry, but I don't know who I was angry with." The Marines made a ready target. "I became very anti. . . . How do you have a militant Marine? You start to change your views and you get into foreign policy arguments at your drill center. You become very disillusioned about the military's role in anything. You question everything. You distrust authority. The military does *not*, does *not* sanction questions. Honestly, it even manifested itself in a bad stomachache going to drill."

He tried his best to get kicked out, going delinquent at drills and showing up late to miss his flight to summer training. He had signed a contract known as a six by two—six years active duty, two years inactive—but tried unsuccessfully to transfer into the Army to do less time. He probably could have quit without serious consequences, he says now, but with less than a year left, he figured he'd ride it out. By then, he knew that he wouldn't fight if he was called up. He told people that—in his unit, on campus, anywhere someone would listen. "That's when the resistance was born, I believe, but it was not really tested," he says. "With CO, you have to put up or shut up. That's when the war came down."

On August 2, 1990, Iraq invaded Kuwait, and the United States began deploying soldiers to the Persian Gulf: some 540,000 troops all told, 265,322 of them reservists.[7] (In contrast, only 15,000 reservists and National Guard members were sent to Vietnam.) Kwame was at Camp Lejeune for summer training in biological and chemical warfare when he and his classmates turned on the TV and heard the news. He went to the map to find out where Kuwait was. Back at school that fall, he got a phone call from his unit—"Looks like we're gonna be called up soon"— so when his orders arrived in the mail on November 29, he didn't open them. He thinks he still has them in their sealed envelope somewhere.

"When I heard that I got called up, I was mad more than anything. I was furious at the war escalating and I was furious before we got called up at how they would televise it and make it like a rallying point. This is one of the most racially divisive times in our history, and the war comes up. My, oh my." He laughs without hiding his bitterness. "I think that the war may have happened anyway, but I don't necessarily think it was necessary."

Almost immediately after mobilization began, soldiers on active duty challenged deployment orders, and when reservists were also called up, military counselors, attorneys, and politicians across the country reported a barrage of phone calls about conscientious objection. The first Marine to go public with his resistance was Jeff Paterson, who sat down on the runway of an air station in Hawaii as his unit was being loaded onto planes bound for the Persian Gulf. Kwame saw the coverage on the national news, which is when he first realized that conscientious objection was an option.

Many CO applicants claimed that they didn't know they were eligible to apply and got little help from the military when they tried to find out about it. It is likely that many reserve command officers didn't know the regulations either, since it came up rarely. Anyone who knows he is a CO is barred from signing a contract with the military, but in recognition that people may change their minds after enlisting, all branches of the military have regulations allowing for CO discharge or reassignment to noncombatant duties. The CO discharge process takes an average of eight or nine months, and responsibility for processing a claim lies with an individual's command structure, giving officers considerable control over applicants.

On August 22, the president authorized the implementation of a "Stop Loss" policy that allowed the military to suspend nearly all discharges, transfers, and retirements. Under the Army's Stop Loss, the most extensive, no one whose unit was on alert, had been notified of deployment, or had been deployed to the Gulf could apply for CO status until arriving there. The language in these new policies was unclear, and many commands failed to alert soldiers to this change until they tried to file CO claims, leaving them the no-choice choice of avoiding fighting only by going to the scene of impending battle.

The right to conscientious objection is implicit in the Universal Declaration of Human Rights and, at this time, was recognized by most European countries.[8] In the United States, it is not a statutory right but has been covered through personnel regulations since 1962 (regulations were revised after the Gulf War). The Uniform Code of Military Justice defines conscientious objection as "a firm, fixed and sincere objection to war in any form or the bearing of arms by reason of religious training and belief." The burden of proof is on the applicant, who must have altered his or her beliefs since the time of enlistment; the objection must be to all wars and cannot be based on politics. Two Vietnam-era Supreme Court decisions broadened the definition of religious belief to include deeply held moral and ethical convictions not necessarily based on the concept of God,[9] though applications are stronger when they are grounded in religious doctrine.

Kwame wrote his application with the help of Bill Ramsey, then a program coordinator at the St. Louis American Friends Service Committee (AFSC). In it, he answers the requisite questions but offers little more. Briefly, almost perfunctorily, he mentions the Catholic doctrine of a "just war," the nonviolent resistance of Martin Luther King, and what he believes to be unjust U.S. policies, particularly in Central America. Yes, he would retaliate if his family were threatened, he writes, but ultimately, "I have come to an ethical and moral belief that this war is not right." Though raised a Catholic, Kwame had lost interest in organized religion but still defined himself as a spiritual person. He read books on philosophy and religion, believed in God, and prayed. He included some of this in his CO application, but the basis of his claim was primarily political, and he is glad for that. "It was not religious awakening that brought it out. It was just my own internal right and wrong. This was all real, all coming from the heart, all live in prime time. I mean wrong is wrong. I don't need a book that tells me what's wrong and right."

Yet the point of conscientious objection is that morality has an individual dimension and perceptions of right and wrong can change. For Kwame, right had once included fighting for what he accepted as his country's interests. Now, both the fighting and the interests seemed unbearably wrong.[10] "The metamorphosis that I went through from the things that I saw, the things that I experienced and the people that I met, I just could no longer have that macho militant attitude," he says. "Even if I put it on and wore it, it would look like a contradiction to me because it doesn't serve the people that I look like. It wouldn't even serve me. And why would I wear that attitude when that attitude hates me? That's crazy."

Kwame's complaint brings to mind the tension W. E. B. Du Bois wrote about at the beginning of the twentieth century: "One feels his two-ness—an American, a Negro; two souls, two thoughts, two unreconciled strivings." "How dare you tell me what my loyalty is and what I should do?" Kwame says, angry all over again at the politics of the war. "You have not put the same heart and soul, blood, sweat, and tears investing in my people. Why the hell should I invest like that with my own? Potentially losing my life, for what? For oil prices? I mean, what is that about? I thought, realistically, if I am fighting for oil, why don't people ride bikes more?"

In the latter half of the twentieth century, the wars with U.S. participation were fought far away and largely over abstractions that tended to
shift midcampaign. When Kwame's turn came, he had already located
his responsibility closer to home. In this he was of his historical moment,
with its suspicion of governmental solutions, glorification of individual
initiative, and Candide-like conclusions about tending our own gardens.
His sense of duty is pretty basic: using the advantages he's had to help
others fulfill their potential, acting ethically, being fair. Fairness comes up
often as he talks, and though "It's not fair" is a few steps short of a political program, it worked as a starting point for his political awareness.
"My duty lies with my people really: African Americans," he says seven
years after he refused someone else's definition. "I think you cannot clean
up anybody else's house until you clean up your own. I don't have a lot
of love for people who always blame white people. Racism is a real thing,
believe me, but there are things that you can clean up first, like how you
treat one another."

He would have given the same answer in 1990, he thinks, though it
has taken him time to find the right words. Of the Marines, he says, "I
think that it overwhelmed them to have a black man make that kind of
analysis of the world and then tell them to go to hell. I just really, really
think they couldn't deal with it."

They didn't deal with it, at least not through the usual multistep
process for reviewing CO applications, which includes an interview with
a military chaplain, a psychological evaluation, an official hearing, and
a final decision at headquarters. Kwame's application went nowhere and,
under military law, became moot as soon as he was charged with a legal
offense.

———

On the day Kwame received his orders to mobilize, Ramsey delivered his
CO application to his unit and was told that Kwame had until sundown
to show up. When he didn't, he was officially AWOL. That put him in
good company: at the end of the conflict, some 4,500 deserters were still
being sought by the military,[12] which comes to about eight deserters for
every thousand troops sent to the Gulf.

Ramsey asked if Kwame wanted to make a public statement. Absolutely, he answered. He called a press conference and booked a room on
campus in his capacity as president of the Black Student Association. The
administration was less than pleased, but Kwame remained unfazed. "It's

almost like shock, because I think if I was conscious of all that may have happened and all that was going on around me, I would have been frightened and I was not." Though he knew no other soldiers who were resisting the war, he felt a part of something. "I looked at a pattern from the Vietnam War and this war, and it seemed that it's the same kind of consciousness as a nation that poor black men should fight and not question and that if you did that, you were un-American and unpatriotic." He had a vivid, early memory of "people busting their nose diving on the floor whenever they heard firecrackers." They were Vietnam veterans returning home to his neighborhood. They're sick, his mother explained, but they didn't look sick to Kwame. "I think a lot of the strength that [young black men] got was from a lot of the things that had occurred in the sixties."

The press conference lasted about thirty minutes and was well attended. Kwame is a natural teacher, powered by his convictions, media-savvy and attentive to his audience, confident that he has a perspective worth passing on. He describes SIU-E as "very Bible belt, very Christian right," but he found a lot of support there for his stance. "For one, I think that the majority of the campus really didn't know what to think. I talked about war and who fights wars and who benefits. If you have all the information you can make better decisions. I mean, that would be an overnight revolution, a bloodless revolution. You choose not to do it. Think about that: You just choose not to do it."

But surely an army can't function by letting its soldiers choose not to fight. The military isn't a democracy in peacetime, and in battle there are very practical reasons for hierarchy. "But you can choose who you want to fight," he insists. "If you had the opportunity and information to choose who you had to fight, then somewhere along the line you're going to make friends. The military has no friends. Anybody can be the potential enemy."

The outbreak of soldiers, sailors, and Marines who had once chosen the military and now were opposed to battle seemed a slap in the face to a public that largely supported the war. It seemed also to baffle and enrage military officials. The COs were excoriated in the press as "sunshine patriots," "opportunists," and "manipulators" who underwent "pathetically convenient" conversions when asked to fulfill their duty. Conscientious objection is not supposed to be easy, but turning your back on all that is expected of you requires a special brand of courage. In what may have been the understatement of the war, Clare Overlander, an attorney defending army CO applicants on trial in 1991, observed, "Given the present climate, we are talking about the most unpopular defendants in the country at this time."

Americans have always been ambivalent about conscientious objection, though pacifist resistance to the military is older than the country itself. The first instance was recorded in 1658 in Maryland; a century later, one of the first laws enacted by the Continental Congress granted exemption from military service on the basis of conscience. James Madison advocated including a CO exemption in the Bill of Rights, but his proposal was defeated by those fearful of federal interference with state militia.

When the first national draft came into effect during the Civil War, the North and South exempted COs, though opposition to military enlistment was often treated as a crime. CO exemptions were allowed again when the draft was reinstated in 1917, the same year Theodore Roosevelt branded pacifists "traitors." During World War I, 450 resisters were court-martialed, and 17 were so mistreated that they died in prison. World War II saw only a tiny number of COs, but even then, the FBI and the Military Intelligence Division kept extensive records on war resisters. The first peacetime draft came into effect in 1948, and a decade later, despite the deep chill of the McCarthy years, over 7 percent of military inductees became COs.[13]

During the Vietnam War, almost eighteen thousand enlistees filed for CO status,[14] with approval rates reaching 90 percent in the later years. From this era comes the prevailing image of the conscientious objector as a white, Christian, middle-class, educated, male draftee, though, beginning in 1965, the majority of COs were not religious objectors. The stereotype obscures the amount of resistance from soldiers from other backgrounds during Vietnam and beyond: by 1972, for every 100 men inducted into the military, 130 others received exemptions, and the government soon ended the draft. Since 1980, however, all men have been required to register with the government when they turn eighteen.

The Gulf War was the United States' only all-volunteer war in the twentieth century. Voluntary enlistment, by definition, involves a choice, so it wasn't such a stretch for people who had joined the military of their own volition to think they should be allowed to choose their conflicts and their enemies. This seemed particularly true in the reserves—probably half the CO claimants were reservists—which had changed from being a safe haven for the middle class during the Vietnam War to a large and diverse group interwoven with active-duty forces.[15] To the military command, the resisters' arguments rang hollow: they had accepted the benefits of enlistment, now it was time to assume the risks. Besides, they responded, CO regulations required opposition to all wars, not a menu of choices. Objection to a specific war is recognized elsewhere, however: in standards adopted by the U.N. Human Rights Commission, in several European countries, and in legislation introduced into Congress in 1992. There is also the rock-hard reality that anyone who resists fighting so vehemently isn't likely to be much of a soldier.

———————

Was Kwame baiting the Marine Corps by making a public show of his opposition at his press conference? "Yes and no. I knew that there would be repercussions. What outweighed it was, I am sick and tired of people of color just doing stuff blindly. I am sick and tired of people not thinking and making the same bad, silly choices over and over and over again," he says, slapping the back of one hand into the palm of the other to emphasize the words. "I mean, stop being everybody's chump, stop being everybody's whore. At the press conference I said, I gotta do what I gotta do and they gotta do what they gotta do."

They did. At 2:30 in the morning of December 12, 1990, twelve days after his press conference, Kwame was awakened by loud knocking on his door. Five U.S. marshals entered while another five stood guard outside. "I was kind of glad it was over," he says. "We were waiting for them to come."

They put him in leg and belly chains and took him away. "It was like I was a drug kingpin. They whisked me out, they put me in a car, and I swore I heard a helicopter. And when I got in the car, cars came from everywhere and met up. Now the marshals were cool. The marshals know the difference between somebody who doesn't want to go to war and kicking in drug dealers' houses in East St. Louis. You could tell on their faces, they were, like, is it really that necessary?" One marshal suggested that Kwame could write a paper about his arrest after it was over, another patted him on the back and wished him luck. Four Marine chasers, the men sent to pick up deserters, arrived. One, a white Marine, made a phone call to report, "We got the black honcho from SIU."

Kwame's caravan drove to Scott Air Force Base, where he was loaded onto a general's private jet and flown to Camp Lejeune, a legal center and the largest concentration of Marines and sailors in the world. It was also where Kwame's unit was preparing to ship out to Saudi Arabia. Immediately on arrival, he was put in solitary confinement, a.k.a. the hole, where he remained for forty-two days.

Kwame knew no one who had been in prison and had no idea what it was going to be like. It turned out to be like basic training, only behind bars. It was Christmastime, he wasn't allowed visits from his family or girlfriend, and he didn't know how long he would be held there. Five to seven years had been mentioned, probably to scare him, since the recommended maximum sentence for missing movement was two years. "You're in the old, one-man cells with the bars and the whole nine. You tell time by when it's time to eat. I think at that time all they had was the Bible and Koran, and I read the Koran."

Nadine Gordimer writes in her novel *The House Gun,* "There's no privacy more inviolable than that of the prisoner." Was it like that? I ask, a little embarrassed because the answer could be yes. Kwame replies slowly and carefully. "I think that when you are in that kind of a situation where your fate is unknown and you're very, very frightened, that it is a time when you constantly confront yourself. You cannot run from your reality, not only physically but mentally. Basically I went through a metamorphosis in the hole because I really stripped myself of anything that could hurt me. I think that was the last time I ever had a term of endearment for Christmas. When you're in that situation, you can tear your hair out by thinking about things that are unattainable, so you kind of empty the program, for lack of a better term. The love for my girlfriend, the longing to graduate with my friends, to go on and prosper. My life was a vulnerable thing that they had taken away, and I could not let them use that to get inside me. I heard people losing it: 'Let me out!' Kicking on the door hours and hours. I had to be the calmest person.

"I've never told anybody this. I remember focusing, finding a spot about all of the good times with my girlfriend, about being home, about college. If you can picture that as a blanket, and my survival in that brig is to find a hole in that blanket and make the hole bigger and bigger and bigger to get to where that did not clog where my mind needed to be to cope with this. . . . I remember visualizing that and that helped me a lot."

In part because Kwame arrived at Lejeune before the other resisters, in part because he didn't define himself primarily as a CO, his involvement was mostly with the nonpolitical prisoners. Many supported the war completely, but some had found their own way to protest. Kwame recalls one who had punched his platoon sergeant and another who was released as soon as he said his being AWOL was not in protest. "The only reason that I got what I got was because I went on TV and quote-unquote embarrassed the military," says Kwame. "So if the military ever comes up with a sheet that says we only had this many [resisters], it's probably triple that because they gave them other charges. Ooh, there were a lot of guys in there."

Lawyers and counselors for the COs in all branches of the military charged that when their clients exercised their First Amendment rights, they were used as object lessons in what happens to soldiers who dissent. Some objectors were sent for courts-martial far from home where they would be separated from their families, supporters, and friendly witnesses. Others were shipped out to Saudi Arabia where their access to the news media could be controlled. According to Ron Kuby, a lawyer from New York representing COs at Lejeune, Marine policy was explicit. Defendants were offered shorter sentences if they pleaded guilty or agreed to join their units in the Gulf; if they went to the media, they were assured of stiffer punishments.

Of the 150 Marines who reported late during the Gulf War, defense lawyers complained, only CO claimants were charged with desertion. The Marine Corps responded that in all cases the disciplinary charges were unrelated to questions of conscience and that COs were treated no differently from others. It cited Defense Department rules requiring CO applicants to abide by military regulations, including transfer orders, until a discharge is granted. Failure to follow orders, especially in time of war, the Marines stressed, cannot be taken lightly.

Military regulations also provide for expediting CO applications and reassigning applicants to duties that conflict as little as possible with their beliefs during the review process. Reports from the COs indicate that the military went out of its way to do the opposite. When Sam Lwin, a Marine reservist from New York, handed in his CO application around the same time as Kwame, his commanding officer responded, "I hope the sergeants and other officers beat the shit out of you." Rather than process the application of Danny Gillis, a black, active-duty Marine from Baltimore, his superiors forced him onto a bus to take him to a plane for Saudi Arabia; black friends coming to his defense attacked his white guards and caused a small race riot. In the Army, five soldiers stationed in Germany were shackled and forced onto planes for the Gulf. Once there, their CO claims were delayed or denied, and they reported being subjected to beatings and death threats—a particularly unsettling prospect when everyone around you is armed.

Some COs awaiting trial at Lejeune were harassed so badly by prison guards that a military judge not known for leniency reduced their sentences in compensation. Amnesty International adopted Kwame and twenty-eight others as prisoners of conscience, the first in the United States since 1987. Several churches offered sanctuary to resisters, and thirty-three Catholic bishops signed a letter asking then-President Bush to grant amnesty to soldiers who refused to fight in the war.

It was in this charged atmosphere that Kwame went on trial. The day after he arrived at Lejeune, he had received a visit from his legal team, which consisted of a local, civilian attorney and Captain Burt Nunley, a Marine lawyer. Nunley was in his midthirties, short and stocky, with a buzzcut and a straightforward manner, and he and Kwame hit it off immediately. "He liked to win. I could see it in his eyes," Kwame says, still surprised at their odd pairing. "At first I didn't know how to take him, but he was impressed with me because I could write very well. I didn't know that was a big deal." From Nunley, Kwame learned that his commanding officer had asked who had put him up to applying for CO status—the question that rankled enough for him to repeat it to me months later. But Nunley also told him, "Your defiance made me see that you're legit." Kwame asked other prisoners how their lawyers talked to them, but apparently his relationship with Nunley was unusual. Quickly, he came to trust that Nunley would do whatever he could to get him the best deal possible.

Kwame's court-martial, the first for the Lejeune COs, took place on January 15, 1991, the day before the United States began bombing Iraq. Confident that he had already made his point, he took Nunley's advice and didn't push the CO issue. "I knew since my views were political and [given who] the judges were, the odds were against me. I knew I couldn't beat the rap."

Military courts operate under the same burden of proof, rules of evidence, and right to counsel as civilian courts, but there are significant differences. Jurors are selected by the commanding officer of the jurisdiction, convictions require only a two-thirds vote, judges have no fixed term of office, and no one is insulated from hierarchical pressures. At Lejeune, all the judicial offices shared a building, with judges on the second floor, defense on one side of the first floor, prosecution on the other. As Captain Jeff Sanky, a senior defense counsel at Lejeune at the time, told me, "The lawyers' community, we're very small."

At Kwame's court-martial, the prosecution submitted a tape of his press conference, highlighting his statements that they considered anti-American. It was a technique used in subsequent courts-martial, as the military regularly tried to introduce newspapers articles and videotapes of public events in which defendants expressed their opposition to the war and their intention to apply for CO status. The speech of service-people is protected by military regulations as long as they do not make public pronouncements in their capacity as soldiers, so the Marines maintained that the tapes were used only as evidence that the resisters were politically motivated and knew they were breaking the law.

In our first talk, when his court-martial was fresh in his mind, Kwame had said, "When you have an older, white authority figure who feels like the Marine Corps is the best thing that ever happened to this black guy . . . I think I pissed the judge off. There was the sentiment that I was ungrateful for this opportunity." Sentiment was moot, however, because Nunley had already cut a deal. Kwame pled guilty to Unexcused Absence and Missing Movement and received a three-year sentence, reduced to eight months for good behavior. "I bet I'm one of the few people in history who got a dishonorable discharge and did less than six months in the brig," Kwame brags. "That's unheard of."

The strategy came from Nunley, but the decision was Kwame's. "I was not interested in reforming the military," he says. "I was interested in getting out and getting to the folks that needed to hear it. I don't think Moses did a song and dance for Pharaoh. The best thing was to get the best deal I could, stand on principle, because I did it, I admit it, okay, fine. And I never backed down and never showed any remorse. I never said, I apologize, never said, okay, I give in, I'm going. Never."

That was an option offered him as he went to trial: apologize, quietly ship out to Saudi Arabia, and get discharged as soon as the war was over. So why didn't he do that?

"Because I had to look at myself in the mirror and say, are you compromising your principles? Most people are not given a chance to really act on what they believe. I'm so glad that I did. I sleep better."

Back when the CO story was unfolding, my impression had been that the dominant response in the military to the amount of internal resistance was surprise. "Not black people," Kwame answers. He found support in unexpected places. He had been promoted to corporal just before going to the brig—military efficiency at work—and some clerk in his unit quietly ensured that he continued to get paid at that level while in prison. Someone else conveniently "lost" his record book in Saudi Arabia. No local charges were filed against him and no permanent felony conviction showed up on his record (he is now trying to change his discharge from "dishonorable"). Had he been active duty, rather than reserves, his punishment might have had a greater impact on his life, but he insists that he still would have done the same thing.

---

Antiwar groups, such as the War Resisters League, Central Committee for Conscientious Objection, and AFSC, which had helped soldiers file CO claims, now found lawyers to defend the resisters. A high-powered legal team calling themselves the Aardvarks flew from New York to Lejeune, while an organization called Hands Off! coordinated publicity. Kwame's sentence seemed to establish a benchmark for those that followed, as most of the COs opted for similar pretrial agreements. Then, in May, Sam Lwin contested the charges against him and received only four months, by far the shortest sentence until then. But two days later, another reservist who also pled not guilty got thirty months. In contrast, a Marine who blamed his absence during the entire war on alcoholism received a twenty-one-day suspended sentence.[16]

Kwame was unimpressed with the theatrics of the lawyers and support organizations, who he thought were putting words in the mouths of some of the COs and using them to advance their own agendas. "They wanted all the COs to line up politically. It was like a dream team for the COs. After a while it got to be like a soap opera. Even the military was grandstanding. My court-martial was so cut and dry. By the time Sam Lwin came, it was like *Matlock*," he says with disdain.

Not surprisingly, given his plea bargain, he thought that the best thing the lawyers could do for their clients was to get them out of prison quickly so that they could go on with their lives and, he implies, act on the beliefs they espoused. "Making a statement is nothing," he says. "I don't bad-mouth any of the COs, but some of them were just scared and searching for a reason not to go. I give them the benefit of the doubt, but I don't think they were as conscious as they said they were. Usually if you make a serious step like this, your views have solidified."

Even in what would seem a very private struggle, star-making mechanisms were at work (in this country, to be well informed is to know who's famous), and the COs who got the most attention were the ones who looked the part or were most comfortable in the spotlight. One of the most public and protracted cases involved Erik Larsen, a Marine reservist from northern California, who stated that, as the son of Danish immigrants, he had joined the Marines because he wanted to repay America for what it had given his family. Fair-haired, strong-jawed, well-spoken, and Henry Fonda–lanky, he was a Marine out of central casting.

After announcing his intention to apply for CO status in August 1990, he spoke against military action at over one hundred events in the United States and Europe, until he was charged with desertion in time of war, potentially a death penalty offense, and sent to Lejeune. Larsen's celebrity did not go unnoticed by the Marines. His lawyer uncovered two "Fact Briefs," written at the highest level of Marine command, that monitored his public statements and the media and political attention they attracted.[17] When I met Larsen at a legal hearing at Lejeune the following fall, I commented, "You were famous."

"We *are* famous," he corrected. Larsen and his lawyer shrewdly used that fame and the outcry it generated to keep his sentence to six months.

"Not to knock Erik Larsen," Kwame says, "but he was the darling of the peace movement. He's a very intelligent guy, but that kind of strong stance doesn't happen over a week in your bedroom. Erik Larsen was sold as a package deal. The other COs would just look at him and, oh, man. I guess he felt obligated to give them some of his mail to read."

Freshly out of the brig, Kwame had told me, "This was about people's potential for growth, not just a peace issue. I think the peace movement needs a tune-up. If they—if we—are serious about antirecruitment, we're going to have to go after the pool the military draws from—minorities, women—going to have to look at social issues, the bigger picture. Economic conscription is the biggest reason people join the military." Now he instructs, "I would like you to put that in there. I didn't see a difference between the racism within the peace movement and the regular Marine Corps."

When Kwame returns that night after work, he tells me that he has been thinking of a lot of things since we talked that morning. "I think when racism deadens people, not to think, not to question, not to look at their own value system and to look at the world with realistic eyes, I think that's much more devastating than lynching somebody."

I tell him about a few of the COs I know of who stayed active in antiwar work, and he says he's glad to hear that. "I was so fortunate that God above and, I think, myself just kept me out of a lot of foolishness. The COs were promised all kinds of crazy things. You know, 'There are a lot of girls. . . .' By that time I was trying to get back into a normal frame of mind, so it was really going over my head." The CO as political pawn is a theme he returns to a few years later in an email reporting on a tenth reunion of COs that he helped organize. "We laughed; we cried," he writes. "We came up with strategies to help others in our past positions and swore that we would not exploit others like many of us were."

Kwame's portrait of publicity run amok intrigues me because at the time it had seemed that few people beyond Lejeune knew the COs existed. The first round of resistance elicited some stories in the mainstream media focusing more on human interest angles than issues. After that, the stories were mostly hometowners, as someone came up for court-martial or got out of the brig. Independent, probing reporting was one of the casualties of the Gulf War in general, but long after restrictions had been suspended for other journalists, reporters covering the COs at Lejeune were accompanied by a public affairs officer whose presence did little for open inquiry. Kwame was satisfied with the local and occasional national coverage he got after his release, though he disliked being portrayed as someone who "pays the price."

"Your fifteen minutes of fame," I say.

"A little bit more than fifteen minutes," he answers, echoing Larsen despite himself. He was released from the brig on June 2, 1991, about six weeks early, thanks to Nunley, who had traded a favor or two. He returned to SIU-E for summer school, but, to his dismay, everyone acted as if nothing had happened. That puzzled him since he felt so profoundly changed; surely it was apparent. "I have really, really, really changed a great, great deal," he repeats. "Even if I hadn't joined the Marines, I think maybe I would be a different person."

---

Six months after his release, Kwame was a featured speaker at an event organized by the head of youth services for St. Louis. His talk was titled "Why Black Youth Should Not Join the Military." Immediately, the Marines sent Kwame a letter informing him that he was prohibited from giving speeches, interviews, or news conferences for the remainder of his original, three-year sentence. The letter cited a difficult-to-find division order that applied only to Marine Corps officials, according to the lawyer who sued on Kwame's behalf to have the gag order rescinded. It was eventually dropped and a settlement negotiated, and that was the last Kwame heard from the Marines, which was fine with him. He was ready to move on, though he's convinced from reading local recruiting material that he left his mark. "They address issues like economic conscription, and I know this area doesn't know anything about economic conscription unless they heard it from Eric Hayes during the Gulf War."

He got his degree in 1993 and, as promised, brought what he had learned from his resistance back to his community: volunteering with AFSC, an African American firefighters organization called FLAME that advocates for multicultural fire departments, and Simba Wachunga, a black youth group that re-creates ancient African rites of passage. (Kwame describes it as "kind of like when a guy gets bar mitzvahed.") His ties to a larger community, to America, are more tenuous. He could leave in a heartbeat, he announces, even as he ticks off all the things he prizes here. "The technology is tight, the medical resources, the whole nine . . . beautiful. How America has struggled with adversity is beautiful. You have a constant struggle in America and I like that. America is as liberal for me to do what I did because it has been so oppressive in the past. My ancestors paid dearly. People fought, bled, died, were torn apart for me to have the right to refuse to do it."

Back in the fall of 1991, after most of the CO trials were over and the defendants were finishing up their time in the brig, I had a phone conversation with Lieutenant-Colonel Gerald Bubsey who, as Staff Judge Advocate for the 4th Marine Air Wing, had advised the commanding general on many of the Lejeune courts-martial. "Obviously these kids aren't criminals," he told me then. "They just made a serious blunder." When I quote that to Kwame now, he doesn't miss a beat. "Well, that's a blunder I'm glad I made.

"It seems like a hundred years ago," he says, waving an old newspaper clipping I've brought to show him. "Hopefully, the book will show a continuum. I hope when you write this, you make it sound like part of something bigger."

The first time Kwame and I spoke, he said of his decision to dissent, "It's maturing, it is growth, spiritually, intellectually, that the path I once chose makes me no longer choose that path."

When I called him again six years later, he said, "It caught me in midstride. It caught me at the time that I was making the transition from sitting on the fence to action."

Now, it's very late, and this battle has been replaced by new ones. Tired, talked out, we slouch in our chairs. "My country didn't need another infantry rifleman," he says firmly. "I served my country a hundred times better by not going."

# chapter three

# BEYOND MERE DISSENT

Margaret Randall

*Albuquerque, New Mexico, June 1997*

On a startlingly clear October day in 1985, Margaret Randall, a writer and poet, walked to the mailbox at the end of her driveway in the hills above Albuquerque and pulled out the fat envelope from the United States Immigration and Naturalization Service that she had been waiting for. She remembers the beauty of the high desert in autumn as she stood reading. It was part of what had brought her home to New Mexico after twenty-three years abroad. Though U.S.-born, she had reluctantly relinquished her American citizenship when she became a Mexican citizen long ago. Now, here was a letter from the INS district director, informing her that her application for permanent residency was denied because, he wrote, "Her writings go far beyond mere dissent, disagreement with, or criticism of the United States or its policies."[1] She was given thirty days to leave the country.

It was true that Margaret had criticized government policies, but she had assumed that she was free to do that as her birthright. Citizenship, she figured, didn't hinge on the propriety or patriotism of one's thoughts. Now the government wanted to send her away because it didn't like her thinking. For the next two years, as both sides contested the case, they would cite history, law, and national sentiment to buttress their positions, but at the heart of the argument is the most basic question about free speech that a democracy faces: How should a government respond to ideas that, rightly or wrongly, it considers dangerous?

All governments, whatever their philosophy or structure, respond with some degree of suspicion, and the United States has been no exception. In 1952, at the height of McCarthyism, Congress indulged the national mistrust of "foreign" ideas by enacting the McCarran-Walter Act, which governed immigration for the next four decades. Provisions in this law allowed the State Department to exclude and deport noncitizens solely because of their beliefs, making the United States the only Western democracy to do so.[2] These provisions, known as the "ideological exclusionary clauses," criminalized a number of vaguely defined beliefs and affiliations, primarily related to communism. When Margaret sought to reclaim her American citizenship, the government invoked these exclusions as necessary limits to freedom and began proceedings to deport her.

---

When Margaret and I meet in the summer of 1997, nearly eight years after her case was resolved, she is settled into her North American life. She lives with her partner, Barbara Byers, a teacher and artist, in a house her father helped her build at the foot of the Sandia Mountains. It is an adobe structure with airy rooms, fine views of the mountains, and walls lined with books, Margaret's photographs, and Barbara's paintings. After dinner one evening, the three of us hike along a trail beyond their house that winds in and out along the mountainside. The setting sun turns the hills the color of wet sand. Below, the city's lights spill in ribbons down to the Rio Grande. You can see for fifty, seventy miles, Margaret tells me, sweeping an arm expansively. It is easy to understand how this land called her back, even from so far away.

The morning I arrive, Margaret makes me pancakes, then we sprawl foot to foot on the sofa. In youthful photos on her book jackets, she is an intense woman with long, dark hair, high cheekbones, and beautiful gray-green eyes. Now in her sixties, the eyes are stunning still, but she has thickened, her hair is gray and short, and she seems at ease with herself, if not yet with the world. As we talk, she kicks off her huaraches and curls up against an Indian blanket thrown over the sofa, so that, with her purple T-shirt and turquoise jewelry, the scene reminds me of an ad for Southwest design. When she speaks, however, it's strictly Brooklyn, an accent that she says marks her Spanish too, though she left New York for New Mexico when she was ten.

Margaret's citizenship troubles began in the late 1960s, several years after she packed up her infant son, Gregory, and caught a Greyhound bus for Mexico City. She was twenty-four years old when she did that and had already dropped out of college, gotten married, lived in Spain, gotten divorced, and moved back to New York, where she began to write poetry. Having a child without a husband was her choice, but then, as now, supporting and raising a baby alone was difficult, and she had a sense that life would be easier in Mexico.

She quickly fell in with a group of writers and artists, who introduced her to the literature of Latin America. Out of these friendships grew a bilingual literary magazine called *El Corno Emplumado / The Plumed Horn,* which she edited for eight years, publishing prominent modernist writers and scholars from all the Americas. She married her coeditor, a Mexican poet named Sergio Mondragon, and they had two daughters. "So that in 1967," she sums up, "I lived in Mexico City, was married to a Mexican citizen, had three young children, all under the age of six. I presumed, I suppose, at the time that I would live with him for the rest of my life."

Mondragon became increasingly involved in Eastern philosophies and decreasingly interested in the workaday world, so it fell to Margaret to provide for the family. Ever resourceful, she translated comic books, did midwifery, and sold tortillas, but, as a foreign woman, she found remunerative work hard to come by. She was advised, somewhat inaccurately, that taking out Mexican citizenship would make that easier. Up to that point, she, like most native-born Americans, hadn't given citizenship much thought. "I love the United States, I love my country, I love many things about the culture," she says, "but I never believed that having that passport or a piece of paper had anything tangible to do with the idea of citizenship, as being a part of, identifying with my country. They were formalities, like having a driver's license."

In fact, about the only obligation of American citizenship is not to lose it, but Margaret found one of the few ways to do that. Mexican law required her to declare that she gave up her U.S. citizenship, and once she did that, she dutifully informed the American consulate. "I said to her [the consular official] at the time that I had no desire to lose my American citizenship, but that I had done this to get a better job." Around this time, the Supreme Court ruled that citizenship is a right that cannot be taken away by Congress and can be lost only when a citizen voluntarily renounces it with full knowledge of the consequences.[3] This made dual citizenship possible, but apparently, word of the change hadn't made it to the American consulate in Mexico City at the time Margaret spoke with them, and she was told that, regardless of her wishes, she was no longer an American citizen.

Soon after, she and Mondragon were invited to give readings at U.S. universities, and they applied for visas as Mexican citizens. Mondragon got his with no problem, but Margaret's was denied. A consular official told her this was because she was a member of the Mexican Communist Party, which was not true. At the last moment—Mondragon and the children were already in the States—she was issued a temporary travel permit after she listed where she would speak, who she thought would be in the audience, and what she intended to say.

In Mexico City, as in much of the world, 1968 was a turbulent year. Students were agitating for economic and political reform, and an uneasy government was growing increasingly repressive. Drawn to the students' politics, Margaret wrote supportive editorials in *El Corno,* helped with translations, fed and hid people who were in danger: "Just what any decent people in Mexico would have done at that point." On October 2, government troops opened fire on unarmed demonstrators at Tlatelolco, the Plaza of Three Cultures, killing probably more than three hundred people.[4] In the aftermath, at least two thousand others were arrested and held without trial, and the student movement was decimated. Thirty years later, Margaret was to write in a letter to family and friends, "From that moment on, I would know what those in power are capable of, what they are willing to unleash in order to preserve their power."

In the crackdown that followed, the Mexican government withdrew its subsidies from *El Corno* and intimidated printers who tried to print it. Support from abroad kept the magazine alive for a few more issues, but like everyone even tangentially linked to the movement, Margaret lived with a sense of threat.

In the fall of 1969, she had separated from Mondragon and was living with Robert Cohen, a young American writer with whom she had just had her fourth child. Margaret was sick in bed when two men, claiming to be representatives of Mexico's social security assistance, arrived at her house. They had been tipped off, they said, that she was not a Mexican citizen and was running an illegal sweatshop in her home. None of it was true, but in an attempt to prove them wrong, Cohen showed them her passport. No sooner did they have the passport in hand than—Margaret snaps her fingers—one pulled a gun as they ran to a car with no license plates and sped away.

Margaret petitioned various government agencies to learn of accusations against her, but the responses consistently came back negative. She wasn't surprised; she knew the men weren't from the government and came to believe that they were paramilitary agents, perhaps with CIA connections. When she asked the Mexican government for a new passport, though, she met with skepticism and was told that they would have to investigate before she could get a new one. She didn't consider asking the U.S. consulate for help. "Certainly the United States protects those it wants to protect, but," she says dryly, "I very soon fell out of that category."

Having exhausted their options, she and Cohen decided to go underground. Just after her passport was stolen, her son had been held by Mexican police for thirty-six hours, and the danger was palpable. But after several months, living clandestinely became too difficult for the children, and Margaret sent them on their own to Cuba. She reports this almost offhandedly, but when I press her—Wasn't she scared?—she concedes, "I had no idea who would be at the other end, and it was scary and it was very difficult, but I felt that it was the right thing to do by them. I felt that their lives were already endangered enough. There was really nothing else we could have done."

She and Cohen had been planning to move to Cuba before they were forced underground. Margaret had visited there twice and found it a sympathetic and appealing culture. Now it was one of the few places she could go without papers. So she brought her children to the Cuban embassy and asked if Cuba would take them, as, she says, it had taken thousands of children from around the world.

She expected to join them within a few weeks, but from this point, her journey sounds like an "Escape from" movie. With the student movement shattered, it was hard to get the false papers she needed to leave the country. She and Cohen heard of someone in the northern border state of Chihuahua who would get her a passport, but when they finally tracked him down, all he had to offer was a temporary document that had to be authenticated by a U.S. consul, making it useless to her. "This guy was, I think, a gangster of some kind. I don't know what he was involved with, maybe guns." But he was inclined to help her out. She doesn't know why. "So Robert took a commercial bus to El Paso and this guy got me out of the country in the back of a meat truck. Robert and I met up in Juárez and we walked across the bridge, as if we were two North Americans who had walked across for the day."

From Texas, Cohen went to New York and Margaret flew to Chicago, then took a bus into Canada, using her birth certificate as identification. From Toronto, she flew to Paris's Orly Airport and stayed outside customs until boarding a plane to Prague, where she was met by Cubans who were supposed to send her on to Cuba. There was only a weekly flight to Havana, though, so when she finally reached Cuba, she had been separated from her children for four months. Ana, the baby, didn't recognize her mother. The whole experience, she says, was both very hard—she was sick and missed her children—and very easy. "Because I guess I'm the kind of person when I have to do something and I figure out that this is the way to do it, then I just do it, you know? I was lucky and it worked."

When she moved to Cuba, she dropped an appeal to regain her U.S. citizenship that she had been pursuing, and at the end of 1969, the State Department approved a loss-of-nationality certificate for her. For the next ten years, she lived, worked, wrote, and raised her children in Cuba. She traveled frequently—to Chile, Venezuela, Peru, North Vietnam, even the United States on a long lecture tour in 1978—using a Cuban identity card. But, she says, "I continued to live sort of as a person without a country."

It was during this time that Margaret began to work with *testimonio,* the populist oral history that grew out of the Latin American revolutionary movements of the 1960s and, for Margaret, was enriched by the writings of second-wave feminists. "Many of my questions about my own life were clarified by feminism," she says. "What that made me do after I looked at my own life was to try to figure out what the lives of women around me were like. My entrance into testimony was feminism. I didn't know what I was doing was, quote, oral history. I didn't know it had a name."

Her first book of *testimonio* was *Cuban Women Now,* published in 1972 in Spanish and two years later in English. *Spirit of the People: Vietnamese Women Two Years from the Paris Accords* followed in 1975. Both books would later be used by the U.S. government as evidence of her subversiveness, and their underlying concept was radical, at least in terms of how history is perceived. She explains, "In revolutionary societies, there was a huge emphasis on ordinary people being the protagonists of history. One of the things that popular revolution does is try to restore a people's sense of their own identity and history. That history is very often different from the picture that they've been given in a book."

Impatience with authority informs much of her work, and the seeds seem to have been planted early on. "It seems to me that I was always a rebel from the time I have memory. My father was extremely encouraging to all of his kids. There was nothing as an adolescent or young woman that I wanted to do that I couldn't do." This confidence—arrogance, maybe—helped her head to Mexico knowing no one, start a mag-

azine with no experience, write about what interested her without credentials, make a life wherever she landed, and fight for the right to her
own voice when the need arose. Still, she's a little mystified about how
she got politically radicalized.

Margaret grew up in a comfortable area of Albuquerque near the University of New Mexico, where the streets are named for East Coast colleges. Her father, a cellist, taught music in the public schools and played
in the local symphony, and her mother did Spanish-English translation.
Her parents moved in liberal circles and championed liberal causes, but
she came of age in the 1950s, not exactly a high point for radical thinking among the middle class. "I grew up thinking that my parents were
quite radical and risk taking. They did interesting, fun things, but [in
their thinking] they didn't veer from the accepted path. Over the years
I've come to realize that my parents were frightened of authority." Some
of that had to do with anti-Semitism, she thinks. Her father had changed
his name to the non-Jewish Randall, and only after his death did her
mother admit that it was because they had wanted to spare their children
the prejudice that they had experienced.

"It's so antithetical to how I believe one should live one's life," Margaret says now. "I understand now in my older age, my mother thought
she was helping her children and I'm sure my father did too, but I would
have liked a more courageous example. Now, given the torture chambers
of Latin America or the concentration camps of Europe, would I have
been able to be courageous? Don't know." Margaret is an atheist and
lived for years in Catholic countries, but she made sure that her children
knew they were Jewish from the time they knew the word. Jewishness,
she says, gave them a history to identify with.

History, power, identity, voice: if lives can be said to have themes,
these are Margaret's. After lunch one day, Barbara, her partner, joins us
and speaks movingly about the learning-disabled kids she teaches, who
struggle with the simplest of expression. Through circumstance, she
points out, they have no voice. Is this censorship? she asks.

Speech is tamped down in many ways: parents scold their children for
swearing, teachers punish students for disrupting class, friends object to
a tactless remark, and the guy behind us at the movies shushes our witty
commentary. The most frequent—and persuasive—limit to speech is
someone else's desire to be left alone. Censorship, in contrast, is an official act, or at least an impulse backed by the means to enforce it. But definitions of censorship sidestep the reality that free speech is not distributed evenly and neither is outrage at its restriction. To feel censored, you

have to believe that you have something worth saying, so censorship probably seems like a more present threat to people who have been congratulated from an early age on their every utterance. Perhaps that is why support for free expression rises with education and income and why its most ardent supporters tend to be white, male, politically active, and young.[5]

"Most people are taught that their stories are not important," Barbara says.

"Or won't make any difference," Margaret adds.

In her case, the government had the power to deny her what she wanted but not, ultimately, the power to make her into a different person. "Say I had been deported and I never could have lived in this country; it would have changed my life. It would have been very painful, but I never didn't have a voice. Even when I had to be careful of what I was saying because of the case, I still had a huge, loud voice."

She describes, with obvious satisfaction, an interview she did with a Cuban woman, an old, unschooled tobacco worker, who told her story vividly. When Margaret returned to read the woman what she had written, she reports, "She kept saying, 'Yeah, that's me, that's me.' And then, 'That's not me,' and it wasn't. It was an incredible process getting something she could identify with as her voice."

"That's why Margaret got in trouble," Barbara says, proudly. "To give a voice to people who aren't supposed to have voices, you're in trouble."

———

In 1979, just after the Sandinistas' victory in Nicaragua, Margaret got a call from Ernesto Cardenal, a poet and, at the time, Nicaragua's newly appointed Minister of Culture. He and Margaret had been friends since her Mexico days, and now he asked her to come and write about the women of his country. It was an intriguing proposition: being involved at the beginning of a revolution, documenting the role of women in that transformation, working in a society that valued artists and writers highly. She visited for three months, collecting material for what would become *Sandino's Daughters,* one of her most highly regarded books, and soon after returning to Cuba, she knew that she wanted to move to Nicaragua permanently.

The problem was how to get there without a passport. Shortly before she was to leave, she read a newspaper article about the new Mexican ambassador to Cuba, and, recognizing him as one of two diplomats who had been particularly courageous during the 1973 Chilean coup, she decided to try once more to get her Mexican passport back. She explained her case as she had to others before, and, she says, "His reaction was unbelievable. He said, 'Of course! You're a national treasure. I have five of your books. I'd like you to sign them for me. You'll have your passport by eleven o'clock in the morning.' " And just like that, she did.

In Nicaragua, Margaret gravitated as usual to political and cultural circles, an easy thing to do, since politics and art were everywhere. But the ongoing civil war made life in Managua increasingly taxing and dangerous, and by mid-1983, she was sliding into a nervous breakdown. She struggles to describe it. "I was tired, I was wearing out. I began to feel that I couldn't write what I wanted to be writing because I was working long days. The kind of work I was doing could have been done by anybody, but the kind of writing I wanted to do could only be done by me, and I had to go home and do that."

It is a refrain she returns to often. "I began to look at my own life as a series of incredibly important places and political times, but I never stopped thinking of myself as New Mexican. I also got toward middle age, and I just had this terrible need to find out how those different strands came together in my life and what they meant and what that produced." She became sicker and more terrified by what was happening to her until, at her request, her employer sent her to a therapist, a Mexican woman whom Margaret credits with saving her life. After two sessions, the therapist said, "You have to go home now."

Home, for Margaret, was the United States, where she had not lived for twenty-two years and was officially an "alien." But the official stance made no more sense to her then than it had when she lost her citizenship. "I wanted to come home and I always felt that this was my home. This country, this part of the country, this landscape, this life, this space, this culture is deeply a part of my identity. I'm a poet, I use this language. But when I wanted to come home, I wanted to stay. And that was the point."

That was pretty much what she told the man at the American consulate in Managua. She doesn't know if he knew who she was, though it's likely he did, since she had some prominence in Nicaragua. He gave her a one-year, multiple-entry visa, the best he could do, and advised her that she would have a much better chance of getting a permanent visa once she was in the States. Charles Peacock was his name. He gave Margaret his card, which she carried in her wallet for years. "You wonder about these people in your life," she says, still surprised to have found compassion where she expected bureaucratic indifference. "I've always wondered about the man in Chihuahua too. What was he? He was so kind to me. People walk into your life and walk right out again, but you always wonder."

———————

Every Fourth of July, my newspaper runs a photo of a veritable United Nations of people, some solemn-faced, some teary-eyed, others grinning, but all apparently pleased to be sworn in as American citizens. It's one of those feel-good photo ops we're meant to regard with pride, and there is something hopeful and moving about people achieving a goal and finding a home. It isn't citizenship that we're celebrating, though, but *American* citizenship, and I think of this as Margaret narrates her thwarted desire to be "American" again.

Margaret returned to the United States in January 1984, coming home to Albuquerque and to Floyce Alexander, an old friend and fellow poet, with whom she had been carrying on a romance by mail over the previous year. They married in February, and in March, she applied for permanent residency status, commonly known as a "green card." Her husband, son, and, later, her father, American citizens all, petitioned on her behalf.

Getting a green card usually takes two to three months, but Margaret wasn't overly concerned when a year passed and nothing happened. She was busy reacclimating to life in the States. In that year, she had begun teaching at the University of New Mexico and had separated from her husband and realized that she was a lesbian. It had taken her a while to figure this out, she admits somewhat wryly, because in the revolutionary circles of her generation, it was considered bourgeois to worry about one's personal life.

Finally, the following June, she was summoned to the INS office in Albuquerque, where some of her books were opened on the table with passages highlighted in yellow marker. A quick look told her that the marked parts included poetry and prose, as well as opinions, hers and those she reported, that were critical of the American government and economic system. Politely, the INS official asked what she meant by these things. Politely, she answered that she meant what she had written. And why had she had written it? "Well," she explained, "there was very little coverage in our press that I considered fair about what goes on in Cuba and Nicaragua, so I think it's important that people hear the other side."

The interview continued for two hours, but, innocuous as it was, by its end, Margaret understood that if she wanted to remain in the country, she was going to have to fight. She phoned her friend Michael Ratner at the Center for Constitutional Rights, a public interest law organization in New York, described what had happened, and asked if she had a case. Absolutely, he replied. CCR soon agreed to represent her.

America's attitude toward immigration is complex and often contradictory. We think of ourselves as a nation of immigrants,[6] accept about one million legal immigrants each year, and allow millions more in on a temporary basis. We also turn millions away, mostly because the demand is great but sometimes because of exclusionary policies. Once immigrants arrive, their constitutional protections are open to debate. Until recently, it was generally assumed that the government could decide whom to let into the country but could not limit the rights of noncitizens living here, and well before Margaret's case, the Supreme Court recognized even illegal aliens as "persons" entitled to due process.[7] Yet for years the First Amendment rights of noncitizens were limited by the ideological clauses of the McCarran-Walter Act, which allowed the government to deport individuals whose presence was considered "prejudicial to the public interest" or who "advocate[d] the economic, international, and governmental doctrines of world communism."[8] These exclusions targeted activities that are legal when undertaken by citizens, so the clauses were more punitive than protective. Nonetheless, from Eisenhower on, every administration invoked McCarran-Walter to deny visas to a total of tens of thousands of people, including Nobel Prize winners, politicians, and writers. Eventually, the State Department would create a computer database of about a million people who could be excluded under various clauses of McCarran-Walter.[9]

When Margaret received the official denial of her visa application that October, she was as prepared as she could be, but the reasoning behind the denial—that she had disagreed with the government and therefore didn't deserve to live in this country—seemed such an abrogation of her basic rights that it renewed her anger and determination to retrieve her citizenship.

---

It is likely that the decision to deny Margaret residency came from higher up than the INS office in Albuquerque, yet it seemed to her that the head of that office had a personal vendetta against her. Sometimes his animosity struck her as funny, as when he declared her an "alien anarchist" on a local television show. Other times it was less amusing, as when she ran into him, the only man there, in the waiting room of her gynecologist. She allows that it could have been a coincidence, but she doesn't think so.

Attacks came from other quarters too: obscenities screamed at her on the street, a physical threat at the University of New Mexico, death threats in the mail. She says, "The attacks were very few compared with the support, but enough so that I never knew when someone rushed toward me what they were going to say. You're always on edge; you don't know what to expect." It was an odd fame, her face becoming so familiar that, years after the case was over, a woman she had never seen before walked up to her in Amsterdam and said, "Margaret Randall, you cut your hair."

Against the insinuations and threats stood an impressive network of support, testimony to the value of political organizing and the good fortune of those who can call on it. Over twenty support groups were organized across the country, and as Margaret's case became something of a cause célèbre among American intellectuals, creative people found creative ways to make her situation public and to raise money. Berkeley proclaimed a Margaret Randall Day, Seattle held a Bowl-a-Thon for Free Speech. Painter Elaine de Kooning made posters, cartoonist Nicole Hollander created postcards, singer Holly Near gave a concert, and the list of poets and writers who gave readings on Margaret's behalf forms a Who's Who of the cultural left.

In Albuquerque, a fifth-grade class at the school Margaret had attended as a child adopted her and wrote her letters. One reads: "I know how you feel. Some days I feel like if I don't believe what my classmates want me to believe they won't like me. But everyone has a right to believe what they want to." When Margaret traveled, Red Caps at the Albuquerque airport signaled their support. On a California street, a man pushed a $20 bill into her hand and said, "Spend it on yourself. We need roses as well as bread." Many donations came from people she didn't know, but she wrote to everyone who helped. "Some people gave $1,000, but the most moving were the ones that gave $5," she says. "That's a very important thing for me to hold onto. It kept me going."

Margaret knew she was lucky. It was much easier to pursue citizenship inside the country than from abroad, she had status and backing among people who knew how to get their views heard, and, though she couldn't afford the legal costs herself, she had access to money. (Her legal bills would come to a quarter of a million dollars.) She also had confidence in the rightness of her cause. "I believe in the First Amendment, that it was an important issue to fight for," she says. "So much so that when I realized that I was a lesbian, although it's not in my nature to hide who I am, I was willing in this case to not externalize that." At the time, "sexual deviancy," a euphemism for homosexuality, was grounds for exclusion. "I believed I had a responsibility, since I was able to fight that battle for people who couldn't."

---

After Margaret's application for permanent residency was denied, the next step was a deportation hearing, which took place in El Paso, Texas, over four days in March 1986. Some eighty of her supporters (including a few elderly men from the 1954 Salt of the Earth strike in southern New Mexico) filled the small courtroom. On the second day, the INS brought in its own contingent. The transcript of the hearing is over eight hundred pages long, though the government called no witnesses and based its case solely on Margaret's writing and ideas.

Americans, I've found, tend to view with suspicion anyone who chooses to live somewhere else, taking it as a form of betrayal. I detect something of this in the government's attempt to discredit Margaret as un-American. As if expatriate life were evidence of bad character, the INS attorney condemned her as "a fifty-year-old malcontent expatriate who has deliberately chosen to live a self-imposed political exile from the United States for the majority of her adult life."[10] Later, an INS appeals board member would oppose returning her citizenship because "she turned her back on her country and chose to embrace a life in Communist dominated countries. A welcome mat should not be placed at her feet."[11]

Her putatively un-American activities included interviewing and attending meetings with communists and anarchists; being an atheist; publishing "anti-American cartoons" and an ad for a book by Karl Marx in her magazine; writing a poem titled "Che"; and, one of her favorites, "disrupting the happiness and good order of the United States."[12] Some of her offending opinions, such as opposition to the Vietnam War, had been held by many Americans, but presumably she, as someone who had "renounced" her citizenship, was not permitted to dissent, or to challenge current popular political assumptions, such as the villainy of Nicaragua's Sandinistas.

The INS subpoenaed everything Margaret had ever published, which came to 2,744 pages, according to Martin F. Spiegel, the presiding judge, who seems to have counted. Much of her work was in Spanish, so the INS had it translated into English, but the translation was so poorly done that Margaret felt compelled to point out inaccuracies. At one point, Guadalupe Gonzalez, the INS lawyer directing the case, who Margaret says spoke no Spanish, stated that Margaret first visited Cuba in January 1967 to meet with the Nicaraguan poet Rubén Darío. That year marked the centenary of Darío's birth, and Margaret had been invited to an event called "Encuentro con Rubén Darío." *Encuentro* in this case meant not an encounter, as the INS translation had it, but a symposium, and Rubén Darío had died in 1916.

It was not just words that were lost in translation as the government and the writer confronted each other, but also how each side thought about language. As evidence of Margaret's danger to the country, Gonzalez presented a description someone had written of *El Corno* as a "revolutionary weapon." That, Margaret told her, was a metaphor, to which Gonzalez replied, "What's a metaphor?" No doubt, many Americans don't know what a metaphor is and are no lesser people for it, but the government based its case on the written word without any apparent awareness that writing can function on more than one level or that meaning may vary with context.

Much of the case against Margaret rested on her oral histories of women in Cuba and Nicaragua, who spoke with quite uncritical enthusiasm about their countries' revolutions. She had struggled not to appropriate their stories for her own purposes, but the INS was haphazard in distinguishing the words she quoted from her own. Still, it is apparent that Margaret sympathized with the women's views. She didn't deny this; she just thought that using it as a reason to deny her residence was itself un-American. Randall is interested in the lives and thoughts of people in countries with communist governments, this reasoning goes; therefore, she must be a communist—that is, guilty by association. Taken a few steps further—as it was with increasing frequency over the next several years—this thinking can be used to condemn journalists, scholars, students, writers, artists, teachers, social workers, medical workers, clergy, and almost anyone with a healthy curiosity.

At Margaret's hearing, the clash of cultures proliferated. There were the social and political systems of Central America that she had functioned in for her adult life contrasting with those of the United States. There was her radical cosmopolitanism chafing against the protective chauvinism of the INS. Finally, there was the style and snobbery of an intelligentsia asserting itself against the state's questionable aesthetic judgment and its restrictive definition of what it meant to be American. All this was apparent in the witnesses Margaret brought to testify in her behalf, which included her mother, a wisp of a woman, who demanded to know how the country dared celebrate the Statue of Liberty's centennial when it didn't honor freedom of expression. Also important to her defense was the testimony of experts, such as the poet Adrienne Rich, speaking to the value of Margaret's writing, and Nelson Valdez, a Cuban exile and sociology professor at the University of New Mexico, who explained that being a member of your block committee in Cuba was not the same as being a member of the Communist Party.

Margaret calls this a "brilliant showing,"[13] but in many ways it was beside the point. Much of her work, particularly in *testimonio,* was significant, but writers can almost always find experts to certify their writerliness, and if insignificance or inadequacy were grounds for banning writers, this country would be covered with a lot more trees. Margaret believes the state has no imagination, and the American state proved itself tone-deaf and literal-minded in her case. It appeared to have no interest in understanding or appreciating her work, but it did pay her the compliment of taking it seriously enough to fear it. "Oh, absolutely. I should hope so!" she answers brightly when I ask if she thinks her writing is subversive. But when I observe that censors always feel that the idea they oppose is too dangerous to air, she corrects me: "You can't use a word like *dangerous* without a context. It has to be, dangerous to what? If we're talking about dangerous to complacency, dangerous to small-mindedness, prejudice, self-aggrandizement, I hope to hell my writings are dangerous. Dangerous in that they can blow up a building? No."

The government has obvious and valid reasons for wanting to keep criminals out of the country. McCarran-Walter, however, made no distinction between dangerous acts and disfavored words, though democracy is supposed to be elastic enough to embrace even inflamed struggles over conflicting ideas. As Thomas Jefferson noted, uniformity of opinion is unattainable, and the effect of coercing it is "to make one half the world fools, and the other half hypocrites."[14] Even if it were possible, homogeneity of thought, though passingly seductive, is hardly desirable. Exclusionary laws and practices are based on the belief that a controlled society is a secure one—the same wishful thinking that creates gated communities—but people are not safe from what they don't know. How else but through open discussion can we refute ideas if they are wrong or learn from them if they are right? And how else to tell the difference between the two? Taking advantage of the unusual convolutions of the case, the government sought to clamp down on ideas and opinions that would have been hard to censor had they come from citizens. But trying to stop discordant ideas at a geographical border is impractical, particularly in a wealthy, mobile, and technology-saturated country like the United States. While Margaret was being threatened with deportation, her books were available in bookstores and libraries and assigned in college courses. They would remain even if she couldn't.

All this put the government in the position of arguing that it was protecting core American values by denying them to an individual who had committed no crime and who posed no physical danger. Neither had she "advocated the doctrines of world communism," a statutory definition so overwrought that, as David Cole, Margaret's lawyer, was to observe, few communists ever advocated it.[15] This was 1986; by the time her case was resolved, the communist governments of Eastern Europe were toppling, and soon after, communism—the doctrine deemed so threatening that we needed the draconian measures of McCarran-Walter to save us—would be declared dead. As we again struggle to locate the source of threat, it is useful to recall that the United States survived intact, and probably not because a bunch of writers and intellectuals had been turned away from its shores.

Margaret's lawyers argued her case on First Amendment grounds—that her writing, even if radical, was protected political speech—and on technical grounds—that she should never have been deprived of her citizenship to begin with. But under immigration law, a defendant is not automatically presumed innocent, which left Margaret to prove her worthiness in a system that gave little value to the past twenty-five years of her life. So, a further irony: in condemning Margaret, the INS set itself up as possessor of the one truth about what it means to be American, but among the things Americans and others learn when they live in another culture is just how slippery truth can be.

The chasm between the two ideas of America was summed up in an interview Holly Near gave before a benefit concert in Albuquerque. Margaret quotes the interviewer as asking her, "Why do you think Margaret Randall should be allowed to live in the United States?"

"Why do you think she shouldn't?" Near replied.

---

By the time of the El Paso hearing, Margaret had been living in legal limbo for two years and the uncertainty was taking its toll. Some of the effects were concrete: losing teaching jobs when the INS intervened or university trustees got nervous, missing the birth of her first grandchildren because if she left the country she wouldn't be allowed back in. She didn't

know how much time she would have with her aging parents, or how she
and Barbara would adjust to another country if she was deported.

Other effects harder are to pin down: "You're not allowed by circumstances to show yourself in a very complex way. I'm not talking
about not telling the truth, but I'm talking about things that are grayer
than that." Throughout her dealings with the INS, she sensed that if she
apologized and said she didn't mean what she had written, all would be
forgiven. "Women are always being urged to say, 'I'm sorry, I was a bad
girl, I'll never do it again,' " she notes.

"I believed then and I continue to believe that we have an absolutely
inalienable right to hold opinions, whatever those opinions are, so I
wanted to be very careful during my case not to even *imply* that I was
ever sorry. At the same time, I've changed some of the opinions that I
held during the years that I was writing these books that were under attack. That was a hard line to walk because I would like to demand the
right to change my mind. On another hand, I think I've grown a lot as a
poet, and my language has developed."

Margaret is a prolific writer out of necessity and desire. Her subjects
have ranged from Christians in the Nicaraguan revolution to cooking,
incest, and women and money. She says, "I used to joke that all my
books are written between eleven at night and three in the morning, and
while that's not strictly true, there's quite a bit of truth in it. The last thing
in the day that I could get to was writing. As a result, I think a lot of my
early books are pretty superficial." Of the early poems under scrutiny at
the hearing she says, "Today, for me that language is boring and stupid—
it was such poor stuff compared to what other people have done—but
at the time it was part of who I was. It was painful sometimes to be seen
in that static way at the age of fifty-something."

Was she ever tempted to recant? "No, I wasn't. I wasn't." She doesn't
move or say anything for a while, then repeats, "It really became a matter of principle for me."

———————

In August 1986, Judge Spiegel, writing as if the case left a bad taste in
his mouth, upheld the INS's decision to deport Margaret. His reasons differed, however. While the district director had used his discretionary
power to exclude Margaret because he believed her political views presented a danger to the national interest, Judge Spiegel determined that
McCarran-Walter gave him no choice but to deny Margaret permanent
residency because of her putative advocacy of communism. Were he free

to decide on discretionary, rather than statutory grounds, he added, he would allow her to remain in the country.[16]

CCR had meanwhile filed a countersuit on behalf of some of the country's most prominent writers, who argued that Margaret's deportation would violate their right to exchange ideas freely. That right doesn't trump immigration law, however, so the suit was a long shot. It lost at the district court level and the Supreme Court declined to hear it.

That left Margaret with a third, and final, chance: an appeal to the Board of Immigration Appeals (BIA), an independent review board operating out of the Attorney General's office and the highest judicial body within the immigration system. Oral arguments were heard in October 1987, and in the fifteen minutes allowed her, Gonzalez, the INS lawyer, quoted from *The Closing of the American Mind*, by Allan Bloom, a seminal text in the culture wars, and reiterated her argument that the government was correct to be intolerant of people like Margaret, whose case, Gonzalez told the board, provided them "an opportunity . . . to keep faith with the American people in their fight against communism."[17]

The BIA took nearly two years to come to a decision, probably because McCarran-Walter was at last being overhauled. Congress had been fiddling with the law for about a decade, and though tolerance for differing views was hardly a hallmark of the era, the ideological exclusions had become a bipartisan embarrassment. In December 1987, Congress enacted Section 901, a one-year provision barring exclusions based on "past, current or expected beliefs, statements or associations" that would be protected if U.S. citizens engaged in them. Briefly, it looked as if Margaret's case would be moot, but when 901 was extended for two more years in 1988, it was limited to temporary visitors, not those applying for resident status, as she was.

Finally, in July 1989, the BIA issued its ruling. In a split decision, it determined that because Margaret had become a Mexican citizen out of economic need, she was still a U.S. citizen and could not be deported. The board denied her a complete victory, though, by explicitly sidestepping the First Amendment question. Even then, the INS requested a stay of the ruling in order to ask the attorney general for a reversal. So it was not until the end of August, when the INS decided to let the decision stand, that Margaret knew she was home for good.

Section 901 was made permanent five months later, and the following year, the Immigration and Naturalization Act of 1990 superseded McCarran-Walter, whose demise was probably spurred on by Margaret's case and others, which were in turn helped by the changing political climate. For the next six years, visa decisions were based on actions, not ideas, and people were excluded almost solely for illegal activities.

Then, in 1996, two laws reintroducing McCarran-Walter's most insidious principles—guilt by association and selective prosecution based on one's thoughts—targeted a new group of undesirables: people associated with "terrorist" organizations. The laws were passed on the anniversary of the bombing in Oklahoma City, and most of the people they caught turned out to be Arabs and Muslims living in the United States, often legally. The Illegal Immigration Report and Immigrant Responsibility Act (IIRAIRA) amended the 1990 immigration law to permit exclusion and deportation of "representatives" of organizations designated as terrorist by the president.[18] It also denied federal courts jurisdiction to review certain INS decisions. The Antiterrorism and Effective Death Penalty Act (AEDPA) made it illegal to support organizations on the list, even in their lawful, humanitarian activities, such as sponsoring hospitals and orphanages.

Both laws allowed the use of classified information in deportation proceedings against noncitizens linked to any group on the government's terrorist list. This included evidence from anonymous sources so secret that defendants, their lawyers, even their judges were not allowed to see it. Thus, the laws discarded two cornerstones of the American justice system: the right to know the evidence against you and the right to confront your accuser. As David Cole was later to write, "Without the right to go to court, all other rights are meaningless."[19]

Until this time, immigration hearings had usually been open to the public, but even before the laws were passed, the INS had tried to deport immigrants who held unpopular beliefs by using information they couldn't see. In one protracted case, when the INS was finally forced to disclose its secret evidence, the "terrorist activities" turned out to be distributing pamphlets for a Palestinian organization on the government's list and organizing events to raise money for humanitarian projects.[20] Here and in other cases, the classified evidence was based on faulty translation, cultural misunderstanding, rumor, innuendo, and self-serving lies.

This use of secret evidence was ruled unconstitutional, most notably in a 1995 decision in which the federal appeals court in California decided that noncitizens have the same right to freedom of association as citizens.[21] But IIRAIRA changed the ground rules, and in February 1999, the Supreme Court upheld the "court-stripping" provisions of the law and freed the INS to use secret evidence without concern for due process or First Amendment protections.[22] "Were my case to have been fought today," Margaret writes me on the tenth anniversary of her victory, "I would not be here."

Eventually, elements in the federal government grew uneasy about this state of affairs. In 1999, legislation to prevent deportation based on secret evidence was introduced in the House; a federal judge in New Jersey ruled against detaining immigrants on the basis of such evidence;[23] and the Board of Immigration Appeals ordered the release of an Egyptian who had been held in custody for over three years.[24] The following May, an INS judge reversed her earlier decision and found Dr. Ali Karim, an Iraqi Kurd who had been detained for three and a half years, eligible for asylum and ordered him released. Karim had been a member of a CIA-trained group opposing Saddam Hussein, but after the CIA evacuated him and five others to the United States, they were declared spies and marked for deportation. Not only was the evidence against them kept secret, but so was the judge's original ruling. Then James Woolsey, a former CIA director with top security clearances who was in high dudgeon over their treatment, joined their defense. He enlisted the help of Congress and the press and, mirabile dictu, about 90 percent of the evidence was declassified and made available to the Kurds' lawyers.[25]

Overnight, the risk to national security presented by these men evaporated, but the impulse to hide information and relationships the government found politically dicey or inconvenient took longer to ease. By March 2001, though, the INS had not brought any new secret-evidence cases for eighteen months, and only one person charged in such a case remained in detention.[26] In June of that year, the Supreme Court recognized the constitutional rights of immigrants in its review of two important cases.[27]

This is where things stood on September 11, 2001. Afterward, the number of secret detentions involving secret evidence soared. In response to a Justice Department directive, Chief Immigration Judge Michael Creppy instructed immigration judges in a September 21, 2001, memo to close all proceedings to the public and the press. According to the Justice Department, in the year that followed, some six hundred immigrants were subjected to secret hearings. As of October 2002, only one hearing had been partially opened, and that under court order. The courts again debated the legality and necessity of closed hearings, though from a starting point much higher on the secrecy scale. The decisions have been contradictory, with one court ruling that the country's "primary national policy must be self-preservation"[28] and another admonishing that "democracies die behind closed doors,"[29] so the matter is likely to go to the Supreme Court.

———

Shortly after she won, Margaret sent a thank-you note to her lawyers, saying she would no longer need the "public mask" she had created to get through the hardest times, though she was different from "the woman I once was." That clarifying process, she says now, "makes you very strong. I learned a lot about myself, who my real friends were, how my family would react. It made me much more palpably conscious of my beliefs, what you're willing to stand up for, how far you're willing to go, what censorship is, how it affects people. Those are very important issues for a writer."

They spill beyond the writer's desk, of course; word anxiety is part of the social fabric now, and dark impulses aren't always dramatic. Like most people, Margaret is ambivalent about the need to control speech, even before 9/11. "I think there are always going to be issues where one's beliefs come up against very hard questions. I'm very suspicious of the U.S. government and its motives in just about every way. I know that if they make war against pornography, for example, they're not going to be against *Hustler;* they're going to be against *Our Bodies, Ourselves.* But I still don't like *Hustler.* So I guess my feeling is that the way to continue to struggle against these attitudes and actions you don't like is to organize at the grassroots level." She concludes, "Ten or fifteen years ago, I had all kinds of lines. I have a lot more questions today."

Margaret has written, "The repressive act always begins with the repression of an idea."[30] Now, she asks, "Would I be happy if the Nazis marched in my town? I'd be terrified. Would I want to be the one to give them the permit? I certainly wouldn't. But do I think they should be denied the permit? I don't think so," she concludes, her voice going alto on "think." Yet having that choice is part of why she wanted to come home to the United States. "Who I am, for better or worse," she sums up, "is a North American in every fiber of my being. I was raised to have the kind of prejudices, loves and fears and feelings and sense of identity that North Americans have, so that the positive aspects of that have been a blessing. For example, the types of freedom we have. The negative aspects, that sense of superiority, that is what I had to wage my personal battle against."

# chapter four

# LA MORDAZA

## Daisy Sánchez

*San Juan, Puerto Rico, March 1998*

The night air in Puerto Rico has the swampiness of a New England August and the fresh, sad breeze of its fall, but it is unlike anything I've felt before. This is the first sign that Puerto Rico is different from the mainland, though that difference is reinforced throughout my time here. Actually, the air is the second sign. As our plane touched down, people around me applauded, not uncommon, I'm told, for Puerto Ricans returning home. So right off, I am introduced to two themes of life on the island: it's a separate place, and Puerto Ricans like it that way.

I've come to San Juan to talk with Daisy Sánchez, a prize-winning reporter for Teleonce (TV Channel 11), who, in 1991, interviewed two members of Los Macheteros, a radical proindependence group. Daisy's interview had aired to the interest not only of viewers but also of the FBI, since the men she interviewed were sought in connection with an armed robbery in Hartford, Connecticut, several years earlier. Puerto Rico is not a large island, so the FBI's failure to find the men was an embarrassment and Daisy's success an annoyance. The government responded by demanding her original videotapes. Fearing that what they really wanted was for her to testify against her sources, Daisy refused to cooperate, even when she was threatened with prison and summoned to Hartford in the dead of winter—punishment itself—to appear before a grand jury.

Daisy's situation was specific to the culture and politics of Puerto Rico, but her situation mirrors run-ins between reporters and governments throughout the United States. Despite constitutional promises of a free press, journalists are frequently pressured to renege on pledges of confidentiality and to provide information to authorities about possibly illegal activity.

In an era when reporters regularly make themselves convenient whipping boys for our confusion over what is public and what is private, journalistic ethics don't make for much of a rallying cry. Moreover, claiming privilege ensnares journalists in the contradiction of arguing that they should be allowed their secrets while pushing governments toward greater transparency. Finally, fighting subpoenas is costly, time consuming, and debilitating, making it tempting for broadcasters and publishers to trade editorial independence for the chance to be left alone. Still, punishing journalists for what they report is meant to have a chilling effect, and when it comes to governmental pressure on a journalist to betray a source, silencing is usually the point.

———

When Daisy and I talk, we face a different obstacle. She understands English but chooses not to speak it, and I speak Spanish, but clumsily. So I ask my questions in English, she responds in Spanish, and I record the conversation to be translated later. Our system works—sort of—and as backup, we're joined by Linda Backiel, an American civil rights lawyer who has lived in Puerto Rico for ten years and who knows Daisy's case well.

Daisy has been on leave from work since rupturing three vertebrae in her neck, so we meet at her home, a new house south of San Juan on a hill so lush its colors seem to pulsate. The area was countryside until recently, but now a forest has been cleared for a shopping center and expensive houses, and a tollbooth has been added at the highway exit to keep the poor away.

Daisy, at forty, is strikingly pretty, with round, dark eyes, a heart-shaped face, and black hair cut mannishly short and slicked tight to her head in a style both severe and chic. Her face grows animated when she talks, which she does rapidly, sliding between sentences with an attenuated "and" or "but" and exclaiming, "*Ave María!*" when she's surprised. A Latin mix of expressiveness and reserve, she is quick to laugh, vague when uninterested in a question, and passionate about politics and her dog. "He's *bobo,*" she says—dumb—"but he's got sex appeal."

Linda, in contrast, is parchment thin and pale: pale skin and eyes, pale hair piled in an elaborate swoop on her head. She came to Puerto Rico to defend a client indicted in the Hartford robbery, and, except for six months in prison in Philadelphia for refusing to testify against a client, has stayed on. The three of us sit around a big wooden table in the middle of a whitewashed kitchen, the door left open to catch a breeze. Daisy and Linda begin by reminding me that to understand Daisy's story, you have to know something of Puerto Rican politics, and to understand Puerto Rican politics, you have to know something of the island's relationship to the United States, or, in the vernacular, its status. Theoretically, Puerto Rico has been a self-governing commonwealth since 1952, but in reality, it is still a U.S. possession. Mainland political divisions and alignments—Democrat, Republican, left, right, center—don't apply, at least not in the same way. Puerto Rico has three main political parties, which represent the three status options: statehood, commonwealth, and independence. Labor unions and other civil groups also come in threes. So do opinions. "Status is everything!" exclaims Linda. So, it seems, is context.

Columbus "discovered" Puerto Rico, then called Boriquén, on his second voyage to the Indies in 1493. He claimed it for Spain, which enriched itself at the natives' expense, a dynamic that continued when the United States acquired the country in 1898 as a spoil of the Spanish-American War. The acquisition, however, came wrapped in a quandary: Acquired in what capacity? Puerto Rico wasn't a state, so a colony, maybe? But we don't have colonies. A territory, then? Well, yes, and then a commonwealth, but figuring out what that means continues to shape nearly every aspect of Puerto Rican life.

Puerto Rico, when it gets mainland attention, is mostly an afterthought, but the United States is much on the mind of Puerto Ricans, and one thing that has rankled about American rule is the distance between its high-minded rhetoric of liberty and the illiberal governance it has imposed. The American general who seized Puerto Rico in 1898 announced, "We have not come to make war . . . but to bestow upon you the immunities and blessings of the liberal institutions of our government."[1] Those blessings have been mixed.

Puerto Ricans are U.S. citizens but cannot vote for president and do not have voting representation in Congress, which controls their government and economy. Though the Supreme Court has ruled that they have rights under the U.S. Constitution, it has also upheld selective application of those rights.[2] The island's economy is shaky, a result of neglect, good intentions gone awry, and short-sighted initiatives seldom designed for self-sustaining growth. Puerto Rico imports nearly all of its food, corporate profits are reinvested on the island only sporadically, and much of the population depends on the government for employment or subsidies. In the late 1990s, over half the islanders qualified for some form of public assistance, unemployment ran close to 20 percent, and the median income was half that of Mississippi, the poorest state. Puerto Rico is an expensive habit to maintain, and those who favor independence argue that what is best in this regard for the island is also best for the United States.

It was in this context that Daisy approached a representative of the Macheteros at the end of a press conference in 1990. She was interested in interviewing Filiberto Ojeda Ríos, a prominent nationalist revolutionary who had been on the run from the FBI ever since he removed his electronic monitoring bracelet and left it in the door of *Claridad,* the newspaper of the Puerto Rican Socialist Party, then edited by the man who was later to become Daisy's *compañero.* When Daisy made her request, Ojeda had been in hiding for the better part of a year, but he loomed large in the Puerto Rican psyche. In the cultures she inhabited—the culture of journalism and the culture of Puerto Rico—the Macheteros merited attention. "This interview with a clandestine group, I considered it was news," she explains. "And it was also very important for me because they never had an interview of that kind. Nobody had seen them or talked to them." The aide was cordial but noncommittal, giving Daisy time to consider the risks and, no doubt, giving the Macheteros time to check her out.

A year later, she got a phone call at work. It had been so long since the first contact that it took her a minute to figure out what the caller was talking about, but she covered her surprise and agreed to what she calls a "blind date" at a nearby cafe. This was the first of three meetings where each side negotiated terms; eventually, Daisy agreed to go to the interview alone and the Macheteros agreed not to preview her questions. At their final meeting, she was told to expect a call and to be ready to go. It came on a Friday in the summer of 1991 at midnight: "We'll see you in three hours." A click and that was all.

Following instructions, Daisy drove into town, arriving precisely at 3 A.M. The street was ghostly and silent, save for the click-click of her heels as she walked to a nearby phone booth. There she found a wad of paper jammed behind the phone. "Look to your left," the note said, directing her past two overflowing garbage bins to an unlit alley. Summoning her courage, she all but ran down the alleyway, and when she reached the other end she heard a noise, the first indication that she wasn't alone. She whirled around, saw nothing, then turned back to face a bus, the kind Puerto Ricans call a *guagua*. "Don't be frightened," someone said as he tied a blindfold over her eyes and led her aboard.

Despite the blindfold and the turns obviously intended to disorient her, she was pretty sure they stayed within the San Juan metropolitan area, though she didn't try to figure out where. When the blindfold was removed, Daisy found herself standing in a room wrapped from floor to ceiling in brown paper, like a bargain-basement Christo project. The monotony was relieved only by a door, an air conditioner cranked up high, and drawings of the Puerto Rican flag and a machete, the group's symbol. She counted six people in ski masks standing guard and recognized an automatic rifle, a pistol, and an Uzi they were holding. Well, she thought, if I'm supposed to be impressed, it's working. In the middle of the room, three chairs had been arranged in a semicircle, as in a television studio. A cameraman sat in one, and in the other were Filiberto Ojeda Ríos and Luis Colón Osorio, the men Daisy had come to interview.

Daisy recognized Ojeda—she had seen him the year before in San Juan's federal courthouse—but his gray hair was dyed black, and he seemed smaller than she remembered, older too, looking his fifty-eight years. A musician by trade, Ojeda had helped found several radical, nationalist groups, the most recent being the Macheteros (literally, the machete wielders), launched in 1976 on the anniversary of the U.S. invasion of Puerto Rico. With approximately three hundred members[3] and a goal of removing all U.S. presence from Puerto Rico, the Macheteros had carried out a series of violent forays against the federal government. They took responsibility for killing two sailors and wounding ten others in an attack on a Navy bus, blowing up nine fighter jets at a National Guard base, killing a sailor returning to his ship, and firing antitank rockets at federal buildings in San Juan. (They were apparently aiming at FBI offices, but missed.) Then, on September 12, 1983, the birthday of Pedro Albizú Campos, Puerto Rico's most illustrious *independentista,* a twenty-five-year-old guard at a Wells Fargo depot in Hartford, Connecticut, stole $7.1 million in the second largest robbery in U.S. history. At first it looked as if he had pulled it off single-handedly, but, in the course of an unrelated investigation, the FBI discovered that he was a Machetero.

Though clandestine, the Macheteros have a flair for public relations. In January 1985, with the robbery fresh in the minds of Hartford residents, three men dressed as kings delivered a truckload of toys to that city's poor children for *Día de los Reyes,* the Epiphany and day of gift giving in the Latin world. Ojeda was reputed to have been one of the "kings," and the romance of the outlaw—particularly a clever outlaw who outfoxes unpopular authorities—was not lost on Puerto Ricans. "Terrorist or patriot?" Daisy asks in *Cita con la injusticia,* her account of her ordeal, even while admitting that at the time she didn't feel so coolly analytical.

Ojeda gave her a charming smile as he extended his hand and thanked her for coming. Then he introduced Colón, about whom Daisy knew little, except that he had long been involved in radical politics and had spent time in prison. A story had made the rounds that, during a prison uprising, he had entertained reporters with a flute concert. According to the FBI, he was the Macheteros' quartermaster in charge of weapons, and he too had fled underground.

The interview proceeded smoothly, so that Daisy reckoned time passing only by the changing of the guard. "We talked about the Macheteros and the robbery of Wells Fargo. I asked, but they obviously didn't give up any information about it," she reports. "We talked about political issues. [Ojeda] even insulted a couple of public figures. We had a dialogue about their strategy. The three of us were sitting in a small room. It was total talking heads."

Toward the end, Ojeda and Colón warned Daisy that the interview could bring her trouble with a grand jury, but she shrugged off their concern. "In Puerto Rico, the grand jury was used to scare the *independentistas.* I was aware of this," she says.

Again, they shook hands, again she was blindfolded, again she was warned not to look behind her as the bus drove away. Back at her car, she was amazed to find that it was only noon. Her son, Gustavo Julián, turned four that day, and she hurried home to prepare his birthday party.

———

On a Monday morning in August, Daisy drove to work with the tapes by her side, reveling in having gotten the scoop, that distinctly journalistic thrill of tracking down an elusive source, getting him on record first, and knowing something no one else knows, knowing too that your story will lead that morning's front page or that evening's newscast. Queen for a day, Daisy calls it. It's part of why people become journalists.

Accustomed to an audience, Daisy has a flair for the dramatic. When she arrived at the station, she went directly to see Linda Hernández, Teleonce's news director and her boss. The year before, they had talked about an Ojeda interview, and Hernández had agreed to run it if it happened, but when the opportunity finally came, Daisy had had to act quickly and had told no one. Now she put the manila envelope holding the two videotapes with the interview on the desk between them and waited.

"What's this?" Hernández asked.

"The interview with Filiberto Ojeda Ríos," Daisy replied casually, as if they had just been discussing him.

As Daisy hoped, Hernández shared her excitement, but before running the interview, she wanted to consult the station's CEO, a customary precaution. The CEO at the time was a North American named David Murphy, new to Teleonce. Daisy had heard a rumor that Murphy had a merger application pending with the Federal Communications Commission, and she worried that his commercial interests would make him cautious. The rumor panned out, but not her concern. It took him half an hour to give the go-ahead. Daisy worked with the editorial director to cut the four hours of tape to about ten minutes of the most interesting talk—what they would do with any interview. By midday, the station was running ads; by six, the interview was ready to air. "We couldn't hold it," she says. "It was simply too good. The only error we committed, I now understand, is that we should have taken those cassettes, broadcast them, and gotten rid of them." That was the usual practice: to recycle videotapes after they were edited. Instead, the station decided to make a copy and give the originals to the station's lawyer, which seemed as good an idea as any at the time.

At some point during this hectic day, Daisy had left a message for her own attorney, Judith Berkan, a civil liberties lawyer experienced with grand juries, and Berkan called back just as the interview was beginning. Watch the news, Daisy told her, then tell me if I need legal counsel. Ten minutes later, Berkan called again to say that she wanted to see Daisy first thing the next morning.

The next morning was when the FBI visited Teleonce to inquire about Daisy and the videotapes. Teleonce normally responded to a government request for a transmission by requiring a letter explaining how it would be used and charging $75 to cover copying costs. Courts can order a broadcaster to hand over material once it has aired, but the status of unbroadcast footage or unpublished notes is murkier. (Online journalism, where it is not always clear what constitutes publication, befogs the question further.) Some journalists destroy their notes as soon as they've written a story, and some broadcasters destroy unaired tapes as a policy.

Once material is petitioned by the government, however, destroying it is no longer an option. Too late, Daisy realized this, but she had no doubt about the consequences of turning her tapes over to the government. To do so would go against her principles as a journalist and would undermine her ability to do her job, since sources would be reluctant to trust her in the future and viewers would question her independence.

Daisy was not at the station when the FBI agents visited, so the first time she met them was in the Teleonce conference room the next day. She arrived to find the station's officials, department heads, and lawyer assembled around a large table. No one was smiling, least of all the FBI. The taller of the two agents wore a military-style buzzcut and an overcoat, an unusual accessory in balmy San Juan. The second agent was a nattily dressed Latino—Mexican, she figured from his accent. After Daisy's ordeal with the Macheteros, the posturing of the FBI must have seemed tame, but she was used to being in control of interviews, so when they began with a series of questions they knew the answers to—her name, her address—she recognized the journalist's trick of lulling the interviewee into carelessness.

"I'm sorry, but I can't answer that," she told them repeatedly.

But these are dangerous men, the agent replied. You don't want to be responsible for harm to innocent people, do you?

"I'm a journalist," Daisy answered. "I know my work and my responsibilities." She set about evading questions or saying "I don't remember" until it became a joke—almost. Then, the agents asked whom the tapes belonged to, and Murphy replied that they were Daisy's, whereupon they ended the interview abruptly. Relieved, she rose to leave, but one of the agents stopped her as he dug into his briefcase and pulled out two subpoenas: one for the station, the other for Daisy.

The subpoenas turned out to be full of mistakes and had no legal worth, but if they were meant as a scare tactic, they had their effect. Daisy got more bad news when she met with Berkan, her lawyer, who informed her that she was mistaken in thinking that she had firm legal protection if she refused to hand over the tapes. So they decided on a strategy: she would comply with a subpoena by showing up at the grand jury, but she would not agree to relinquish the tapes or confidential information. As she and Berkan finished their meeting, Daisy got an urgent message from the station's lawyer. The FBI had been to his office, demanding the tapes. He had refused, but he was nervous and wanted Daisy to come get them. She did, and from then on, they were in her possession, which seemed right, since they were made on her time with no station equipment or assistance and so belonged to her.

A week later, another subpoena arrived. This time, it was correct, making it clear that the government was serious. To Daisy, it meant she was going to jail.

---

Federal grand juries were originally designed to protect citizens against false accusations by the state, but they have evolved into investigatory tools of prosecutors, who now have almost total power. Proceedings are closed, transcripts are usually sealed forever, defense lawyers cannot accompany their clients into the courtroom, and prosecutors are allowed to present evidence obtained illegally or to withhold exculpatory evidence, all with little judicial review. Not surprisingly, prosecutors usually get the indictments they seek: between 1994 and 1998, only one of every 1,480 charges brought to a federal grand jury was rejected.[4] Given this setup, prosecutorial abuse of the grand jury's subpoena power and secrecy is perhaps inevitable.

Puerto Rico does not have a grand jury system and views the federal grand jury as a tool of colonialism. Says Daisy, "[To use] an organization like the grand jury that doesn't have anything to do with Puerto Rico to demand information and documents from the press of this country, [you] can't be any more obviously imperialist than this. In reality, as they say, I got myself into a mess of problems 'with the empire.' "

As a way out of the mess, the station decided to broadcast the interview in its entirety. It was the suggestion of Daisy's then-husband, who pointed out that the tapes would then be available to the FBI as well as the public. In a country where everyone follows politics (the voting rate is among the highest in the world), TV is the most popular news medium, and everyone owns one. "One, two, three," Daisy laughs. "One in each room." So eleven days after the short interview was broadcast, the unabridged version went on the air, along with commentary and analysis. Talking heads, stationary camera, unedited footage, brown-paper backdrop, and all, the uncut version got the highest ratings of any television program in Puerto Rico.

Daisy has independence sympathies, as, she claims, many Puerto Ricans do, despite the Independence Party's dismal showing in elections.[5] "I believe in independence. I guess that I belong to the middle class and that influences the way you face life. I am convinced that my country has the right to be free." But she insists that she can separate her politics from her work. "The government should not use us to find information in their behalf. I am not saying that other reporters aren't doing it. What I am saying is that I will not do it."

Daisy was born in San Juan, the middle child of a labor unionist and a teacher. She studied communications and film at the University of Puerto Rico, and before coming to television news, she wrote for the paper *El Mundo* and the magazine *Vea*. Teleonce was her first real reporting, and when the FBI demanded her tapes, she had been there for about a year and a half. Of her refusal to cooperate, she says, "I wasn't saying no just because. I was defending a basic principle of my job: the right to inform people about what the opposition is saying, even if that opposition is not the best. Somebody told me that they [the Macheteros] used me. Maybe they used me, but I did use them. That's the way journalism works: I had the means, they had the information. At that time I was more romantic about my ideals. I firmly believed in the freedom of the press. I don't believe in objectivity, but that's another story. I was a girl in love with my career, willing to defend my ideals."

---

Without intending to, Daisy found a test of those ideals in the Macheteros, who, like other *independentistas,* figured prominently on the FBI's lists of terrorists. Puerto Rican nationalist groups were targeted in the 1960s under COINTELPRO, a covert program against domestic dissidents,[6] and again during the Reagan administration, when domestic surveillance of criminals had a habit of sloshing over into spying on law-abiding citizens with opposition politics. *Independentistas* continued to preoccupy the FBI: according to FBI testimony to Congress in 1998, radical Puerto Rican groups had committed about 44 percent of terrorist incidents in the United States and its territories.[7] (The FBI connects the Macheteros with Cuba, where the Wells Fargo robber and money probably ended up—only $85,000 has been recovered—but by most accounts, the Macheteros are independent-minded in every sense of the word.) The Macheteros were considered among the "most active and violent" of the groups,[8] and five years later Ojeda remained on the FBI's Most Wanted list with a half-million-dollar bounty on his head.

Terrorists, by rhetoric and deed, place themselves beyond human sympathy. They mock the conventions of legitimate protest and spread fear through acts of violence meant to appear random, uncontrollable, and unfathomable and, therefore, terrifying. (The Macheteros claimed to attack only in retaliation, but their victims included people with no direct involvement in the injustices they sought to avenge.) But because *terrorist* is a serviceable label for a government to affix to its enemies, it is applied selectively and often for political purposes.[9] From 1983 to 1985, the FBI spent about $8 million tracking people it believed to be Macheteros, bugging every phone it could and coming up with some thousand hours of tapes,[10] although wiretapping is expressly forbidden by the Puerto Rican constitution. It is interesting, then, that when twelve alleged Macheteros were arrested, they were charged, not with a political offense, but with a criminal one: involvement in the Wells Fargo robbery.

The arrests came on August 30, 1985, when two hundred FBI agents descended on Puerto Rico in the largest antisubversive operation in the island's history. Eventually, they arrived at the town of Luquillo, where Ojeda was hiding. He held off the FBI for two hours while burning documents in his bathtub. During the standoff, a ricocheting bullet hit an FBI agent in the eye, and assault was added to the charges.

The legalities that resulted from these arrests and additional indictments were complicated, and, in the interest of expedience, the case was divided in two. The first set of trials ended in April 1988 with one acquittal and four convictions. Ojeda was released in May along with the remaining defendants (he had spent the longest time in detention of any defendant in federal history), but he was rearrested a few months later and sent back to Puerto Rico to stand trial on the charges stemming from his standoff with the FBI. There, after four hours of deliberation, a Puerto Rican jury acquitted him.

"But this case is a good example of what we are," Daisy says. "In the federal court in this country, you must speak English. The defendant's lawyer must speak English. The prosecutors must also speak English, and the jury must also know English, and the judge as well. When someone speaks in Spanish, it is translated into English, although everyone understood."

Linda adds dryly, "But when the judge had something really important to say to the jurors, he said it in Spanish. What did the judge say to the jurors? 'We're gonna recess for lunch now. I want you back at here at two o'clock.' *That* they say in Spanish because they don't want the case to start late."

Daisy picks up the narrative. "But you have to understand: Filiberto is a Machetero who defended himself with an Uzi. He spent two hours shooting at everyone. They come at him like an army; there was even a bazooka. This case was heard in Puerto Rico with a Puerto Rican jury in a federal court. And Filiberto walked. Free." She and Linda jump up, fairly cackling with glee as they imitate Ojeda brandishing the gun, spent ammunition at his feet. "And since he's a Puerto Rican, it's as if they [the jury] were proud. You know what Filiberto said? He used Spanish, so that the jury could understand it. It is something very cultural. He said, 'I was at home with my wife, and these people arrived and grabbed my wife, who was in her bathrobe. And like you men would have done and like you women would have wanted, I defended my home and I defended my wife.' The message was clear to the jury: Ojeda was defending, not just his house or his family, but also his country and his right to determine its future. And he won the case!" Daisy says with a satisfaction that seems widespread on the island. "Remember that they presented him in court as an assassin, anti-Yankee. They presented him as the worst, and the Puerto Ricans decided he wasn't guilty. That was the message. And his pride."

Ojeda was convicted in absentia in Connecticut on the Wells Fargo charges in 1992 and sentenced to 55 years in prison, but by then he had disappeared underground, where Daisy interviewed him and where he remains to this day.

———————

Once the FBI had served Daisy a valid subpoena, the Bureau set about reminding her of its presence, sometimes subtly, often not. She looked around when she left work to see if she was being followed, checked her rearview mirror as she drove, invented new routes home. She listened for the telltale click that would indicate that her phone was being tapped and thought she heard it one day during a conversation with her brother. After that, she monitored her words carefully. She trusted no one, and that probably was the point: to make sure she knew that the government was keeping track of her. "It was like a game of nerves. That's how I see it."

This second subpoena was Daisy's introduction to John Danaher III, the chief prosecutor in the case. Amused by the pomposity of his name, she seldom refers to him by less than his full patrilineal glory. Danaher never came to Puerto Rico, so they didn't meet until she went to Hartford, but, as with Margaret Randall and her local INS director, Daisy felt that he nursed a personal grudge against her. It's not surprising that both women would feel this way, since their lives were turned upside down by officials who seemed to savor their power, nor is it surprising that the pursued were women and the pursuers men. Their relationships, elusive and charged, illustrate the strange intimacy between censor and censored, who, whether they meet or not, figure hugely in each other's imagination.

In Daisy's case, the prosecution obviously wanted her to give in to its demands, but since it would gain no new information from the original tapes, something else had to be at stake. "Who's the guy who is causing these subpoenas to be issued?" Linda asks rhetorically. "He's the U.S. attorney who brought the case against the Macheteros. Now the two main guys in that case"—Ojeda and Colón—"manage after three years of incredible battles to get out from under him completely, come back to Puerto Rico, do a whole lot of public speaking and organizing and then they say, 'We're going back underground,' while they're on bail from his jurisdiction. And what does Daisy do a year later? Interviews them. Well, he takes this as a personal insult. So who does he take it out on? Daisy."

As we drove to their house earlier, Daisy's *compañero*, Manolo Coss, observed that the FBI probably thought Daisy was an easy mark. "She's petite," he said, with obvious amusement. Daisy is just over five feet tall, but the FBI underestimated her to its disadvantage. Given the politics, she thinks they would have gone after a man as well, but adds, "Yes, this must have occurred to them, that I was more susceptible to intimidation because I was a woman."

Intimidation, harassment, and humiliation were the weapons of choice. When Daisy went to New York to drum up support from journalist organizations, Danaher sent a fax to her hotel to remind her yet again that she had to appear before the grand jury or go to prison. (Linda notes that it is unethical for a lawyer to contact directly anyone he knows to be represented by legal counsel.) Daisy doesn't know how he found out which hotel she was staying at, but she does know that employees there could have read the message and guesses that Danaher knew that too. "The guy was a fascist. *Ave Maria, que tipo!* He called and called to remind me that I had to be in court on such and such day and that if I didn't show up, I wouldn't go to a grand jury and he would throw me into jail."

A grand jury had been convened in Puerto Rico, but Daisy was subpoenaed by one in Hartford, purportedly because it was investigating the bail-jumping charges against Ojeda and Colón. Daisy thinks the real reason is that, had she gone to court in Puerto Rico, the outcry would have been a public relations nightmare. As it was, the government postponed her appointment twice, apparently hoping the protest would die down.

The outcry was over what Daisy insists is the real issue. "We are defending the freedom of the press and the right of that reporter to do her job without coercion—including [from] the courts," she says vehemently. Teleonce's management was giving her its full backing, and she had support from most of the other media on the island, with the exception of rival TV stations, of which, she says, "It is sad, because after all it wasn't my fight only; it was a fight that affected all the other reporters." The other holdout was *El Nuevo Día,* the largest daily newspaper, which reported and commented on the case only after it was settled.

Support came from outside her profession too. Strangers stopped her at the grocery store to give her their blessings, and on the day she was called to the grand jury, a huge demonstration took place in front of the federal courthouse in San Juan, while a smaller group marched on Hartford's Federal District Court. "The public felt impressed that I was being persecuted for being a journalist," she says. The Association of Puerto Rican Journalists (ASPRO) reached out to labor unions, who declared their support for Daisy, as did religious groups, the College of Lawyers and other legal organizations, the governor, both houses of Puerto Rico's congress, leaders of all three political parties, and the Puerto Rican Institute for Civil Rights. In a country where political divisions define nearly every facet of public life, outrage and disbelief that Daisy might go to prison for doing her job may have been the only thing all the factions agreed on that year.

---

Daisy's situation is both typical of American journalists who stand up to governmental bullying with sparse legal protection and distinct to Puerto Rico, where journalists are regarded highly. Daisy talks of their role as *fiscalizamos,* which she translates as meaning "we watch out for the interests of the people." While she was resisting cooperating with the federal government, the Puerto Rican government was in the hands of the Popular Democratic Party (PPD), which favors a commonwealth or free associated state, the status quo since 1952. The PPD's main rival is the New Progressive Party (PNP), which champions statehood. The third main party is the small but vocal Independence Party (PIP). All politicians have their run-ins with the press, Daisy says, but the PPD has been less confrontational and repressive, and Rafael Hernández Colón, who was running for governor at this time, enjoyed relatively friendly relations with journalists.

It was not always so. In 1948, the Puerto Rican government instituted *La Ley de Mordaza,* or "the gag law," a broad and harsh piece of legis-

lation modeled on 1940s federal sedition legislation aimed at communists in the United States. The targets in Puerto Rico were the *independentistas,* whose popular support threatened the more accommodating
power structure of the island. Among other repressive measures, *La
Mordaza* made it a felony to "print, publish, edit, circulate, sell, distribute, or publicly exhibit any writing or publication which encourages,
pleads, advises, or preaches the necessity, desirability, or suitability of
overthrowing the insular government." *La Mordaza* became law as
Puerto Rico held its first gubernatorial election, and, as intended, it
scared a normally chatty society into silence. Though it was repealed in
1952, its foul taste lingers, influencing political discourse to this day.

Repression turned the press combative and made it into a popular institution with the Puerto Rican people. The media are now owned primarily by large mainland conglomerates and powerful Puerto Rican families, but for much of the twentieth century, journalism was a kind of
cottage industry, nurtured by the island's chief intellectuals. Barred from
governing their country, they became journalists, poets, lawyers—and
anti-American nationalists. "Here, we have a tradition of journalism that
is incredible," Daisy boasts. "People like the press. They believe in it, they
believe the news they read. We are a small country. Nevertheless, we have
[access to] over one hundred TV stations, we have five national newspapers, plus ten regional papers. The press is part of our history."

When the Puerto Ricans got to write their own constitution in 1952,
they made their respect for the press clear. Not only does Puerto Rico's
Bill of Rights guarantee freedom of the press, but it also includes an unusual clause forbidding the government from declaring eminent domain
over a building that houses a printing press. The Puerto Rican constitution was pruned considerably by the U.S. Congress before it approved it,
and it is still trumped by the U.S. Constitution as interpreted by American courts, but the sense of press freedom is broader in Puerto Rico than
in the United States, a point Daisy's lawyers used to argue her case.

Pleasing as prestige is, legal protections are more reliable, so American
journalists summoned to testify in court or to turn over material to the
government claim the "privilege" of guarding secret information dis-
closed to them in a professional capacity. Claims to journalistic privilege
are frequently challenged by authorities, however, who argue that journalists have the same civic responsibilities as anyone when it comes to cooperating with legal investigations. The only Supreme Court case to address the question was inconclusive. In 1972, a fragmented Court ruled
in *Branzburg v Hayes* that the First Amendment does not give journal-

ists "absolute privilege"—that is, immunity from testifying before a grand jury—but dissenting opinions acknowledged "qualified privilege," thereby opening the door for state shield laws. Thirty states and the District of Columbia have shield laws giving reporters varying degrees of protection, and several other states recognize some kind of qualified privilege. These laws are still subject to interpretation by the courts, though, and their constitutionality has yet to be tested.

Puerto Rico does not have a shield law, but the Code of Ethics of ASPRO, the journalist organization, spells out a reporter's responsibility vis-à-vis legal proceedings. Journalists should not identify sources who wish to remain anonymous, it states, nor is it a journalist's role to help the police in their investigations. The exception is when the journalist takes part in or is an eyewitness to a serious crime—which leaves Daisy's resistance well within the mainstream of journalistic principles.

The FBI's hounding of Daisy was not just a clash of professional ethics but also a skirmish in the ideological and cultural struggles that have defined Puerto Rican–U.S. relations for a century. "You have to understand," Linda says, her voice rising, as she adds commentary to translation, "Daisy is saying that the imperial mentality is alive, and they have managed to continue as an imperial power, enforcing policies of imperialism, because they never got it that it was a separate reality. Never. And Daisy is part of that different reality."

"But, but," Daisy interjects, "just so you can see how some of us resist assimilation, how we've resisted in the fact that we still speak Spanish. I am speaking to you and I understand what you are telling me and I'm resisting speaking your language. It is a cultural issue that they tried to impose on us, they tried to impose it on me." She learned English at school and from the American music, movies, ads, and television programs that pervade the island. When she is on the mainland, she speaks English, she says, but we are in her country now, so she speaks her language. "And the majority of the people in this country, for all their talk, resist English," she concludes firmly.

A Puerto Rican living in Hartford will tell you he is Puerto Rican, not American,[11] notes Linda. Daisy nods and murmurs, "sí, un huh," then tells of hearing a Puerto Rican politician describe them as a community, not a nation, and thinking, "This is only going to make people in Puerto Rico feel more like a nation, because can you deny that Puerto Rico is a nation? We speak differently. We are different—in all aspects. Five hundred years of history. Five hundred years! And to say, no, we are a community. . . . That's like telling us that we're a bunch of people on a rock. It's as if Puerto Rico was a festival in some random location."

———————

Through the fall of 1991, the FBI continued its cat-and-mouse game, while Daisy did all she could to avoid prison—except to give in. With each new summons, she prepared herself to explain to the grand jury why she could not comply; with each unexplained postponement, she grew more anxious. At a remove of a few years, Daisy recognizes the magnitude of what happened to her and takes pride in her response, but at the time, it was no fun. The station covered her legal expenses and, if she went to jail, would keep her on salary, but probably not fully, meaning that money would be a problem. So would leaving her young son for who knew how long. Already, she felt guilty for being so busy and distracted and absent in his life. Still, at no point did she consider giving in to the government's demand—not out of stubbornness or martyrdom or a desire for fame or higher ratings, she insists, but because she was certain that what the FBI really wanted was information. "I would have gone to jail, probably for being stupid, [but] it is important to have a principle, and not only to have it, but to defend it. While the rights are written on paper, there aren't people to defend them for you. Many people like Linda united to support me, but I was not crossing my arms to cry so that they would resolve my problems. The moment came when I had to demonstrate that I believed in this above all else."

Daisy wasn't surprised at her response. She has a temper, she admits, but, more to the point, "Fighting has always been a part of my life, like breathing. So really, this was nothing new for me. I wasn't a heroine and I didn't want them to see me as one because sometimes people think heroes aren't afraid—and I was afraid. I simply wanted to be true to myself, and that meant not giving up on what I believed."

Of Danaher, she observes, "He thought I was a journalist in the U.S., where they put a journalist in jail every month and nobody cares." An overstatement, I object, but Daisy continues, "It happens much more than it should in such a democratic country. As such, Danaher thought that it was just another journalist in the U.S. and they put her in jail and she is going to give up and give them the tape." In 1999, when the most recent figures were tallied, 1,326 subpoenas were issued to news outlets, primarily TV stations, across the country, and, in most cases, journalists complied or negotiated a settlement.[12] By the reckoning of the Reporters

Committee for Freedom of the Press, seventeen journalists were jailed between 1984 and 2001.[13] Daisy knew of only three reporters in Puerto Rico who had been pressured to provide material to the government, and none had been threatened with imprisonment.

Punishment of a journalist who refuses to cooperate with a legal investigation is not necessarily partisan, but when governments try to restrict information or influence its purveyors, power and political maneuvering take center stage. In Daisy's case, with no new information at stake, the government's message seemed to be that dissident voices are not to be heard. To the FBI, giving criminals like the Macheteros a platform for their ideas—in essence, free publicity—was not enterprising journalism but a challenge flung in the face of lawfulness and security. Governments understand well the risks of letting their adversaries near the microphone. Hence, British media were barred from broadcasting the voices of representatives of "terrorist organizations," a.k.a. the Irish Republican Army, from 1988 to 1994 (they got around this by having actors read the IRA's words), and, in 2000, Russia made it illegal for the media to quote Chechen guerrilla leaders.

What governments seem to understand less well is that journalists are able to report ideas they don't agree with, though that should be obvious for a profession that prides itself on being bloody-minded. This is not to say that news outlets don't create their own restrictions or that the press is not restrained in multiple ways. In the United States, "family" newspapers delete obscenities, keep grisly photos off front pages, and seldom name victims of sexual assault; TV news programs avoid stories that don't lend themselves to visuals; and for many news media, vast sections of the world barely exist until someone dies there violently. Add to that the coalescing of ownership (nine corporations own nearly all the major media outlets in the United States at last count), pressure for instantaneous news, and the glorification of gossip. (Ah, but hasn't gossip always, blessedly, been a staple of news?)

Then there are journalists themselves, whom nobody likes, not even other journalists.[14] The list of their transgressions is well rehearsed, but equally pernicious are the internalized constraints that seldom get discussed because they're so slippery.[15] As journalists increasingly share the interests, values, and status of the newsmakers they report on, it becomes harder for them to resist the seductions of power and self-importance or the ease of reporting on what is familiar and readily grasped. Like most people, reporters probably find too much independence a burden, and reporting against the grain is pretty unrewarding. (When journalists report on the trappings of power, they're seen as combative but effective; we feast on unmasking the rich and famous and, particularly, politicians, as if this proves that anyone really can be president. But let a journalist examine the structures that keep these people in charge and he or she is considered disloyal, hostile, and not ready for prime time.)

Still, it ought to be possible to want the press to do a better job without devaluing the enterprise itself. A reporter's latitude to tell the government to go to hell when it grows ham-fisted or deceitful or just gets in the way of a good story lies at the heart of journalism—and of democracy. Tantalizing, though inconclusive, evidence suggests a correlation between the number of newspapers in a country and its level of corruption,[16] and a government's treatment of its press is a good indicator of its treatment of its citizens. A host of dangers flows from a citizenry with the power to govern itself without the information to do so, but information is in endless supply these days when even the Macheteros have a Web site. The greater danger is in the narrowing of acceptable thought and discussion, particularly in our politics, where we traverse a small strip of the ideological spectrum and confuse crotchety opinion with original thinking.

Efforts to keep the press from reporting on what people think are futile. Governments may be able to keep people from saying things publicly but not from thinking them privately—and cherishing the thought more for its being forbidden: witness Ojeda's hero status. Conventional wisdom is not immutable fact, and bad ideas don't always announce themselves as such. Those opposed to airing disfavored ideas worry that the ideas will find new adherents, but it is unlikely that independence never occurred to Daisy's viewers before they watched her interview. In any case, we can defeat ideas only if we know about them, and the more we know, the better prepared we are to address the circumstances that make them appealing. Puerto Rican independence may not always seem an extreme position, even to the FBI, and in the meantime, radicals like the Macheteros make news. Writing of Daisy's case, José Delgado, a former president of ASPRO, reminded his readers that the role of a free press is to inform fully, not to limit information to a sanctioned or even a legal point of view.[17] Nor, I'd add, is it to soothe.

The value of journalism's gadfly function has not been lost on statesmen and jurists throughout our history. Thomas Jefferson wrote, "Were it left to me to decide whether we should have a government without newspapers, or newspapers without a government, I should not hesitate a moment to prefer the latter."[18] Nearly two centuries later, Supreme

Court Justice Hugo Black affirmed the sentiment, saying, "The press was to serve the governed, not the governors."[19] For all the high-minded rhetoric, though, it is probably the rare politician who believes the press is just doing its job when it attacks him or her, and courts do not consistently back up reporters in their watchdog mode. In 1998, a federal appeals court rejected the argument that subpoenas against the media interfere with the journalistic process, opining that "to the extent that the lack of a privilege may affect editorial decisions, it seems that this effect may well accrue to the public's benefit" by making editors more accountable.[20]

Accountability to what and to whom is one of the great, endless debates in journalism, where suggestions for reform frequently come down to ways to limit bad news in favor of fads like civic journalism or "news you can use." However you define accountability, punishing a reporter for presenting ideas, even those of avowed enemies of the state, is a classic case of shooting the messenger, but, more to the point, governments and citizens need at times to hear more than just what they want to hear.

Even as I write that, it sounds suspiciously like "Eat your peas," as so many prescriptions for a good society do. And as if to reinforce the power of counterarguments comes the reminder that the day I write this is the fifth anniversary of the bombing of the federal building in Oklahoma City, a horror carried out with explosives, not words, but spawned by a poisonous ideology. What I mean to say is that for a healthy society, a freewheeling, unruly press is not an evil we must tolerate but a cause for celebration and pride. The premise behind press freedom is forward-looking and hopeful and deeply American because it assumes a capacity for change. Our system of governance is a work in progress, where divergent views duke it out in the hope of getting it right someday and where journalists, when they're good, are among our most joyful brawlers. Their responsibility, as independent journalist Amy Goodman has said, is to "go to where the silence is and say something."

On December 9, 1991, Daisy boarded an early morning plane for Hartford, accompanied by a representative of the Puerto Rican Institute for Civil Rights and her lawyer, Roberto Roldán, a partner of Berkan's. Daisy's husband, her boss, and a group of supporters were following on the noon flight. For someone anticipating prison, she felt surprisingly tranquil, having prepared as best she could—for instance, making tapes of herself reading her son's favorite stories so he could hear her voice before going to sleep each night. She hoped to be allowed to return to San

Juan to ready her affairs, but she couldn't count on it, and she didn't know when she would see him again.

They were met at the airport by John Schoenhorn, a lawyer representing Daisy in a motion to quash her subpoena, who greeted them with news: the judge had moved the hearing forward, and they were to appear before him in an hour. It was a good development, though the chance of success was slim. The judge, T. Emmet Clarie, was known to be conservative and about to retire. Worse, when he presided over the Wells Fargo trials, he had refused even to consider the political aspects of the cases. "How could we think that he would grant us this favor? It was quite the opposite," Daisy says.

The new schedule created another problem. She was casually dressed in cropped pants, and her more appropriate clothes wouldn't arrive until that afternoon with her husband. There was nothing to do but brazen it out, though: she would enter the courtroom wearing the long overcoat she had bought for the trip north and unwrap herself only when she had sat down and hidden her legs under the table.

A few minutes after Daisy got to the courtroom, John Danaher, the prosecutor, arrived. He was younger than she had imagined him, but his hauteur was precisely what she expected. Judge Clarie too was in character, perched God-like on a podium high above everyone else in the well-appointed courtroom. To Daisy, he looked like an Irish Santa Claus. The sole spectator was her friend from the civil rights institute. Damn! she thought, here she was sitting in the middle of a great story and she couldn't even report it.

Efficiently, each side presented its argument to the judge. Danaher contended that the government needed the original tapes to ensure that no changes had been made and cited *Branzburg* to argue that journalists are not exempt from providing evidence to grand juries. Schoenhorn too used the protean *Branzburg,* but he claimed that it gave Daisy qualified privilege, so that the government's interest in the tapes was not direct enough to trump press freedom or to compel Daisy to breach confidentiality. The debate between the two lawyers grew heated—Danaher suggesting Daisy might be shielding other suspicious sources, Schoenhorn accusing Danaher of abusing his power to get evidence for a case already pending—until Clarie gaveled them into silence and announced that he would issue his ruling the following day.

When she arrived at the courthouse the next morning, Daisy learned that the decision would not come down until five that afternoon. It was going to be a long day, and, preferring to spend it alone, she passed her supporters demonstrating outside the courthouse and wandered through the city. She passed an appealing store, thought about shopping, then remembered that she was about to go to jail. "I didn't regret my decision," she writes, "but I was scared."[21]

At five minutes to five, Daisy returned to the courthouse, determined and resigned. "We won!" her lawyer shouted, waving a copy of the decision, as he ran down the hall to her. Clarie had upheld journalistic privilege, using a three-part test proposed in *Branzburg* to balance constitutional and societal concerns and concluding that Daisy's First Amendment interest in avoiding disclosure outweighed the government's need to present the original tapes to the grand jury. She was instructed to keep the tapes, but she did not have to turn them over to anyone, and she was not going to prison. "Politics and political games work after all," Daisy says, with appropriate wryness. "They didn't want a Puerto Rican journalist in jail in the U.S. because for the U.S. it would have been the most shameful portrait of what they are in this country. That they, the great empire of free press and democracy, would have put a journalist from one of their colonies in jail. . . . Imagine the scandal that would have caused!"

Daisy's subpoena was the last for a journalist in Puerto Rico, but she worries that in the years since she went to Hartford, the island's press has become increasingly embattled. An assault on a cameraman in a courtroom, shots fired at colleagues: the motives are unclear, though she maintains that the government's animosity toward journalists encourages the public's hostility. She is certain it would be much harder to get the government to support her if she were subpoenaed today. A second act isn't inconceivable, since her ideas haven't changed. "On the contrary," she says, "as time went by, I realized that I was really right when I fought not to turn [the tapes] over because that was a small step for us, the Puerto Rican press, and that won us respect. Moreover, I can always raise my voice and say something because I never went back."

And, true to form, she raises her voice regularly. Eight years after her defiance of the federal government, at a press conference about the future of Vieques, the Puerto Rican island then occupied by the U.S. Navy, the governor responded to her questions by accusing her of being an *independentista*. Daisy defended herself well, Linda reports, answering that she understood his job to be policy making about Vieques. Hers, she reminded him, was to ask questions.

# chapter five

# POINT OF VIEW

## Susanna Styron

*Martha's Vineyard, Massachusetts, August 1996*

"You might want to turn that on," says filmmaker Susanna Styron, pointing to the tape recorder. "I'm about to say something." We sit on the floor of a gazebo in the middle of a grassy slope above the harbor, where boats dance at their moorings. After threatening to rain all morning, it is now coming down hard, much to the delight of the kids splashing noisily in the puddles around us. Halfway up the hill, a flag unfurls on a gust of wind, then droops in the rain. The scene is pure Americana.

So is our conversation: Susanna's pronouncement is about the inviolability of the First Amendment, though it took a decade of legal wrangling before the federal government agreed to apply that premise to one of her films. During those ten years, Susanna led several documentary filmmakers in a legal battle to obtain the educational certificates granted by the U.S. Information Agency (USIA) that made it possible to distribute films internationally without charge. Susanna's film, *In Our Own Backyards: Uranium Mining in the United States,* which she made with Pamela Jones, tells the story of a nuclear waste spill on Navajo land in New Mexico. It was clearly a documentary, and she and Jones meant it to be educational, but the USIA disagreed, finding it ineligible because of its point of view.

"I was raised in a very political atmosphere where I was taught to speak my mind. It's also my personality," Susanna explains in a deep voice that grows more deliberate with the weight of the topic. "It came naturally to say, Hey! you can't do that to me! I guess I grew up always being suspicious of the government on some level. I was an adolescent during the Vietnam War and my parents were always taking me off to marches in Washington. And what I saw as I was becoming a person was that if you don't insist on finding out for yourself what's going on, then, one, nobody's going to tell you, and, two, unjust things will happen."

In August 1996, about a year and a half after the lawsuit that seemed as if it would never end ended, Susanna and I talk on Martha's Vineyard, where she is spending the summer, as she has since she was eight. There was confusion over the ferry schedule, so it has taken all morning for us to meet, pick up sandwiches, and then cast about for a place to talk where we won't be disturbed and, she cautions, she won't be self-conscious. The warning surprises me. She seems quite able to hold her own in the high-powered company she keeps. She is, she states matter-of-factly, the child of celebrities: the Pulitzer Prize–winning writer William Styron and the poet and human rights activist Rose Styron.

Susanna is forty-two, loose-limbed, long-jawed, angular, with quick, sharp movements that manage not to feel hurried. She has a sudden laugh, even, white teeth, a dimple in her chin, and red hair ("That's how you'll recognize me") made redder by a punk-pink rinse. She is staying at her parents' place a little ways out of town with her daughters, Emma, 8, and Lilah, 6, while her husband, actor Darrell Larson, remains at their home north of New York City. Martha's Vineyard, a summer watering hole for the East Coast's cultural elite, is a place of casual stylishness, where kids come equipped with nannies, people use summer and winter as verbs, and car ferry reservations must be made six months in advance. But Susanna's Vineyard is also a homey place, where everyone who passes on the street says hello and doors remain unlocked.

She made her first film about the winter people here. It served as her senior thesis at Yale, and Carlos Fuentes, then Mexico's ambassador to France, was so impressed by it that he recommended Susanna to Luis Buñuel, who hired her to work in Paris on his last movie. Next, she went to Los Angeles to work as assistant to director Ken Russell on *Altered States*. Susanna mentions these connections casually, save Buñuel, whom she idolized, but when I say something about privilege, she bristles, pointing out that those with privilege have the choice of how to use it. Raised to use it for the greater good, she is determinedly bringing up her daughters the same way. And that, as she sees it, includes fighting injustice where you meet it.

————————

For Susanna, the injustice against her and Pam Jones, her partner on the film, began when their distributor, Bullfrog Films of Oley, Pennsylvania, submitted a routine application to the USIA for a Certificate of International Educational Character. These certificates were issued under the Beirut Agreement, an international treaty meant to promote "the free flow of ideas by word and image . . . and the mutual understanding of peoples"[1] by eliminating duties, broker fees, and cumbersome paperwork on the importation of documentary, educational, and scientific films. The idea behind the agreement was to give documentaries a boost, since they can be valuable sources of information and perspective but rarely make any money.

Since UNESCO negotiated the Beirut Agreement in 1948, it has gone into effect in about seventy countries. The United States ratified it in 1960 and put it into law six years later, at which point Congress gave implementing responsibility to the USIA, the federal agency that disseminated information about America to other countries. The USIA then added an elaborate set of regulations, including a stipulation against certifying materials "which by special pleading attempt generally to influence opinion, conviction or policy . . . to espouse a cause, or, conversely, when they seem to attack a particular persuasion."[2] Another rule eliminated material "which may lend itself to misinterpretation, or misrepresentation of the United States . . . or which appear to have as their purpose or effect to attack or discredit economic, religious or political views or practices."[3]

Government-speak aside, these guidelines had the potential to limit governmental approval, and the benefits that flow from it, to films that meshed with official policy or doctrine. For about twenty years, that seemed to make little difference: between 1973 and 1987, the USIA granted 64,148 certificates and turned down only 471,[4] and if the denials were for ideological reasons, no one called the agency on it. Then Ronald Reagan appointed his pal, Charles Z. Wick, a former businessman and writer/producer of the film *Snow White and the Three Stooges,* to head the agency, and ideology became central to its activities.

The problem of where to draw the line between information and propaganda had plagued U.S. diplomacy since the end of World War I, and not until 1953 was the USIA formally established as an entity separate from the State Department. The agency's status and name have varied depending on domestic politics, international relations, and the strength of its leadership. (In 1999, it was stripped of its autonomy and reincorporated into the State Department.) When Wick was appointed, he announced, "We are engaged in projecting an accurate image of American society and in explaining to foreign audiences the nature, meaning and rationale of our foreign policies."[5] This translated into a series of assaults on the free exchange of ideas, perhaps the most egregious of which was a blacklist of over eighty prominent Americans whose politics made them, in the eyes of the government, unsuitable representatives of American culture.

The agency also began to interpret the Beirut regulations to suit the political agenda of Wick's boss, Ronald Reagan, and the selective application of the regulations raised the question of whether the government should be reviewing films in the first place. In the early 1930s, Hollywood set up the Motion Picture Production Code, commonly known as the Hays Code, as a system of review, precisely to convince the government that no standardized federal licensing would be necessary because the industry could police—and, if need be, censor—itself. The benefits of the code and its successor, the Motion Picture Association of America (MPAA) ratings that we now use, are open to debate. They never covered noncommercial documentaries like *In Our Own Backyards* anyway, but having a movie labeling system in place gave legitimacy to the USIA when it applied a code of its own.

*Backyards,* hardly a booster of the official and commercial sentiment about nuclear power, was turned down for certification because, the USIA Chief Attestation Officer wrote, its "primary purpose . . . appears to be less to instruct or inform in an education sense, than to present a special point of view."[6] This attempt to make the image of America fit Reaganite politics didn't sit well with Susanna, in part because her politics were diametrically opposite and in part because she knew that the government is supposed to remain neutral on the content of speech it allows. Though she didn't yet know the terminology, she suspected that any regulation that "burdens" speech had dubious legal standing.

———————

Setting legal precedent was not on Susanna's mind in 1979, when she and Jones were tossing out ideas for a film and she recalled reading something about uranium mining in the Southwest. They were drawn to the topic but lacked a way to dramatize it until Susanna did some work with MUSE, Musicians United for Safe Energy. A board member introduced her to Larry Anderson, a Navajo and one of the founders of the American Indian Movement, and Anderson, who appears in the film, put her in touch with other Navajos, who served as sources.

Then in July 1979, shortly before Susanna and Jones began filming, a dam broke at a holding pond for United Nuclear Company's operation near Church Rock in northwestern New Mexico. About one hundred million gallons of radioactive waste spilled into the dry riverbed of the Rio Puerco, creating a flash flood of contaminated water that flowed ninety miles downstream.[7] This, then, was their story, the effect of and response to the spill—lucky for them, but disastrous for the Navajos in the area, who had to contend with polluted groundwater and poisoned livestock. "It was a massive nuclear contamination," Susanna says, "but because it was in New Mexico, because it was on a Navajo reservation, because it wasn't threatening white people, it didn't get nearly as much publicity as Three Mile Island."

She and Jones traveled to New Mexico to check it out. Susanna was twenty-four, too young to rent a car. What they found alarmed and frightened them: not only environmental devastation but also what looked like an attempt to cover it up. *In Our Own Backyards* is straightforward and slightly dowdy, mostly talking heads and grainy shots of bleached-out landscapes. It presents the views of people who seldom appear in official accounts, and it makes its charges without equivocation but not without evidence to back them up.

On the Navajo reservation, Susanna and Jones filmed a former uranium miner dying of lung cancer, a miner's widow, and tribal officials. Off the reservation, they filmed Dr. Jorg Winterer, a pediatrician with the Public Health Service in Gallup, who describes being threatened with a court-martial for stating publicly that the Church Rock spill continued to present a grave danger. When asked why the Public Health Service wasn't doing something about it, he claims his superiors told him they "didn't want to antagonize the business community in the area." The film also includes Dr. Joseph Wagoner, who had worked with the Environmental Protection Agency and, at the time of the film, was with the U.S. Public Health Service. Commissioned by the government to perform an epidemiological study of lung cancer in Indian uranium miners, he had learned that they were dying of the disease at five times the rate of a similar, radium-free population.

They talked to a veterinarian who admitted to them what he hadn't said to others: that he didn't think it was true, as officials claimed, that it was safe to eat the livestock. "And the way that they determined that," Susanna recalls, "he said, 'We largely just eyeballed them.' How do you just look at an animal and say, this animal looks okay to eat? The contamination, the radiation levels in the water were way, way, way too high for people to be using that water. But it was only Navajos who were using it."

Uranium is a radioactive element used as fuel for nuclear power plants and in nuclear weapons. Around the world, it tends to be found on land owned by indigenous people. It is land that appears on the surface to be useless—which, as Susanna points out, is the kind of land conquered peoples end up with. *Backyards* also includes interviews with southern Vermonters who, when uranium was discovered near their town, fought successfully to keep mining interests out of the state. Susanna believes that they won, in part, because they were white.

In the United States, uranium mining began in the Southwest after World War II as the country was entering the nuclear age and the Navajos were struggling to make a living. According to the Navajo Uranium Miner Oral History and Photography Project, companies such as Kerr-McGee, John Good, and Trimax were originally welcomed to the Four Corners area, where New Mexico, Arizona, Colorado, and Utah meet, because their uranium mines and mills provided employment close to home. But uranium was subsequently linked to cancer, lung diseases, and other serious ailments, and the miners and their families were later to charge that no one warned them about these dangers. Ventilation in the mines was poor, and miners were not provided with safety devices, such as respirators. They built houses nearby, their children played in piles of uranium waste, and in the summer, when no other clean water was available, they brought cool water from pools inside the mines to drink.

Conditions have improved—one of the USIA's complaints was that *Backyards* didn't acknowledge that sufficiently—and, after years of lobbying, the miners got a measure of official recognition when the Radiation Exposure Compensation Act of 1990 included "compassionate compensation" for people who had worked in uranium mines between 1947 and 1971.[8] Aboveground miners and millers were added to the program in 2000, but the next year, the new administration sought to delay payments to them.[9] Susanna, who hasn't returned to the area since she made her film, is aware of some changes. "I don't know what the long-term effects have been of the Church Rock spill," she says. "There's a certain level of consciousness of Native American issues, but it's not very high."

*Backyards* alleges that the government knew about the health dangers of uranium mining since 1976 but did nothing (this charge was substantiated in testimony before Congress in 1979),[10] and the filmmakers' hearts are clearly with the Navajos. But Susanna and Jones had both worked in journalism, and they were good enough documentarians to seek out the perspective of the nuclear industry, notably Kerr-McGee, the nation's largest uranium producer. Kerr-McGee was reluctant to talk with them until they pointed out that, absent the company's cooperation, their film would have only the Navajos' views—whereupon the manager of Kerr-McGee's operation at Grants, New Mexico, agreed to appear on film. They were also allowed into a uranium mine. Susanna and Jones show up briefly in their film, two young women in hard hats and very bulky, very white protective suits, signing a statement that Susanna reads aloud before going underground. They are not pregnant, they swear, and if they are, they will indemnify Kerr-McGee "for any and all incidents and injury, including but not limited to radiation exposure, that may happen to the unborn child."

Further "expert opinion" came from Toby Moffett, then chairman of the House Subcommittee on Energy, Environment and Natural Resources and a friend of Susanna's, and from a nuclear physicist at Vanderbilt University, who comes across as half apologist for the nuclear industry, half disinterested theorist. Susanna says the USIA ignored the physicist in its assessment of the film's objectivity. "They said there weren't expert opinions, so I guess they deliberately overlooked him. But that's why I really liked having him in there. He didn't really have an investment in either point of view."

Though the mining companies apparently tried to hush up the consequences of the spill and the government seemed willing to help, Susanna and Jones weren't attempting to uncover something no one knew about so much as to highlight something few people thought about. The working and living conditions of Navajo uranium miners in 1979, even granting the government its caveats, were bad, and bringing an inequity to light has long been a valid documentary enterprise. In short, the film has a clear point of view, as, Susanna argues, all documentaries do. "When a person puts something on film or on paper, presents it in any form, it's going to be from his or her point of view. You can't go into making a documentary without any preconceptions and without any ulterior motives and without any desire to see it come out one way or another."

This question of bias and objectivity is a central one for documentary filmmakers and other journalists, as well as scholars, and anyone drawn to unlocking a puzzle of what really happened and what it means. Journalism, we're told, is supposed to be "balanced"—a mantra that replaced "objectivity" when the idea of a journalist as neutral observer was called into question. But when reporters investigate a situation and find

that, on balance, the weight of evidence is on one side, they draw conclusions, as we expect them to. Part of the journalist's function is to sift
through undigested data and make sense of it—in other words, to bring
to bear an informed subjectivity. Their conclusions can be influenced by
a host of factors—researchers don't necessarily enter an investigation
with an open mind, and the more you examine something, the less disinterested you usually become—but by disqualifying *Backyards* because
it had a "special point of view," the USIA implied that documentaries
and, by extension, journalism and scholarship that make judgments have
dubious educational value.

Susanna has little patience for this reasoning. "You try to be as balanced as you possibly can. If you've got a really strong point of view in
one way—which we certainly developed in the process of making this
film—then that's what you're going to be trying to get on film. We set out
to do an investigative reporting piece, but all of that is irrelevant to the
application of that law. Because the USIA was trying to make a judgment
that is preposterous," she says, accenting the second syllable. "The
problem with the USIA regulations is that they pretended that you can
be objective."

A film's point of view is honed in the editing process. Here the editor
decides what to keep and what to take out, juxtaposes interviews to support or undermine ideas, cuts to give some statements greater weight
than others, and determines where to enter the story and what to leave
as the final images. "And believe me, *60 Minutes* does that too," Susanna
says. "I worked for ABC documentaries. That's the whole point, the
power and the drama of getting across this information."

Back in New York, she did most of the editing since Jones had another
job, or, as she describes it, "Pam would come in every day, and I spent
my life on it. I literally would be there from ten in the morning till two
in the morning and then I'd go home to sleep. Then I'd go back. Then I
started to lose my mind." That's when they brought in an editor for the
final cut. The film cost about $50,000 to make, and, as is typical of in-
dependent documentary makers, they funded it with grant money, other
jobs, and savings. They also called on useful connections. The writer
Peter Mattheissen, a Styron family friend, narrates, and James Taylor,
Carly Simon, the Aga Khan, Jack Lemmon, and Walter Matthau are
among those thanked in the film's credits.

"And then that was sort of that," Susanna says. She went to work for
ABC News, Jones went to law school, and *In Our Own Backyards* was
released in 1982. It was shown on PBS and at the Museum of Modern

Art, made the round of film festivals, and collected prizes and accolades. The *Bulletin of Atomic Scientists* called it "an excellent summary of the problems of uranium mining." Peace activist Helen Caldicott said, "It is absolutely wonderful."

To distribute their film, they signed on with Bullfrog, which specializes in films about the environment. Bullfrog sent it around the country and, as is routine with documentaries, planned to distribute it abroad. But when Bullfrog applied to the USIA for certification, it was informed that the film fell "outside categories of material which the Agency may properly certify in accordance with established criteria of judgment."[11]

The USIA's review committee consisted of nine career bureaucrats from various government agencies. (In a distinction that would amuse Rick Nuccio [Chapter 1], the agency was later to insist that the process was safe from politicization because no political appointees were involved.) Since the committee knew little about uranium mining, they sent the film to the Department of Energy for expert review. The DOE has its own point of view: it regulates uranium mining and was criticized in *In Our Own Backyards* for doing it badly. Later, the USIA official in charge of certification admitted that this could constitute a conflict of interest,[12] but it seems to have been standard operating procedure at the time. Bullfrog appealed the decision, but eighteen months later, the USIA turned the film down again.

An appeal to the USIA's director, the last chance for certification, was denied in February 1985. *Backyards,* the agency said, was inaccurate in implying that the uranium industry was "callous to the public need and unwilling to spend the money for adoption of adequate safety measures," that "the government [was] too concerned with pleasing industrial leaders to protect the public interest," and that "the American society [was] once again taking advantage of the Native American Indians." Also, foreign audiences might misinterpret the film, which "would therefore not augment international understanding."[13]

The denial came as a bombshell to John Hoskyns-Abrahall, Bullfrog's co-owner, because none of their films had been turned down before.[14] He asked Susanna and Jones what they wanted to do: pay the duty themselves or not distribute their film abroad. They chose neither option. Says Susanna, "We didn't do this lawsuit because we couldn't afford it. We did it because it was wrong. My feeling is that if there was five cents for one film and none for another and if they had an equally strong so-called point of view, then it's censorship. It's a way to deter a certain point of view from being aired."

Besides, the reasons given for the denials made Susanna and Jones suspicious. "We were, after all, in the Reagan administration and this was the USIA," she says. "We found out that almost without exception the films that were getting the certificate were basically, for lack of a better term, right-wing, films that did not in any way criticize a point of view that would be consistent with the government's at the time. There were some very radical, very heavily opinionated films about how good and safe nuclear power is, how women are supposed to be subordinate to men in the family, and how God is our master.[15] And we went, hey, wait a minute. I think we have a First Amendment case here." I observe that not everyone who meets with bureaucratic injustice says, "We've got a First Amendment case." True, Susanna says, but she and Jones didn't ask to have their work discriminated against, and when it was, it made sense to them to make a federal case of it—literally. Jones was in law school at the time, and political activity is central to how Susanna defines herself. It has been since childhood.

Susanna grew up in southern Connecticut in a family marked by wealth, accomplishment, fame, and connection to power. A premium was placed on involvement, opinions, and political action, and, as the oldest of four children, Susanna learned the lesson well. "In my family, my parents were always watching the news, reading the newspaper, talking about it, doing things about it, whether it was marches or letters. I remember my father always writing articles and writing letters to newspapers, which of course got published because he wrote them. There were always strong moral issues, political issues." Her mother was very involved in Amnesty International, PEN, and other human rights groups, and activism seemed natural.

When she was twelve, her mother took her to Washington to march against the Vietnam War, a defining event for her, and one that she replicated with her daughters, who first marched on Washington in a reproductive choice rally in 1992. "I thought it was important to have children there, and it was important for them. Both of them remember it," Susanna says with pride. Politicians frequented her parents' home, giving her uncommon access to the workings of the system, which continue to fascinate her. "The operations of politics were always familiar to me. And by extrapolation, how the government works: all about who's doing what, who's covering what up, how to get the information out, how to fight it, how to change it, how to make it better."

So that's why she chose a lawsuit? If you don't like something, you don't foment revolution; you sue and evoke the Constitution? "It's you do what you can do," she counters. "I mean, certainly the protest against the [Vietnam] War wasn't about the legal system. It was about having a voice and having the voice be heard. I guess it made sense when it came to this [lawsuit] because it was a government agency that was preventing us from disseminating information. The logical way to fight it was to sue."

She felt a commitment to the people in the film to get their voices heard, but the lawsuit wasn't about them. "It's not like their battle would be lost if this film didn't get distributed in Australia or Canada," she says, though she knows of at least one Canadian distributor who refused to accept uncertified films. Nor did she want to talk with anyone at the USIA about the decision. "I wasn't particularly interested in getting a reasonable point of view from some perfectly innocent employee of the USIA. I wanted to win a case and make a point." She repeats, "It was the principle. It was the right of free Americans to speak their mind versus the desire of a potentially repressive government to shut us up to repress a point of view. It's sort of the whole concept of democracy right there."

The Center for Constitutional Rights agreed to take their case and encouraged them to add other films to the lawsuit, so Susanna got to work convincing filmmakers who had been denied certificates to join them. Some had appealed, but none had, as she puts it, "stopped and said, 'Hey, wait a minute, I don't have to put up with this!' " When the group was assembled, it was apparent that the films that had been rejected tended to criticize U.S. policies and practices, especially concerning nuclear war, the environment, and Central America. Among them was *Save the Planet,* a 1979 film opposing nuclear power, which the USIA had found unacceptable because it portrayed "anti-nuclear protesters as heroes, as intelligent and highly motivated," while undoctored footage showed politicians and government officials "giving speeches which appear to be simple-minded, lacking in understanding of the problem, and in some cases, almost maniacal."[16] *Whatever Happened to Childhood?* another of the films, won an Emmy and several other awards for its examination of broken families but was denied certification because it "distort[ed] the real picture of the universe and youth in the United States."[17]

The other films named in the suit were *From the Ashes: Nicaragua Today; Ecocide: A Strategy of War;* and *Peace: A Conscious Choice,* a brief, impressionistic film with New Age music, squiggly images, and disembodied voices repeating "I don't want war" in English and Russian. The seventh movie in the suit, *The Secret Agent,* which is about the defoliant Agent Orange, had gotten certified on appeal when the USIA decided to overlook its point of view because it "showed the American 'system' at its best."[18] Susanna says the producers joined the lawsuit because that rationale was so ludicrous.

*Bullfrog v Wick,* filed on December 5, 1985, on behalf of sixteen filmmakers and distributors, charged Charles Wick and John W. Mendenhall, a career bureaucrat who had served as Chief Attestation Officer at USIA for many years, with using the certification process in a politically biased manner to prevent certain films from being seen abroad. The suit asked that the films be reconsidered and the regulations be revised to fall more in line with the Beirut Agreement and the First and Fifth Amendments.

*Bullfrog* was filed in federal court in Los Angeles because Susanna, who had taken on much of the responsibility for the case, was living there. Disillusioned with trying to raise money for documentaries, she had gone to work in Hollywood and then to the American Film Institute, where she spent three years as a directing fellow, making a short film and getting her MFA. (She continues to make feature films, including the 1999 *Shadrach,* based on a story by her father.)

By 1985, *In Our Own Backyards* seemed distant history, but she had invested a lot of time and energy in preparing the case and representing the filmmakers, and as the trial approached, all the old anger, disbelief, and edgy excitement returned. The CCR lawyer arguing the case was David Cole, who later represented Margaret Randall (Chapter 3). He was twenty-seven years old but looked younger, and this was one of his first cases. "I remember meeting him the first day and thinking, Oh, my God!" says Susanna. "I have a twelve-year-old trying my case." Her fears were soon allayed. "We got in the courtroom and I was stunned. It was like seeing Laurence Olivier for the first time. [David] was so brilliant, he was so articulate." She wasn't testifying, but she was still nervous. "I had never been in a courtroom. I had total stage fright just sitting there. For David. I mean, I'm sure he was totally cool, but I suddenly realized what a sort of performance it is. And there's so much more at stake when you're a lawyer. It's like you have these people's—in my case, not lives— but in a lot of cases, people's lives in your hands. We had this fabulous judge, Wallace Tashima. He's Japanese American, very handsome and kind of graying. He was very even. And very sharp. He didn't miss a thing."

She watched the trial with a director's eye, and it both lived up to and disappointed her expectations. It lasted only a few hours, and since there was no jury, the courtroom was empty, save for Cole, herself, and the government's lawyers, whom she lumps together as "five guys in suits."

Yet a drama unfolded. "The thing that struck me about the lawyer's argument, it's a performance not for an audience; it's for the judge. It's all happening right then. You can't edit it, you can't rehearse it, you can't cut and start all over again."

Essentially, Cole was arguing that the First Amendment axiom that governmental restriction on speech cannot be politically motivated also applied to what was basically a government subsidy of speech. It was a harder argument to make than if the issue had been an outright ban on speech, but Cole claimed that the USIA regulations were too broad and too vague, making the review process unconstitutional. Why did that matter, beyond creating a nuisance for a handful of obscure filmmakers? The problem, as with all ambiguous and overreaching rules, is threefold. First, murky rules make it difficult for people to know what is expected of them, so they can be caught in noncompliance without warning, as happened to Susanna and company. Second, the absence of clear guidelines gives officials undue authority to make decisions on a subjective and capricious basis; in this case, it turned bureaucrats into film editors as well as arbiters of the truth. Third, the fear of running afoul of sanctioned points of view creates a chilling effect on speech. Arbitrarily applied rules are a method of control and a popular one in a democracy where it is preferable for people to police themselves.

The government argued back that this was not censorship because no speech was stopped; the certificates were merely advisory and the filmmakers were free to show their films wherever they wanted. Furthermore, the First Amendment does not guarantee government subsidies, nor does it require that assistance to one kind of speech be extended to all kinds of speech. The government regularly distinguishes among the messages it supports and, on occasion, attaches strings.

"Frankly, they didn't have much of a case," Susanna says now, and apparently Judge Tashima agreed. On October 24, 1986, he decided against the USIA and instructed the agency to review the films again under revised guidelines. "Once the government makes benefits available, it may not withhold them on the basis of 'unconstitutional conditions,' " he ruled. "In a nation that prides itself on the protection of the right to express unpopular ideas and the right to dissent, can the expression of such dissenting views ever be 'misrepresentation'?"[19]

Susanna remembers screaming into the phone in excitement when Cole called her from New York to report the decision, but their victory was short-lived. The government quickly appealed, and the case stretched on for nine more years in a series of rulings followed by appeals that became repetitive and anticlimactic. "David would call me every six months or so and say, well, we won the appeal"—she laughs—"and they're appealing again."

It all seemed a little remote: not only the deliberations but also the costs. CCR covered the legal expenses, and she hadn't been counting on any profit from *Backyards*. Nor could she claim much personal cost. "I felt all through this that it was an incredibly important case, but there was no personal sacrifice or risk for me involved in bringing the suit. Although, if it had been a higher-profile thing, I'm sure on some level somebody would have tried to get even with me. Not like run me over with a car in the middle of the night, but try to discredit me somehow. I don't think I was a big enough threat to make anybody bother."

The first time the USIA appealed, it made no changes to its regulations. Cole went back to court and got Tashima to compel compliance—whereupon the agency created a "propaganda" stamp, which, as Susanna points out, was worse than no stamp at all. *Backyards* was reviewed under the new guidelines and was turned down again, this time because the USIA found certain statements unverifiable or out of date. For example, they said, "There is a definite link between cigarette smoking and lung cancer. . . . Accordingly, the agency is unable to verify that uranium was the cause of the lung cancer of the miners."[20] Baloney, replies Susanna; none of the miners in the film smoked, which could have been verified easily by talking to the doctors she and Jones had interviewed.

CCR went back to court in what became known as Bullfrog II to challenge these revised guidelines, which Tashima ruled, in May 1988, were impermissibly vague. Accusing the USIA of "foot dragging," he ordered it to certify the films, regardless of the regulations. So six years after Susanna and Jones first applied, *In Our Own Backyards* finally received a provisional certificate, and four days after Tashima's ruling in Bullfrog II, the Ninth Circuit Court of Appeals unanimously affirmed his 1986 decision in Bullfrog I. Once again, the USIA appealed.

Around this time, everyone begins to sound fed up. Tashima gave the USIA sixty days to come up with new regulations, Wick threatened to withdraw from the Beirut Agreement, and the USIA suspended all certification, then reverted to the second version of the guidelines, which Tashima had struck down.

In the fall of 1991, Congress added language to the Foreign Relations Reauthorization Act that would grant certificates to films on a viewpoint-neutral basis, which meant that certain aspects of the case had to be argued anew. Meanwhile, the USIA continued to propose revised guidelines, which CCR continued to challenge, until, all appeals and apparently all patience exhausted, the USIA decided not to take the case to the Supreme Court and, in January 1995, agreed to a settlement. All the films were granted educational certificates, and regulations that passed constitutional, and CCR, muster were adopted.

Says Susanna, "They kept appealing it because they're the Justice Department. The lawyers are there. I mean, why not keep going all the way to the top?" Says Cole in an e-mail, "As to why it stretched on so long—that's litigation for you."

So Susanna and Jones finally got what they wanted, although *Backyards* never did travel abroad because by the time it got its certificate, the material was dated and the buzz a new film generates was lost. (Bullfrog continued to list it in its catalogue "for sentimental reasons," Hoskyns-Abrahall reports.) Which means that the USIA also got what it wanted: a limited audience for the film and its point of view. That the government would go to such lengths to do that still perplexes Susanna. "Oh, I can't believe that the USIA really could feel that threatened by [my film]," she says in a scathing voice. "Well, I'm flattered that they think it could have that kind of power. I think it tends to be a habit of government, which is just the thing that makes it so dangerous, that it can come down to not even having to do with something wildly inflammatory. It's like classified information. They totally lose perspective on what's a threat and what isn't.

"This became about a commitment to a certain type of freedom. It sounds really grandiose, but it's really something that affects everybody in this country and I feel very, very strongly about it. I feel [freedom] is wildly more endangered than most people ever realize. If you let it start getting eroded and slipping away in little cases like this, then before you know it, it's gone. What the ability for everybody to speak his or her mind does is prevent any one person from getting too much power, any one point of view from being the law of the land."

She stops, slightly abashed at this ringing affirmation of democracy, but even as Susanna and I were talking, *Bullfrog*'s core tension—the First Amendment's doctrine of neutrality pitted against the patron's right to call the tune—was resurfacing in an angry, public debate known as *Finley v NEA*.

---

In 1990, four performance artists who came to be known as "the NEA 4"—Karen Finley, Holly Hughes, Tim Miller, and John Fleck—had charged the National Endowment for the Arts with violating their First Amendment rights when it denied them grants because of political opposition to their work. They sued, and as in *Bullfrog*, *Finley* was taking its time getting resolved.

Since 1965, the NEA, along with its counterparts in state and local governments, had been sponsoring art on the largest scale in U.S. history and with considerable success. A government agency probably can't call forth great art, but the Endowment had acted on the reasonable assumption that good art is more likely to come from plenty than from deprivation. In its twenty-three years, it had distributed over $3 billion in some hundred thousand grants and had also leveraged support from other sources, spread the cultural wealth around the country, and fostered the idea that art is a valid activity. The NEA was also one of only a handful of sponsors supporting experimental, demanding, or disquieting art and the resolutely impolite artists who made it.

Though the Endowment was designed to be insulated from political interference, from the beginning, it was plagued by an internal contradiction: it took what is an essentially undemocratic process—patronage—and gave it a democratic gloss with open application procedures, peer review panels, and support for the kind of art most patrons avoid. Then, in 1988, the moralist right, whose political influence was on the rise, began to target the NEA, singling out for censure the marginal arts groups and artists who were most dependent on public funding and therefore most vulnerable. The NEA and its supporters responded to the attacks by noting that only a minuscule number of its grants had been controversial, as if this were cause for pride, not shame. They could have denounced blandness and named bullying for what it was, but instead they tried to play the game of the politicians who had never liked the agency to begin with and who, at the behest of moral extremist groups, now demanded to know if certain works of art offended too many people—whatever that number might be.

In response to the controversy it had abetted, Congress set out to try to legislate taste through content restrictions on what the Endowment could fund. This was not censorship, politicians protested predictably, but a question of proper use of "tax dollars." Like the USIA insisting that it shouldn't have to certify films it disagreed with, the NEA's detractors argued that "taxpayers" should not have to pay for art they didn't like— as if all taxpayers couldn't make lists of things they would prefer their taxes not cover, and as if that makes any difference.

Though this sent artists, arts advocates, audiences, administrators, and funders into a tailspin, the NEA proved to be hard to kill off, so Congress tried instead to hobble it. Finding language that would restrict the NEA without violating the First Amendment, however, proved to be even harder. An early attempt, inserted in a 1989 appropriations bill, was a provision known as the Helms amendment, which prohibited the NEA from funding obscene or homoerotic work. (Its immediate effect was an expansion of the national vocabulary, as "homoerotic" started tripping off everyone's tongue.) Soon after, the NEA took a stab at placating Congress by requiring grantees to sign a pledge not to create anything that "may be considered obscene." Bella Lewitzky, a dancer in her seventies, who had lived through other governmental attempts to coerce conformity, immediately challenged this requirement in court, where both the pledge and the Helms amendment were struck down as unconstitutional the following year. (The NEA apparently doesn't hold grudges; it awarded Lewitzky a National Medal of Arts in 1996.)

That's where things stood when the NEA 4 filed their lawsuit to get the grants they believed were rightfully theirs. The group included two lesbians and a gay man, favored targets of the moralist right, and all four addressed sexuality in their work, though, in the ensuing spin cycle, it was hard to tell how or to what extent. They had applied for fellowships, which had been approved by a peer review panel, whose decisions had previously prevailed. But the panel's recommendation was overridden by the Endowment's chairman, a Bush appointee named John Frohnmayer, who justified his decision by saying that he had to "live in a political world."[21] Just how political was soon revealed. In the *Finley* discovery process, lawyers for the NEA 4 found that political interference had reached as high as the president, who wrote to Frohnmayer in June 1990: "I do not want to see censorship, yet I don't believe a dime of taxpayers' money should go into 'art' that is clearly and visibly filth. . . . We have to find a way to preserve the independence of the arts, yet at the same time, see that in egregious cases such as those mentioned above, the taxpayer will not subsidize filth and patently blasphemous material."[22]

That December, Congress amended the NEA's enabling legislation to require that its chairperson, and consequently everyone in the grantmaking process, consider "general standards of respect and decency for the diverse belief and values of the American public." The NEA 4 and their supporters again accused the Endowment of caving in to political pressure and amended their lawsuit to challenge the constitutionality of this "decency" clause.

In court, the government insisted, as always, that it was not censoring. It pointed out, accurately, that no one is entitled to a grant and that the NEA grant-making process discriminated among applicants by design. In response, David Cole, as one of the lawyers for the NEA 4, resurrected his winning argument from *Bullfrog:* while the government is not required to assist art, film, or other creative endeavors, once it has set up mechanisms to do so, it cannot pick and choose among viewpoints in dispensing its benefits. *Bullfrog* had established the principle that to make such decisions on a political basis went against the First Amendment.

Once again, it looked as if the government didn't have much of a case, and in 1993, the Endowment settled part of the lawsuit, reinstating the artists' grants and awarding them damages. The challenge to the "decency" clause continued for years, however, crossing paths with and echoing *Bullfrog* at several points. It was Judge Tashima who had ruled in the artists' favor, thereby putting the "decency" standard on hold and establishing that First Amendment principles pertained to government funding of the arts. When the government appealed that ruling, William and Rose Styron were among twenty-seven writers who petitioned President Clinton to drop the appeal, and when it went ahead, the Ninth Circuit, the same court that had affirmed Tashima in *Bullfrog,* affirmed him in *Finley.*

But the parallels—and victories for the artists—ended there. This time, the government pursued its appeal at the Supreme Court, which, in 1998, decided that the "decency" language was neither too vague nor too onerous to fit under the First Amendment. Instead, the court declared it "merely hortatory" (as the USIA had declared its certificates merely advisory) and reasoned that since NEA guidelines were already subjective, consideration of "general standards of decency" would be no worse.

The arts world tried to put a good face on it, pointing out that the Court had strongly suggested that a direct NEA ban on "indecent" art would be unconstitutional. Still, determining what "general standards of decency" are remains a hopeless tangle, and, absent agreement, the determination will be made by those in power—on the basis of their point of view. That may well have been the purpose of the "decency" language, which serves less to preserve public sensibilities than to place certain views beyond the pale, or, in the language of the moral extremists, to name the damned. Despite its rhetoric of freedom, in both *Finley* and *Bullfrog,* the government ended up playing the role of disciplinarian, forced in anger or disappointment to rein in those it felt went too far. As *Finley* plaintiff Holly Hughes wrote about hearing her case argued before the Supreme Court, "You're not here because you're a citizen participating in a democratic institution. You're here because you've been bad."23

Susanna too had been "bad" in criticizing the government and its probusiness creed, and this was hardly the first time a government resisted giving its imprimatur to an unflattering image of itself or to a perspective at odds with its own. The point of the USIA was to make America look good in front of the neighbors, and though a confident country, like a confident person, can withstand criticism, even unearned criticism, almost no one welcomes it. "Well, I'm sorry," Susanna answers, when I suggest the propagandist's view, "but this is America. There's uranium mining in America. It's mostly on the Navajo reservations. It's mostly where people don't care what happens to them. It's Indians dying of lung cancer. And it's the whole attitude of the nuclear industry based on profits over everything else. Which is pretty damned American. I think what's harmful to America is for it to be seen as a place where any point of view is valued less than another. The whole point of America is that people can speak their minds.

"And if you talk to anybody who comes from any dictatorship or any country that's even mildly repressive in terms of speech, they're just like"—she mimics breathless awe—" 'This is the greatest country in the world. You can say what you want, you can publish it in the newspaper, you can speak it on the street and nobody will put you in jail.' I see a lot of that because my mother spends her life trying to help people in other countries who are victims of that, so, I've met a lot of survivors and it's a very ugly, awful thing. I'm not saying we're on the verge of putting everybody who dissents against the government in jail, but there's a starting point for everything."

───────────

When Susanna and I finish work for the day, we move to the larger of the two houses in the Styrons' compound, where we pour ourselves glasses of wine and retire to a generous porch to look out across a well-tended lawn to the sea. A hammock slung between two trees, orange daylilies along the white fence, the plonk-plonk of a tennis game nearby: the starched orderliness of the scene puts me in mind of a *New Yorker* cover in July. She loved to read here for hours when she was younger, she reports, wrapped in a blanket against the weather.

And so our talk turns to children, returns, really, because the subject is never far from Susanna's mind. That's where the protection needs to be, she pronounces, and where her activism is focused now. But when we get to the question of protecting kids from odious speech, her response is less certain. Working it out aloud, she compares the First Amendment and the death penalty. "There are times that, as a mother especially, I may say of someone, if he did that to my child, I would want to kill him. I don't know if I'm capable of killing anybody, even when it comes to my children." She laughs uneasily. "I might. I'd want to kill him and afterwards I might think, oh, I shouldn't have done that, it'd be better to put him in jail." This answer, this muddle, is so unedited that we both laugh, knowing the queasy moment when you recognize that the great font of tolerance you advocate is about to blow up in your face and the best defense you have is a theoretical "robust exchange of ideas."

"There's stuff I hope I never hear," she continues. "There are all sorts of hateful, hateful forms of speech. But I think to take away the right of people to express them is more dangerous than the expression of them. I wish it, censorship, could just be applied to the people I don't want to say things, to people who don't have my point of view," she concludes wistfully. "Which is what the government wishes too. But it can't. That's the problem with it."

In an essay Susanna wrote about her response to an earthquake in Los Angeles, she asks, "Can we teach our children to be safe without teaching them to be afraid?"[24] Confidence and shelter: Is that what she wants for her kids? Without hesitation, she answers, "I want them to speak up for themselves. I want them to grow up knowing that if they see something they believe is wrong or hurtful to themselves or other people, they will feel that they have a voice and that they can speak up about it. And believe me, they do."

part two

# FREELANCE VIGILANTES

OVER THE PAST DOZEN YEARS, we have been gripped by a holy justice run amok that takes as its target, not the standard stuff of censorship, but the everyday interactions and pastimes of the American people. It is a culture war, we are told; these are the battles. Sometimes it seems the war is over, but then a religious group declares a "Victims of Pornography Month," or a congressman rallies his troops for an "aggressive counterattack" against "a cultural coup," or a school superintendent justifies pulling Allen Ginsberg's *Howl* from the classroom by saying, "Academic freedom is one thing, but what we tell our students is another"—and the hostilities resume. The lid must be kept on, the lid must be blown off. Each prospect is frightening to some, exhilarating to others. It is this definitively American tug-of-war between puritanism and license that underlies the stories in this section.

Annie Sprinkle appeared in porn movies for years, but it wasn't until she crossed into performance art that she incurred the wrath of everyone, from fellow feminists who believed sexual representation harms women to politicians who held her up as a symbol of government profligacy. Context, it seems, is all—or nearly all. For the many artists ensnared in fights for control of the culture, vague regulations, bureaucratic cowardice, and uneasiness about art's power played a role too, as James Montford, Denise Marika, Michael Willhoite, Hans Evers, Jay Critchley, Ifé Franklin, and Maxine McDonald learned when their work was attacked, defaced, and banned. In a roundtable discussion, these seven visual, performing, and literary artists attempted to understand why culture has become a lightning rod for social anxieties.

Many of the attacks on art, as well as on popular culture and education, came from the religious right, and Skipp Porteous, once a pastor in a fundamentalist church that brooked no deviance from its doctrine, used his insider knowledge to track groups that capitalized on cultural conflicts to advance their theocratic aims. These groups recognized that a key to changing public perception is changing public education, so they assailed curricula, books, and teachers whose ideas clashed with their own. Caught in this dynamic, New Hampshire high school teacher Penny Culliton was fired for insubordination after she asked her students to read two novels with gay or lesbian protagonists.

The kind of censorship that appears in this section is usually portrayed as protectionist, a shield for the weak and vulnerable, and no one is deemed more vulnerable in present-day America than children. For decades, we have been caught up in moral panics over material we don't want kids to see or hear; recently, we've shifted our anxiety to what kids themselves say and create, and when they are perceived to step out of line, punishment can be harsh. When Mike Diana drew gross-out comic books in Florida, he was convicted of obscenity. When graffiti artist Richard Taylor painted a mural that Los Angles police found disrespectful, it was destroyed. When Paul Kim, an honor student in suburban Seattle, created a Web site satirizing his high school, his principal retaliated by undermining his college applications.

Where did you find these people? I get asked, and I'm surprised, because for each argument, each story appearing here, I know of four, five, ten like it. What they share is a kind of freelance censorship. Since the impetus to control comes mainly from groups or individuals acting in unofficial capacities, the result is not usually a violation of the First Amendment, but the intention to silence offends First Amendment values.

No one persuades or is persuaded in these fights because what is being fought over are buried intentions. People in disputes over their beliefs or identity tend to resort to an Explanation of All Things, the theory or principle or catchphrase that acts as a sieve for all conflicts, so that issues come out at the other end simplified and clear. And when they don't, when the Explanation doesn't explain quite enough, we can always say, "Well, I believe in diversity" or "Kids must be protected" or "I'm a free speech absolutist." Trying to organize discordant ideas is human nature and necessary at times if one is to act, but it makes discussion difficult and resolution nearly impossible. That may be why there is a sadness to all of these stories. No matter what side you're on in a speech fight, victory is transitory. There will always be words and pictures that upset or annoy, and there will always be someone somewhere who will want to banish them.

For people not easily offended by speech, it can be hard to give credence or sympathy to those who are. Even trying to explain the censorious impulse implies a dismissal. Passion deconstructed is passion deflated, and we're talking politics here, hardly a haven of disinterested inquiry. The issues raised in this section are not easy to resolve, but if we're ever to move on, we need to understand why trying to shut people up has become such a comfortable habit.

In these stories, concern over expression falls into three categories:

danger, immorality, and offensiveness. Expression considered dangerous usually involves sex or violence. Although images are sometimes deemed psychologically damaging in themselves, the greater harm is said to lie in what they will lead to—that is, sexual or violent behavior. Despite the best efforts of scientific research, a causal relationship remains unproven. Predicting how people will behave on the basis of how they react in a laboratory setting is dicey, particularly since researchers can't ethically incite violent acts, which leaves them to test for amorphous things like "arousal" and "aggression." Findings are hard to interpret, not only because of context but also because it is difficult to know if the images cause the behavior or appeal to viewers who already tend to behave that way. Finally, claims of causality ignore a host of other factors, such as neglect, poverty, and abuse, that contribute more to violent and sexist behavior than Mike Diana's comics or Annie Sprinkle's monologues.

Lack of scientific proof seldom deters anyone from feeling afraid, however, and people who believe they are surrounded by enemies will accept strict defensive measures. Yet for all the "protections" against speech advocated recently, no one seems to feel very safe. Instead, each faction in the culture wars appears to believe that its adversaries are more powerful precisely because their arguments are more attractive. So the antisex contingent assumes people will be drawn to sin, while the prosex bloc assumes people will readily believe that what gives them pleasure is bad. (This may help explain why we perpetuate a state of affairs—fearing sex—that makes us so unhappy.)

In an old comedy routine, Mike Nichols and Elaine May observed that a moral issue is much more interesting to intellectuals than a real issue, and as a reason for censoring, morality taps into astonishing wells of passion. Though the speech confrontations we hear about are usually played as revolts of the fed-up—spontaneous outbursts by individuals brought together over burning issues—many of these quarrels have been nurtured or orchestrated by organizations of the moralist right. Well organized, well financed, and well aware that little attracts attention better than controversy reduced to sound bites, these groups espouse a morality of sexual prudery and brittle authoritarianism and wish to limit government intervention in everything except speech.

The moralist right has honed its strategies to marginalize and vilify those it goes after, and because the techniques work, they are now routine among the unaffiliated as well. Words and images get taken out of context and treated on a literal level only (as Richard Taylor was to learn, censors dislike ambiguity, preferring to pin down ideas like butterflies on velvet). These bits are then magnified to represent all that is wrong with whatever is under attack: art, education, the Internet, kids. Another method is to create supposedly irreconcilable dichotomies, so that people like artist Ifé Franklin, who is both black and lesbian, are pressed to make a choice. Stealth is also valuable. For nearly everyone in this section, the challenges to their work, thoughts, or being came out of the blue, leaving them scrambling, drop-jawed, to defend what had already been portrayed as indefensible. These strategies make it hard for the people under attack to avoid victimhood on one hand, false heroics on the other.

This campaign from the right to punish antisocial speech has been paralleled by one on the left to institute prosocial speech as a corrective to a society judged badly out of whack. Women and racial and sexual minorities are portrayed as victims of bad speech, fragile as Victorian ladies taking to their beds the minute an infelicity enters the room. Not content with substituting better speech, some factions have pushed for measures to outlaw certain expression—laws banning pornography as a civil rights violation, speech codes at universities—though the left more often relies on self-righteousness and browbeating. (Conservatism is seen as a political position, liberalism as a way of behaving.) It was this brand of sanctimony that greeted James Montford, an African American artist whose subject is racism, when he tried to talk with college students after they ripped apart his installation because they found it racist.

Censorship is a prerogative of power, but the less powerful give legitimacy to censorship as a solution when they restrict words and images in an effort to gain leverage or balance. The upshot of antidiscriminatory speech campaigns is a kind of fascist chic, the sense that it is not just okay to shut people up but also kind of cool.

The triumph of the word police, no matter what their politics, has been to turn their precepts into common wisdom. Pornography is harmful, the Internet is dangerous, artists are corrupt, tolerance is capitulation, and discussion, imagination, plain old talk must be corralled and controlled. Even liberal-minded people who are aghast at the prospect of censorship talk easily of "limits." The implication is that reasonable, well-meaning citizens will behave civilly toward each other, and embedded in that are two assumptions that recur in the stories that follow: that the defense of individual speech rights has brought a riot of dangerous expression that needs to be throttled and that depending on the civility of strangers will resolve conflicts over what is good and bad speech. The first of these propositions will be debated forever, though the dangers of censorship usually outweigh the dangers of speech. As for the second, I think civility is great, depend on it to get through the day, and get upset when it's breached. It isn't a panacea, though, and pretending that it is smothers all the things that are not civil but still need to be said.

We have been worn down by these squabbles, especially as they erupt over matters of less and less consequence. The republic probably will not fall if a kid can't wear an obnoxious T-shirt to school, and words, art, books, and ideas generally outlive the forces that try to destroy them. The people those forces censor sometimes do too, but never unscathed. Speaking of his native Mexico, Octavio Paz asked, "How can we create a society, a culture, that will not deny our humanity, but will also not change it into an empty abstraction?" The answer, should we ever find it, is why these arguments matter.

chapter six

# THAT SPECIAL SHIMMER

Annie Sprinkle

*Telephone Conversations to Provincetown,
Massachusetts, July 1997, Sausalito, California,
July 1998*

It is hard to know how to describe Annie Sprinkle. There is the sound bite: Prostitute! Porn star! Performance artist! The self-description: Multimedia whore, sexual revolutionary, pleasure activist. The biography: Born Ellen Steinberg in 1954, the oldest of four children in a middle-class family. The politics: Feminist, lesbian, champion of sex and all its manifestations. The obvious: She has very large breasts, which she bares often. And finally, what may be most notable in our time: Annie seems to feel little guilt or shame about her body or its functions.

It has been remarked so often that we are in the throes of a sex panic that I feel foolish writing it here again. American culture has never made peace with the erotic, but these days we seem able to talk about sex only at a fever pitch, as if whatever it touches has a special shimmer, and as if we can imagine nothing more perilous, especially to women and children. That unease influences not just what we say, see, and think but where and how we live, whom and how we love, how we raise and teach our children, how freely we touch or laugh with each other, how often we look over our shoulder when we walk down the street, and, not long ago, whether our president was guilty of an impeachable offense. When the charge of sex meets the license of imagination, both become ready scapegoats for a multitude of anxieties and a heap of hypocrisy, and nowhere is this more apparent than in the age-old argument over pornography.

Annie is one of a number of feminists who champion sexual expression, but few women have acted on their sexual philosophy as whole-heartedly as she. In the thick of controversies for the past twenty-five years over how sex is portrayed, she has managed—sometimes gleefully, sometimes not—to run afoul of the FBI, the postal service, cable TV stations, customs officials, university administrators, antisex feminists, and Senator Jesse Helms, who denounced her so harshly from the floor of Congress that eight years later, her name would still be synonymous with the supposed sins of the National Endowment for the Arts.[1] Little wonder that she says, "Censorship for me is almost a daily occurrence."

Annie and I talk by phone as she is about to move from Provincetown, Massachusetts, to a houseboat in Sausalito, California. I have seen her show *Hardcore from the Heart* a few months before, and we planned to meet, but things change suddenly and she is moving the next week. In photographs, Annie has an almost caricatured hourglass figure, a mane of dark hair, a megawatt smile, and kohl-rimmed eyes that look like she's enjoying a very good secret, but the phone being our medium, it is her voice that sticks in my mind. It's a good-natured, Minnie Mouse voice, alternately dreamy, fizzy, and firm. I picture the words dripping from her mouth as she murmurs assent, drops articles, elides verbs—*wanna, gonna, hafta*. So one way to describe Annie is to note the disjunction between expectation and reality. Her talk is blunt, her sexual tastes are unconventional, her press teeters on the sensational (my favorite: "She makes giving blowjobs for pay sound like a summer-camp crafts activity"),[2] yet there she is, sounding much as you'd imagine a sweetly generous Ellen Steinberg to be.

---

Annie was born in Philadelphia and raised in a "very white-bread, middle-class" suburb of Los Angeles. Her grandparents were Eastern European Jews (her maternal grandfather was the graphic artist who created the Morton Salt girl), her parents were liberal-minded Unitarians. Her father was a social worker, and when she was thirteen, the family moved to Panama for his work.

Annie describes herself as shy and virginal until she was seventeen, which is when she discovered sex and found that she really liked it. She moved to Tucson with her lover, a man ten years her senior, and put her predilections to work. "My journey definitely starts with prostitution, and then I went into pornography," she explains. "So first of all, I started with something that was totally, absolutely illegal, even though I personally find the fact that it's illegal as absurd as making hot fudge sundaes illegal. I was a hippie in Tucson, Arizona, and a friend of mine was working in a massage parlor, and I just came down to answer the phones one day for a little extra money. One thing led to another and for three months I worked. I thought I was a horny masseuse. Finally, it hit me that I was actually a prostitute, although no one ever said the word. I just kind of fell into it, but being a creative kind of person, I always saw prostitution as a very theatrical, expressive act. You know, sex in general, paid or unpaid. I'm forty-two now. I've been doing sex stuff a quarter of a century."

When she was eighteen, she got a job selling popcorn at a movie theater showing *Deep Throat,* the first porn film she saw. Within weeks, the theater was closed down on obscenity charges, and when she was called to testify at the trial,[3] she met the film's director, Gerard Damiano, who, she writes, gave her "deep throat lessons." She became his mistress, followed him to New York, and soon after made her first pornographic movie. It was called *Teenage Deviate.*

Silly and misogynistic as those films seem to her now, Annie has fond memories of the underground porn industry of the early seventies. "When I made a porno movie, it's not like the Hollywood films make it out to be. My experience is, we're making a movie and isn't this fun. And isn't the sex feeling good. People can't even imagine taking money for sex, but if that's your job and you like it, it doesn't feel bad, for the most part. My days in porn were some of the happiest days of my life." As for the claim that women are invariably exploited in pornography, she counters, "My experience is that women are exploited in most businesses or aren't treated as well as men. But in fact, women porn actors make a lot more money than male porn actors.[4] It's not an ideal world, but where is there an ideal world?"

In all, Annie acted in some 150 films and directed a few, including *Deep Inside Annie Sprinkle,* the second-highest-grossing sex film of 1982. (She's been told that after her trademark golden shower scenes of urinating on her sex partner were edited out of most copies, the uncut version became a collector's item, demonstrating once again the marketing power of official disapproval.) By then, the industry was changing, regulating itself in response to police action and new technology, such as VCRs and pay-per-view, which brought porn out of red-light districts and into the living room.

———————————

Mass market porn is a post–World War II phenomenon, but depictions
of sex have been around as long as people have drawn pictures and told
stories. The word *pornography*—literally, "writing about prostitutes"—
first appeared in print in English in 1850.[5] If it ever was a purely de-
scriptive term, it is now heavily freighted, with the debate ranging narrowly from "It's offensive and dangerous" to "It's offensive but not
dangerous." Only a small group of people have anything good to say
about pornography, and until recently its producers weren't writing
books. (Writing *about* prostitutes is different from writing *by* prostitutes;
mistresses have had their say throughout history, but whores are not supposed to kiss and tell.)

In the United States, pornography is not a legal category. Neither is
erotica, its dress-up name, or indecency, whose definition is anybody's
guess, although the term appears in federal broadcast regulations and
National Endowment for the Arts guidelines. It is obscenity that ranks
among the few categories of speech not protected by the First Amendment, though the courts have yet to formulate a good reason why. Rather
than try, policy makers and lawmakers have concentrated on defining
obscenity, and two themes central to Annie's story appear again and
again in these efforts. First is the largely unchallenged assumption that
dirty words and pictures have a dangerous effect on susceptible populations; and second is the hope that if we try hard enough, we can wall off
"unworthy" pornography from "worthy" art. For all our apparent sophistication about sex, we have made little progress in proving or dis-
proving these propositions, so the issue, as in most censorship controversies, becomes, who decides and who polices?

Angela Carter, the British feminist writer, argued in a 1978 essay that
when pornography "serves . . . to reinforce the prevailing system of values and ideas in a given society, it is tolerated; and when it does not, it is
banned."[6] In colonial America, blasphemous speech was punished as
harshly as wrongful acts, and in the nineteenth century, state laws
against profanity were widespread but rarely enforced.[7] Then, in 1873,
the federal government got involved when a young and ardent Anthony
Comstock persuaded Congress to outlaw the sending of obscene material through the mail. Comstock's eponymous law was the model for
American antiobscenity legislation into the 1930s, while his rhetoric
characterizes antivice campaigns to this day.

Meanwhile, jurists, failing to define obscenity, resorted to devising
tests to determine if something fell into that category. For a long time,

the defining test in the United States came from *Regina v Hicklin,* an 1868 English case that focused on the effect of sexual material: specifically, whether it tended "to deprave and corrupt those whose minds are open to such immoral influences and into whose hands a publication of this sort may fall"—that is, the lower classes. (This posed a problem to our American pretense of being a classless society, which we resolved in part by focusing on women and the young.)

The beginning of the twentieth century saw an increase in obscenity trials, and after World War I, when the courts began to tackle First Amendment law in earnest, the obscenity versus art, and particularly literature, debate took center stage. In the landmark *Ulysses* case of 1934, a federal court in New York decided to allow James Joyce's novel into the United States because, in the pungent words of the judge, the effect of passages was "somewhat emetic, but nowhere does it tend to be an aphrodisiac."[8] This ruling created a new test that would hold sway for nearly twenty-five years: taken as a whole, and in the judgment of a "man of average sexual instincts," was the dominant effect of the work in question to arouse lust? Thus, the judgment of the average man supplanted that of the impressionable lad, the *Hicklin* yardstick, and literature was protected as long as it wasn't a turn-on.[9]

The *Ulysses* episode was unusual in that several of the central actors—as opposed to the victims—were women. When Margaret Anderson and Jane Heap were the first to publish chapters of the book in their literary magazine, the *Little Review,* between 1918 and 1920, the only print shop in New York willing to do the job consisted of a man whose mother had been the poet laureate of Serbia and his two daughters.[10] Charged with publishing obscenity, Anderson and Heap were fined fifty dollars each, but *Ulysses* did not become a litmus test for another decade because their fine was paid by a woman who hated the book to keep the publishers from becoming martyrs to the cause.[11] When *Ulysses* was published in its entirety in 1922, it would be another woman, Sylvia Beach, who published it from her Paris bookstore, Shakespeare and Company.

For all the legal ferment, not until 1957 was the Supreme Court asked, in *Roth v U.S.,* to decide if the First Amendment protected obscenity. It did not, the Court ruled, because it had always been assumed that it didn't. Thus, *Roth* codified obscenity as second-class speech and sanctioned punishment, as Justice William Douglas noted in his dissent, for "thoughts provoked, not for overt acts or antisocial conduct."[12] (As a positive side effect, the ruling explicitly sheltered art under the First Amendment; this made little difference to Roth, a pornographer, but has proved useful to artists fighting censorship ever since.)[13] *Roth* was a setback to sexual-speech advocates, but it also paved the way for increasingly narrow definitions of obscenity.[14]

Eleven years later, Lyndon Johnson convened a congressionally authorized commission, known as the Lockhart Commission, which spent two years and $2 million but, to its apparent surprise, found no clear evidence that pornography causes antisocial behavior. The commission recommended launching "a massive sex education effort" and getting rid of laws that banned the sale of sexual material to adults (children, as always, were another story), but Richard Nixon, who received the report in 1970, rejected it. In the familiar refrain of word-Cassandras, he warned, "If an attitude of permissiveness were to be adopted regarding pornography, this would contribute to an atmosphere condoning anarchy in every other field."[15]

Ignoring the commission's recommendations, the courts continued to tinker with tests for obscenity and, in 1973, arrived at the Miller Standard, which prevails today. This test establishes that material is obscene only if, taken as a whole, it (1) appeals to prurient interest, as judged by "the average person applying contemporary community standards"; (2) portrays sexual conduct in a clearly offensive manner; and (3) "lacks serious literary, artistic, political or scientific value."[16] (When I worked at the National Endowment for the Arts in the early 1980s, we talked, somewhat tongue in cheek, about our grants conferring a Good Housekeeping Seal of Approval. This koshering process had legal ramifications when Congress later tried to prohibit the agency from funding "obscene art": if, as was generally agreed, an NEA grant proved "serious artistic or literary value," the Miller Standard would seem to exempt anything the agency chose to fund, making "obscene art" a legal oxymoron.)

For a while, the effect of *Miller* was to make obscenity convictions increasingly rare. Then, in 1985, Ronald Reagan appointed what became known as the Meese Commission and stacked it with people who did their best to prove the dangers of sexually explicit material. Even so, its findings were inconclusive, though that made little difference. When it comes to matters of taste, morality, or habit, we deem "evidence" valid when it confirms what we already believe. The Meese report called for vigorous enforcement of federal obscenity laws, and American legislatures and courts became increasingly amenable to regulation of all kinds of sexual material.

Despite this crackdown, once the pornography business adjusted, it thrived. By 1998, Americans were spending anywhere from $2.6 billion to $10 billion on sexual devices and sexually explicit entertainment and an additional $1 billion on phone sex.[17] In 1999, they rented 711 million hard-core videos, close to ten times the 1985 rate.[18] By 2001, there were seventy thousand pay porn Web sites worldwide,[19] the top five of which received four million individual visitors daily.[20] Porn, in fact, is the only consistently profitable category of online sites, probably accounting for more than 10 percent of all electronic commerce.[21]

The adult entertainment industry is an American success story, catering to a mind-popping range of tastes and markets, offering health insurance and HIV testing to its workers, spearheading technological innovation, and making sizable profits, not only for its creators and distributors, but also for related businesses, including video stores, Internet providers, hotel chains, and telephone companies—all of whom pay taxes.

---

This explosion happened as Annie was moving away from pornography. Through her twenties, she had made hard-core films, modeled for sex magazines, sold a line of sex-related products, worked on and off as a prostitute, experimented with all manner of kinky sex, and hosted the Sprinkle Salon, a kind of ongoing sexual house party. (Annie is nothing if not enterprising.) As long as she made no bones about selling sex, she was left pretty much alone. Then she began to think of herself as an artist and everything changed.

When I ask when her art career began, she says, "That depends. I think that a lot of the prostitution and the porn movies I did were like performance art." She claims to have created a form of burlesque called "strip speak," which does sound like performance art monologues, but her first foray into what is more generally thought of as art came in 1978, when she became involved with Willem de Ridder, a Dutch artist, who had been prominent in the avant-garde Fluxus movement. As she, de Ridder, and a couple who published a sex magazine called *Love* were finishing up a special issue based on her diary, their typesetter revealed herself as an undercover policewoman—I picture Superman bursting from a phone booth—and hauled them all in. Annie spent forty-eight hours in jail for "conspiracy to publish obscene materials," among a host of other felonies, the only time she has faced criminal charges for her work. All charges against her were dropped, but it was an eye-

opener to find that other people had the power to take away her freedom, and it scared her.

By the time she turned thirty, Annie had grown bored with the commercial sex scene, so she enrolled in the School of Visual Arts in New
York and emerged with a degree in photography. She also apprenticed
herself to Linda Montana, an avant-garde artist, who created a ritual in
which she baptized Annie an official artist. It's interesting that Annie,
who had embarked on sex and film careers with no training, felt the need
for certification in art, which may be the field in which credentials are
most elusive.

Further authentication came in 1984, when she appeared at Franklin
Furnace, a downtown performance space in New York City. Franklin
Furnace was hosting a multimedia exhibit about "feminist pornography" called Carnival Knowledge, and Annie and several friends from the
sex industry performed "Deep Inside Porn Stars," a stylized reenactment
of their support group meetings. Carnival Knowledge was a hit and also
something of a portent. When a Christian morality group (mis)informed
Franklin Furnace's supporters that it was showing pornography to children, Exxon and Woolworth cut off their grants, and the NEA, which
normally seeks credit wherever possible, requested that Franklin Furnace
refrain from mentioning its name unless it expressly funded an exhibit.[22]

Annie continued to make forays into the more progressive precincts
of New York's art world. She gave an erotic Bible reading, created an installation called Porn Star Fan Mail—Open to the Public, which consisted of a crate of her fan letters and signs urging the audience to take
some home to answer, and appeared in a show called "The Prometheus
Project." That's where she first presented her "pornstistics" that charted
her commercial sex career through, for instance, a graph comparing her
weekly income from burlesque with the weekly income of the average
American woman. Stripping was about sixteen times more lucrative.

She began weaving her short pieces together to create a one-woman
show, which she called Post-Porn Modernist and performed after hours
at a burlesque theater owned by a friend. The curator of the Kitchen, another downtown art space, saw it in 1990 and booked Annie for an un-
usually long run of twelve performances. Post-Porn was a breathless
compendium of skits, slides, monologues, and jokes about her porn career and reflections on art, politics, sex roles, and feminism. By turns
playful, mocking, and compassionate, Annie demonstrated absurd sex
toys, such as a dildo shoehorn; showed slides of women she had transformed into "sex star" pinups; danced her breasts to the strains of the

"Blue Danube Waltz"; and told stories about past lovers, a group diverse enough to warm the heart of the staunchest multiculturalist. In form, the show was typical of performance art. Where it broke new ground was in its context. When Annie moved downtown, she crossed the line from sex in its place (prostitution, hard-core films, magazines kept literally under wraps) to sex as a subject for artistic exploration. Then she went on, as she has all her life, to smudge more lines: between male and female, straight and gay, beautiful and ugly, good and bad, good and evil, and sex and nearly everything else. This erasing of boundaries may be what appeals most to her audiences; it certainly disconcerts her detractors.

From her first appearance in front of an art crowd, Annie, like a century of jurists before her, was struck by the difference context makes. "A porn audience wants to get turned on. It's generally all men of all ages and races. The art audience was more students and intellectuals and academics. It had women." This makes her laugh and makes me ask if performing for women is different. "In terms of what they want to see," she answers. "Basically what I did when I got in front of the art audience, I started telling *my* truths and sharing about *my* kind of sexuality, whereas when it was for a porn audience, they had a certain fantasy or ideal that I was fulfilling. It's kind of hard to play their game. Like, I could never have gotten away with showing my cervix in a strip club, but I could show it at the Kitchen."

Ah, yes, Annie's cervix.

A favored strategy for belittling art and artists is to reduce the work to its least part by snatching elements out of context. Annie's performances must have seemed an embarrassment of riches to her attackers: How to choose? Not, of course, that most of the people who claimed to be horrified by her show saw it, another time-honored tradition. Some audience members were troubled by what they saw, but they generally weren't the people trying to ban it. That fell to politicians, who relied on self-appointed monitors, who got their information from press releases and scandal-eager journalists. When Annie's turn came, this alliance latched onto the part of her show called the Public Cervix Announcement, in which she instructed the audience about the female reproductive organs—"Let's all say *fallopian tubes* together now. Very good"— then inserted a speculum into her vagina and invited audience members to look. "So it sounds almost like shocking and disgusting, like I'm being provocative, but it was actually the total opposite. It was taking something that was kind of all those things and making it normal and natural," she insists. "Hearing about it and seeing it were really two different things because when people saw it, it was like, you know, no big deal."

Whatever else Annie accomplished, she made it clear that peering at someone's cervix isn't sex or voyeurism; it's gynecology. She learned the word for cervix in seven languages and estimates that nearly twenty-five thousand people around the world have seen hers. This was long before performances of *The Vagina Monologues* became a chic Valentine's Day celebration, and she did the piece, she says, to counteract shame and myths about the vagina ("No teeth in there") and to give people perhaps their one chance to look at a cervix. There may have been a degree of aggression too. Among her reasons for doing it, she notes, "I wanted to say to certain guys, 'Hey, you want to see pussy? I'll show you more pussy than you'll ever want to see.' "[23]

On stage, Annie is all id and no superego, which is both liberating and alarming to experience. This becomes manifest in *Post Porn*'s grand finale, "The Legend of the Ancient Sacred Prostitute," in which Annie masturbates, as she says, "into ecstasy." She calls it "a kind of experimental sex magic, masturbation ritual," and it is sensual, sexy, enigmatic, and potent to watch. But its ritualistic quality—hypnotic chants, chimes, rattles and drums, flickering candlelight, stylized movement—tends to get lost in the recounting.

"I would go into sexual frenzy or sometimes sexual meditation, depending on the energy of the mood," she says, since everyone wants to know if her orgasms were real or faked. "I learned more from doing that than anything I've ever done in my life. People were either really into it and crying and having spontaneous orgasms or people would run the hell out or be angry or be freaked out. I just held up a mirror and said, okay, we're sexual beings, I'm going to masturbate, you're going to see me. How do you feel about this?"

Among the debates about porn is whether it demystifies sex or whether that's impossible. Possible or no, I wonder if we want it demystified. When I ask if she has an inner censor, she laughs and says, "Those are the things that interest me in talking about, things that are hidden and taboo, scary or bizarre. Like, at the moment, I'm really wanting to talk about money a lot. In my world, hardly anybody talks about it. Everyone I know talks about sex all the time."

"You do know that your perspective is an unusual one," I suggest, but she doesn't bite.

"My perspective?"

"Yeah. About sex. I'm curious why you think you're the way you are."

"Just personal experience," she says, and I imagine her shrugging on the other end of the line. "I was told about menstruation and the sperm fertilizing the egg and it was this big, scary thing. But when I got right down to it and learned from firsthand experience, then just somehow the fears went away."

———————

The tension between sex as danger and sex as pleasure is an old one, but when the danger argument was resurrected most recently, its support came from a surprising direction: radical, second-wave feminism. What began in the late 1960s as protests against mainstream representations of women (beauty pageants, bridal fairs, magazines, billboards) by the beginning of the 1980s had grown into a movement, led by groups such as Women Against Pornography[24] and informed by books such as Andrea Dworkin's *Pornography: Men Possessing Women,* which became something of a sacred text for sex-protectionist feminists.

These new antiporn crusaders combined the old idea that pornography is morally dangerous with the new argument that it is a form of discrimination against women. By diminishing women to their body parts and sexual functions, they argued, pornography validates and promotes sexual violence: that is, it is harmful. By "institutionaliz[ing] the sexuality of male supremacy,"[25] pornography suppresses the voices of women and makes it impossible for them to navigate the world with equality: in other words, it causes discrimination. Thus, because women are victimized through contact with pornography as participants and unwilling viewers and again because others view it, pornography is a violation of women's civil rights and should not be allowed to exist.

The rhetoric of antivice campaigns is never a model of restraint, but testimony from "victims of pornography" rivals the hardest of cores in luridness. The antiporn feminists presented horrifying, sad, distressing stories from women who had been preyed upon sexually and silenced by sexism and gender-related poverty and violence. This testimony is not easy to read or hear and harder still to ignore. It makes you angry, makes you want to do something so that the brutality and depredation won't happen again. That something, these feminists insisted, was eradicating the images as a prerequisite for eradicating the violence itself.

In the 1980s, Catharine MacKinnon, a legal and feminist scholar, teamed up with Andrea Dworkin to propose what they hoped would be pioneering legislation outlawing a broad range of sexually explicit material as discriminatory against women. They joined forces with right-wing religious organizations and conservative legislators, with whom they shared few other goals, and enjoyed favorable publicity that presented them as representing all feminists. But despite initial victories in Minneapolis, Indianapolis, and Cambridge, Massachusetts, the legislation was eventually voted down or ruled unconstitutional on free speech grounds. This encouraged other feminists who had championed open discussion of sexuality and mounted spirited rebuttals to the MacKinnon-Dworkin strategy, most notably a legal brief filed in 1985 by the Feminist Anticensorship Task Force. Feminist thinking in the 1980s remained sharply split between those who would improve the lot of women by protecting them from sexual imagery and those who would do it by freeing them from sexual constraints, a conflict that Annie and other female artists were then beginning to explore and dramatize.

Defeated in the particulars but not in the war, the antiporn faction continued to advocate measures to limit sexual speech. They had a significant victory in 1986 when the concept of "hostile environment" was incorporated into sexual harassment law (see Chapter 11), and another in 1992, when Canada enacted legislation using a MacKinnon-like definition of pornography as gender inequality. But censorship invariably leaks beyond the boundaries constructed for it, and it is folly to assume that everyone who enforces a law restricting speech will share the intentions of its creators. As opponents of her position never tire of pointing out, two of Dworkin's books were among the first stopped by customs officials under the Canadian law.

Ironically, as our tolerance of variety in sexual conduct increases, so does our punishment of sexual expression. The twin responses to the latter—prudery and prurience—are connected to a third, portentousness, which takes anything other than sanctity about sex as an insult. In all three instances, the image is given great power, as if pornography creates sex and not the other way around. This, then, is the antiporn feminists' greatest triumph. Catharine MacKinnon, who has made a career out of claiming to be misrepresented, may be portrayed as extreme, but her basic premise—that sexual images harm women—is widely accepted. MacKinnon and company didn't accomplish this attitudinal change all by themselves—American feminists are not that powerful—nor would it be the first time moral prejudice was given an intellectual gloss. But by stirring the language of social science and progressive politics into the mix, they made a morally regressive position palatable to people who might balk at the language of sin and retribution and who would be less likely to accept censorship of other forms of speech.

Some factions within feminism have proved to be as repressive and moralistic as the patriarchy they set out to overthrow, but women have long been given a list of shoulds and should nots that end up making them feel guilty, ashamed, or afraid about sex. In contrast, Annie is refreshingly unprescriptive. "Misogyny and sexism are dangerous and harmful," she maintains. "I don't believe sex is. I think that there's harmful things in society and sometimes they get reflected in pornography, but the same with Hollywood movies or certain books. That doesn't mean it should all be stopped." Still, she is not wholly unsympathetic to the MacKinnon-Dworkin argument. "They're pointing out where women are exploited or manipulated or even violated, and those are important things to look at and acknowledge, but they absolutely refuse to acknowledge the other side.[26] I looked at Andrea Dworkin's Web site and a lot of what she talked about made sense to me. I would totally love to hang with her. I think that she's a reasonable woman."

I'm not surprised that Annie is intrigued by Dworkin, who doesn't play by good-girl rules either. When I joke that her next performance could be *An Evening with Andrea Dworkin,* Annie says "I don't think she would want to go near me, which is sad. But most of the people I know wouldn't want to go near Andrea Dworkin either." Genuine discussion between the two camps has been rare, in part because the antiporn faction dogmatically maintains that all women react to sexual images in the same way—their way—and that those who say they don't are dishonest, benighted, or victims of false consciousness. Annie counters, "As a friend of mine says, the only answer to any question about sex is always, 'It depends.' It's the same with porn. What's really great for one person might be horrible for another."

———

Although these left-wing attacks on pornography coincided with right-wing attacks on artists, the antismut feminists largely ignored the art world, even as artists were creating work that would easily fall under their definition of pornography. The reason, I think, has to do with our ideas about art and artists. A while after Annie and I talked, I was invited to speak at a seminar for college freshmen called "Pornography and Society." My topic was porn and art, and I presented Annie's story as a case study, talking about her performance, the outcry, the free expression issues, and how all this related to ideas about sex and representation. The students listened politely, then turned to what they wanted to talk about, which was how Annie's work could possibly be art.

"I think it's bullshit," said the first student to speak, proud to expose the emperor naked. Other students, probably kids who had been taught that art is what your teachers say it is, came to Annie's defense, while still others said nothing but nudged their neighbors as they thumbed through the copy of Annie's graphic autobiography, also called *Post-Porn Modernist,* that I passed around. Underlying the discussion was a suspicion that Annie and I, in calling what she did art, were playing them for fools, and underlying that was an abashed anger, because nobody likes to seem foolish.

Walter Kendrick, in *The Secret Museum,* makes it clear that as long as erotic books and pictures remained available only to a small group of upper-class men who were sure they shared intentions and reactions, no one paid much attention to the books or their readers. It was only when the material became widely available that "erotica" turned into "pornography" and alarms were sounded. A similar dynamic seems to be at work in the attacks on publicly supported art that began as Annie's art career was flourishing. Had the National Endowment for the Arts stayed with the symphony orchestras that lobbied for its creation in 1965, it might have been allowed to go about its business, but the agency created programs with baffling names like Expansion Arts and Inter-Arts and gave its money and blessing to, if not Annie, then the likes of Annie. At a time when art was regularly being turned into scandal, she turned scandal into art, and in the battle of symbols known as the culture war, what better summation of all that was wrong with government support for culture than Annie's show?

As *Post-Porn Modernist* closed at the Kitchen, a story in the conservative *New York City Tribune* raised the specter of tax dollars going to support a live sex show. (Annie's response: "I had done live sex shows, and believe me, this definitely was not one.") Someone sent the article to the Kitchen's corporate funders and to Dana Rohrabacher, then a Republican Congressman from California, who was playing Sancho Panza to Senator Jesse Helms's Don Quixote as he tilted at the NEA. Annie became the subject of an anti-Endowment diatribe from Rohrabacher, in which he implied that she had received government funding. The Endowment scurried to distance itself from her, but, unfazed, Rohrabacher denounced her in a "Dear Colleague" letter. Meanwhile Helms offered up *Post-Porn,* "a sewer of fetishism, depravity and pornography," as proof positive of the NEA's decadent agenda.

Annie soon became Exhibit A in arguments both against and for the Endowment. Never mind that she never got a penny from the agency;

venues where she performed did, though they insisted that no federal money was used to present her show. "Frankly, prostitution and pornography are what supported my art career," she observes. "In fact, I always say that the sex business supports more artists than the National Endowment ever could."

If and how a government supports art are valid topics for discussion, but smearing Annie was hardly a fair, or productive, mode of debate. She had broken no law, requested no government benefit, and aspired to no position requiring legislative review, yet she was singled out for ridicule on the floor of the Senate. It was not censorship—Annie was free to perform, her First Amendment rights remained intact—but it was an abuse of power, and the message was very clear: anyone who crossed the congressional righteousness brigade could expect the same.

Still there's nothing like controversy to sell tickets, and *Post-Porn Modernist* played to solid audiences and generally positive reviews in the United States and abroad. (Annie has collected a loyal following, as evidenced by an outpouring of money and goodwill—much from people who knew her only through her work—when her houseboat burned in 1999.) In retrospect, Annie is more amused than dismayed. "I just said, thanks for the publicity, everybody, and I just kept making my work. I did feel that, even though people were attacking me, I was still bringing some of my ideas to light. Just the fact that people are talking about a woman showing her cervix on stage, I thought that I was accomplishing my goal, that it was all part of the educational process."

She isn't always so sanguine about how she and her work are treated. Early in the conversation, she declares that she experiences prejudice—her word—on a daily basis. In the last few months before we talk, for instance, a printer in New York has refused to print her stationery because its drawing of a many-armed goddess with naked breasts offended his workers; police at the University of South Florida have seized a videotape of her *Sluts and Goddesses Video Workshop* when a student screened it outdoors; and, in order to get a video of another show through Swiss customs to the Montreux Film Festival, she had to relabel it *Annie's Football Game*. (Bureaucracy is censorship's friend.) It occurs to me that this list of complaints will come as comfort to the people behind morality-based regulations; they mean to make things difficult. Most of the harassment she encounters, however, involves expression that is legal. Also, the attacks can be vicious. She mentions taking *Post-Porn Modernist* to Australia, where, she says, "We had a little bit of a problem." It seems a radio talk-show host reviewed the show, which, incidentally, he had not seen, and asked about Annie, "Where's Hitler when we need him?"

---

"Sex is one of our most basic human interests. Everyone has that in common," Annie pronounces as we talk about why her performances cause such an uproar.

We have already gone down a list of reasons, starting with the uneasiness that swirls around most aspects of the body in America, where we talk about health and sickness, youth and aging, appearance, exercise, appetites, and bodily functions in the language of morality plays—guilt, denial, capitulation, betrayal—as if we must punish our bodies for being wayward or needy. Next is the shift in attitudes toward sex during the 1980s, when Annie was working most publicly. The sexual revolution, with its disconcerting freedom, had turned sour; in its wake came a backlash against sexually independent women, while the scourge of AIDS and other sexually transmitted diseases tied sex to danger and death. "Life was a sex cabaret," Annie wrote. "Then suddenly, seemingly overnight, friends and lovers were getting horribly sick and dying."[27]

Now she brings up puritanism, and to illustrate what she means, notes that female ejaculation is banned in porn films because it is considered a golden shower. "So first of all, I don't think it's fair—it's not a golden shower. But second," she continues in her it's-all-perfectly-reasonable voice, "What's so bad about a golden shower either? Everybody pees."

Yes, I agree, but not necessarily on someone.

"Exactly," says Annie, as if that proves her point. "So there's a lot of jealousy of people who are enjoying their sexuality [from] people who don't. You know, a lot of these people who are fighting against sexuality have absolutely miserable sex lives and they just can't stand the fact that other people are having five-minute-long orgasms. Real spoilsports, a lot of them."

Well, true, Americans can be prudes, though surely not everyone who opposes pornography is sexually repressed or dissatisfied. Alongside priggishness, we have a tradition of singing the body that goes back at least as far as Walt Whitman, and it is impossible to imagine our contemporary culture or our economy devoid of sexuality, implied or explicit. H. L. Mencken defined puritanism as "the haunting fear that someone, somewhere, may be happy," and in that way it probably does figure into the equation, along with a sense of inadequacy or the concern, not so much that someone is having a good time as that someone is having a better time.[28] Our puritanism is marked, not just by opposition to sexual pleasure, though, but also by barely or uncontrolled longing for sexual abandon. Look at our long line of great puritan hypocrites that stretches from Hawthorne's fictional Arthur Dimmesdale to real-life televangelists Jimmy Swaggart and Jim Bakker, not to mention politicians too numerous to name. No wonder Annie figures both as puritan America's wildest dream and as its worst nightmare.

Sex is disruptive of the social order because it is more powerful, but it is probably Annie's sex-positive attitude that has made her so controversial. Sharing with her attackers a talent for embodying complex ideas in simple, arresting images, she touches on all the great themes: sex and money, sex and religion, sex and taboo, sex and death. What gets short shrift is sex and misery. Oh, she gives the nod to difficulties, acknowledges bad times, but her take on sex is basically unapologetic and celebratory, and that has made her a lightning rod for other people's anxieties. Moreover, in contrast to many female performance artists whose subject is sex, her stage persona is disarming and coy. Even now in her postporn incarnation, she slips easily into sex goddess mode—only now she wants to talk about it.

Contemporary pornography is primarily visual—despite a history of book censorship, no written work has been found obscene in this country since 1965—so Annie's loquaciousness stands out. Sex put into language is particularly problematic because it changes our relationship to the act and tells us something we suspect we shouldn't know. It also raises the question of who does the telling. In culture wars and other censorship fights, the central question is whose voice will be heard, with the traditionally silenced demanding their say and the traditionally talkative feeling threatened. This tug-of-war between teller and told-about is apparent, not only in antismut campaigns, but also in the testimony we are now getting from sex workers, some of whom have college degrees and writing workshops under their belts.[29] Sympathetic as segments of the feminist movement may be when they take up the workers' cause, it is still someone else speaking for them.

When Annie recast herself as an artist, she claimed the right to speak for herself and to choose her own sexual identity, an option not available to all women, or, as she points out, to her for most of her career. Yet her former coworkers weren't uniformly pleased. "Sometimes there's been strippers that said to masturbate on stage is absolutely the most disgusting thing they ever could imagine. Because I do it for real. It's not stylized, show erotic. It's raw. I don't consider any of my work entertaining particularly."

———————

Entertaining or not, Annie's work continues to cause controversy. Take what happened in Northampton, Massachusetts, a hip, staunchly feminist college town that ought to be Annie Sprinkle country. In the spring of 1997, she was slated to do her new show, *Hardcore from the Heart— My Film Diary of 25 Years as a Porn Queen,* at the Center for the Arts, a nonprofit, producing-presenting organization, where she had appeared twice before to sold-out audiences. The center's new director, a woman, maintained incorrectly that Annie had done "something illegal" in those earlier shows and refused to let her perform. "A lot of people were really outraged that she did that," Annie reports. "She wouldn't talk to me on the phone even. It was all done through the media. I think she was just so afraid of me. It was very weird."

What followed was by now routine. The ACLU protested the director's remarks, academics testified to Annie's art-worthiness, the local arts council gave a bland endorsement to variety in programming, and the center's board of directors issued a sort-of apology along with a statement of support for artistic freedom. Annie thinks the board's public apology means she won this round, but *Hardcore* ended up at an ill-suited, cavernous rock 'n' roll club, where audience members were carded and the performance had to finish early to clear the place for Teen Night.

*Hardcore* was a sentimental trip down Annie's sexual memory lane, illustrated by clips from her porn films, a dose of New Age philosophy, and pungent one-liners like "As long as you've got a pussy you'll never starve." She had added lesbian to her sexual identity, and this, along with her then-partner, figured prominently in the show. At intermission, as a fund-raiser ("We want to buy a boat this summer"), Annie posed with her breasts on the head of audience members, while an assistant snapped Polaroids for souvenirs. It cost ten bucks. "They're soft," someone said as Annie arranged her breasts carefully for the shot, and she laughed. Performance art monologues tend to point up the banality at the center of most lives, and somewhere in here, it became clear that part of Annie's message was just how ordinary sex is. Her show wasn't exactly good, clean fun, but it didn't turn anything on its head, either.

"*Hardcore from the Heart* was very different [from *Post-Porn Modernist*]," Annie says when we talk a few months after her Northampton performance. "It's a more critical look." Annie's voice is soothing, especially when she's being vague, as she is now. She has been performing *Hardcore* for a few months, but it has drawn much less attention, both positive and negative, than the earlier show. "I think that's what I've come to, the main answer to what is sex all about; it's just change. And the same thing with censorship. When I was in my twenties I was known as the Queen of Kink and I did really outrageous movies. Now I look at these girls doing such-and-such movies and go, God, how could they do that! It's because I've changed, times have changed, young women have changed."

A major change is that Annie and academia have met. She contributes to scholarly publications, appears on women's studies reading lists, lends her expertise to panel discussions, and recently earned her Ph.D. in human sexuality. It is hardly surprising that scholars have gotten around to studying pornography, or that Annie, who has dedicated her life to deconstructing sex and bringing the subterranean to light, would be a popular figure on campuses. What this signifies about American tolerance of sexually graphic pictures and speech is less obvious. The academy routinely vets a few outsiders and allows them in, and it is much easier to change the canon than to change attitudes, especially about sex.

And how does she respond to these vicissitudes? "You know what? Having started out in prostitution, my inclination was just to try to not be there for the bust. So, for example, in Cleveland, Ohio, when I first was doing *Post-Porn Modernist*, the police were in the audience and they said, if you show your cervix we're taking you to jail. I had tickets for Europe the following day. I didn't really want to go to jail, so I just didn't do it. But in retrospect, I think I missed an opportunity. When the Jesse Helms thing happened at the Kitchen, the world was watching. I could have been a fighter, and I just really didn't understand the issues because I was from a world where what I did was constantly censored and illegal. So I didn't get it that artists have privileges. I really admire Karen Finley, who is such a fighter, and the NEA 4 people [see Chapter 5]. I was very inspired because they won, partly."

Annie won partly too because she declined to play the victim, but the mockery still rankles. "Just the fact that I was made a joke of because they said, 'Oh, she's a porn star, she couldn't possibly be an artist.' It seems very unfair to me because whether it's art or not shouldn't matter.

If really, really talented, well-educated, arty kind of people have more freedom than other people, it's just outright not fair. It's snobbism."

---

When Congressman Rohrabacher's press secretary was asked what criteria they used to select examples of "outrageous" NEA funding, he replied, "It's so obvious. . . . This is hardcore, triple-X stuff."[30] Others, however, have found the distinction less clear. Talking about masturbating on stage, Annie asks, "Why should that be any more hidden than anger or betrayal or any of the other things that are explored in theater or romance?" Theater and porn do have a lot in common: public enactment of private tensions, heightened emotions, audience manipulation, ritual, catharsis. But the law implies that art and pornography are mutually exclusive categories, and society gives special, if grudging, dispensation to art, so which category we assign determines who gets to do what.

In making that determination, we—juries, legislatures, the public— weigh several factors, some consciously, others at a gut level. As with the original legal tests for obscenity, we typically begin with the motivation of the maker and the response of the audience. Annie offers a long list of intentions—exploring, teaching, learning, amusing, healing. She doesn't number shocking, offending, or arousing among them, but neither does she tailor her work to ensure that these won't happen. As for her audiences, they attend her performances by choice, hoping to be amused or taught or healed, and so they usually are. As participants in an art event, they know what is expected of them and know too that if they want to pant and leer, there are better places to do it. Annie sums up this distinction with her usual candor. "With my porn audience, the whole thing was to try to make their penis hard and in some cases get them off, right? With an art audience, the intention was to reveal some truth, to heal myself and others, to explore ways to do sex-explicit art and to take kind of lowbrow culture into a higher-brow world and see what happened. It was a social experiment."

The aims of the artist and effect on the audience create a frame, and in dividing art from nonart, we judge this frame on a kind of raunchy-classy scale, reading signs as if tracking prey:

What are the parallels and associations? If it's slides in art history class and friendships with modern dancers, it's art. If it's a marquee in Times Square and friendships with lap dancers, it's porn.

Who are the sponsors? Nonprofit by this reckoning is purer than profit, though the government isn't supposed to pay for it and neither is the Playboy Foundation.

How is the subject treated? Can we establish "serious artistic, political or scientific value"—the legal definition—but not so much that it's really convincing and therefore arousing?

What vocabulary do we use to discuss it? Opaque and arcane is good, blunt and accurate, bad.

Who likes and dislikes it? If it has been reviewed by critics and boycotted by people who never had any intention of seeing it, it is probably art.

These are the gatekeeping distinctions of a guild with an interest in limiting its membership, but read another way, they are class discrimination—what Annie calls snobbism—and it is disingenuous to defend her performance at the Kitchen while condemning a similar show on 42nd Street. Context does matter. So do production values, the maker's intent, the audience's receptivity, and everyone's socialization and sophistication. But none of this purges a performance of its sexual quality, or certifies that it won't be titillating or just plain dirty. Politically useful as it is to put art on one side, porn on another, Annie's work is both.

It may be impossible, as Kendrick points out, to "display things . . . and keep them hidden at the same time,"[31] but it is very possible to condemn something and allow it to exist at the same time. About thirty years ago, Willard M. Gaylin, a psychiatrist, took an informal poll among his acquaintances and found that the only group unconvinced that pornographic books "do not corrupt" were other psychiatrists. He went on to say, "They made a distinction between the reading of pornography as unlikely to be per se harmful, and the permitting of the reading of pornography, which was conceived as potentially destructive. . . . To openly permit implies parental approval and even suggests seductive encouragement. If this is so of parental approval, it is equally so of societal approval."[32]

This, then, is our accommodation, to excoriate and entice simultaneously, or, as public moralist William Bennett suggested (tongue in cheek?) as an alternative to the government censoring depictions of sex and violence in popular culture, "Maybe we should just feel bad about it."[33]

That may be the only workable solution and not a bad one at that—until people are punished for providing what we are so obviously unwilling to do without. As Annie learned, the central problem with merging art and porn is that it gives the gloss of artistic respectability to the sexual material we are not supposed to condone.[34] It calls the bluff of our convenient hypocrisy, leaving us confused and ashamed of our confusion.

# chapter seven

# SOMETHING TO OFFEND
# NEARLY EVERYBODY

Jay Critchley, Hans Evers, Ifé Franklin, Maxine McDonald,
Denise Marika, James Montford, Michael Willhoite

*Boston, Massachusetts, September 1996*

In June 1989, 108 members of Congress signed a letter to the National Endowment for the Arts, complaining that two traveling photography exhibitions it had funded contained offensive art. One, including work by Andres Serrano, had ended the previous January. The other, a one-man show by Robert Mapplethorpe called *The Perfect Moment,* was to open the next month at the Corcoran Gallery, a private museum in Washington, D.C., with some NEA funding. Hoping to head off controversy, the Corcoran canceled the exhibit, but the Senate voted to restrict what the Endowment could fund anyway, including a five-year ban on grants to the two institutions that had mounted the now-problematic exhibits.

The art world leapt up in protest, doing what it does well, which is to get attention creatively. The Washington Project for the Arts picked up the exhibit, and a gallery-restaurant flashed slides of the photos on an outside wall of the Corcoran. Artists canceled upcoming shows there, the curator who had booked the show resigned, and all that summer, as the exhibit traveled around the country, the *New York Times* made an industry out of Mapplethorpe commentary because by then everyone had an opinion on the subject. Even people who had no intention of ever looking at art photography knew that Serrano stuck crosses in "body fluids" and that Mapplethorpe did kinky things with a bullwhip. (There are second acts in America: in 2000, the *New York Times* featured celebrity portraits by Serrano in its Sunday magazine.)

Jump to 1999, when New York mayor Rudolph Giuliani threatened to cut off city funding to the Brooklyn Museum of Art if it didn't cancel an exhibit of contemporary British art called *Sensation*. The title was apt. The show featured artwork that sensationalized sex, violence, and other charged subjects, leading some critics to suggest that the museum had been banking on a scandal from the start. The mayor focused his pique on a painting of the Virgin Mary by Chris Ofili, who used, among other media, cow dung for her breasts and clips from porn magazines for her halo. Again, it was the (reductive) talk of the town, but the museum refused to buckle under, instead taking the city to court to block punitive action.

On one of the numerous talk shows about the controversy, televangelist Pat Robertson opined that, while Giuliani knew he wouldn't win the legal fight, he would win political points for appearing tough on porn and blasphemy. And so it went: the museum won in court and in attracting large audiences to its show; Giuliani won on the political stage, eighteen months later, responding to another piece of art he didn't like by creating a panel to determine "decency" standards for the city's publicly supported museums.

*The Perfect Moment* and *Sensation:* bookends to a shameful, silly, cynical era in which it became clear that nothing is sacred—that, no doubt, being the point. Since then, the number and ferocity of attacks on art have abated somewhat, in part because restraints are so neatly in place that we barely notice how well we have absorbed their message. After all, enough bad press and pretty soon everyone thinks twice before creating or supporting art that has the potential to cause headaches. Why bother?

If the incidents are less frequent, though, they are no less predictable, as public arguments over what art does and where it belongs unfold with the ritualization of Chinese opera. A representative of the government, a church, or a community group learns of an exhibit, performance, or book and, generally without having seen the work, declares it outrageous, offensive, dangerous, pornographic, blasphemous, or all of the above.

Quickly, artists and their supporters rally and, as if taking a multiple-choice test, maintain that: (1) the work is misconstrued, (2) art must be considered in context, (3) the complainers are Philistines, and (4) artists are shocked and/or saddened to be so misunderstood. Equally quickly, critics explain what we are supposed to make of all this, eventually getting around to: (1) artists didn't always enjoy the supposedly privileged position they now do, and (2) how unfortunate that they, the critics, must defend second-rate art in the name of free expression. Meanwhile, scandal being the marketing tool of our time, offending artists and whomever they offend bask equally in the limelight, with all the perks that implies. Moral entrepreneurs find fund-raising a breeze, politicians find moral indignation a plus at election time, and artists find their work garnering attention and prices that would otherwise require them to die young and spectacularly. It's so commonplace that it feels as if it were ever thus—and maybe it was.

---

America has never been at home with art—too hard to pin down, too effete, too feminine, too undemocratic, too, well, un-American. As for the conundrum of what art is, we hope to resolve that by making it a matter of taste, but this creates more problems: democracy and intellectual fashion deem all tastes equally valid, but art can't be created by ballot, at least not to any productive end. (When the brilliant conceptual artists Vitaly Komar and Alexander Melamid polled Americans on what kind of painting they wanted to see, they came up with a realistic landscape with lots of blue, a few wild animals, and George Washington fully clothed.)[1]

Attacking art is an old way of attacking social structures, but the recent round of attempts to govern the imagination began in the mid-1980s. By then, according to the Center for Cultural Conservatism, a project of the Free Congress Foundation, "America's culture was turning into a moral sewer. Clearly, a new conservatism was needed in response—a conservatism built not on economics but on defense of traditional Western culture."[2] Religious right organizations, such as the American Family Association, which had previously busied itself totting up inches of skin on TV shows, now declared that in order to preserve cultural values, noncommercial art had to be reined in too. "High" art, with its priesthood, acolytes, and claims to deeper truths, posed a sort of rival religion. Serious art combines an aesthetic sensibility with an ethical one, but it is not the ethics of conventional morality, and artists, with their cultural values of explicitness and transgression, were obvious foes. With little political or economic clout, they were also convenient to pick on. (It is not irrelevant that the 1980s were the first time a significant number of American visual artists could actually make a living from their work.) As quickly as you can say "offensive," artists throughout the country found themselves in the uncomfortable position of being victims of a smear campaign and beneficiaries of a publicity one.

The cultural friction of the 1980s and 1990s was part of a larger social upheaval that changed our language and our relationships. The divisions between kinds of art had been weakening for decades. Mod-
ernism, in borrowing from popular and folk culture, blurred the line
between "high" and "low" art. Postmodernism, with its emphasis on
content over form and its embrace of technology, commerce, and glob-
alism, obscured the line between art and other categories, such as politics and consumerism. By the 1990s, art came to be viewed as an attitude
as much as an artifact, and where "culture" had once meant art for the
gentry, now, just as often, it referred to a set of social or communal values. A positive effect of these changes has been to make audiences comfortable with all kinds of culture. Another effect—positive or negative,
it's unclear—is that art to which only a self-selected elite previously paid
attention is now open to review, criticism, and attack by anyone who
wants to bother.

Originally, the conservative cultural warriors exhorted against smut,
blasphemy, and a kind of free-floating contamination in which you didn't
actually have to see, hear, or read something to be harmed by it. Then
they cannily hit on the charge that tax money was being used by elitist
artists to run roughshod over the sensibilities of the American public.
Missing nary a buzzword, Louis Sheldon of the Traditional Values Coalition testified to Congress that "the NEA then uses our scarce tax dollars
to fund works which are intended to shock Americans into an acceptance
of dysfunctional behavioral lifestyles and to destroy the family."[3]

This winning combination—money, sex, and snobbery—struck a responsive chord with those politicians who didn't like the NEA much to
begin with. The rather touching idea that taxpayers get to choose what
their taxes pay for, as if government were a shopping mall or favorite
charity, played well with those who thought of the arts as someone else's
hobby—and a rather nasty one at that. Early in the twentieth century,
Anthony Comstock, granddaddy of American antismut crusaders, proclaimed, "Art is not above morals." Part of the anger directed at the Endowment was that some artists appear to think it is.

From 1989 on, political moralists gained ground by using artists for
target practice, but for all the attempted repression, American art still
pushed at boundaries. What was sacrificed was less artistic freedom than
the belief that art and artists have something to contribute to our society. Congress created the NEA in 1965 in a flush of nationalist pride. "If
art is to nourish the roots of our culture, society must set the artist free
to follow his vision wherever it takes him," President John Kennedy said

then.[4] This support for the *right* to make art also had symbolic significance: it announced to the world that, in America, artists were free to create unorthodox, challenging, and diverse art.

If you give artists money, however, chances are they will use it to create their own art, not Jesse Helms's or Donald Wildmon's art. When the political winds shifted and Congress decided to use public funding to dictate taste, morality was a good excuse, but the real issue, as in all censorship, was control. Father Timothy Healy, then president of the New York Public Library, wrote in 1989, "Government aims in its subsidy of the arts to enhance the quality of life of the people, or, in more political terms, to foster an educated citizenry. That is a great national good."[5] Increasingly, this argument fell on deaf ears. The following year, a national survey found that, while nearly 74 percent of respondents supported the right of artists to display potentially offensive work, 72 percent opposed spending tax money for art that might offend.[6]

Artists have their own contradictions to reckon with as they try to fortify their position in society while reserving the right to make antisocial art—or, put less generously, to violate taboos expressly to excite. Just as censors routinely deny that censorship is what they intend, people who shock usually protest that this was not their purpose. But it smacks of bad faith when artists defend themselves by asking, "What's the big deal?" when they obviously meant to make a big deal. At the same time, artists, like others, may want to share the blessings of a prosperous society. Government support for art has given them something to lose; not much— we're talking an allocation to the Arts Endowment that amounted to sixty-eight cents per American at its highest—but enough to make grantees, and anyone with hope of becoming one, cautious.

The success of public arts agencies and associated institutions, such as art schools, writing programs, and exhibition and performance spaces, has taught that to be an artist is to get grants, be affiliated, make the gossip columns. This includes the self-styled avant-garde, which, in good avant-garde fashion, went about its business of *épatant les bourgeois* and then sending them the bill. That worked for a while: artists got to imagine freely and reinvigorate the culture, patrons got to hang with the hip and boho, and audiences got to look and think afresh. But where the postwar American vanguard had once exuded optimism and a sense of freedom, by the 1990s, the art scene had turned essentially conservative, and to be avant-garde without being radical is to be merely irritating. It's hard to be avant-garde in America—everything gets sucked in and ground down and then sold back to us—but when nominally cutting-edge art relies on grants from the structure it is purportedly challenging, just how radical is that challenge going to be?

It doesn't take radicalism to get censors going, though. As South African writer J. M. Coetzee noted of the dynamic of censorship, "There is a world of difference between subversive ideas and morally repugnant representations. In practice, however, the same censors patrol the boundaries of both politics and aesthetics."[7]

---

In 1996, as attention to art brawls, if not the brawls themselves, was winding down, I organized a roundtable discussion among seven artists from New England whose work had recently been pilloried, banned, or defaced. (Throughout this chapter, I use the term *art* to cover all visual, musical, literary, filmic, and performance media.) We met in Boston at Mobius, an artist-run space on the top floor of a brick building that had once housed a shoe factory. Like other low-budget arts operations that have reclaimed decaying industrial districts, the space gets adapted to a multitude of uses. The day we meet, it houses an exhibit organized to complement a conference on "difficult" speech hosted that weekend by the Boston Coalition for Freedom of Expression (BCFE). The exhibit is called *Palladia: The Dismantling of Safe Havens for Critical Thought* and includes work by two of the participating artists.

We sit around a long wooden table: Maxine McDonald, a photographer; Michael Willhoite, a writer and illustrator; Ifé Franklin, a visual artist; James Montford, a conceptual artist; Hans Evers, a sculptor; Denise Marika, a video sculptor; and Jay Critchley, a performance and environmental artist. The circle is completed by three people whose work and sympathies have involved them in art controversies: Kathleen Bitetti, a visual artist and director of the Artists Foundation, who curated the exhibition; and the founders of the BCFE, playwright Jim D'Entremont and his partner, Bob Chatelle, then chair of the National Writers Union Political Issues Committee. Since 1989, the BCFE, under Jim's leadership, has unwaveringly defended artists, writers, and others when their free expression was threatened, and he has helped me organize this gathering.

So, an honor roll, or rogue's gallery, or perhaps both. The group is typical of moderately successful artists around the country, with their awards, degrees, commissions, shows, publications, and bodies of work that are seldom commercially viable. They are typical too of artists who have faced censure when they addressed one of the explosive topics of the era—child nudity, homosexuality, racism, or religion. These artists had other things in common relevant to our discussion: many created art for public spaces, all were attentive to the communities in which they worked (some communities went to bat for them, others turned their back), and all got hit with publicity that was out of proportion and out of control. Reluctant to assume the role of victim, they nonetheless felt vulnerable to misconceptions about artists and their work, as, one after another, they talked about being hurt and being afraid. The legacy of censorship, they had learned, is fear: of offending, of looking foolish, of losing support, of getting hauled into court, of seeing your work destroyed, of being stopped from making the art you want and need to make.

Only a few of the participants know each other—censorship is meant to be isolating—but they slip easily into the camaraderie and gallows humor of shared persecution as, for three hours on an unseasonably warm September afternoon, we throw open the windows to catch a breeze off the nearby harbor and we talk. The discussion is videotaped, and later, as I fast-forward through the tape, I watch images skitter by: a bunch of people sitting around a table lurch back and forth in their chairs, reach for a Chocolate Orgasm (brownies that have also been banned in Boston), break into laughter and just as suddenly into seriousness. Meaning is obscured, movement disjointed, as in a very old newsreel. Then I push "play" and everything shimmies into place.

———————

It is Maxine McDonald's turn to tell her story. She points to pictures in the exhibit around us, soft-focus, homage-to-nature photographs that feature her granddaughter, then six years old, naked and coy in an off-hand, little-kid way. These are some of the photos that brought the police after her. As if this were an AA meeting, she announces, "I'm Maxine and these are my photographs."

Maxine makes an unlikely outlaw. She is fifty-eight, the oldest of the group, pale-skinned with dark hair waving over her shoulders, and artsy-looking in a loose-fitting, red-and-purple jacket. She is well known in her community, a small town about an hour west of Boston, where she has been a popular art and photography teacher at the high school for years. She explains that she moved from black-and-white to color photography when she got access to processing facilities; she took the photos of her granddaughter for a class in experimental photography that had appealed to her, in part, because it offered an affordable way to develop color film. For an assignment in the summer of 1994 to explore nightmares and dreams, Maxine photographed the child as she played on a beach, planning to overlay the prints with salt water, sand, and other textures from nature. She took the film to be developed by a photo lab that she used regularly, but when she returned a few days later to pick up this roll, she was told it wasn't ready, could she come back in a little while?

At this point in her story, everyone in the room mutters, "Uh huh, right," but she thought nothing of it. She took care of some tasks at her school across the street, then returned for her film. "It was ready," she says, "but they were ready with the police for me."

The chief of police, whom she had known for years, and another policeman took her out back, read her her rights, and asked who the "young lady" in the photographs was. "I told them she was my granddaughter," she says in a low, monochromatic voice, sounding uneasy still. "They wanted to know how old she was, and I told them she was six. They wanted to know about the photography, and I explained. They said, well, this is against the law in Massachusetts." Maxine didn't know what the law said, but she repeated that this was her own granddaughter, that the girl's mother, Maxine's daughter, had been present, that she would never take a photo that hurt any child. Besides, she explained, this was art. "Photography is considered reality," she points out. "If these [photographs] were drawings, there would probably be very little trouble."

The police weren't interested in discussing aesthetics. "They didn't treat me like they knew me at all. They didn't treat me like they knew that I was a teacher." They sent her home but kept her photos. When she asked what would happen next, she was told the district attorney would decide.

As soon as she got home, Maxine began to rid herself of anything that might be seen as incriminating. She knew about other artists who had faced legal sanctions for photographing nude children, most famously Jock Sturges, a California photographer, whose home and studio were raided by the FBI in 1990 after a photo lab employee turned him in for creating child pornography. Maxine says, "I called everybody that I knew who knew I did this kind of photography. I said, would you hide my work?"

"And sure enough," she continues, "the Department of Social Services intervened." DSS, apparently alerted by the police, interviewed her twice, her daughter and granddaughter separately. "Basically they frightened her," she says of the child. "They kept asking her questions and pressuring her: Do you like it when your grandmother takes pictures of you? Do you like it when she takes pictures of you nude? And on and on. She didn't know what to make of all this."

———————

When it became clear that she couldn't fight this battle alone, Maxine hired a lawyer, who traced the photographs to the office of the district attorney in Gloucester, the city where they had been shot. There they sat, evidence of something, while the investigation continued for several months. In the end, the state found nothing untoward, but it took repeated calls to the DA's office to get the photos back. In the background, Maxine's lawyer told her, she heard people laughing about the "child pornography case."

Defining child pornography is as problematic as defining other kinds of pornography, with the added complication that pictures of children in various stages of undress show up in family photo albums everywhere. Where is the line between cute and lewd, or between natural and imposed sexuality, and who judges? As Maxine was being investigated, laws in twelve states required photo lab employees—with no training and usually no guidelines for making such subjective determinations—to alert law authorities if they thought they were being asked to develop "child pornography." Child endangerment laws in other states included similar provisions.[8] Massachusetts has no such law, but many labs there have turned photos over to the police nonetheless.[9]

We have been moving in this direction since the late 1970s, when public anxiety fixed on a purported epidemic of child pornography, based on wildly exaggerated reports.[10] People under seventeen had been denied access to material deemed "harmful to minors" since 1968,[11] but the protectionism now turned to minors involved in producing the material. At the urging of religious groups, who worried about sex, and child advocates, who worried about exploitation—in Jim D'Entremont's words, "your right-wing prudery connecting with left-wing victim culture"—Congress passed seven laws aimed at outlawing child pornography between 1977 and 2002. Heavy penalties were imposed for producing or possessing child porn, enforcement was stepped up as a result of the 1986 Meese Commission report (see Chapter 6), and soon America's commercial child pornography industry closed down. Child porn is still available, however (rumor has it that the largest distributor in the United States is the government, selling it in sting operations), with access made easier by the Internet.

By the 1980s, concern had shifted from what is in the frame—naked kids in sexual poses—to what is outside—the intent of the photographer—and more protective measures were deemed necessary. In 1982, the Supreme Court ruled that the Miller test for obscenity doesn't apply to child porn, which is obscene by definition and therefore outside the First Amendment.[12] Congress outlawed distribution of child pornography by any medium, including computers, in 1990, the same year possessing or viewing child pornography in one's home was ruled illegal.[13] A few years later, then–Attorney General Janet Reno said that children didn't have to be naked for photos to be pornographic.

Child pornography was redefined by Congress in the Child Pornography Prevention Act of 1996 (CPPA) to include any image that "appears to be" or "conveys the impression" of a minor "engaged in sexually explicit conduct."[14] This included pictures of young-looking adults as well as "virtual" child porn, or photographs generated by computer that involved no actual children in their creation. The rationale for limiting sexual images of children had thus evolved from protecting children from the harm of looking at the pictures to protecting children from being harmed in the making of the pictures to protecting everyone because the existence of such pictures was harmful. Two of the three provisions in CPPA were struck down in April 2002 when the Supreme Court ruled that they were overbroad and unconstitutional—whereupon Congress and the Attorney General immediately set to work crafting a new law.

Meanwhile, stories similar to Maxine's continue to surface around the country, and it is the ambiguity of the law that scares Maxine most. She could be caught—doing what?—again. She says, "It's frightening to put work out in a gallery. It's not that they're going to take it down. They're going to come to my house and arrest me."

Politicians, police, parents, everyone, it seems, worships at the altar of child protection—as long as what children are being protected from are pictures and words. Our laws—and pressure to come up with laws—assume that while "we" are able to distinguish the sensual pleasures of a child's body from sexual abuse, no one else can.[15] Anxiety at this level over child nudity seems perverse in itself, as if our society is seeking out eroticism under the guise of preventing it. Michael Willhoite, wondering at the response to Maxine's photos, muses, "Sex is one of the most absorbing things in the world for children from a very early age. They're very curious about it and always will be. It's like certain parents are terrified that their children are going to develop healthy attitudes toward sex."

That gets the artists going on why such alarm over nudity and sex in general. Fear of intimacy, someone suggests. Someone else says Americans are uptight. A third notes the advantages to capitalism of manufactured desire, while a fourth reminds us that a lot of sex *is* scary. Bob Chatelle says, "My theory is that the people in power have a real need to create monsters because they can tell the people, 'These monsters are your enemy. *We're* not your enemy, and we are here to protect you from these monsters.' " Hidden expression like child pornography makes for particularly fertile monster-fantasies since its true scope is unknown, so while pornographers are unlikely to slip down to the corner film lab for a quick fix, the many parents and artists who do so risk prosecution in the name of some equivocal protection of minors.

---

Artists seem an odd choice of bogeyman to scare the children with, but mistrust of them goes way back. A tenet of puritanism that informs our culture still is that sinning in thought is tantamount to sinning in action. Artists, with their task, their talent, for imagining human frailty and depravity fully enough to make them *seem* real, are therefore marked as sinners. In 1837, Nathaniel Hawthorne wrote, "Thus a novel writer, or a dramatist, in creating a villain of romance, and fitting him with evil deeds, and the villain of actual life, in projecting crimes that will be perpetrated, may almost meet each other half-way between reality and fancy."[16] That halfway point continues to trouble, not only those on a moral crusade, but also those who think art should be better, purer than reality. As a letter to the editor about Hans Evers's sculpture asserted, "True art is in touch with life, people, and all that is good. It believes in life and in the people and in the community it portrays."[17]

In sharp contrast, when the roundtable artists talk about what they want to do in their art, they spend little time on beauty or uplift, though their work may be inspiring and pleasing. Instead, they sound like artist provocateurs as they talk of reflecting and revealing, pushing boundaries and prompting questions, making people uncomfortable enough to see anew. Perhaps clearest about what he hoped for and from his audience was Michael Willhoite when he wrote and illustrated his children's book *Daddy's Roommate* in 1991. The book, the first in a series created for children with gay and lesbian parents, portrays a day in the life of a young boy, his father, and his father's male partner. One of sixteen books Michael has published, it received good reviews and a Lambda Literary Award. He expected the book to sell for a season, but it was included in

Children of the Rainbow, a determinedly multicultural curriculum for elementary schools in New York City, and when that curriculum came under attack for "promoting homosexuality," *Daddy's Roommate* got slammed. "I had no idea!" says Michael, a compact man of about fifty, with a round face, round glasses, tidy mustache, courtly manners, mordant wit, and traces of his native Oklahoma in his speech. "It was the most banned book in the country for two years running."[18]

We greet this announcement with a chorus of congratulations, wows, and reallys, but none of us is surprised: gay artists have been targeted disproportionately since this round of art attacks began. Three of the NEA 4 (see Chapter 5) were gay or lesbian, and by 1995, 35 percent of the challenges to artistic freedom compiled by the liberal group People for the American Way concerned work with homosexual content that was condemned as "indecent" or "pornographic."[19] In 1989, the NEA had revoked, then restored with reservations, a grant to Artist Space in New York for an exhibit of art about AIDS called *Witnesses: Against Our Vanishing.* The title proved apt in more ways than one, since censorship is often used to render ideas and the people who hold them nonexistent. When antigay activists turned to *Daddy's Roommate,* they took the tack of insisting that if gays weren't invisible to children, they certainly should be.

Even accounting for the tenor of the time, opposition to the book was surprisingly fierce, given its sweet drawings, innocent portrayal of a loving, monogamous relationship, and no sex whatsoever. Michael holds the book up for us to see the pictures as he reads: " 'Work together . . . Eat together . . . Sleep together . . .' " One man is pictured getting under the covers, the other is sound asleep. " 'And bathe together.' " "Someone actually objected to this," he marvels. "They said we're going to change the whole of the U.S. Navy—which I was in—into a brace of raving queens."

*Daddy's Roommate* fills a need, he insists, "teaching other children about gay men and lesbians and also teaching children who find themselves in this situation that this is life as it is." But life as it is is unacceptable to some people, particularly those who believe that to read something is to swallow it uncritically, or, as the conservative Concerned Women for America claims, that children are as impressionable as "wet cement."[20] This fear of influence seemed to underlie objections to Michael's book, which centered less on the portrayal of gay men living together than on gay men living together happily and, worse, making a child happy. "The way it usually happens is that some young mother or father will bring a child home from the library and the kid has an armful of books, as we all did at that age, and this parent sees this child reading *Daddy's Roommate* and goes ballistic." He imitates outrage—"This man's trying to teach my child to be a queer!"—waits a beat and adds, "You can't learn it. You are or you aren't."

At a library board meeting in Florida, a parent said, "*Daddy's Roommate* lays on the shelf like a loaded weapon."[21] In a dispute in Massachusetts, a Baptist minister warned, "Ten years from now, you'll be debating whether to put books on pedophilia in the library."[22] The newsletter of a right-wing group in Colorado described Michael's publisher, Alyson Books, as "work[ing] out of a seedy, run-down warehouse next to a crime-infested housing project in Boston" and "cater[ing] to adults who want to have sex with children."[23]

Librarians, heroes in Michael's saga, regularly went to bat for *Daddy's Roommate,* fighting attempts to ban it or move it to restricted shelves, and when the publisher offered free copies to libraries, it was inundated with requests. But if the would-be censors failed to banish the book, they succeeded in making Michael weigh his words carefully. Describing his internal debate over whether to include a kiss in a sequel called *Daddy's Wedding,* he sighs deeply and concludes, "I filter what I do with what my publisher thinks they can get away with."

As the controversy raged over Michael's book, two overheated and oddly complementary modes of self-representation were all the rage: memoirs, with their overtones of confession and rebirth, and identity politics, with their insistence that people assigned to a certain category come with a set of preordained and immutable beliefs. When these ways of thinking meet up with the American creed that all human transactions are, at base, a version of salesmanship, the artistic enterprise makes sense primarily as a form of evangelical hucksterism. What else to conclude then, but that Michael was out to convert his young readers?

"You're not converting, but you're obviously supporting it," Maxine points out, and Michael agrees readily. He meant *Daddy's Roommate* to have an effect, but he sees that as different from indoctrination.

This reminds Jay Critchley of the response to a plan he once submitted to Boston's Institute of Contemporary Art to turn New Hampshire's Seabrook nuclear power plant into a national nuclear monument. The ICA couldn't figure out if he was against nuclear power or for it, he tells us, so they turned it down.

"For complexity?" someone asks.

"For ambiguity," comes the reply.

---

"It was interesting," begins Denise Marika, who says that when she means something bothers her. Referring to her video installation that drew public outrage precisely because it was enigmatic, she continues, "I think ambiguity is a flashpoint, because while the piece that I had censored was up, there were Calvin Klein ads on billboards with pants kind of unzipped and ripped off. Nobody had any problem with that because everyone knew they were selling underwear. But where there was ambiguity [as in her installation], then people were very upset because they didn't know *what* to think. They'd rather have you tell them to some degree."

Unlike many contemporary visual artists, Denise doesn't do much telling in her work, relying on fluid images to make her point. The piece that came under attack in May 1994 was called *Crossing*. It consisted of two photographic projections overlaid on a crosswalk signal in Brookline, the Boston suburb where she lives with her husband and two children. The Brookline Arts Council, a nonprofit artist group, had commissioned it and paid expenses, but Denise earned nothing from the project. The images were of a woman and a toddler, Denise and her son. Both figures were naked, but seen in outline, so features and gender weren't easily discernable. For the Walk signal, the adult held the child's hand, for Don't Walk, she hugged him, presumably to restrain him from running into traffic.

Denise is forty-one, tall, slender, and stylish in beige linen shorts and spiky hair. She studied stone carving before moving on to video while a graduate student at UCLA and combines both traditions in her work, which she calls video sculpture. Her medium is the body, hers and others', which she uses to explore physical relationships and tensions among image, form, and time. According to one review, her work "gets under your skin." Another calls it "ethereal and powerful." No one who sees it seems unmoved.

Denise put up *Crossing* on a Friday before a weekend art walk, so it got immediate exposure, and by Monday, the town hall was fielding calls demanding its removal. "Some people were very upset because they thought it was a man and a child," she says, still puzzled by this response. "This was very interesting to me because if it was a man and a child, their interpretation was that it was pedophilia. I felt so bad for every man I

know that the immediate interpretation [was] that if a man touches a
child there is something potentially very wrong about the situation."

The next morning, Denise got a call from the Brookline transportation department, which had helped her install *Crossing*, saying they had
been told to take it down. Astonished, she pleaded with them to do nothing for twenty-four hours so that she could document the piece. They
agreed, but, in the meantime, the owner of a nearby liquor store complained to the news media, who, Denise says, "were all over this." Here,
to their delight, was controversial art innocuous enough to show on TV.

*Crossing* got the most coverage of any of Denise's work up to then,
with headlines like "Flashing lights! Residents bare their anger over nude
signs." One woman was so incensed by the reports that she came from
Cambridge to try to smash the piece with a hammer. Denise's phone rang
nonstop as she attempted to insert some accuracy and proportion into
the coverage. She watched with the queasiness that comes from hearing
a story you know well told all wrong as a TV reporter stood in front of
*Crossing*, a microphone in one hand, Denise's proposal and budget in the
other. "He was telling people it was taxpayer money. Brookline Arts
Council money is lottery money. It has nothing to do with your taxes,"
she says with disdain. "And he inflated the budget by about ten times."

As the week wore on, things calmed down a little, in part because arts
and civil liberties groups got to work reminding town officials of the
legal implications of removing public art precipitously. Though some officials were troubled by the piece—a selectman was quoted as saying, "It
just seems so out of place. It probably belongs in an art gallery"[24]—ultimately, they decided to keep *Crossing* up for its planned two-month run.

"I think if I were to have the opportunity to do it again, I'd try to get
some of the educational aspect up front rather than have it follow after
a crisis," Denise says. The education—for the public and her—came primarily though a forum the arts council organized. About eighty people
attended, most spoke favorably about the work, and others approached
Denise on the street afterward to talk about how their thoughts on the
piece had changed and deepened. She was relieved. Making art for her
neighborhood had been part of the project's appeal, but when the controversy exploded, being so visible had made her uneasy. Everyone knew
where she lived, her children were in the public schools. "It was nice
when people started to rally to realize that you're not out there all by
yourself," she says.

Denise's story has all the elements of the arts quarrels of the time: hys-
teria over portrayal of the body; a small, local argument magnified into

a crisis; accusations of wasted public funds. Yet even if the media do caricature artists and the "taxpayers' revolt" is no more than a cynical ploy, such strategies wouldn't work were it not for what Denise calls the many myths about artists—for instance, that they grow rich from public coffers creating stuff that nobody wants.

While the merits of a work of art may be open to debate, the economic reality of the artistic life is painfully clear: Few artists make a living from their art.[25] Typical of American artists, those at the roundtable subsidized their art with other, unrelated jobs, giving the lie to another myth: that artists are unstable, unreliable, and parasitic. "And God forbid, if you're a woman that you have children!" Denise concludes with mock horror. "You're supposed to have given that up!"

———————

Five months later, Hans Evers found that a male artist with children can be vulnerable in a different way. Hans is Dutch, born in Curaçao and educated in the States. Blond and handsome, he is a slight, soft-spoken man in his early thirties and the father of two young sons who figure in his work. At the time of the show that got him in trouble, he was teaching art at the University of Massachusetts at Dartmouth and negotiating, none too cordially, with his soon-to-be-ex-wife over custody of their children. Like Denise, Hans uses body images in his sculpture. His focus is male sexuality and "who we are as fathers, as sons, as lovers," questions he explored in *Identidem,* his one-man show in Cambridge, Massachusetts, in October 1994. He had been selected by a three-person jury of the Cambridge Arts Council, a city agency, to present a month-long show at a gallery in the second-floor foyer of the City Hall Annex, and he was pleased with the opportunity, even though he would be paid nothing and would have to cover expenses himself.

Hans's work incorporated a variety of media: photography, film, bronze casting, found objects. Among the pieces in the show were photographic self-portraits, a filmstrip of his sons, a plexiglass case with vibrators, and a sculpture, titled *Critical Proportions,* which consisted of large wooden boxes with latex dildos mounted inside. As with many artists, his art and intentions make a lot of sense when he talks about them and very little sense when his critics do. He passes slides of the exhibit around the table, confirming the murmurs. "Dicks and cocks and dildos, that's right," he says mildly, though a display of sex toys wasn't what he had in mind. Using the phallus as a symbol of male power, as have many before him, he meant *Critical Proportions* as a wry reference to male obsession with penis size—obviously no joking matter.

As Hans and the gallery staff were installing the show, William Walsh, a city councilor, who had had very public disagreements with the arts council in the past, stopped by. This time, he took matters literally into his own hands, ripping dildos from *Critical Proportions* and grabbing a photograph of a penis from another piece. Booty in hand, he marched to the city manager's office to demand that the exhibit be canceled and the arts council punished. "I didn't like the artwork," he later testified.[26]

"Then," Hans sums up, "he called the media and created the scandal because that's what he wanted. Of course, even though we quote-unquote self-censored the show already, there was a big media circus anyway." More good headlines: "Is it art or obscenity?" and "No sex please, we're Cantabrigians." More quotable outrage from Walsh, who, incidentally, was awaiting sentencing on multiple counts of bank fraud: "We've lost a sense of propriety in government. If God is banned, and nudity is condoned, I don't know where we are going to end up."[27]

For an artist, to have his work destroyed is the cruelest form of censorship, short of destroying the artist himself, because it is so final. When art is suppressed, there remains the hope that it will reemerge some other place or time. "Bans, along with the governments that impose them, do not last forever," South African writer Nadine Gordimer reminds us.[28] But art, once ruined, can never be resurrected. "I wasn't looking for any controversy like this," Hans says. "Obviously, I was very hurt and offended that someone could actually [remove] a piece and partially destroy another and he would get away with it and I was going to look like the bad guy."

In public disputes like this, it can be hard to figure out who exactly is harmed, since most artists want media attention. They'd like it to be for their art, though, and they'd like it to be accurate. Hans says, "I had never been in a situation like this, but I assumed that the media would be on my side. It turned out when that when you told them how the finances actually worked, you were completely misquoted." The others agree that this is typical of what Denise labels "here's-another-crazy-art-thing-isn't-this-amusing kind of attitude." When the mainstream media bother addressing art, they very often treat it in terms of personalities, profit, or power struggles, so when the art scandals broke in the 1990s, the terms of coverage had already been set. All that was left for the press was to slot names into the simplistic descriptions and outlandish-artist stories.

As the conflict escalated, Hans began to hear complaints from city workers in the building about sexual harassment, though it was unclear who was being harassed or how. "They felt somehow impeached in their freedom of speech in the sense that they were forced to see something that they didn't want to see and that they felt was offensive to women," Hans says, trying to sort out rumors from substance. "Somehow they felt that vibrators, for example, were more offensive to women than to men. Some were actually interested in having a discussion, but they would say things like 'Aren't you worried about offending lesbians?' So all these prejudices on their side were filtering in how they were interpreting my artwork."

The arts council managed to negotiate a compromise: *Identidem* would open as planned but would be screened by wall partitions with advisories about what lay beyond. Jim D'Entremont, who, through BCFE, had advised Hans, says, "This was more like a peep show, basically telling people what to think of it before they'd seen it." BCFE urged Hans to sue Walsh for malicious destruction of property, but he balked at putting himself and his family through a legal battle. His wife was threatening to charge him with sexual abuse over pictures he had taken of their sons naked (the Department of Social Services was investigating his family when we met). In the end, he did file a criminal complaint, but it proved a bad strategy. When the case came to trial the following spring, the jury, like the people at the Gloucester DA's office who laughed about Maxine's photos, seemed more amused than concerned. They acquitted Walsh, simply reckoning the cost of the materials and ignoring any First Amendment issues.

Cambridge, where you can't spit without hitting an academic, fancies itself progressive and freethinking, surely worldly enough to take a dildo or two in stride. But apparently it couldn't, and, as with Denise's work, context was the issue. Says Hans, "The argument was, we all know that dildos exist and we all know they live in the Combat Zone [Boston's erstwhile red-light district], but we don't want them to live in our public space." He had worked closely with the gallery's curator to select what went into the show, deciding against including his most explicit work. "I didn't have a problem with that because I think there's something to be said for a curator and an artist in a mutually cooperative way coming to some kind of a compromise which is dictated by the specifics of that situation. Curators and artists make those decisions all the time."

Denise is less sanguine about this vetting process. She is preparing to show a new work at the Museum of Modern Art in New York, where she anticipates no trouble because museum visitors come knowing more or less what to expect. Curators count on this to avoid controversy, but to Denise, that knowledge is more confining than comforting. "It's always been clear to me that because of the subjects that I deal with, [physical] conflict between people, that I'm pretty much forced into gallery and museum venues, the white box, almost exclusively," she says in frustration, adding that she doubts she'll be offered the opportunity to do a public piece again.

When art shows up in public places, questions of ownership and access inevitably arise: Who gets to use public space? Who decides what goes on communally owned property? Who controls what we pass by and see? Public art arouses the censorious reflex more readily than gallery art because people who have to live with an object feel, fairly enough, that they should have some say in their environment. Never mind that our cities are full of structures and commercial images that we have no control over; in contemporary America, advertising feels inevitable, art optional.

Public space is connected in the public mind to public funding, which may account for the assumption that Hans and Denise were using up tax money, but traditional settings for art—theaters, libraries, Denise's white box of museumdom—are not immune to attack. In 1995, nearly one-fifth of recorded challenges involved sponsors, public and private, backing away from commitments to show various kinds of art.[29] This faintheartedness is much more common than outright censorship, but the consequences are similar. Denise describes curators dropping references to delicate local sensibilities as they suggest she omit a piece from a show. They sound quite reasonable, she says, except that she knows where such "suggestions" are leading. As Hans wrote in a letter to the editor in the aftermath of his dispute, "What we see again and again is that these controversies around 'difficult' art turn into pyrrhic victories where, in the end, funding is cut and/or selection processes are compromised."[30]

---

It's sneaky how caution turns into suppression and suppression into habit, how the desire to sidestep controversy becomes the controversy itself. Ifé Franklin begins her story: "I'm an African-American, lesbian, artist, human being . . ."

"Did they know that?" someone asks.

"Yeah," she answers a little uncertainly, since her bout with censorship implied that she would be permitted to diverge from the majority in only one way at a time. Ifé, an expansive woman in her early thirties, works with art, dance, and media literacy projects in Boston. She has arched eyebrows and peroxided braids tied with beads that click softly as she turns her head, and when she talks, her face, hands, shoulders, whole body get into the act.

She backs up to explain that the past spring, she had been invited to take part in an exhibit at Northeastern University. It was to be called *Sweetpotato Style (Sisters Cookin' Together)* and would celebrate diversity and unity among African American women. The show was organized by another African American artist, who knew that Ifé was a lesbian, though she had never shown art that would be labeled "homosexual." (The word sounds so clinical to her that she speaks it in quotes.) She said she would be showing new work, but tells us, "I didn't feel like I had to say, 'You know, this is, you know.' "

The you-know was a smallish collage called *Yo! Black Lesbian and Gay Pride,* which included photographs of writer Langston Hughes, a gay man, and blues singers Ma Rainey and Bessie Smith, bisexual women. Ifé included it among the title sheets that she and the three other participating artists turned in shortly before the exhibit was to open. A few days later, she got a call from the show's organizer. *Yo!* could not be included, she announced, though she had yet to see it, because it was inconsistent with the theme of black sisterhood.

"I was hurt, I was infuriated, I couldn't believe it," Ifé says, waving her hands and leaning into the table. "The woman, she's a minister. So she gives me this, I can't put it in because it goes against the word of God. And I'm like, what does that have to do with the show?" The organizer insisted that her decision had nothing to do with her views of homosexuality; she just wanted to avoid politicizing the exhibit. This makes no sense to Ifé. "I said, your work is Afrocentric; isn't that a political statement? Every day you walk out of your house and you're a woman. That's a political statement. Or anybody can walk out of their house and just be sane. These days that's a political statement!"

There is a central conflict between the artistic values of accuracy and authenticity and the civic value of getting along, which may require keeping certain things unexpressed. Add in the disinclination to give attention to ideas one finds distasteful, and you have the tensions that exploded in Ifé's exchange with the exhibit's organizer. *Yo!* was out; the woman wouldn't budge on that, but she seemed to see no reason why she and Ifé couldn't get past that and go on with the show. Ifé did. "Do you understand that you're an artist and you're censoring my work?" she demanded. "I said, if that's your stance, then I'm going to expose you. I'm going to go to every newspaper because"—she articulates each word—"I will not allow you to do this to me."

There wasn't much of what could be called discussion after that. A dean at Northeastern, a black man, who got involved when Ifé copied him in on a letter of complaint, officially canceled the exhibit, though who actually dealt the coup de grâce is open to debate. Ifé charges that the dean sidestepped the issues of censorship and homophobia, instead making it sound like "a catfight." "I don't get in the middle of grown folks' business," he told the *Boston Globe*.[31]

As is often the case, Ifé's troubles brought her new opportunities, including a one-woman show through Northeastern the next year, but she worries about being branded a troublemaker. Though Michael reminds her that in our celebrity-besotted culture, notoriety is a form of success, she doubts that this kind of attention serves her purposes. "I want to have conversations with my community, the African American gay and lesbian community and the African American heterosexual community, because I'm so tired of these divisions," she says, angry all over again. "I refuse to be discriminated against by my own people. I think they're still going to have the show. They're just waiting for all of this stuff to die down. They're not going to invite me and then when I find out about it, I'm going to protest because I feel like this is not dead because you close your eyes or your ears." With a flourish, she concludes, "Silencing me by acting like I don't exist?"

———

It is a refusal to be silent, or polite, or politic, that drives Jay Critchley, who embraces opposition as a goad to ever more extreme postures. "I'm provoking people," he admits cheerfully. "Then that becomes the work. That's sort of how I see my role as an artist, to redefine the boundaries. I expect that there will be controversy, but that controversy becomes the seeds for future exposés of hypocrisies."

At forty-nine, Jay is tall and loose-limbed. With his long head and short chin, heavy-lidded eyes, and prominent ears, he looks like a cartoonist drew him. He is gay, a father, and recently a grandfather. Jay's oeuvre consists of installations and performances that he creates for commissions, such as a project he did in connection with the 1996 Olympics; for residencies, such as one at Harvard in 2000; and for the hell of it. We have moved to a windowless room so he can show us slides, which prove to be useful, since what he does defies easy explanation. Conceptual art? Performance art? Environmental art? Art at all? "I was an activist before I became an artist [he has helped raise over $1 million for AIDS programs], so a lot of my work is based on working publicly," he explains as he clicks through the pictures and narrates with deadpan delivery.

He dates his first artwork to 1981, when he parked a sand-encrusted VW bug in a public lot on the waterfront of Provincetown, Massachusetts, the fashionably funky beach town favored by gays and lesbians, where he lives year-round. The response gave him a delicious taste of things to come. Town officials declared the piece a public nuisance but lacked any legal basis to remove it, so they called a public meeting. Stymied after hours of debate over whether it was a sculpture or a car, they threw up their hands and let it be. Jay's take? "The average person on the street really liked the fact that I stood up to city hall and won."

After the car project, he continued to tweak the noses of bureaucrats and aesthetes, who invariably rose to the bait. One of his most elaborate projects is *Old Glory Condom Corporation,* created for an exhibit of political art at MIT in 1989 and inspired by the pro–safe sex and anti–flag-burning campaigns of the time. Old Glory is a corporate entity that markets condoms with the American flag emblazoned on their package. Its slogan is "Worn with pride country-wide." At the exhibit, Jay, as Old Glory's CEO, stood in front of a wall-sized logo in a three-piece suit, looking for investors to back the corporation and thus complete the piece. "I've set up a challenge for myself as an artist: to become what I'm satirizing," he had told me then. A decade later, his satire—instant fortune based on a bright idea—became the reality of IPOs, testimony to the drawbacks of satire when excess is the norm.

At the roundtable, he explains, "This is one way that I find my voice as an artist. I was saying it's patriotic to protect and save lives; it's not just patriotic to be thinking about war and killing." The government begged to differ, denying his application for a trademark on the grounds that it was immoral to associate the flag with sex. Jay and his lawyer, the indefatigable David Cole, argued his First Amendment rights, and eventually the U.S. Patent Office, like the Provincetown officials, gave in and became part of Jay's art.

But even Jay, cheerleader for provocation that he is, was unprepared for the response to *Blessed Virgin Mother Goddess—Immaculate Protection,* a piece he and two collaborators made for World AIDS Day in

1994. "Most of the things we've been talking about today have to do with sex, but let me tell you, when you start talking about religion, this is much more controversial," he says. The project, which linked the destruction of the rainforest with the emergence of the HIV virus, consisted of prayer-ads placed in local newspapers that entreated the goddess to "restore the precious immune system of the earth" and shrines with votive candles and more prayers at Boston's Institute of Contemporary Art.

Jay was raised Catholic. He claims to have been visited by the goddess, whom he places in the Christian tradition of seeking saintly assistance in times of need, but a right-wing Catholic group was unimpressed. Their pitched protest led to an editorial in Boston's Archdiocese newspaper, which demanded, "What perverse pleasure, what political advantage, what possible social good was done by deliberately trashing the woman whom Christians hail with such great affection as the 'Mother of God'?"[32] When Jay and his partners offered to provide several good reasons, the paper declined. "The ICA was inundated and scared to death by all these calls from Catholics," Jay says, with relish. "They were out there saying the rosary for World AIDS Day, which I thought was appropriate." Within the week, posters of the goddess were removed from a glass display case in the subway that the MBTA, Boston's transportation authority, had lent to the ICA to advertise its shows. The posters disappeared, apparently thrown away, though two years later, the ICA and MBTA are still disavowing any responsibility for the destruction of Jay's art.

———————

Like Jay's work, James Montford's occupies an equivocal space between idea and action, play and attack, amusement and irritant. James makes conceptual pieces, mostly for galleries and museums, but despite the traditional art venues, his work regularly draws fire. For several years, James, an African American, has been doing installations and performances involving racial stereotypes and racist language, expression that, in an example of how social disapprobation can change the way we talk, seldom shows up in routine conversation now.

In his late forties, James is sturdy, dark-skinned, bespectacled, and mustachioed and wears his hair in miniature dreadlocks caught in a bunch at the nape of his neck. He lives in Norwich, Connecticut, has exhibited throughout New England, and, like Hans, subsidizes his art by teaching. For much of the discussion, James has been leaning back with his arms across his chest, saying very little and exchanging glances with his teenaged son who has accompanied him, as if to gauge his reaction. Now he smiles—affably? warily?—and takes his turn.

"I want to make good work," he begins in a low, soothing voice. "I want to make work that has integrity. I'm not very concerned about what I owe the audience. I could get away with not putting it out there, given what happens with all the political and social ramifications I have to work out: Who's going to accept it, who's going to reject it. Why put yourself through all that?"

His focus on racism emerged from a Ku Klux Klan rally he attended in 1982. "That sort of changed my life. There were twelve guys in white robes standing there condemning me as a person," he says. Eventually, he began to incorporate the experience into his work, using art as a kind of disinfectant. An early piece in this vein was *A Myth and a Metaphor,* a map of downtown Hartford on which he renamed streets with racial epithets, such as Jigaboo Street and Tar Baby Plaza. When *Myth* was exhibited in 1991 at the Old State House in Hartford, the executive director, a white man, took it down because, he told the press, "I was educated to believe that one does not tolerate this sort of thing."[33] James's point, then and now, is that "this kind of thing" has too much power over us. Our time would be better spent, he suggests, combating, not the symbolism, but the reality of racial injustice. But like some black comedians and contemporary artists, James makes this point by using symbols of racism, and so he threatens twice: once in showing what he is not supposed to, and again in pointing out the vulnerability of the walls we've built to hold the taboo at bay.

A couple of years later, for an exhibit at the University of Rhode Island, James filled thirty-four baggies with locks of hair and arranged them in a grid on the wall above the question, "Can You Find the Nigger Hair?" You can't—there isn't any—though in looking for differences, the viewer is implicated disconcertingly. The effect is sly and hard to shake off, but when the protest came, as of course it would, it took a surprisingly literal form: someone ripped the word *nigger* from the caption and left everything else intact. *Nigger Hair* is part of James's contribution to the exhibit at Mobius, and it decorates the wall behind us now. Close up, the hair samples look like sterile forensic evidence, but from a distance, the whole is unnervingly pretty, an abstract collage of texture and hue.

James likes to discomfit, something I learned firsthand at the exhibit's opening the night before, when he did a performance piece in which he teased the audience that he was about to pull something out of his pants.

Told that way it sounds like a silly schoolboy joke, and he milked it for a good ten minutes. I sat in the front row and smiled a lot because I was uncomfortable. James smiled back. His work isn't particularly subtle— what he pulled from his pants was a banana—but it makes his point: while he's in charge, we're going to see what he wants us to see, and euphemism be damned.

This friction between artist and audience exploded when, in 1993, James was asked to join a group show for the art gallery of Hampshire College, a small, elite school in Amherst, Massachusetts, that a local paper describes as a "bastion of liberal rectitude."[34] James's installation consisted of basketballs strewn across the floor, some connected by black tape to create a constellation, and an invented mythology involving fried chicken and a Negro League team called the Gator Aid boys, documented in extensive wall text. He called it *The Lipper Constellation*. "So," he narrates, "I went to the opening. It was a sleeper, nobody was there. Then a week later, I get a call from the curator, saying"—here his voice drops to a frantic stage whisper—" 'Everyone's going crazy all of a sudden. I've been in the president's office the last three days for hours on end, I've met with faculty, I've met with students. Please come up here!' "

James arrived at Hampshire to find the campus up in arms. His work had been kicked apart by scandalized viewers and altered by a "response wall" added by the administration. When he tried to discuss the piece in a gallery talk, he was hooted into silence. When a professor proposed that the faculty affirm "the right of all members of the College community to the free expression of views in speech or in art," he was voted down. Where did the attacks come from? we ask, confused. Everywhere, he answers, blacks, whites, students, faculty, administrators; even now, he's perplexed by the demands for enforced civility that he reads as political correctness run rampant. "A strange sort of crucifixion," he calls it.

We shake our heads in bemusement until Bob brings up an e-mail he has just received from a white woman, "a friend of free expression," he says, who had been at the opening the night before. "She was really troubled and puzzled," he tells James, "because of your use of the word, ah . . . the word . . . ah, ah . . ." He stops. Something shifts, like a tiny tear in time. "Nigger," he says at last.

All afternoon, when we talked about sexuality, the artists have made easy villains of those who tried to suppress it, but now that we're talking about racism, the tone changes. I start to point that out, but when I come to the word *nigger*, to my surprise, I can't say it either. I know it's just a word, symbol, sound, know it's shaped by who says it and how and why, but when it comes to saying it now, in this room, something takes over. People who say it are people I don't want to be, and in my mouth right now, it makes me someone I don't want to be. I do say it eventually, but stumbling and too quiet.

"Maybe [the point of James's work] is to push your comfort zone," Ifé suggests, "because it's really hard for me to say *nigger* now and. . . ." She stops short in a contagion of self-consciousness. "I can't even say *white people*. You can't say *nigger* and I can't say *white people*! It's like if we don't have a dialogue, how the hell is this going to change?"

---

James tells a story. He attended an invitational exhibit at a community arts center in Hartford, which, despite the city's large Latino and black populations and the center's significant public funding, included no artists of color. "So I said, okay, I can't stand it. I said to a friend, give me some lipstick. I took the lipstick and I wrote on the walls under the exhibit on opening night"—someone gasps at the prospect—"NO COONS HERE." He wasn't invited back, but, in a notably cool curatorial response, his graffito was left on the wall as part of the show. "No one knows where to place me," he concludes. "I make work that's really questionable and edgy. It's not pretty work. In my case, the censorship centered around somehow not being connected."

"Maybe they just didn't like your work," says Jay, insisting against our laughter that he's serious, so that we have to acknowledge his point. Artists get spurned all the time: art involves making distinctions, and patronage disappoints more petitioners than it pleases. Yet while rejection by grant makers, curators, editors, directors, or critics is painful, it isn't usually censorship and would be hard to prove if it were. The market probably confounds censorship as often as it causes it, and artists don't get to control how their art is received, perceived, or used. The roundtable artists weren't just denied a grant or a gig, though. Someone wrested control of their art, not for interpretative purposes, but to prevent it from being seen, heard, read, or argued with by anyone else. While they had very practical reasons for resisting these attempts to make them toe someone else's line, their experiences also make clear what they were fighting for.

Art may not change us, but it can show us a way to change our mind. It allows us to muck about in the unimaginable, no small gift, and to do that requires license in all senses of the word—permission, liberation, boldness, immoderation, unruliness, any of which can be alarming. Art works by hitting its beholders directly, circumventing reason and other defenses we use to mediate between us and difficult ideas or emotions. When it succeeds, the response is charged too. The opposite of license is suppression, and though creativity may survive that, what is gained, save a certain cunning on the part of the creator and greater skill on the part of the audience at reading between the lines?

So do artists deserve special treatment? The easy answer is no, just the same freedom as everyone else. The more complex answer has to do with the modern, romantic ideal, battered but still alive, that exhorts artists to reckon by an inner compass, pandering neither to patron, ideology, nor profit. Art for art's sake: a credo we embrace, I suspect, because it implies that art isn't good for much else. But irrelevance wasn't these artists' problem. They got nailed for being too relevant about realities and fantasies their detractors thought better left alone. Yet they and hundreds of other artists around the country who were similarly attacked did nothing destructive or corrupt, let alone illegal. Their offense was to make art that somebody didn't like. Censorship seems an unduly harsh form of criticism.

# chapter eight
# THE SEDUCTION OF ABSOLUTES
## Skipp Porteus

*Great Barrington, Massachusetts, July 1997*

"The most savage controversies are those about matters as to which there is no good evidence either way," wrote Bertrand Russell.[1] This applies acutely to controversies over matters of faith, since faith needs no evidence, more often resents and rejects it. Still, Americans who feel their religious beliefs have been offended lay claim to protection both constitutional and divine. However the divine may manifest itself, the U.S. Constitution is very much of this world, albeit somewhat ambivalent when it comes to religion. Religion is addressed in the "conscience clauses" of the First Amendment: the free exercise clause prohibits the government from interfering with religious belief or practice, and the establishment clause bars the government from endorsing any religion. At times, these rights—to worship freely and to be free of religious coercion—conflict. That tension is particularly apparent when it comes to religious speech.

These internal contradictions are not lost on Skipp Porteus, who spent ten years as a fundamentalist pastor, then two decades as an anti-fundamentalist activist dedicated to tracking and exposing the religious right and groups that share their theocratic plan for America. "I was once one of these people," he writes in his memoir, *Jesus Doesn't Live Here Anymore*, and, even now, when he talks about fundamentalism, he sometimes slips into the first-person plural.

"It's sort of a weird place to start," he says, "but I remember that after I left fundamentalism, I felt ripped off. Fundamentalism was so horrible in so many ways, I felt like I had escaped. I never wanted to talk about it again. Maybe I wouldn't have if it weren't for Barbara." Barbara is Barbara Simon, Skipp's wife and cofounder of the Institute for First Amendment Studies, the nonprofit organization they have run since 1984. Skipp is fifty-three, average height, stocky. His face, a nice face, looks slightly owlish with its full cheeks, rosebud mouth, and high forehead. He watches me earnestly when he talks, listens thoughtfully when I do, clearly likes to laugh. So does Barbara, though she's more ironic. She looks like an Alice Neel portrait, with her prominent eyes and nose and a toothy smile that cracks her face wide open. She's wide open too, milking her stories for dramatic effect, swooping her fingers through the air, angling her long body across the coffee table toward where I sit, as if to pull me along.

The past year, they moved the institute from their home into a two-story building on Main Street in Great Barrington, a pretty town in the southern Berkshires that swells to bursting with tourists each summer. House-proud, Barbara shows me "before" photos—it was a derelict SRO hotel, knee-deep in junk when it was given to them—then gives me a tour, admiring the spanking new spaciousness herself, as if for the first time.

Fundamentalism is another world, Skipp says. It's meant to be, and to understand it, you need to know some basic concepts. "There's three things [fundamentalists] fear: the world, the flesh, and the devil. They believe the devil is literally around trying to tempt them. They're in a cocoon, a heavenly world, and everything else they call the world." In addition to the unsaved, that "everything else" includes nonfundamentalist Christians, and Skipp (along with the mainstream media at times) uses "Christian" when he means "evangelical Christian." He illustrates this mind-set by citing a fund-raising letter in which Pat Robertson called on "all 45 million Christians" to vote, though evangelicals constitute a little more than one-fourth of the Americans who call themselves Christian. "We were," he concludes, "very special."

Only apparently not too special. "To become a born-again Christian, you've got to believe that you are a rotten sinner destined for hell. But the good news is that Jesus can save you. They're always harping on sin and guilt. Guilt is what gets people into born-again Christianity and guilt is what keeps them there."

"They should be Jewish," I say, which is when Skipp informs me that he is, having converted the year before. More observant than Barbara, who was born and raised a Jew, he keeps kosher, doesn't work or use a computer on the Sabbath. As a former insider who knows the Bible, speaks the language, and once shared the beliefs of the born-again, Skipp must have offered a tantalizing challenge to those who would rescue him anew. "People used to call me up after I left the church, saying they have a few scriptures they want to share with me," he says.

"That and they were always praying for you," Barbara adds.

"They have this superior attitude, which is why I think what we do today is because of hatred," Skipp continues. "Not hatred on our part, but on the Christian part. Many of these Christians are full of hate. They don't want to find middle ground. They just feel they're absolutely right and everybody better fall in step with them." In a survey of conservative Christian activists the institute commissioned, one-third of respondents identified the ACLU as the most dangerous group in America (only 5 percent said private militia were), and over 80 percent believed that these dangerous groups should not be allowed to operate legally and that their members should be barred from making speeches and running for public office.[2] "I believe in the separation of church and state and the Constitution and all these things that we base what we do on, but the biggest reason I'm doing this is because these people in many cases are so bad that I think they need to be countered, slowed down a bit."

So I couldn't have this conversation with a fundamentalist? Sure I could, he says. Evangelicals want to talk about their faith as a way to bring others into the fold. "We were taught in Bible school that every human being has a God-shaped hole that only Jesus Christ can fill."

That's nice, a God-shaped hole. The vocabulary of evangelism, so ripe and evocative—*glossolalia, backsliding, slain in the spirit*—appeals to me and soon I find myself speaking in apocalyptic tropes and metaphors too. Except that, for evangelicals, apocalypse isn't a metaphor. They read the Bible literally, which is probably why some read everything else literally as well. The Bible is believed to be "inerrant," never wrong, never in doubt. All you need to know is there; you just have to puzzle it out.

In the early years of the institute, Barbara reports, they included a glossary of fundamentalist terms in their newsletter as a translation service. What bowls her over still is the Rapture, during which, as she describes it, "Jesus was going to come back and, like a major Electrolux vacuum, suck up all the true adherents and the rest of us will be left here to be destroyed in a nuclear holocaust." Skipp jumps up to rifle in a desk behind me and returns with a colorful, naive-art postcard depicting believers levitating through the skies, their arms outstretched like newly minted wings, while an alarmed-looking pilot steers his airplane around them. "Everything about fundamentalist Christianity is negative," he says, "all leading up to Armageddon, the destruction of Israel, the Third World War, and Jesus coming back."

"Why is that comforting?" I ask.

"Goodness should be rewarded. Badness is punished," Barbara recites, adding that this absolves you of responsibility for your actions or their consequences.

"I used to make prayer lists," Skipp tells me. "I'd write down a list of what I prayed for, and when God answered the prayer I'd [write down] the answer. It's amazing how all these needs were met by God. So after I left Christianity, I made a mental note of what I needed and wanted and kept mental track of how these things came about, and it always happened anyway."

---

I live in a secular world. That's not to say that people in it don't confess all the time. A magazine article extolling the joys of spanking or a play-by-play of a session on the couch is commonplace, but almost no one I know talks about faith, at least not without quotation marks or apology and never as simply and directly as Skipp. As he instructs me in the ways of fundamentalism, it feels too intimate and my inquisitiveness feels wrong, like sightseeing in a land where the natives talk of nothing else.

"Ever since I could remember," Skipp says, "I always felt something spiritual, a relationship with God." He grew up in a close-knit family in Hillsdale, New York, a small town in the Grandma Moses country between the Hudson River and the Massachusetts border. Named Charles after his father and grandfather, he was called Skipper, which he shortened to Skipp and later took as his legal name. His grandparents owned the town's hardware store, his father worked there, his mother ran a boardinghouse, and the whole family attended the Methodist church. Religion was a Sunday morning sort of thing, but even then Skipp excelled at the "sword drills," which are races to find specific Bible passages to use as weapons against nonbelievers.

He was a mischievous kid and an indifferent student, but he liked art class, so when a fundamentalist couple moved to town and began an arts and crafts club, he joined. That they showed Billy Graham movies was an added treat, since the nearest cinema was ten miles away. Little by little, he was drawn into fundamentalism until, at age eleven, he "went forward" to be born again. "It's a step-by-step process," he explains. "This is calculated on their part. I was vulnerable." He spent two summers at what he calls "a Holy Roller camp," where he learned to box, met a young Pat Robertson (once also a boxer), and planned to preach the gospel on the streets of his town until his mother squashed that idea. Then one day, the Bible seemed no more than an adolescent infatuation, and he put it away. He had it practically memorized anyway.

After high school, Skipp moved to Manhattan, where the world opened up for him. He worked at decorating department store windows, roomed with a born-again Christian and then an atheist, met gays and lesbians for the first time, attended performances at Harlem's Apollo Theater, and had a very good time. When his draft board started breathing down his neck, he applied for a conscientious objection exemption. His CO was rejected, but he remained determined not to fight in Vietnam, so when he fell in love, it made sense to take advantage of the marriage exemption. His wife, Linda, was sixteen; her father gave his permission to marry if she promised to finish high school.

That was in 1964, a fine time to be young and footloose. They packed up their Mustang and headed west, landing in Los Angeles, where Skipp got a job at a munitions factory and a coworker introduced him to the People's Tabernacle of Faith. The first time he and Linda attended a service, the singing and preaching and dancing in the spirit, the call and response and speaking in tongues, were like nothing they had ever seen, but it got into their heads and they found themselves returning. Soon Skipp was listening to Christian radio, attending services and prayer breakfasts diligently, and building his life around the church. First, it was Pentecostalism, then a charismatic subsect that embraced the spiritual gifts of faith healing, prophecy, and speaking in tongues, or glossolalia. Finally, they landed in something called End Time Ministries, whose adherents believe themselves chosen to usher in the Second Coming.

For all its emphasis on "traditional values," Protestant fundamentalism barely predates the twentieth century. Its tenets were established in 1895, and Pentecostalism began on New Year's Eve of 1901. For the next quarter-century, fundamentalists were active in the political sphere, notably in the evolution-versus-creationism debate surrounding the 1925 Scopes trial. Creationism won in court, but fundamentalism lost in the court of public opinion, and, according to Bruce Bawer in his 1997 book *Stealing Jesus,* it "proceeded to withdraw from the public square and remained essentially withdrawn from it for nearly half a century."[3] Out of the secular public eye, however, fundamentalist churches continued to thrive and were undergoing a growth spurt in the 1960s, when Skipp became involved.

The kind of zealotry he found is distasteful to him now, but at the time, the bright division between right and wrong was comforting. Absolute faith moored him, gave him a community, made him feel safe and valuable and, best of all, right. He quit his day job, sold insurance at night, and enrolled in LIFE—Lighthouse of International Foursquare Evangelism—Bible College, which had been founded by the flamboyant revivalist Aimee Semple McPherson. He wanted to preach, to "win souls," and Hollywood's Sunset Strip offered an abundance of opportunity. With friends, he rented an office across the street from the Playboy Club, called it the Chapel on the Strip, and, entrepreneurial by nature, projected Billy Graham movies on a huge rockface behind the chapel. The movies were popular, the mission less so. A lot of the lost souls they encountered were runaways, young kids who had fled as far west as they could and had nowhere else to go. "I could see this need that was so visible," he says. "They left Iowa with the shirt on their back, they had no job, no food, nothing. First obligation was to see that their needs were met, to help them physically, and then you talked about the gospel and saving your soul." His fellow evangelists disagreed, arguing that there was no need for social work, since once you accepted Jesus, everything else would take care of itself. Frustrated, Skipp left the chapel.

Around this time, he was introduced to radical doctrine embraced by various factions of what would soon unite as the religious right, including *Dare to Discipline,* in which James Dobson, the Dr. Spock of the movement, advocates corporal punishment for children, and *The Protocols of the Elders of Zion,* an anti-Semitic tract that, though a forgery, is taken as authentic by the paranoid right. Skipp found things in these books and his studies that sounded suspect, but he swallowed his doubts and dedicated himself to deeper faith, and in May 1968, he was ordained by the Harvest Fields Missionary and Evangelistic Association. What followed was a busy time, as a weekly Bible study group he led grew into a small ministry, then a church. It was officially named Eagle Rock Assembly, but everyone called it Skipp's church. He performed dozens of exorcisms, hosted a weekly radio program called *Pastor Porteous Shares,* started a home school (he and Linda now had three children), and established a ministry in Indio, California, and a second church in Baja, Mexico.

In 1974, his mother got sick and he wanted to raise his kids in the East, so he took a job at the West Copake Dutch Reformed Church near where he had grown up. Fundamentalist groups were beginning to return to politics, and in 1976, Skipp agreed to be New York State coordinator for "If My People," a lavish, gospel musical that he calls a God-and-country rally. The plan was to present the show in the capital city of every state. "Our feeling was if we could start a revival in a state capital, it would affect politicians and start turning things around. That was very naive." The auditorium in Albany was half empty, and the take at the door didn't cover expenses. "See, they'd been testing the waters, trying to figure this out," Skipp says of those planning a political-religious revival. "They started rethinking how they were going to approach politics as Christians, and then they set out to try to teach Christians there was a new way of thinking about politics." Heeding the call, he ran for school board on a Christian platform and almost won. "We thought this was supposed to be a Christian nation, but it had fallen away and in order to save it, we had to make it a Christian nation again. See, America is so crucial because it's like a missionary outpost of the world. If America falls, the rest of the world is going to fall."

---

In a country defined by Enlightenment faith in individual responsibility, the centrality of debate and compromise in governance, and the rule of civil law as separate from religious law, the insistence that America is a Christian nation is confusing. The Declaration of Independence does talk about rights endowed by the Creator, but the founding fathers' take on religion was essentially practical. They saw it as a constructive social force.[4] In contrast, the religious right reads the Bible as a blueprint for society, in which religious principles transcend democratic ones, and therein lies the problem: not that religion has no place in politics, but that the politics of the religious right are aimed at undermining the rights of others.

The religious right emerged as a significant political force early in the 1980s, when veterans of Barry Goldwater's 1964 Republican presidential campaign, who saw in conservative Christians a large, untapped constituency, joined forces with right-wing religious leaders, who saw an opportunity to impose their morality through government. Conservative Christians had been taught that they were citizens of heaven, a loftier affiliation than any on earth; now they were encouraged to stop being "the silent majority" and to register to vote. In 1979, Jerry Falwell founded the Moral Majority, which was joined by groups with similar philosophies, such as Concerned Women for America, Focus on the Family, Citizens for Excellence in Education, and the American Family Association. Ten years later, after his failed bid for the Republican presidential nomination, Pat Robertson founded the Christian Coalition and ushered in a second wave of religious right activism with a mission repackaged to be more widely palatable but no less theocratic.

America goes through cycles of confusing civic virtue and private morality, and in the 1980s, several factors came together to make the country receptive to the message and tactics of the religious right. Triumphant at the ending of the Cold War, the United States anointed itself the world's moral leader, but losing our common enemy left us feeling unmoored, and we turned our discontent inward. New technology made it easier for people to share that discontent by communicating their beliefs and opinions widely. It also broadened the reach of a popular culture dedicated to pushing at boundaries. In the backlash that ensued, evocations of "family values" resonated with some baby boomers who were reassessing their values—and apparently concluding that parenthood led inexorably to buying a station wagon and voting Republican. Meanwhile, political alignments shifted. Without communism to battle, conservative politics lost their focus, creating a vacuum that political-religious groups were only too happy to fill with a rhetoric of absolutism that, in contrast to the increasingly priggish and whiny confusion on the left, sounded refreshingly clear.

Within the decade, the religious right had made its political mark. By 1992, 42 percent of the delegates to the Republican National Convention would be evangelicals.[5] Two years later, the religious right would dominate the Republican parties in Virginia, Texas, Minnesota, and Iowa. Two years after that, the Christian Coalition would claim two million members and a $26 million budget, and Concerned Women for America would bill itself as the country's largest women's organization with six hundred thousand members. These membership figures proved to be exaggerations, and the vitriol of the 1992 convention scared off a lot of voters, but the religious right regrouped and returned in 1994, helping conservative Republicans take control of both houses of Congress for the first time in forty years.

Adept at framing issues, the political-religious right gained ground through shrewd use of the law, mass media, and marketing techniques pioneered by direct-mail whiz Richard Viguerie. They created organizing kits, lobbied Congress, staged boycotts, got elected to school boards, distributed voter guides in churches, and repeated their themes on radio and TV, in newspaper ads, and in overwrought funding appeals that named a roster of villains whom only they could vanquish. ("Do you remember when you could go to the corner store without locking the doors of your home . . . those were the days before terrorism and AIDS . . . when abortion was a horrifying rarity instead of a political cause," says a fund-raising letter from the Coral Ridge Ministries in Florida,[6] neatly blending nostalgia, fear, and a soothing rewrite of history.) These are legal and mostly standard political strategies, including demonizing opponents to raise money, but the religious right routinely betrayed a contempt for democratic processes—for instance, fielding "stealth candidates" who kept their philosophy and affiliation secret until after being elected.

In the administration of Ronald Reagan, these groups found a government conveniently disdainful of the First Amendment and comfortable with their vision of an American society delineated by moral pieties. As the government promoted policies that weakened the boundaries between public and private and made it clear that intolerance would be tolerated, it became easy for some people's lives to become other people's crusade. According to Skipp, abortion was a "nonissue" within fundamentalism for the four years between 1973, when it became legal nationally, and 1977, when he left the church. Soon enough, the religious right made it *the* issue, along with homosexuality, pornography, independent women, and, for good symbolic measure, the National Endowment for the Arts, demonstrating that it isn't a big leap from trying to save souls to trying to save institutions.

It would be nice if, as contemporary revivalists claim, America did have a special relationship with God. We need all the help we can get. But our Constitution is a secular document, concerned with the rights and duties of men here on earth, and it locates power in the people, not in some higher force. Nowhere does it mention God, and when it alludes to morality, it is to moral autonomy. (Its neutrality on this score is what ends up ticking off nearly everyone eventually.) Our civic-religious incantations are relatively recent too: "In God We Trust" didn't show up regularly on coins until 1908 and didn't become our official motto until 1956. "Under God" was added to the Pledge of Allegiance in 1954 in a bout of anticommunist fervor.

Still, religion is important to our country, which has always been fertile ground for spiritual quests and new religions (all that wilderness) and generally welcoming to those fleeing religious persecution. Despite, or maybe because of, our identity as a secular nation, Americans are a theistic people. Nine out of ten adults say they believe in God, and six out of ten voters claim to attend religious services regularly.[7] Such self-reporting merits a grain or two of salt, but, even so, these percentages are higher than in many countries that make less fuss about church-state relations. At the same time, Americans have never liked being told what to believe, especially by the government, so we resist anything that smacks of official doctrine. What we want, it seems, is a secularism blessed by God.

---

Skipp probably would have become active in this religious-political efflorescence had the world not caught up with him in a different way. About a year after they moved east, his wife left him. She returned a month later, but by then it was clear that they had never shared much more than religious fervor, and he too wanted out. When she walked out a second time, leaving their kids, aged ten, seven, and five, behind, he knew that the marriage was over.

In a small town, nothing stays secret for long, so his fractured family was soon common knowledge. Contributions to his radio ministry dried up, speaking engagements got canceled, friends shunned him. He says, "I have the three kids and my wife is gone. I was being criticized a lot by people in the church, especially people on our board. We had an elders meeting and there were a couple real strong critics that felt they couldn't have confidence in me until my home was back together again. There's something in the Bible about how if you can't manage your own house, how can you manage the house of God?" (Despite this sentiment, born-again Christians are slightly more likely than the rest of the population to have been divorced.)[8] The best thing to do, he decided, was to leave his church and move his family from the rectory to an apartment in his parents' house a few towns over. He would take a sabbatical and make time for reflection, he figured a year at most.

Skipp's first job out of the ministry defined secularism. At a small-town newspaper, he did a little of everything: sales, layout, photography, the police beat. "I was working seven days a week, so I never went to any Bible study or any of that stuff that they use to keep you going," he says. "At the end of that year, I just started seeing things more clearly. I started thinking these people are nuts. I just felt so good."

One night, Skipp shadowed a police officer as research for a news story, and as he and the cop sat in the cruiser shooting the breeze, he asked what the county was doing about the drug problem. What drug problem? came the reply. Skipp knew a fair amount about local drug use through his ministry, so he called the sheriff to talk about it. A few days later, the sheriff called back to offer him an undercover job. He took it, keeping his day job at the paper as cover.

My eyebrows shoot up at this bit of news, as I imagine most journalists' would. But Skipp's concern had to do with betraying his parishioners' confidence, not journalistic ethics. "Most of the people in the bars didn't know who Reverend Porteous was, but rumors started getting around, apparently," he says of his new identity. "I grew my hair pretty long for the job."

"He missed the sixties," Barbara explains gently.

His task was to get in with the local dealers and buy as much dope as he could, since the bigger the bust, the longer the sentence. Skipp relished the cloak-and-dagger (he later became a licensed private eye), and it was fun to hang out at bars with an expense account and the law on his side. One assignment was to follow an arsonist, a student at the local community college, who had been cast in a play by none other than Barbara, who had recently moved up from New York City to teach. Skipp made up a story about being a graduate student and sat in on rehearsals, but his cover was blown when one of the actresses whispered to Barbara, "You know he's a narc."

Annoyed, she confronted him, demanding, "Are you a narc?"

"Absolutely," he replied.

"And I thought, yuck!" Barbara finishes. But they got to talking, he convinced her that his purpose was honorable, and pretty soon, they were friends, then more than that. Barbara didn't date non-Jews, which is what she told Skipp when he asked her out. The problem was that she really liked him. "I thought, am I going to make my life a life of labels or a life of substance?" she says now. They got married four years later.

By then, the newspaper had closed, Skipp's sleuthing had wound down, and rumors that he was on a hit list discouraged him from accepting a uniform police job. Meanwhile, Barbara had quit her professorship the day she got tenure. They were living in Great Barrington with his younger daughter, and they were ready to move on to something new.

---

In 1984, Skipp watched with alarm as evangelists Jerry Falwell and Pat Robertson were given pride of place at the Republican National Convention in Dallas. "It brought back to me what the movement that I left was trying to do and I thought they'd never be successful," he says. He and Barbara were vacationing in England and reading the *Herald Tri-*

*bune,* he recalls, when something clicked. "I said, I know these people and I don't like it. I started explaining this whole thing to Barbara and we felt, let's do something about it." They decided to chart the activities of the religious right and publicize them through a newsletter. They called it the *Freedom Writer,* gave it the slogan, "A hard look at the hard right," and sent the first issue to one hundred people they hoped would be interested. (Its circulation grew at one time to over fifty thousand.)

Like dominoes, each piece of activism led to another. Barbara returned home one day, steaming over a program devoted to ultraconservative political views that she had heard on the Albany public radio station. They called to ask for equal time, and though the station refused, it offered to interview them. A teacher at Simon's Rock College in Great Barrington heard the interview and invited Skipp to speak. It had been seven years since he had spoken in public and he was nervous, then startled as the room filled to capacity. His talk about the philosophy and aims of the then-obscure religious right got the attention of the local newspaper, the *Berkshire Eagle,* which gave it front-page coverage.

The next step was to set up the Institute for First Amendment Studies, a rather grand name for an organization that consisted of two volunteers—them—working out of their living room. They decided to concentrate on information and education, and their method boiled down to getting hold of speeches, interviews, testimony, and documents from religious right organizations, then skewering the groups with their own words. To avoid ambiguity or misrepresentation, they ran lengthy quotes in *Freedom Writer:* for example, reprinting in full Pat Robertson's rambling exhortation to stone those who believe in UFOs and space aliens.[9] Barbara got a law degree to be able to speak authoritatively on constitutional issues, and Skipp used his familiarity with the thinking of the religious right. With his undercover skills, he was able to infiltrate some organizations and plant moles in others. They had "someone inside" the Council for National Policy, an elite group of the far right, which closed its meetings to the press and kept its membership list confidential until the institute posted it on its Web site. When another volunteer became publisher of the newsletter for the Albany chapter of the Christian Coalition, the institute printed the mailing labels, which allowed them to see the newsletter before it went to the printer. Skipp brags that their guy even got invited to a party at Pat Robertson's house.

Perhaps their biggest coup came in 1986, when Skipp penetrated the inner sanctum of the National Federation for Decency, the cultural watchdog group in Tupelo, Mississippi, that Donald Wildmon founded and later renamed the American Family Association. Though Wildmon wasn't yet well known, Skipp sensed he would be a player, so he got on the NFD mailing list as "Reverend Charles Porter" and organized a local chapter. On the strength of trumped-up press coverage, he became their fair-haired boy. He went to Mississippi and got a tour of the facilities, candid responses to his questions, and time with Wildmon before someone checked out his bona fides and called in the cops. Skipp was escorted out unceremoniously, but he writes with obvious satisfaction, "My sources tell me that Wildmon loves to tell this story to his friends in Tupelo."[10]

The institute was among the first organizations to monitor the political-religious right and one of the few to get its hands dirty. As a pay-off, Skipp and Barbara have come across remarkable material. In 1994, a volunteer bought a photocopy of a *Field Manual of the Free Militia* (at that point not yet published) from a pastor leading an antiabortion meeting in Wisconsin. Apparently intended as a primer for anyone contemplating joining a private militia, it provides a rationale for a citizens' army to protect religious freedom, other individual rights, and gun ownership, then offers practical advice for arming, organizing, and avoiding detection. The institute was never able to learn who wrote it, but a note under the copyright notice reads, "Any American citizen who desires to secure and defend the blessings of liberty for himself and his posterity may freely copy from this material." Reasoning that it's a good idea to know how your enemies think, they published it.

Skipp sends me back to my hotel with a copy, which makes for creepy bedtime reading, especially when it's not unhinged enough to dismiss. There is standard-issue patriotism—"The fact that rights are unalienable [*sic*] by a government and cannot be outweighed by the interests of the majority is incontestable"[11]—sermonic imperatives—"If you are a Bible believer, you must be committed to following its moral standards"[12]— and exhortations that would resonate with civil libertarians—"If you become convinced that the federal government is bent on systematic violations of our personal liberties, it is your moral duty and obligation to join with others so convinced to restore true liberty for all Americans."[13] The rub comes when political critique turns into fanaticism and the rhetoric of resistance into a call for armed rebellion. "It's one thing to talk about militias, but it's another thing to show from their own writing what they believe, why and what their intentions are," Skipp says. The manual became one of their best-sellers, particularly during the trial of Oklahoma City bomber Timothy McVeigh.

The institute became a resource for people who, in Barbara's words, were "getting their first taste of what it's like to stand up for the constitutional right to be free from religious intrusion in public life." Many requests for help came from mainstream Republicans, alarmed by the religious right's inroads into their party. The mainstream media also found Skipp and Barbara reliable—and in Skipp's case, exotic—sources. He did hundreds of talk shows, including debates with Jerry Falwell, Donald Wildmon, Tim LeHaye, and textbook censor Mel Gabler. He also had an instinct for making news: for the Fourth of July in 1989, he responded to the debate over a flag-burning amendment by selling flags treated with flame retardant. "The best reason not to burn the flag is because we can," he reasoned,[14] leading the *New York Times* to laud him on its editorial page.

But publicity is double-edged, and the institute was no more able to control its public image than other small organizations. "People don't have a true picture of who we are and what we do," Barbara complains. "I think it has been shaped by the way the media characterizes us."

"Antireligious sometimes, which we're not. Troublemakers," says Skipp.

"Antimilitia," adds Barbara.

"You wouldn't think that would be bad," Skipp comments.

Ironically, their worst publicity came from their being good citizens. Within two hours of the Oklahoma City bombing, while the government was still focusing on foreign terrorists as the perpetrators, a source faxed them that the bombers were members of the Christian Identity movement, which places Christian doctrine above the Constitution and rejects the federal government as illegitimate. The fax was followed by a computer disk with an annotated mailing lists of forty-five thousand right-wing sympathizers and activists in the western part of the country.

Skipp and Barbara called the Bureau of Alcohol, Tobacco and Firearms (ATF), the federal agency investigating the bombing, to tell them what they knew. "We don't usually go out of our way to write to the federal government and say, hey, hey," Barbara says, "but we had this and we thought, if it could help, we wanted it to help." The ATF said it would send agents to pick up the list, in hard copy, please, so Barbara and Skipp dedicated the weekend and nine reams of paper to printing it out. On Sunday afternoon, logy from the task, Skipp went to the drugstore, where he ran into a pal who worked for the *Berkshire Eagle*. What's new? his friend asked, and, forgetting that reporters report, Skipp told him. The next morning, the story was front-page news, and by noon, the national media descended, followed by anonymous phone threats from local militia members, nervous about what the list contained.

Not long after, they were at home one night, Skipp in the front room talking on the phone, Barbara in the back brushing her teeth, when they heard a car slow down, then speed up as something seemed to hit the house—"whup it," Barbara says—and ricochet off, perhaps into the woods behind. They couldn't be sure, still aren't, but it may have been a bullet. After much discussion—Did it happen? Are we paranoid? Will the police think we're paranoid?—they reported the incident. Nothing was found and the matter was dropped, but not before a local paper ran the headline "Shots Fired at Porteous."

Skipp describes himself as politically conservative and Barbara says she's mainstream, but in shining light on extreme ideas, they attracted extremist ire. "Perhaps we do become more of a focus because we do stand for democracy and pluralism and there are many people in our midst who don't support that notion," Barbara suggests. About a year before we talk, Eustace Mullins, an author of anti-Semitic tracts clothed as commentary on monetary policy, was invited to speak in a neighboring town. When Skipp reported on the visit in a column he wrote for the *Berkshire Jewish Voice*, Mullins's host sued Skipp and the newspaper for libel. Libel lawsuits are an important way for people to preserve their reputations, but they can also be used to silence opposing views and intimidate those who hold them. Though Skipp eventually won his case, the paper canceled his column and stopped reporting on extremist activities in the area. Mullins himself tried a different tack; he brought a $34 million First Amendment lawsuit against Skipp for conspiring to prevent him from speaking and, according to documents in the case, "fabricat[ing] this assault . . . with the expectation that the shock would prove too much for his fragile health, and would eventually cause a fatal stroke or heart attack." Two years later, that suit was thrown out of court, but it was costly to fight, and, as Barbara points out, "Whenever you've been sued, the public impression is you must have done something wrong."

———

The freelance militia Skipp reported on and the hate-mongers who sued him represent a radical minority within the religious right that is itself a minority. Estimates of its size range from 22 percent of the electorate,[15] to 5 percent of the population, or fifteen to twenty million adults,[16] to one-third of Republicans.[17] "The religious right . . . knows by sheer numbers they can't take over," Skipp says firmly. Yet it has had a disproportionate effect, and he and Barbara suggest several reasons: impressive organization, healthy funding based on the concept of tithing, unified goals and large national events to reinforce that unity, a divvying up of causes to avoid overlap, and an authoritarian tradition. "The religious right . . . cooperate[s] much more than liberals do," Skipp says. "They're like a snapping turtle who grabs something and never lets go. We see the school board taken over by the religious right, so next year we vote them all out and we think we've done our duty and we go on to something else. Meanwhile, they sneak back." And get voted out again. In American politics, we gravitate to the middle, and it is human nature to react more to crisis than stasis.

Skipp isn't opposed to politicians drawing on their religious principles, or to evangelicals being politically active. "Just because someone is a minister or priest or rabbi doesn't exclude them from the political process. Your religious views affect the way you think and live and vote." This echoes Flannery O'Connor, a writer of a deep religious faith, in her advice to young writers that "your beliefs will be the light by which you see, but they will not be what you see and they will not be a substitute for seeing."[18] It is the substitution, the clouded vision, that concerns Skipp. "What I object to is more [when] an organized religious body wants to impose its will on people. For many years, evangelical Christians weren't registered to vote. So Ralph Reed [then head of the Christian Coalition] wants us to come to the table. That sounds nice but they want the whole damn table!"

In the early days of the institute, he says, "People saw democracy as under attack by the religious right. Today, the religious right is part of the democracy. So you talk about the religious right, what else is new? That's your danger." Skipp observes that "for all the years and all the effort and all the money they put into their work, they haven't accomplished a lot." Except, of course, for a sea change in public opinion about what it is acceptable to talk about, teach, or read.

---

J. M. Coetzee identifies a range of attitudes about public moralism and the censorship that enforces it. The liberal position, with its origins in John Stuart Mill's 1859 essay "On Liberty," gives individual rights priority and seeks to shield them from imposed morality; hence, it opposes censorship. A moderate position sees shared morality as a kind of social glue and moral infractions as attacks on the social order; therefore, it tolerates some censorship as necessary. The conservative position, valuing morality in itself, condones anything required to protect it, including censorship.[19]

The religious right upped the ante by embracing censorship, not just as necessary for morality, but as a desirable end in itself. Tolerance holds little charm for true believers, regardless of what they believe in. For fundamentalists, dissenting words and ideas are not just dangerous but Satan's playthings, and, Skipp asks rhetorically, why should you tolerate evil? If the ideas, books, and people you reject are forces of darkness, then they must be destroyed before they lead the innocent and unsuspecting astray. By this thinking, disfavored speech merits little protection and—a dispiriting prospect—the only possible resolution to arguments over what falls into that category is the eradication of opposing views.

The Christian Coalition and friends didn't fight the culture wars single-handedly; the tensions grew in response to large social changes, including those brought by liberation movements in civil rights, feminism, and gay rights. The religious right would not have been able to commandeer the debate as it has, however, if more moderate people weren't also drawn to moral correctives to stubborn social problems. It's easier to ban books than to ensure that everyone knows how to read them, or to arrest parents for photographing naked kids than to stop domestic brutality. When a culture is in upheaval, words and images make particularly appealing scapegoats, and the religious right has shrewdly played on our longing for a time when the costs of our culture of liberty seemed less extravagant. "The country has become more diverse and people have to realize that," Skipp argues. Except that the country has always been diverse. We just didn't talk about it. Now we talk about it so much that it sometimes seems as if what binds us as a country are the divisions between us. Religion is part of that diversity, one of the identities by which Americans define themselves and their role in society.

---

In his postfundamentalist incarnation, Skipp purports to be for "open expression of everything. I just think all kinds of ideas are permissible to have and promote. Their truth and righteousness and goodness I think will always settle on top eventually." I'm less optimistic about the triumph of truth, or maybe just less patient, so I test. What about the students who are told they can't read their Bibles in study hall?

Barbara dismisses this as propaganda: "Pat Robertson on every *700 Club* will tell you about some poor child who's prohibited from reading his Bible in public school because God has been kicked out of the class-room." But there are documented instances of students and teachers barred from praying in school, usually because they are proselytizing and disrupting class, but not always. Taking a page from the ACLU, the right has set up legal organizations, such as the Rutherford Institute and American Center for Law and Justice, to defend individual religious rights in court. The Rutherford Institute alone says it responds to "hundreds of complaints of free speech violations each year."[20]

"It's interesting to try to verify these things," Skipp says. "Obviously there's freedom of religion in schools. But if a teacher says, 'All right, class, it's time to pray,' that would be wrong because the state would be teaching . . .'"

"It's state-sponsored prayer," Barbara interjects. "Once you have state-sponsored anything, you have coercion, and state-sponsored prayer is violation of the establishment clause." The Supreme Court made this resoundingly clear in a landmark ruling that supported Jehovah's Witnesses, whose beliefs restrained them from saluting the flag: "If there is any fixed star in our constitutional constellation, it is that no official, high or petty, can prescribe what shall be orthodox in politics, nationalism, religion, or other matters of opinion or force citizens to confess by word or act their faith therein."[21]

This decision, written in 1943, signaled a shift in the reading of the First Amendment's conscience clauses, but the principle of isolating education from religion has long been used to serve conflicting purposes. According to Jeffrey Rosen, writing in the *New York Times,* opposition to government funding of religious schools began as anti-Catholic sentiment when public education began to flourish after the Civil War, then got a boost after World War II from Jewish groups who took it up as a shield against discrimination.[22] Later, as public schools were integrated in the South, white students fled to parochial schools, thereby perpetuating de facto segregation.

Still, the trend toward clearer separation continued as indirect support for parochial schools was ruled unconstitutional in 1947,[23] and mandatory prayer was banned from schools in 1962 and Bible reading in 1963. (A graph in an American Family Association publication purports to link the decline in SAT scores with the prohibition on school prayer.)[24] In 1971, the Court disallowed states from trying to equalize per-student expenditures by supplementing salaries of teachers who taught secular subjects at religious schools. This case, *Lemon v Kurtzman,* was the high-water mark of church-school separation, and it held for nearly two decades until the political-religious revival of the 1980s brought pressure to reverse it.

During the 1990s, courts went back and forth on religion-and-school issues. The Supreme Court has permitted student fees to be used for religious journals of opinion, tax money to be spent on educational materials at religious schools, school buildings to be open to student religious groups after the school day, and, in 2002, the use of school vouchers, most of which go to pay tuition at parochial schools. On the other hand, it has continued to forbid prayer in classrooms and at school-sponsored events. (After the Supreme Court ruled against prayers at school football games, some southern communities, where football seems to be a religion in itself, planned "spontaneous" prayers.)

In June 2002, a three-judge panel of a federal appeals court in California found the inclusion of "under God" in the Pledge of Allegiance unconstitutional and ruled against its recitation in schools in nine western states.[25] Amid much hue and cry (President Bush called the ruling "ridiculous," the House condemned it in a 416 to 3 vote), the judge who issued the opinion blocked it from taking effect pending an appeal, which came soon after.

Legalities aside, students and teachers continue to pray in public school, as they have for most of our history. Where once they did it with official sanction, now it is with officials turning a blind eye because school prayer is very much in line with public sentiment. In a 2000 poll, only 19 percent of respondents opposed all prayer, including a moment of silence, in schools, and only 37 percent agreed that school prayer violated the Constitution.[26] Interestingly, evangelicals split evenly over supporting or opposing a constitutional amendment on the issue.[27]

"The government has to be neutral toward religion, not for or against it," Skipp says as if he's said it a million times, which he probably has. But religious organizations do receive special treatment from the government, including exemptions from taxes and some regulations, such as nondiscriminatory hiring. (This last has been a bone of contention in the congressional debate over a faith-based initiative championed by the Bush administration that would permit federal funding of religious groups providing social services.) "I agree that students should be able to pray any time they want to at school," Skipp continues, "but if you're doing it in a gathering where people are required to attend, then you're forcing religion on people who may not want to have it."

Schools are full of speech people don't want to hear, as we shall see in the next chapter. Is religious speech a special category, more intrusive, more powerful—the argument made for restricting sexual expression—than other speech? Or is banning prayer in school simply a practical decision, since the variety of religious practices, beliefs, and nonbeliefs in America makes it impossible to deal with religion objectively? Individual, silent prayer has never been at issue, and Skipp asks, why do you need official or communal praying in school, anyway? The religious right has pushed the issue, he claims, not for greater godliness, but out of missionary zeal.

Not a way to teach morality or values? "You can teach that without teaching Christianity or any other religion," he shoots back.

———

I need only open my city's newspaper to find examples of what is at stake in these conflicts, starting with the annual argument over erecting a crèche on public property. This year's skirmish took place on the Lexington Green, where the American Revolution began, which made for fine rhetoric when the town council invoked the First Amendment and said no to a manger scene there. A group of people protested by performing a live crèche, which strikes me as an improvement over the plastic reindeer and snowmen added to sanitize religious scenes elsewhere.

Then there is the city north of Boston that, as a fund-raiser, sold bricks for a park pathway to individuals to inscribe with personal messages. All went well until officials rejected two bricks reading "Jesus Loves You" and "For All the Unborn Children." When the author of the unborn-child brick sued on First Amendment grounds, she claimed that she was commemorating a child she had lost and expressed amazement that anyone could assume her message was political.[28] How disingenuous that sounds probably depends on your views about abortion, but the free speech claim seems solid, since, once the government permits personal expression on public property, it's not supposed to discriminate among the messages it allows.

As I think about these controversies, I return to my own public education, when, for years, the school day began with a reading from the King James Bible and recitation of the Lord's Prayer. Though my religious heritage put me in a tiny minority, I can't say these rituals of Christianity made much difference to me one way or the other, except that I learned all the verses of Christmas carols. Like many kids, I learned to slough off what I didn't connect with, and like most minorities, I learned a lot about the majority. I don't mean to generalize from my experience, or to propose it as a basis for legality, but as I pick my way through the controversies, I'm nagged by the suspicion that when separation of church and state is interpreted to prohibit, not just state endorsement of religious speech, but any public display of religion, the result may be a form of censorship.

So where to draw the line between religious speech as protected expression and religious speech as coercion or interference? Seldom is the struggle more acrimonious than over antiabortion protests. Since the federal Freedom of Access to Clinic Entrances (FACE) Act was enacted in 1994, governments have striven to balance the right of protesters to make their views known with the right of women to obtain health care unimpeded. "Buffer zones" seem a pretty good compromise, fair and constitutional, yet, inevitably, imperfect. To me, a woman's pregnancy is nobody's business but her own, but limits on public protest are problematic. The whole point of protest is to make a nuisance of yourself, and throughout our history, raucous civil disobedience has been invaluable to activists we like as well as to those we don't.

It is a central misfortune of the abortion debate that this and much else get drowned out by venomous argument. In 1995, following the murder of two workers at a Planned Parenthood clinic in Boston, six women active in abortion politics—three advocates, three opponents— began to meet privately to try to talk with one another. Just that. One of the most painful tasks, they reported when they went public with their project, was finding a common vocabulary: prolife or prochoice, unborn baby or fetus, partial-birth or late-term abortion? Six years later, this was still unresolved, yet they continue to put faith in the power of words to heal as well as to sunder. One participant, an abortion opponent, concluded, "Toning down the rhetoric is critical. It's not just better manners, but it turns out it's also better politics."[29]

The politics of abortion defy free speech nostrums, in part, because abortion protests blur the line between speech and action: taunts can turn into shoves, sidewalk counseling to some is sidewalk blocking to others, and protest speech may sound a lot like a call to "imminent lawless action," the legal standard for "fighting words" that are not protected by the First Amendment. The sense of threat reached a new level in 1996, when the since-disbanded American Coalition of Life Activists (ACLA) launched the Nuremberg Files to collect information about people involved with reproductive rights. This included everyone from clinic escorts and security guards to federal judges and Mary Tyler Moore, but the site focused primarily on doctors and nurses who provide abortions, for whom it created what many people viewed as a hit list.

The site was a thing to behold: festoons of babies' limbs dripping cy-berblood; "Horrible Pictures Smuggled From Baby-Butcher Lab!"; bold-face exhortations to "Take Action Today!" all in the name of some vengeful God; and, the pièce de résistance, a "baby butcher" list cata-loguing over two hundred names and home addresses. The data were purportedly to be used in Nuremberg-like trials—hence the name—some time in the future, when abortion would be illegal, but in the present, x-ed out names represented people who had been killed, those shaded in gray, people who had been wounded.

The Nuremberg Files were both menacing and ludicrous, and, it's safe to say, loathsome to all but a small band of fanatics, yet the First Amendment implications are far from clear. All of this information was publicly available, and though the site encouraged spying, intimidation, and less-than-meticulous reporting, it pointedly skirted illegal activity. Planned Parenthood won a judgment of more than $100 million against the ACLA in 1999 for the Nuremberg site and for "Wanted" posters of doctors, two of whom had been murdered. The site's host was not a de-fendant, but after the trial, his service provider closed Nuremberg down for violation of an "Appropriate Use Policy." (He has since launched his own Internet service provider for "The Abortion Abolition Movement.") The antiabortionists appealed, and, in 2001, a three-judge panel of the Ninth Circuit Court, affirming the value of permitting even invasive po-litical speech, overturned the lower court. Within weeks, forty members of Congress requested that the full court review the ruling, and in May 2002, by a six-to-five vote, the Ninth Circuit reversed its earlier decision.

So, pure speech or pure threat? The jury in the original case decided on threat because of the highly charged context of the speech. The panel of judges ruled that, while inflammatory, the site presented no explicit or imminent threat of violence. The ACLU, in an amicus brief, argued that it was possible to remove violence and preserve free speech at the same time, while some electronic-speech activists warned about overreacting to the medium or, as Jonathan Wallace wrote, "look[ing] for nuances to make the behavior which shocks us illegal."[30] Skipp, who reported on the ACLA meeting where the Nuremberg Files were launched, says, "I think they're appalling and I don't see how any good Christian could do that—or anybody else. I find it very disturbing, but I think it probably falls within the area of free speech."

I think so too, but I'm not sure, which brings us back to where we began: Why is the separation of religion and government such a good idea?

When I had asked the question earlier, Barbara had bucked back as if punched. Her eyes grew huge, her smile incredulous. "Why was this country founded? What is religious freedom about?" she had demanded with rhetorical flourish.

Tell me, I said, and she did. "If you believe in religious freedom and you believe in political freedom, then you certainly must believe that the government has to remain neutral in matters of religion, because if the government isn't neutral, your political standing in that society will be defined by your religious beliefs. If you don't believe the government should be telling you what your religious beliefs should or shouldn't be, you must have neutrality. That's the bottom line." In other words, keeping religion out of government and government out of religion protects both democratic and sacred principles.

"I didn't think up neutrality," she continued. "Years and years and years ago, someone else had this great idea. I love the idea of democracy, I love the idea of pluralism, and I want to be viewed in my political community as okay, even if I am totally at odds with every single religious belief that exists around it. And if I'm not, then I'm not really welcome."

---

When Skipp and I talk by phone a few years later, much has changed. He and Barbara are living in Manhattan, but they have separated, amicably, it seems. They're winding down the institute and *Freedom Writer,* having accomplished their goal of getting the word out about religious right activities. Skipp's new occupation is writing, which includes a techno-thriller about the religious right and a nonfiction book too hush-hush to tell me about.

The political landscape has shifted too. When we had met in 1997, the frenzy over religion in politics was ebbing and, within two years, *Freedom Writer* would characterize the religious right as being "in disarray." By then, the fundamentalist-friendly "Gingrich revolution" had wound down, membership in religious right groups had declined, federal agencies had challenged the Christian Coalition's political activities, and the Supreme Court had struck down the Religious Freedom Restoration Act of 1983, which had limited government regulation of religious practices. Paul Weyrich and Cal Thomas, founding fathers of the religious right, were publicly advising conservative Christian leaders to back off from politics, in part because they no longer believed they could be effective in that realm, in part because they figured out that power corrupts. The latter, Skipp suggests, should have come as no surprise; everybody loves catching the self-righteous with their pants down. More generously, he adds, "With the religious right we're talking about people who are presenting a moral platform as well as a political platform. And being human beings, they have a hard time with a moral platform."

Now, when we talk again, it is January 2001. The country has just finished the most religion-sodden presidential campaign in memory, and the new administration's first action was to gag foreign health organizations with U.S. funding to prevent them from discussing abortion with their clients. An Office for Faith-Based Initiatives has been established in the White House to promote "charitable choice," or government funding of social programs run by religious groups, a reflection of the widespread belief that religion can solve societal problems.[31] Americans are still ambivalent about holier-than-thou politicians—70 percent of the electorate wanted the president to be a person of faith, but 50 percent didn't want him to talk about it so much[32]—but religion has become an inescapable feature of American life. Every third TV program has "angel" in its title; every magazine, an article about religion and you name it—crime, academia, sports, atheism. Madalyn Murray O'Hair, who led the fight against school prayer in the 1960s, has returned from the dead, albeit in pieces, and the Christian Coalition has returned from a near-death experience to help appoint as attorney general a Pentecostal so convinced of the place of religion in government that he had once anointed himself with Crisco before taking his Senate seat.

Skipp sounds of two minds also, pointing to the ineffectuality of the religious right in one breath ("More people have boycotted the Baptist church than are boycotting Disney"), warning against letting our guard down in another. Earlier he has argued that if churches had as much influence as they claim, their members would have cleaned up their act a long time ago. Nothing indicates that religiosity increases moral behavior (for what it's worth, over 60 percent of federal prisoners identify as Christians and almost none as atheists),[33] yet even if there were a link, attempts to enforce religious beliefs as official policy end badly. When the government has undertaken morality campaigns—prohibition, drug wars, antiporn sweeps—the result has usually been a mess, and though religious leaders have long participated in our governance, the most constructive have focused, not on compelling righteousness, but on achieving justice.

The problem with God in government is that religions are inherently antidemocratic. They draw lines between those who believe with them and everyone else, fostering at best a class of tolerated minorities and at worst outright bigotry. The men who wrote the Bill of Rights knew this—hence, the conscience clauses—and their prescience has spared us religious warfare of the shooting kind. What we get instead are culture wars, which, though usually not lethal, take their toll. They also put us at risk of forgetting that the rights we claim proudly as Americans are civil rights, human and temporal and hard won, often in the face of religious opposition.

# chapter nine

# INSUBORDINATE

**Penny Clinton**

*Wilton, New Hampshire, March 1996*

Penny Culliton believes fiercely in many things. She believes in American literature, the Constitution, pet rats, and the right of students, all students, to be treated with respect and understanding. In 1995, when Penny acted on the last of these—she disobeyed instructions from her school board by assigning two novels about homosexual characters that had been approved, then disapproved, by her supervisors—she was dismissed from her job as an English teacher at Mascenic Regional High School in New Ipswich, New Hampshire. The school officials who fired her will tell you that the cause was insubordination, but Penny will have none of it. "Think about this," she insists, "teaching Emerson, Whitman, *To Kill a Mockingbird, The Crucible,* all the standard works of American literature we teach in high school, after having acquiesced to a wrong like the one they were asking me to do."

Arguments over what kids should and shouldn't know regularly escalate into battles for their souls and, by extension, for the future of our society. Penny's story is a classic of such fights, in which supposedly heretofore apolitical citizens rise up in alarm to banish "inappropriate" books from a school or library so that the innocence of students may be preserved. Challenges to books and curricula reached a high point in 1995, when Penny came under attack, and though the target may shift—within a few years, evolutionary science and whole-language reading programs would be the bugbears—the antidemocratic impulse remains the same. It is hard to be the object of such campaigns, but the greatest cost may be to students because the teachers who were willing to stick their necks out—often the ones who make learning an adventure and a triumph—now proceed with caution.

When we meet in the spring of 1996, Penny has been out of work since the previous fall and is deep into contesting her dismissal. She is thirty-five years old, a small, ardent woman with a sleek Dutch boy haircut and porcelain doll features that make her look both younger and older than she is, especially when her mouth grows tight. She speaks quickly, turning her voice up at the end of a statement when she is incredulous or upset, sweeping an arm to reinforce a point, and often telling her story in the present tense, though it is nearly a year since her fight began.

Penny and her husband, Randy Wright, then lived in a small, rented apartment at the back of a house that sits partway up a hill among other unprepossessing houses. (They have since bought a house in another town.) We sit at a kitchen table tucked in among a spinet piano, a clock that chimes the half-hour, and two lovingly groomed rats in a large wire cage. The apartment has a cramped, make-do air, but there are graceful touches, such as the delicate cups and saucers Penny pulls down from a top shelf when she makes us tea.

This is south-central New Hampshire, with its postcard charm and hardscrabble lives, but in mid-March mud season, harshness wins out over charm. Prosperity touched down briefly here in the 1980s, then took off again, leaving half-completed housing developments with names like Mill Pond Estates and shopping centers such as Salzburg Square with its faux-Tyrolean architecture. Frequent signs for businesses run out of homes, and probably second jobs—exterminating, hair styling, well drilling—seem better indicators of the economic reality.

The state's economy improved after my visit, but the benefits have remained unevenly distributed. In 1995, Penny's embattled year, Mascenic High School drew its 380 students from three small towns—Greenville, New Ipswich, and Mason—that form a triangle just north of the Massachusetts border. In property value per student, Greenville was then the second poorest town in the state, New Ipswich was fourth.[1] Only about 10 percent of adults in the three towns had college or advanced degrees. "For the most part, if you can, you leave," she says.

Penny grew up in a similarly poor part of the state, so she learned early on about the price kids pay in communities with few resources. Unique among the states, New Hampshire has no broad-based sales or income tax. Nearly 90 percent of school funding has been raised locally, primarily from property taxes, but this system created such disparity among communities that, in 1997, the state supreme court ruled it unconstitutional and gave the legislature sixteen months to find a fairer way to pay for education. Five years later, a workable solution is yet to be found.

Though low taxes are a point of pride among New Hampshirites, in communities like Mascenic's, a weak tax base translates into limited school funding. Facilities are inadequate, teachers' salaries are about 10 percent below the state average,[2] and resources for helping students through family and social problems that may impede their learning are limited. In 1995–96, the Mascenic school district spent $4,565 per student, well below the state and national average.[3]

---

Penny's story starts simply, then spirals out of everyone's control. Early in 1993, after attending two conferences on discrimination in schools based on sexual orientation,[4] she approached her principal, Dana McKenney, about applying for funding from a local program called Respect for All Youth, a name Penny has said so often that it sounds like one word. McKenney agreed, and, that June, Mascenic was awarded a grant of $800 to buy books with lesbian and gay protagonists to supplement the curriculum. The grant would also fund a half-day workshop, rather ponderously titled "Recognizing and Confronting Homophobia and Heterosexism in the Classroom." Penny was in charge of both projects, which she worked on during the summer, taking care to keep McKenney involved and informed.

It is a tradition at the high school that the student council host a brunch each fall for elderly people in the area. In 1993, it was scheduled for the same day as Penny's faculty workshop, so she arranged for participants to stay for the meal afterward. When she checked last-minute arrangements with the student council president, a former student of hers named Israel Saari, he asked about the workshop and, Penny assumes, passed the information on to his stepfather, Charlie Saari. Soon after, she was called to a meeting with her principal and superintendent, who told her that they had received a spate of phone calls from parents objecting to the workshop, all in pretty much the same terms. "I was told that the student council was planning on protesting by refusing to serve the participants at the brunch," she says. "This all sounded pretty crazy to me because this had been no secret that we were giving this workshop. I was very upset. The point is that these are kids we supposedly educated, and we're doing a real poor job of educating them if this is really what they're planning on doing."

McKenney and the superintendent considered canceling the workshop, but Penny suggested that instead they call participants to warn them that they might meet with hostility. When the decision was made to hold the workshop as planned two days hence, she assumed McKenney would make those calls. Quite late in the evening of the intervening day—Veterans Day and a school holiday—she got a phone call from a gay man she had invited along with his partner to speak at the workshop. He was confused, he told her; the principal had indeed phoned, but to tell them that it would be better if they didn't show up.

Penny has been leaning back in her chair, speaking slangily, but at this point, she juts forward and her voice rises about an octave in wounded indignation. "I was floored that this would happen because to me that just defeated everything we were trying to do with the workshop. The next day I went into school, and the first thing I did was talk to the principal and tell him that I didn't approve at all of what he did, that I wanted to go on record as opposing it." McKenney, who was then in his late fifties, had came to Mascenic in 1992. Of their relationship up to then, Penny says, "It was fine. That was the point at which it became not fine." This was not their first run-in over how homosexuality would be addressed at the high school, however.

Penny is straight, but she has always been especially attuned to gays and the prejudice they encounter. She was scrupulous about, and known for, including gay students in all aspects of the school. In the teachers' room, she posted the schedule for a conference on gays where she was speaking to educators. It was removed. In her colleagues' mailboxes, she distributed an article on gay, rural youth. She was charged with accusing the faculty of homophobia. In the computer room, she tacked up a newspaper profile of a computer prodigy who had recently come out as gay. When McKenney told her to take it down, she refused. "If someone's offended, send him to me," Penny told him. "We've been through this before."

"I have a list of these somewhere," she tells me, rifling through papers, not finding the one she wants, continuing anyway. "I felt like I was constantly being told to do things I thought were not right, so I couldn't do them. This is a very high-risk group of kids. They need positive images in the curriculum. They need people who understand where they're coming from. They certainly don't need to be discriminated against. Don't come to me and tell me to take things down and not teach things!"

As Penny recites these events, she circles back to clarify a point, correct herself, hone an argument. Sounding accustomed to justifying her actions, she tells a reporter shortly after we speak that "these issues are important to me because they affect real people with real lives."[5] Who trusts earnestness anymore, I think when I read that. And then, when people care deeply about something, how convenient to paint them as zealots or cranks, so easy to do now when irony rivals baseball as the national pastime. Penny is seldom ironic; her way of undermining an idea is to imitate its proponent, which she does with relish and skill.

---

Despite the threats, the workshop went well, and students and participants talked amicably over lunch. "So from that point on, one very important lesson I learned is that you take everything that these guys tell you with a *real* big grain of salt," Penny sums up. "Don't let it get to you unless you've heard it right from the horse's mouth."

She did hear directly early in December, when Charlie Saari organized a meeting with Mascenic's teachers to explain objections to the workshop. About eighty members of the community showed up, plus the faculty, who were told to attend. It was billed as a public meeting, but students were barred from attending, and Penny says few community people in sympathy with the workshop knew about it beforehand. As she describes it, "It wasn't a protest meeting with signs and banners and pickets. It was just sort of a little homophobia rally, if you will, where people got up and spoke."

Penny thinks the charges against her and the program were unfounded, but she responded philosophically. "At the time I didn't have any objections, because I figure if you give these people enough rope, they'll hang themselves. You can see what they have to say and only that way can you argue against it. As I said to my principal, hey, you let people say what they have to say, because if I try to shut them up, they'll try to shut me up."

Hoping to put the accusations to rest, Penny agreed to an investigation of her curriculum, which, she later learned, had been requested by Charlie Saari. Her department head examined her teaching materials and found nothing untoward, but his report saying so never made it into her personnel file. Instead, a memo from McKenney, describing the charges, stood as part of her permanent employment record until she filed a grievance to have it removed. The memo ends with what was to become a familiar refrain: "In view of the volatile nature of this situation and the concern of both the public and the [school] board, I am directing you to avoid any further discussion of [homosexuality] in your classes. . . . I am concerned that if this perception of you as an advocate for the Gay and Lesbian agendas in the classroom isn't changed, it could seriously impact on your professional reputation. This is not something I would want to see happen to an individual whose knowledge of her subject and skill as a teacher I have come to admire and respect."[6]

That spring, Penny selected books that would, as her grant stipulated, add positive portrayals of gays and lesbians to the curriculum. With Kevin Corriveau, head of the English department, she set up a committee of parents, students, community people, and a school board member to review the dozen or so books that she proposed. She and Corriveau then made the final selection, which McKenney approved. Much later, at a Boston meeting of the writers' group PEN, where she was a featured speaker, Penny insisted that self-censorship is "moral cowardice," but the line between self-censorship and prudence can be blurry, as the selection process proved. After their committee reported back, Penny and Corriveau eliminated any books that could be perceived as promoting sexual activity among teenagers. For example, they decided against *Annie on My Mind,* an award-winning novel by Nancy Garden about a high school lesbian romance, which had been burned by a fundamentalist minister in Kansas the year before. "Basically we were very aware that we wanted to pick books that were not going to cause controversy," Penny says.

To anyone familiar with the literature, they succeeded. The final selections were *The Drowning of Stephan Jones,* by Bette Greene, a young adult novel about a teenager who is pressured by friends to harass a gay couple; *The Education of Harriet Hatfield,* by May Sarton, which follows a sixty-year-old lesbian who uses an inheritance from her partner to start a woman's bookstore; *The Complete Poems* of Walt Whitman, portions of which were already in the curriculum; and *Maurice,* E. M. Forster's posthumously published novel about an Englishman coming to terms with his homosexuality and living happily thereafter. (In a "Terminal Note" added in 1960 to the then-unpublished novel, Forster suggested that the book would be more acceptable and easier to publish "if it ended unhappily, with a lad dangling from a noose or with a suicide pact.") About the only agenda these books could be construed as promoting is the belief that homosexuals are human.

When the 1994–95 school year began, *Maurice* and *The Education of Harriet Hatfield* appeared in Penny's lesson plans with no objections, which is about the only thing everyone still agrees on. From this point on, the story takes on a Rashomon-like quality, though certain phrases and details get plucked out of context and repeated over and over until no one remembers where they originated. When you read multiple accounts of a story you know well, it becomes clear how myths are made. Take, for instance, an implementation plan for use of the books. Purportedly written by Corriveau and presented to the school board in closed session on October 3, 1994, this plan required permission from the English department head and signatures from parents before the books from the grant could be taught. It also stipulated that the Green, Sarton, and Forster books would not be used that year but that the Whitman poems could remain in the curriculum because they "should not be subjective [sic] of the sensitive issues practice normally followed by this department."[7] The administration was later to claim that Penny should have known about this policy, but she insists that she never heard of it until the following summer. She remains skeptical of its provenance, in part because of the grammatical and factual errors she is sure Corriveau, an English teacher, would not make. Most telling was a reference to the death of May Sarton, who died, not in October 1994, when the plan was supposedly written, but in July 1995, a few days before Penny first saw it.

---

As the year wore on, Penny had another argument with McKenney, this time over displaying information about a new gay-lesbian youth support group she had helped set up in a nearby town. When she noticed that the publicity she had brought to school was not displayed with other announcements, she challenged McKenney, saying, "That's discriminatory. I'm going to do everything I can to make sure it doesn't happen again."

Penny calls this confrontation the last straw, and the administration had evidently reached a threshold, too. On January 23, 1995, a week after the first notices about the youth group appeared in local newspapers with Penny named as one of the founders, the Mascenic Regional School Board went into nonpublic session to discuss what they termed "negotiations," one of the few categories under New Hampshire law for which public meetings may be closed. Included in these negotiations was a "sense of the board" that the books from the Respect for All Youth grant should be removed from the school's shelves.

The next day, McKenney called Penny to his office to report the board's decision and, he later testified, to tell her not to use the books.

Why? Penny demanded. She claims he answered "something like, they don't want students reading materials dealing with gay and lesbian issues," but in all his subsequent statements, McKenney denied saying this.[8] Penny's narrative continues in this thrust-and-parry vein. "I said, 'Well, listen, I'm using Whitman already.' He said, 'Not Whitman, but the other three.' Now one wonders, if I said, 'Well I'm also using Bette Greene and May Sarton,' he would have said, 'Well, just *Maurice*.' "

Penny's response, she admits, was precipitous. "I did a couple of things immediately. One was I panicked and I took the books off the shelves and put them in boxes, which I probably never should have done. I just should have left them there and if someone else was going to come and get them, it would be something they did and not me." She also wrote to the school board chairman to ask what was going on. She never received an answer. She now thinks that she should have told her students what was happening and not let the administration hush it up. "They can't get you for insubordination if you haven't done anything insubordinate," she points out. But she feared she wouldn't be believed or would be branded a troublemaker. "I was feeling that I was totally alone."

Penny's sense of isolation was not without basis. Worried about her job for some time, she had looked for allies with little success. Now she contacted the New Hampshire Education Department's Equal Education Opportunity Office, which sent her to the U.S. Department of Education's Office of Civil Rights, which told her that it had no jurisdiction over discrimination based on sexual preference. She finishes plaintively, "I didn't feel there was anybody I could trust who would say to me, you know, what they're trying to do is illegal."

Perhaps because the Respect for All Youth grant gave her position legitimacy, Penny fixated on what had become of the funds, since they were not used to pay for the books. Amid confusion about invoices and payments, the awarding foundation advised Penny to have her superintendent contact them to try to figure out a way to salvage the grant. There was a new superintendent, Francine Fullam, whom Penny now called repeatedly. Unable to get through, she wrote a letter, detailing events and demanding an explanation in less than deferential terms: "As I have for the past two years, dotted every i and crossed every t, all the time jumping through innumerable hoops to complete this project successfully, I am demanding to be informed in writing of all the details leading up to the current situation—precisely how, when and why this project has been totally subverted. . . . It seems to me that what has happened is just the latest in a long string at Mascenic of discrimination against sexual minority students and against me in my efforts to have an inclusive curriculum and classroom put in place."[9]

The books were eventually paid for with general school funds, and the foundation money was returned. When Fullam replied to Penny's letter—nine weeks later—she addressed only the question of payment, saying nothing about the decision to pull the books or the change of heart concerning the grant.

---

Although the Mascenic administration avoided discussing its reasons for wanting to keep these books out of the classroom, the justification for banning books in schools usually centers on the sense that words, ideas, or imagination can be too dangerous to roam free, or on the magic thinking that if you don't talk about something, it will go away. Once these premises are accepted, it follows easily that children (who provide a wonderful excuse for adults to enforce their prejudices) must be protected from "harmful" material. As a Mascenic parent reportedly said, "We don't allow our kids to smoke in school. Why should we let them read these books?"

One of the most comprehensive records of attempts at book banning in American public schools comes from the liberal People for the American Way. From 1982 to 1996, it published an annual report, *Attacks on the Freedom to Learn*, which reads like a roster of books approached with as much literalness and as little joy as possible. These "attacks" were not parents voicing negative opinions or choosing for their child not to read a book but attempts to make sure that nobody else's children would read it either. In the 1994–95 academic year, Penny's troubled year, PFAW recorded 338 attempts in forty-nine states, half of them successful, to remove or restrict books and other educational material from schools and libraries. The Intellectual Freedom Committee of the American Library Association, which also keeps track, has estimated that for every reported incident, another four or five go uncounted. What appears on these lists is not *Protocols of the Elders of Zion* or *120 Days of Sodom* or any of the presumably unteachable titles that are supposed to call the bluff of people who believe kids will survive what they read. More often, lists of banned books leave people scratching their heads in wonder.

In the mid-1990s, stated objections centered on a sibilant trio of transgressions: sex, swearing, and Satanism. Sex has consistently topped the list, with some objectors opposing any mention of any aspect of sex, human or otherwise, while others tolerate only negative references. Still others complain of age inappropriateness or insist that parents alone should talk to their children about the topic. Along with antisex complaints come concerns about material that "promotes" homosexuality—which apparently accounts for a California parent's objection to kindergartners watching *Sesame Street* because the puppets Bert and Ernie live together. The second most popular reason for attacking a book has been use of profanity or other "objectionable" language, which is generally plucked out of context and counted up in a kind of three-damns-and-you're-out reckoning. Next come complaints about "anti-Christian" messages, defined at one time or another to include everything from New Age fads and Halloween masks to the peace symbol, which was reviled in one Texas town as a sign of devil worship.

Interestingly, a fourth "s"—subversion—is seldom cited as a reason for denouncing a book, though the fear that books will make readers dissatisfied with their lot probably figures into many complaints. A book can create an uncomfortable itch that is scratched only by knowing more. For kids especially, books offer a chance to learn that there is much more to the world than what they yet know, that it is rich in ways of seeing and thinking and being. "Just imagine!" a good book calls to us. But censorship, under whatever guise, is the enemy of imagination.

The majority of these episodes involved people on the political right, often encouraged and guided by religious right organizations, such as Citizens for Excellence in Education, which boasted of helping to elect nearly five thousand school board members around the country in 1992 and 1993;[10] Concerned Women of America, which offers a leaflet entitled "Six Action Steps You Can Take to Oppose the Homosexual Agenda in Your Community's Schools"; and the Christian Coalition, which distributed half a million voter guides during New York City's heated 1993 school board elections.

People for the American Way is clearly happier pointing its finger rightward, but about 5 percent of the documented challenges that year came from the left. These include objections to books and language said to be sexist, racist, anti-Semitic, or otherwise "offensive." *The Adventures of Huckleberry Finn* is a perennial on the most-challenged list because of objections to how it portrays black characters and its frequent use of the word *nigger,* and Merriam-Webster drew criticism for its treatment of that word in its dictionary. Words again are invested with great power, although here the power is not to corrupt but to wound.

It is not only people who mistrust books who assume that their purpose is to teach or reinforce an idea or set of values. Anyone who goes into a bookstore looking for a story about a little girl planning to be a doctor or astronaut or unmarried woman is doing the same thing, and, in schools, the role of books as teaching tools is explicit. Because we expect a lot from books, we favor those that reflect the world as we see it—and by "we," I mean people with a range of ideas about what is right or tolerable. At the extreme, this conflation of depiction and advocacy turns into the desire to rewrite certain books. That seems to be the spirit behind a letter from a member of an Illinois school board that was trying to ban Luis Rodriguez's *Always Running*. "If Mr. Rodriguez had wished to keep kids from using drugs and entering gangs," the board member wrote, "he would have written a book based on his experiences of what young people should do!"[11]

Literature presents a host of problems to its readers. Narrative can seduce and abandon, disturb, provoke, and frighten. It can focus attention on topics we'd rather not think about and lodge them in our heads long past their welcome. Fiction may lie about the literal truth to get at another kind of truth (perhaps this is what bothered the parents who objected to a novel with a blurb saying the story was told with "deceptive simplicity" because they didn't want their children taught any kind of deception). Recently, postmodernism, technology, and plain old laziness have muddied the distinction between fiction and polemic or factual reporting. All this complicates the question of what students should read and when. But imagining a life or examining an idea is not the same as swallowing it whole; it is not necessarily even endorsement, and assuming otherwise doesn't give teachers or students much credit. The best way to keep kids "safe" from "dangerous" ideas is to teach them to think for themselves.

———

Late spring of 1995 was the time for Penny's seniors to read *Maurice* and her juniors to read *The Education of Harriet Hatfield*. She argues that, since the books had gone through a review process and neither the superintendent nor the school board chairman had answered her questions about their removal, it was not clear to her that they were still forbidden. Whether she acted out of ingenuousness and conviction, as she claims, or defiance and arrogance, as her critics charge, or simply from the desire to force the issue, Penny assigned the two books as scheduled.

Mascenic is not a large school, so it wasn't long before McKenney came across a student reading *Harriet Hatfield.* He called Penny to his office, demanded an explanation, and ordered her to collect all the books from her students immediately. "I don't know why, I mean in the technical sense of why," Penny argues in lawyer mode, though McKenney's anger was obviously over something other than technicalities. Yet if it was over something beyond her disobedience, that something was never made explicit. Mascenic has a policy for registering complaints about teaching materials, but no formal complaint against the books ever surfaced.

A labor arbitrator was later to report, "Apparently, the Board would have preferred that the students know nothing of the reason why Ms. Culliton had to take the books away from them without any type of discussion with the students."[12] Penny, however, was not about to make it easy for the board. She returned to her class of seniors, about half of whom were reading *Maurice,* and, as she had warned McKenney, told them what had transpired. Here her narrative stalls. "See, I felt guilty about collecting the books at all," she says, then sits very still and says nothing more. The clock chimes the hour, the house falls silent. "I felt I had to collect them, but I didn't feel right about doing it because that was lending myself to something that I felt was wrong. So I said to my students, this is how I feel about it. I just want you to know that because I am doing something that goes against everything that I teach."

By all accounts, Penny is a popular and respected teacher. Her knowledge and love of American literature are infectious, her evaluations are very positive, and her concern for her students has led to long-lasting friendships. So it is not surprising that her students were upset and angered by McKenney's order. When Penny told them they would not be finishing *Maurice,* they proposed walking out of school in protest, buying their own copies of the book, or telling the principal to come collect the books himself. Penny advised against the first, recommended the second so they could address the controversy knowledgeably, and made it clear that the third wasn't going to happen. The students settled for bringing their books to McKenney's office as a group, a gesture read as a protest that heightened the already palpable tension.

A few days later, McKenney called a meeting with some of Penny's students; the press was asking questions, and, he later testified, he thought the situation was volatile. Penny was not invited, but a student reported back that the school was completing the approval process and would use the books the next year. "I said, 'That's not true!' Those were the first words out of my mouth. The administration's story changed.

Now they said, 'Oh, the board just didn't approve them yet.' The board hasn't approved any books for use in English classes that anyone remembers in twenty years!"[13] (The board did eventually approve the books to be used in a new course called Literature in Society, but it was canceled twice for lack of enrollment. "If you believe that, I've got some really great swamp land in Florida," Penny comments.)

On May 15, 1995, Penny was suspended from her job. She was, Superintendent Fullam wrote her, "guilty of insubordination, failure to conform to rules," and "incompetent in that [she had] failed to exercise the degree of judgment that would be required of a classroom teacher."[14]

To Penny, the issue is individual conscience: one must do what is right, even if that breaks the rules. In e-mail, she appends a quotation from Thoreau on resisting unjust laws, but she didn't set her compass to civil disobedience from the start. Like most teachers, she taught what she thought her students should learn, believing that she had the knowledge, experience, and obligation to do so. Whether or not she also had the right was, of course, at the heart of the controversy, but she can point to a tradition of academic freedom as well as to legal precedent to back her up. As the Supreme Court wrote memorably in *Tinker v Des Moines*, "It can hardly be argued that either students or teachers shed their constitutional rights to freedom of speech or expression at the school house gate."

"I shouldn't have tried to ride off on my white horse," Penny acknowledges, though even if she had been more politic, she seemed to be on a collision course with the school board. As is common in clashes over books and curricula, the board steadily denied that censorship was their intent, but in flouting McKenney's instructions, Penny handed them the perfect excuse to change the subject. From that moment on, neither the content of the books, nor the purpose of the grant, nor the rights of gays, nor what a teacher may discuss in class was addressed again. The issue became her behavior; the problem with Penny, the board claimed from the moment the controversy went public, was insubordination, which was not supposed to have anything to do with ideology.

Penny's firing came on the heels of a plan in the neighboring town of Merrimack that was billed as the most far-reaching antigay educational policy in the country. It was enacted while the press was in New Hampshire covering the 1996 presidential primary, so the policy and Penny got national attention. News accounts picked up and repeated the term *insubordination*, sometimes in quotation marks, usually without comment. It is the language of teacher contracts and academic administration, but each time I come across it, I stumble.

Insubordination is why the army busts someone down to private or why smart-mouthed kids get no dessert, but hierarchical and hidebound as schools can be, they are meant to be places of learning, and I have always understood learning to involve examining assumptions and trying ideas on for size. Obviously, this is not a universally held belief, though it hasn't been news since Socrates. What learning is and how teachers should foster it are two hot zones in contemporary cultural and political debates, with everyone claiming to be a reformer. The progressive camp, dominant in the 1970s and early 1980s, defines education as a process by which students develop the intellectual skills and curiosity to gather, use, and create knowledge. It values independent thinking, cultural heterogeneity, and the questioning of social norms. The conservative camp, which has gained influence over the past two decades, contends that education's purpose is to mold productive citizens by passing on information, providing training in marketable skills, reinforcing tradition, and inculcating prevailing values and norms, which include respect for authority, faith in progress, and ambition to succeed.

"If a person can't be fired for not obeying her superiors, it can lead to chaos," a Mascenic school board member tells a local newspaper about Penny's dismissal.[15] Order in the hierarchy: at each stage of the firing and appeal process, the board insisted that this was what was at stake and defended that position despite considerable ill will and expense, an estimated $16,000 to $17,000 before the issue was resolved. "We have been publicly maligned, received hate mail, and overwhelmed with phone calls. Those who preached tolerance didn't practice it," says another board member.[16] Yet the board could hardly have been surprised that Penny fought them—she had challenged everything up to then—or that their action would create discord. Insubordination does smack of things better left unsaid, things Penny insisted on saying directly and often.

"These decisions are definitely not educational," she charges. "They're political." By refusing to go along with a policy she thought wrong, she strode into the realm of the political, censorship's natural habitat, and once there, her best hope was enlisting some authority, such as her union, in her effort to get her job back.

———

Her first step was to negotiate with her employers at a meeting that took place the summer after her dismissal. What an odd scene it must have been, with adults in no mood for the humor of it facing off around a refectory table in the cafeteria of an old elementary school that now housed the School Administrative Unit. The negotiations seemed to end in agreement, though, with Penny and her attorney, Steve Sacks, charged with drafting the terms for her reinstatement in the fall. But the administration rejected their draft without explanation, and, shortly before the fall 1995 term began, Superintendent Fullam wrote Penny not to return.

For her dismissal hearing in September, Penny tried to get Charlie Saari, now a member of the school board, and others who had opposed her to recuse themselves, but they declined. "Of course, they voted to fire me," she says without emotion. "In my view and in my attorney's view, this decision was theirs in the beginning anyway." The vote was unanimous.

Her firing became official on September 25, 1995, which, in an irony too good to be planned, coincided with National Banned Books Week. In protest, some hundred students signed a petition, and about forty walked out of class two weeks later. A few parents joined the demonstration, and a few took their kids home. One of the protest organizers was the daughter of the Mason police chief, who was quoted as saying of his children, "They have beliefs and they should be able to express them."[17]

Amid all this, Penny was becoming famous for being fired, and though less interested in doing a star turn than in getting her job back, she recognized that she had a platform for her views available to few other teachers. She learned quickly to make her points specific and hard to misinterpret, but, she says, "The one thing that's always been problematic in talking about this is trying to make it clear that while I want positive images of gay and lesbian people in the curriculum, I *don't* want to remove those books which have negative images. I often get lumped together with people who would like to do that, with politically correct people."

It is still baffling to Penny that her teaching became so controversial, since she thinks of herself as a serious teacher of American literary classics. She suggests reasons that are a combination of fear, misunderstanding, and opportunism. "Some people want to have a group to look at and say, at least I'm not that. That faction, the real hate-mongers, it happens to be gay people they're scapegoating today. Tomorrow it could be another group. I don't think there's anything that I could say that's going to make a difference for them.

"There's also the parents who, when I say 'gay,' think that means, oh,

you want my son to move to a large city far away, use drugs, never talk
to us again, have promiscuous sex in back rooms with a bunch of anonymous men. It's shorthand for something that terrifies people, and that's
largely because of the way that other group who objects to [homosexu-
ality] has portrayed it. For the folks who are concerned that their children are being taught something that's going to hurt them, obviously educators need to make it real clear that that's not what's going on. That
indeed we may save your child because your child could grow up to be
gay, and if your child thinks that what it means is that he will have to go
to some city far away and lead this horrible, degrading life, he's likely to
kill himself. Or he is likely to fulfill that prophecy and die a very early
death. That is a concern too of most educators. We wouldn't be teachers if we didn't care."

———————

It has never been disputed that Penny cares. The students at Mascenic are
the kind of kids she was determined to teach since she was their age. To
understand why, she says, you have to go way back. Penny grew up
about fifty miles from where she lives now. Her parents divorced when
she was very young. She didn't know her father, and her mother—unstable, alcoholic—moved in and out of her life. Penny thinks their last
contact was fifteen years ago. She was raised by her great-grandmother,
Florence, who was living comfortably with her third husband, Jim Culliton, a retired business executive, whose name Penny took.
    She describes her early childhood in Elysian terms: a Civil War–era
house filled with wonderfully strange collections of books and pets, acres
of land with moose wandering by. Religion was important to her family,
and Penny deems herself still devout, having recently rejoined a Congre-
gationalist church after several years away. "I didn't feel this huge need,
as if the only time you could talk to God was in church," she says about
the hiatus. "It's always weird to me when people say you can't pray in
school. I do it all the time."
    Like her detractors, Penny values families highly, but experience has
taught her that they come in many configurations—a liberal view, but
hardly a radical critique of the institution itself. "I thought our household
was fine until I went to school and people threatened to run me over with
tractors because they think it's queer," she says of her family arrange-
ment. "That word was used and, the funny thing is, I'm not a lesbian, but
I remember being called that. It was just a nontraditional family."

When Penny was eleven, Jim Culliton died, and Florence changed into someone Penny barely recognized. The tension between them came to a head when it was time to choose between two regional high schools. Florence selected the smaller, more convenient one, promising Penny that she could transfer if she didn't like it. "I not only didn't like it, it was just a disaster!" she says. "There were a lot of drugs and alcohol, a lot of violence, but the worst was the pressure to conform. I thought, I'm not probably even going to finish school if I stay here. I felt really powerless."

Sometime during that awful year, Penny decided she wanted to teach. "I knew that I couldn't change things at that school, so I wanted to get an education and go back to a school like that and work with the people who really were my people." A major influence was Jonathan Kozol's *Death at an Early Age,* which reinforced her sense that rural schools were largely ignored in education debates. She cites a passage about a black child who is a good artist but attends a segregated school with no art classes. "Kozol laments the fact that she has to go to the Museum School for art classes, and I'm like, what is with this guy? Doesn't he realize that there are millions of kids in this country who don't have art classes and who can't just get on a bus and go downtown? It costs much more per student to educate well in a small rural district than in a large urban or suburban one."

Penny eventually switched high schools and became a top student, going on to study literature and education at Brandeis University. Eager to return to New Hampshire after graduation, she took a job at Pinkerton Academy, a quasi-public school in Derry, where Robert Frost had taught early in the twentieth century. In 1990, the position at Mascenic opened up, and it looked like what she had been preparing for all her life. In her interview, she explained why and, to make it clear what kind of person and teacher she was, showed samples of her writing, including a persuasive piece on gay rights. It was a rigorous interview, lasting three hours. Penny says of the woman who was then principal, "Clearly this was an administration that cared about whom they hired." She was selected from about one hundred applicants.

Earlier Penny said that most of her colleagues had supported her or stayed neutral during her disputes with the administration. Now she returns to the topic, saying wistfully that by the time of the meeting protesting the workshop, almost everyone who shared her concern for "a more inclusive classroom" had gone. They left for better-paying jobs, a trend that would continue at an alarming rate; in 1996, shortly after

Penny was fired, Mascenic's budget was frozen, and by the end of the 1997–98 school year, the school had lost thirteen of its thirty-five teachers.[18] They also left, Penny says, to avoid the battles she took on.

---

Regardless of how the argument is framed—and it is framed in controversies across the curriculum and throughout the country—at base, it is about who determines what is taught in public schools and ultimately what a society will teach its children to value. In an ideal system, trained, skillful educators cooperate with informed parents and are supported by enlightened community members, responsive unions, and generous politicians. Most central to a school's success, though, is what teachers do in their classrooms, and good teachers, understandably, want flexibility and control over what they teach. Standards and accountability, the new buzzwords in education, and the strategies to reinforce them, such as standardized testing, undermine teachers' autonomy and imply distrust.

Still, most parents seem comfortable enough leaving teaching decisions to the teachers and administrators hired to make them. Only about one-quarter of parents in a 1999 survey by the nonpartisan Public Agenda said they would be comfortable being involved in curriculum development or in changing how teachers teach.[19] Nor have battles over curricula and books reached the epic proportions those who denigrate public education would have us believe. Assuming that each of the 338 curriculum challenges People for the American Way recorded in 1994–95 occurred in different schools, fewer than four-tenths of 1 percent of public schools in the country faced censorship attempts that year. Even applying the ALA's multiplier of five, we are still talking about fewer than 2 percent.

Schools have long been battlegrounds for social and political conflicts, and second-guessing teachers is an ingrained habit, so that some tension between parents and educators is inevitable. Around the time Penny was fighting her dismissal, Gary Bauer, then head of the ultraconservative Family Research Council, explained, "When a government restricts what its citizens can read, that's censorship. In contrast, when parents have input on what local officials do in the schools, that's democracy."[20] Parental input involves making suggestions or complaints; that, as Bauer maintains, is democracy. But parents who agitate to remove a book from the curriculum or library to make a political or moral point aren't just guiding what their own children read; they're trying to control what other parents' children read. When they succeed, they close down discussion and suppress differing ideas, and that is censorship.

In an editorial condemning Penny, the Manchester, New Hampshire, *Union Leader* wrote, "Administrators are hired to implement policy. School boards are elected to determine policy. . . . Teachers are hired to teach. Period."[21] Under local control, a community's interests are supposedly represented through school boards or school committees who are appointed or, as at Mascenic, elected. More democracy in action, though Penny is unimpressed. "My case proves what James Fenimore Cooper said in the 1830s, that democracy works well for many things, but in the arts, education, and acquired knowledge, it leads to mediocrity. . . . I think schools need to educate for democracy. Therefore they need to be removed from it."

Probably the best way to educate for democracy is to practice it, but classrooms, as every student knows, are not democratic institutions. Teachers select the teaching material, create the learning environment, and evaluate the performance of their students. Though many schools, including Mascenic, have "opt-out" policies, under which a student who objects to a particular lesson can skip it or substitute another, students are essentially a captive audience.

Students do not have the same First Amendment rights as adults, though the courts have gone back and forth on what rights they do have. In *Tinker v Des Moines,* a 1969 case involving an anti-Vietnam protest, the Supreme Court decided that most political expression of students is protected. This position was reaffirmed in 1982 in *Board of Education v Pico,* when the Court ruled that school officials cannot remove books from school libraries just because they disagree with ideas contained there. But two subsequent decisions point toward a more restrictive view of student speech rights. In *Bethel School District v Fraser,* a case regarding a student's sexually suggestive nominating speech, the Court ruled in 1986 that the state's interest in education can trump a student's guarantee of free expression. Two years later, in *Hazelwood School District v Kuhlmeier,* it decided that school officials may restrict student newspapers and other "school sponsored expressive activities" in the name of "legitimate pedagogical concerns."

---

That returns us to the central question: Who decides which pedagogical concerns are legitimate and which are not? According to "parental rights" measures that enjoyed a vogue in the mid-1990s, the final decision should not be made by educators. In its 1996 session, New Hampshire's legislature considered a parental rights education bill that, in an early form, included a model letter intended for parents of public school students that read in part: "Pupils have the right to have and hold their values and moral standards without direct or indirect manipulations by the school through the curricula, textbooks, audio visual materials or supplementary assignments."[22] The bill died in committee, but it's a safe bet that the wishful thinking behind it did not. Who doesn't, on some level, long to be free to hold onto his or her preconceptions and prejudices without scrutiny or challenge?

Parental rights make for a rousing slogan, but willful ignorance as an educational policy is hard to defend. (Should schoolwork come with an advisory label: "Warning: Contents may make you think"?) What, after all, were Penny's students being protected from, and to whose benefit? She had strong opinions and didn't hide them, but her students were not children. Sixteen- to eighteen-year-olds, they were probably well along in their sexual awakening and their encounters with the larger world—both places where parental control is limited—and only in a society like ours with its bloated definition of adolescence would they be sentimentalized as innocents. Part of Penny's complaint is that "having students read only boring, hacked-up, watered-down texts in schools run like prisons produces apathetic citizens who do not even realize there are constitutional freedoms to be protected and perfected."

For all their shortcomings, public schools are the bedrock of democratic opportunity and participation. They are the largest governmental function in the country, the social institution the vast majority of Americans have in common, and the fruit of the revolutionary concept of universal education of which Americans are justifiably proud. But what about a democratic process that produces undemocratic ends? And what should be done when a community acts to exclude or stifle or withhold rights from some of its members? "Do you think that the principal would have ever said, 'Well, we have to take out all the books with positive portrayals of Native Americans'?" Penny demands. "I don't think so. 'Sorry, we can't put those pamphlets out; they deal with children of alcoholics'? Yet, evidently, it's okay for him to say, 'We can't have those books out because they deal with gays and lesbians.' "[23]

In 1996, the Supreme Court ruled that an antigay law in Colorado was unconstitutional because "a State cannot so deem a class of persons a stranger to its laws."[24] This sentiment is at the core of Penny's argument with her employers It is central to the equal protection and due process provisions in the Constitution and in the spirit of the First Amendment, which is meant to ensure that neither majority nor minority enforces its prejudices by outlawing ideas it dislikes. This is what distinguished the Mascenic conflict from differences of pedagogical opinion or questions of literary taste.

I ask Penny why the rights of gays matter so much to her, enough to endanger her job, her friendships, the life she wants to lead. It turns out to be the hardest question to answer because it seems so obvious to her. Dutifully, she roots around in her memory to find me a reason and comes up triumphant with the explanation that her great-grandmother, having worked in the theater and the antique trade, knew gay men. "So I was just raised with the idea that some men love men the way most men love women. So that resistance that most straight people would need to overcome?" She shrugs. "I skipped that part. You see, that's just the way it was for me, so I don't think about it that much."

The injustice bothers you too, I say.

"Ask me why. I don't know." She pauses, then, "I think that at a crucial point in my life there was no one with a great deal of sanity there, so I read a lot of literature. A lot of the moral compass that I might have comes from that. I read *The Scarlet Letter*. Remember how you get inside Hester Prynne's head through the narrator? It's said that she's had a very strange life and it's taught her different things and it's taught her much amiss. And you're never sure whether Hawthorne thinks it's amiss or Hester thinks it's amiss or it's just puritan society at large that thinks it's amiss. I don't know if the reader's supposed to think that it's amiss, but it's different. That's the only thing I can think of to compare it to. It was a very different life."

———————

Penny continued to fight for her job by submitting her case to binding arbitration, as provided for in her contract. She preferred that to a lawsuit because if she sued and won, the money would come from the meager school budget. "I think the best way to fight this sort of thing is through education," she says, "through people not shutting up and going away." In April 1996, the arbitrator issued a mixed decision. School authorities have a legitimate interest in requiring teachers to obey directions, and Penny's insubordination was a serious infraction, which merited discipline, he ruled, but dismissal was too harsh a penalty. He

reduced her punishment to a one-year suspension without pay or benefits, which meant a loss of about $30,000 for her, but allowed her to re-
sume teaching the following September.

Despite its partial victory, the school board appealed the decision.
When I call Penny that summer, she sounds weary of battle and uncertainty. "I think there are people who'll go to great lengths to be comfortable in their prejudices," she says. Meanwhile, she has been working
as a cosmetician at a department store in Manchester. It is something she
has done in the past to supplement her income. Now it is her only income.

The teachers' union filed counterpetitions on Penny's behalf, asking
that she be reinstated immediately, so that, in June, thirteen months after
she was suspended, yet another hearing was held, this time before the
New Hampshire Public Employee Labor Relations Board. Penny felt optimistic that this board would rule in her favor too because the Mascenic
school board was unable to produce evidence of the pattern of insubordination they alleged in their appeal.

The week before school was to resume, Penny still did not have a final
ruling. She prepared her classes, but when she called the school to ask
how many students she would have, McKenney informed her that, as far
as the school board was concerned, she was no longer an employee. The
next day, a rumor reached her attorney that there would be protests and
boycotts if she showed up to teach.

At last, on August 23, 1996, the labor board issued its ruling: it upheld the arbitrator's decision of the previous spring, meaning that Penny
was to be reinstated immediately. Once again, though, the school board
would not allow it and barred her from the first day of teachers' meetings while they considered filing a challenge with the state supreme
court, and she and the teachers' union prepared to go to court to force
compliance.

Then, just like that, it is over, so that Penny's e-mailed announcement
reads almost as an anticlimax:

> Monday night the Mascenic Board met with their attorney, who evidently
> convinced them to give up this fight and not block the reinstatement. We
> did not have to go to court and I was back in school for the second prepara-
> tory day. Students returned today. Let's hope this is an end to all the non-
> sense of the past two years.

The previous spring, Penny had summed up why she did what she did
by saying, "I guess I was raised with the idea that this country is special
because it's a constitutional republic and because this is the way that we

do things. Those things did not come from literature. They were reinforced later on but they were there from the time I was a little kid.
Throughout the whole controversy, I've been concerned with keeping my
integrity by practicing what I teach. The public schools exist to turn out
citizens who can function in a democracy. They need to promote the free
exchange of ideas, not bigotry."

# chapter ten

# BLAME THAT TUNE

Mike Diana, Paul Kim, Richard Taylor

"Are you as outraged as I am at how TV is undermining the morals of children . . . encouraging them to have pre-marital sex . . . encouraging lack of respect for authority and crime . . . and shaping our country down to the lowest standards of decency?" asks Steve Allen from beyond the grave in an ad appealing to television sponsors.[1] Never mind that he used to know better back in the days when he pointedly hosted Lenny Bruce on his TV show. Even if their umbrage is less intense, thoughtful adults regularly equate distastefulness of expression with danger and warn of contagion, as if adolescent attitudes were a communicable disease. The focus is usually that perennial of parental concern, popular culture. With its glorification of anarchistic impulses, casual violence, and half-formed sexuality, what entertains America's—and increasingly the world's—kids is a lightning rod for societal anxiety and an ideal target for reformers bent on saving the young from themselves.

When enough adults hop on the blame-that-tune bandwagon, the result is a moral panic, a term first used in 1971 by British sociologist Jock Young,[2] although the phenomenon has been around for a long time. It begins when an interest group, such as a church or school organization, condemns some aspect of the culture as an attack on the social order. Though the original target is usually one specific thing—crime comics in the 1950s, crime-glorifying rap lyrics forty years later—the campaign quickly expands into an effort to stop many things—all comics, all hip-hop—and to blame those things for all that goes wrong in kids' lives.

What these reformers really want is censorship, but since they don't have legality on their side, they rely on public pressure. They deploy research to prove a causal relationship between the thing under attack and antisocial behavior, enlist the support of politicians, who hold hearings to give a gloss of impartial assessment, and bring their cause to the media, which push for a governmental response. In time, other groups form to champion what is being disparaged or to defend civil liberties or to say that kids aren't so bad or to charge that the campaign misses the real cause of societal breakdown. They too marshal evidence to buttress their position and call for action, since, in moral panics, doing something is more important than doing the smart thing.

Nowhere have moral panics played themselves out with more drama and dudgeon than in postwar America, where the marketing of adolescent rebellion, combined with new technologies, created a separate youth culture that many parents don't understand, don't like, and can't control. The dominant anxiety centers on depictions of sex and violence in a variety of media that are said to lead (usually young) viewers and listeners to act sexually or violently or both. Rather than ask why Americans find violence so entertaining and sex so scary, we warn each other that the words and images are "harmful to minors," a charge that is occasionally debated in degree but seldom rejected outright. Popular culture does influence our attitudes and behavior, just as it reflects our concerns and interests, but how and to what degree this happens is less clear than campaigners on any side of the debate claim. Absent good understanding of cause and effect, we end up confusing moral positions with safety measures.

The three young men in this chapter knew their creations stuck a finger in the eye of grown-up propriety. Mike Diana drew nasty comic books, Richard Taylor painted antiauthoritarian graffiti, and Paul Kim created a Web site lampooning his high school. They never imagined such harsh responses, though, so when the punishments came down, free speech changed for them from a political abstraction into something worth standing up for. Paul speaks for all three when he says, "Adults have already been exposed to a lot of different things, so they have a pretty good chance of being able to form opinions. But while you're growing up I think you need even more exposure. I think that's especially true for teenagers. That's when we learn who we want to be and what we want to think like and what our beliefs, our morals are. So when is it more important to speak freely than then?"

## QUEENS, NEW YORK, DECEMBER 1998

Mike Diana's real troubles began in December 1990, when he returned home from Christmas shopping with his mother in Largo, Florida, to find two policemen waiting for him. He wasn't unfamiliar with the local police; he had had run-ins with them for, as he tells it, driving with long hair, and once when neighbors lodged the bizarre complaint that he and his brother were Satan worshipers who had sacrificed a virgin in their yard. But these were state police, conducting a nationwide manhunt for the murderer of five students near the University of Florida in Gainesville that past August. One policeman pulled out a copy of *Boiled Angel*, a comic book Mike had been publishing for a couple of years. It was issue #6, the one with a cover drawing of a tumescent man slicing open a naked woman over the caption "I love engaging in antisocial behavior." Did Mike publish it? the officer asked.

Mike said he had.

Well, then, he was informed, you're a suspect in the Gainesville murders.

Mike seems to have taken this bombshell with customary nonchalance, but when the police showed the comic to his mother, he got upset. Though his parents encouraged his drawing, they didn't much care for his death-infused images—his father said it was no wonder Mike was depressed—so he tried to shield them.

This is the only time Mike uses the word *depressed*, though he certainly sounds it. He has a cold, making it painful for him to talk, but he seems to speak habitually in a low monotone that goes nasal and whiny on the words he backs into—"weell" and "yeeaahh"—when he's only half-agreeing. His enthusiasm the night we talk is reserved for his art and his tattoos: a race car on his ankle, a devil on the back of his calf, a leggy cicada on his shoulder that reminds him of his childhood. He pulls at his clothing to show them off, amused at himself and me. Mike has sleepy eyes, slightly bucked teeth, and platinum-blond hair hanging down his back. His face is sweet, almost girlish, but with the long hair and tattoos and discontent, it's not hard to see how authorities might have pegged him as trouble.

And then there was *Boiled Angel*. "The police started flipping through the issue, and they said that I would be arrested for obscenity if I didn't stop printing it. And I said, 'What about freedom of speech and freedom of the press?' And they said, 'We don't like your attitude.' I didn't like being threatened like that and I saw how much they upset my mom. I knew that they didn't think I actually killed the people. That was just a way for them to come after me."

Much later, Mike read that there had been thousands of "suspects" who, like him, were told to take a DNA test. The test cleared him and the police let him go, but not before suggesting that he use his artistic talent in more constructive ways. Mike, who is narrating this without emotion, concludes, "So I printed my next issues."

Mike was twenty-one then, finished with high school, disgruntled with Florida and the menial jobs he did to get some money together. What he liked to do was draw, and he had been drawing as far back as he could remember. He has a favorite story about an after-school art class his mother enrolled him in when he was six and living in Geneva, a small town in the Finger Lakes region of New York State. On a trip to Seneca Lake, the class was instructed to collect shells, stones, and other beach items to make a collage, but while the other kids picked up pretty things, Mike scavenged for broken glass, cigarette butts, dead fish. The lake was polluted then, and that was what interested him. "I felt that I was doing it as a statement that I couldn't ignore the things that were wrong with the beach," he says. His collage got a lot of attention at open house, since it looked and smelled like no other. "So that was one of my first things that I did kind of unknowingly using my artwork as a protest."

When Mike was nine, his father quit his job as a science teacher and moved the family to Florida. They settled in Largo, then a backwater, now one of the suburbs that march up the coast from St. Petersburg. Mike hated it, and much of his energy seems to have gone into burnishing memories of New York. His disaffection increased four years later when his parents divorced, and he blamed Florida. "Just the change of life from being the happy New York life, living in a big house, and moving to Florida to go to a different school, trying to adjust to a totally different atmosphere where there was no wintertime, only one long, hot season."

Again, drawing came to his rescue. In school, he drew caricatures and what he describes as "weird and gross-type things," which earned him reprimands from his teachers and sniggering approval from his friends. "I think the fact that Florida was so repressive and such a close-minded or religious place, it made me want to do even more. I felt that that was the only way I could rebel against the system and everyone telling me to be nice and just have nice thoughts and draw pretty things," he concludes.

Eventually he collected his work in a handmade magazine, which he called *Boiled Angel* and distributed to friends. Someone suggested he advertise in *Fact Sheet 5,* a magazine about 'zines. A review there called *Boiled Angel* "revolting," and that drew new readers. As Mike's subscription list grew, so did his print run, reaching a high of three hundred for the final issues. He usually knew his readers; they were mostly contributors, mostly guys. It felt, he says, like a club.

'Zines are underground publications that blend fan magazines, alternative newspapers, and literary journals. They cover an array of topics so vast and eccentric as to give proof, if any is needed, that the human mind is a very strange place: *Bowel Movement Quarterly, Book of Dead Animals and Explosions, Eraser Carver's Quarterly, Hot Geeks, Killing Times,* and that's just the first half of the alphabet. What 'zines have in common is a homegrown quality, enthusiasm for free-floating colloquy, and the very human desire to say "I am." About twenty thousand 'zines existed when Mike was publishing his. *Boiled Angel* fell into a subgenre known as "splatterzines," which focus on sex and violence, and he had standing among splatterzinesters, both for his 'zine, which was typical of the category, and for his contributions to others.

Mike had originally called his 'zine *Angelfuck* before he decided to tone it down a little. "I just thought of an angel boiling, like for soup or something," he explains about the revised title, as if it should be obvious. The angel part came from his hatred of religion. He had been raised a churchgoing Catholic, but religion confused and agitated him and, in his mind, was wrapped around the mayhem that is a staple of the nightly news. "Reports about children being molested by Catholic priests and teachers abusing children and murder and rapes," he enumerates, "just all the crazy things that happened, it seemed, every day. I felt like people in the community were being desensitized to the problems around them because it seemed so common. So I was putting my horrors I was hearing about in my comics to show people how horrible the world really is." The world's ugliness remained theoretical—he was never abused, nor did he know anyone who was—but by his midteens, he refused to accompany his father to church anymore.

Mike shows me two issues of *Boiled Angel.* They're full of lurid, violent images, icky sex, crass insults to religion, and gross humor of the kind adolescent boys and practically no one else finds funny. Issue #7, published soon after his DNA test, features drawings of big penises, grotesque women, dead babies, raped babies, Christ with a venereal disease, and a story by a serial killer serving a life sentence in a Florida prison. Issue #Ate, from August 1991, includes more of the same, plus a manger scene with the lyrics: "You better not shout, you better not cry, you better be good, I'm telling you why; Satan Claus is gonna beat the shit out of you."

I thumb through the magazines and hear myself saying prissily, "I'm not offended by pictures of sex, but there's stuff in your comics. . . . Pictures about raping babies are disturbing to me." Disturbing? Hell, yes. But dangerous? I stack the magazines carefully on the kitchen table and push them away.

Mike intended to shock, of course: "When I first started, I was trying to go for a certain look of being as crude as I could in the way the artwork was drawn and also the subject matter. I wanted to give the people the illusion of wondering what kind of crazy person was drawing it and distributing it. Even though I was a very nice person. . . . Some people would write me letters and say that when they saw my first drawings, they would actually have nightmares. It made me feel like I accomplished what I was trying to do, just because it was so weird and scary. I felt people would have to remember it." His influences were the E.C. horror comics from the 1950s and underground cartoonists from the 1970s, like R. Crumb and Ed "Big Daddy" Roth, but he wanted to go them one better. "So," he finishes, "I added in the things about babies."

Mike saw things differently, and in focusing on the difference, became typical of the guerrilla warfare that adolescents wage against adulthood and its necessary hypocrisies. But his satisfaction in shocking others didn't preclude being shocked himself, and not in the pleasurable, fleeting way of scary movies or amusement park rides. "I would read in newspapers about real things that happened and that would disturb me. I would have nightmares about it sometimes. So I felt it wasn't that big of a deal if I drew it on paper, even if I was trying to make it humorous."

---

In 1991, Mike received an order with a local postmark for two issues of *Boiled Angel*. He hadn't sold his 'zine to a stranger so close to home, so he suggested they meet, but the subscriber wrote back to say he was too busy. In fact, he wrote several times, insisting that he wasn't a cop and demanding his magazines. It didn't smell quite right, but Mike told himself he was being paranoid. Besides, he was winding down *Boiled Angel;* publishing it alone was hard work, and he wanted to concentrate on his drawing. He sent the two issues to the subscriber, who was indeed a cop, which is how Mike's comics ended up in the files of the state attorney, where an assistant state attorney named Stuart Baggish came across them nearly two years later and slapped Mike with a three-count obscenity charge. With the disarray that sounds typical of his life then, he didn't pick up the summons until a few days before he was to appear in court, so he was ill-prepared when he showed up at the county courthouse. He was greeted by a crowd of antiporn feminists and religious conservatives calling for his imprisonment and by the media, who routinely paired early reports of his indictment with film footage of the dead Gainesville students.

Mike knew enough to plead not guilty, then contact the Comic Book Legal Defense Fund, a civil liberties group in Northampton, Massachusetts. CBLDF referred him to Luke Lirot, a First Amendment lawyer from Tampa, and also paid his legal bills, which totaled about $56,000. Over the next year, Lirot tried to get the case dismissed by claiming entrapment. When that failed, he tried to get the trial moved to Miami for a more sympathetic jury. When that failed too, he and Mike began to plan their defense. Florida law defines obscenity similarly to the federal Miller Standard (see Chapter 6): as judged by community standards, a work as a whole must be patently offensive, appeal to prurient interests, and lack serious literary, artistic, political, or scientific value. They decided to argue that, though *Boiled Angel* might push the bounds of legal expression, it was protected on artistic and social commentary grounds. It was the first time Mike had analyzed his drawings. "I had to think of the reasons why I drew what I did," he says. "It was interesting and annoying at the same time. I said that I was trying to make people aware that these things were going on around them so they would actually do something about crime."

The case came to trial on March 22, 1994, before a jury of six people who had probably not cracked a comic books in decades. One member, an older woman, explained during jury selection that she knew about pornography because she had found a copy of *Playboy* in her grandson's underwear drawer. "I had nothing in common with them except being stuck in the same courtroom," Mike complains. "They didn't have any understanding really of art and they certainly didn't know about comics."

For four long days, Mike alternated between boredom and curiosity. Baggish, the prosecutor, charged that *Boiled Angel* was neither entertaining nor funny—what the government determined cartoons should be—nor was it art. (The standard cited was Picasso's *Guernica,* one of the world's most moving depictions of horror.) The real Gainesville murderer had confessed shortly before the trial, but that didn't stop the prosecution from noting that Mike was once a suspect. A psychologist who had testified at Florida's other student murder trial, that of Ted Bundy, said that Mike's drawings would appeal to "the borderline personality, the marginal personality, the bizarre, unstable, libertine thinkers."[3] The message was clear: the drawings had no redeeming value, and their creator was a danger to society.

For the defense, the publisher of *Fact Sheet 5* explained what 'zines were, an artist explained what art was, and a psychologist gave the rather tepid defense that people who are incited to antisocial acts by pictures prefer photographs to drawings. Mike spent about three hours on the stand, explaining his artwork, but "Pretty much nothing worked." It took the jury ninety minutes to find him guilty on all three counts, giving him the dubious distinction of being the only cartoonist, and probably the only artist, ever to be convicted of obscenity in America.

The verdict came late on a Thursday, so Mike was sent to jail to await sentencing on the following Tuesday. He was put in a windowless cell with a bare, metal bed. Fluorescent lights stayed on round the clock, and meals were a baloney sandwich and glass of Kool-Aid shoved under the door. When other prisoners asked what he was in for, he answered, "Drawing pictures."

Though the prosecution argued for imprisonment, Mike was sentenced to three years on probation. He was to pay a $3,000 fine, complete 1,248 hours of community service, maintain a full-time job, take a journalism ethics class, get a psychiatric evaluation at his own expense, and stay at least ten feet from anyone under eighteen. (This included a little girl he had been giving plastic animals to when she came into his father's convenience store because she was too poor to buy herself treats; when his probation officer learned of this, Mike was reprimanded for talking to a minor.) Finally, he was not to draw anything that might be considered obscene; the police were allowed random visits to check. "I had enjoyed creating art since I was three years old," he says, "and now that was gone."

The whole process—indictment, trial, jail, sentence, probation—was frightening and isolating, but it was also exciting. It made Mike think about art and politics in new ways, introduced him to people he wouldn't otherwise have met, created demand for back issues of *Boiled Angel* in the thousands, and brought him a modicum of celebrity. It also, at last, got him out of Florida. He appealed his conviction, convinced the judge to put his probation on hold pending that ruling, and moved to New York City in the spring of 1996.

———————————

When I visit Mike, he is living in a Polish neighborhood in Queens, where food shops spill onto sidewalks, crowded even on this cold December night. He takes me to the front and nicest room of his apartment, which serves as a sort of gallery for his recent paintings. Combining prettiness (chubby-cheeked kids, primary colors) and the bizarre (severed limbs, floating penises), this work is decorative, visually arresting, edgy, and more accomplished than his earlier cartoons. His art has changed because he has; the early, crude comics were a thing of youth, he admits, and the trial was a wake-up call. "Now I want to do a lot of comics about the trial and about the freedom of speech issues, which is something back then I never thought I would do."

Mike has lost his appeal in Florida, and the Supreme Court has declined to hear his case, so his conviction stands. He is now twenty-eight years old but seems younger, maybe because of his languor and diffidence, maybe because of his insistence that what happened to him was unfair. He points to problems with the "community standards" by which obscenity is determined: Given their vagueness and subjectivity, how was he to know he was breaking the law? Moreover, if he was creating art, as he believes he was, by definition, it could not be obscene.

"So anything someone draws should be legal?" I ask.

"I think so," he answers.

"And nothing should be prohibited?"

"I think things that are illegal, like child pornography—if it's real child pornography, not the type that Barnes and Noble got in trouble for. . . ." That would be *Radiant Identities,* a book of photographs by Jock Sturges, which a few states brought obscenity charges against and later dropped. But Mike's caveat about "real" child pornography circles back to the core question of who decides. His experience with the issue is concrete, but he gets tied in the same knots as theorists when it comes to distinguishing between bad pictures with sex in them and good pictures with sex in them: in other words, between porn and art. Like Annie Sprinkle (see Chapter 6), he makes a point of violating taboos and calling it art, but, as an utter outsider to the art world, he was particularly vulnerable. His peers are cartoonists, and their reputation has been dicey since comic books debuted in 1934, although sophisticated narrative comics, such as Chris Ware's *Jimmy Corrigan* and Art Speigelman's *Maus,* are held in high repute as "graphic novels."

Comics were, as one scholar puts it, "a new medium altogether . . . that relied on the interaction of words and pictures to tell stories in a unique way."[4] They challenged authority by removing kids' entertainment from adult control, and adults reacted predictably. In the 1930s and early 1940s, critics complained that comic books would spoil their readers for better literature—plus, the small print would ruin their eyes. The Catholic Church and education groups pressed newsstands not to sell comics, and some communities even staged public burnings.

Then, in 1948, a child psychiatrist named Fredric Wertham was quoted in *Colliers* magazine as saying that comic books had a harmful effect on children's psyches, and the charge shifted from comics as bad books to comics as a cause of juvenile delinquency. Wertham was a social reformer with impressive credentials, and his argument was more nuanced than he is given credit for, but he assumed the mantle of head anticomics crusader willingly. Using anecdotal evidence from his practice, he testified that comic books caused "psychological mutilation" of children.[5] "Educated on comic books, they go on to a long postgraduate course in jails."[6] Presaging an argument of antiporn feminists, he wrote, "There are laws according to which it is a punishable offense to 'contribute to the delinquency of a minor.' Yet the text, pictures and advertisements in crime comic books do that constantly."[7] Also like the antiporn feminists, he aligned himself with conservative religious groups to push for legislative sanctions.

As usual, the argument was that such sanctions would be, not censorship, but necessary protection of children, a sentiment nicely embodied in *Seduction of the Innocent*, the title of Wertham's influential book on the harm of comics. *Seduction* was published in 1954, just before the Kefauver congressional committee held hearings on juvenile delinquency, and since delinquency was by then assumed to be linked to comic books, they got investigated too. The committee buried evidence and discredited witnesses who didn't support its position, but its central purpose seemed to be to get the comic book industry to police itself, and in that, it succeeded. Later that year, the Comics Magazine Association enacted a comics code. Modeled on Hollywood's Production Code, the comics code read like an early, enthusiastic manual for political correctness, proscribing, among many things, disrespectful portrayals of "established authority," divorce treated humorously, double entendres, excessive slang, and bad grammar.[8] Distributors refused to sell comic books that didn't display a seal of compliance. As a consequence, horror and crime comics publishers went out of business, but after a period of readjustment, other publishers thrived, and today comics may be as violent and sexual as before, if not more so.

Mike argues that it's a mistake to assume that those who create or enjoy disturbing images are themselves disturbed or dangerous. "I feel like I was ignorant to think that they wouldn't come after me for such a thing," he says, summing up his experience. "I know now how the legal system works and how they screw people and put people on probation for anything they can just to keep them under the thumb of the authorities. . . . One of the things in Florida, it's a hundred times easier to get an automatic weapon than it is to get my magazine."

## TELEPHONE CONVERSATION TO LOS ANGELES, CALIFORNIA, AUGUST 1998

Just off the boardwalk on L.A.'s Venice Beach, cool central for skateboarders, hip-hoppers, filmmakers, tourists, and freaks, stands the Venice Pavilion. For two decades, its palm-studded patio, known as the Graffiti Pit, provided a showcase for graffiti artists, but by 1997, layers of paint had turned it into an eyesore, and a misguided cleanup—walls, benches, tables, even some trees painted bland beige or gunmetal gray—only made it worse. Stymied, the city turned for help to the Social and Public Art Resource Center, a respected community arts organization that has fostered murals throughout the city. SPARC came up with the idea of a giant, all-day Paint-Out.

Among the first to respond to SPARC's call was Richard Taylor, then a twenty-two-year-old muralist who had been working under the alias "xpres" since junior high, when photographs of New York's fever-bright subway painting had caught his eye. "Junior high is when you start to form an identity," he says, "but I was from the suburbs. I wasn't from the inner city, so . . ." He lets the implication hang. An innate artist like Mike, Richard was soon hanging out in an abandoned train tunnel in West L.A., apprenticing in graffiti.

It is August 1998 when Richard and I talk by phone. A newspaper photo from the year before shows him to have pleasing features and a shaved head, save for two rows of spiked hair jutting out like upturned rakes. Richard's suburb was the affluent Pacific Palisades, and creativity and open-mindedness were his family's values. His father, the son of an Air Force colonel, is a graphic artist who designed the *Enterprise* spaceship for the first *Star Trek* movie. His mother is a dancer, fashion designer, and portraitist, and both eventually came round to accepting his graffiti.

People have been making their mark on walls since Paleolithic times, but modern spray-can graffiti developed in northeastern cities in the 1970s and hit the West Coast the following decade, acquiring its own

customs, social structure, and vocabulary as it spread. A creator of graffiti is a "writer," who puts up "tags"—stylized-script names or aliases—
or paints ambitious murals called "pieces." Graffiti is ephemeral and
anonymous; the pleasure is in the doing and in demonstrating one's artistic and athletic prowess. Writers' status depends on their skill, and they
practice and protect their work by banding together in loose-knit groups
called "crews." "Spray paint's a very contemporary medium, and it can
be used to create these beautiful murals and pictures and lettering, or it
can be used to deface private property," Richard instructs. Gangs use it
to mark their turf, while graffiti artists aim to enhance their reputation
by putting their tags up as widely as possible. In general, graffiti defies
authority and orderliness and reflects the hip-hop culture from which it
stems. "Graffiti, for the youth, is always going to be a movement of resistance. Graffiti just shows the discontent in the city."

Graffiti is a form of expression and communication. It speaks elo-
quently to those who speak its language; to others, it can bring a smile
for its wit or sass. A poor man's art, free and freewheeling, it takes the
"I am" of 'zines and adds an "I was here," often in places you can't imagine anyone reaching. In 1974, Norman Mailer wrote enthusiastically,
"What a quintessential marriage of cool and style to write your name in
giant separate living letters, large as animals, lithe as snakes, mysterious
as Arabic and Chinese curls of alphabet, and do it in the heat of a winter night when the hands are frozen and only the heart is hot with fear.
No wonder the best of the graffiti writers . . . are known, famous and lu-
minous as a rock star."[9]

While in high school and eager to avoid the gang image, Richard got
involved with CBS, a well-established crew from Hollywood with thirty
to forty members. (He says CBS stands for Can't Be Stopped, but, like
most crews' names, it seems to have multiple meanings.) It was the diversity that appealed to him, he says, rattling off what sounds like
Woody Guthrie updated: "White kids from the Hollywood Hills whose
fathers were CEOs, kids from East L.A. who were just scratching their
names on bus windows, Asian kids from down south near Huntington,
a black kid from Echo Park named Show who was a skateboarder. They
all came together for mural painting and the creativity and the bond of
that."

Richard began writing as a personal statement—his stories all have to
do with the artistry and challenge of getting a piece up—but after high
school, his ambitions shifted. He was impatient with education and
structure, and the death of a close friend seems to have spooked him. "I

was like eighteen," he says, "and I started to think, this is my mark on the city. I'm going to do big artwork in as many places as I can and get my name up as many places as I can, and when I die maybe some of this stuff will still be around."

He moved into a warehouse in a dangerous downtown neighborhood and earned barely enough to live on by painting commercial murals. He liked that no one was telling him what to do with his life, but within a year, he got arrested for doing graffiti and for carrying a concealed weapon—self-defense, he says—and one night when he was drunk and got locked in the hallway of the warehouse without his elevator key, he punched through a wired-glass window and severed the tendons in his hand, making it hard to draw. When the downscale allure faded, he rented a place in Venice and through a roommate got into a kind of anarchist-punk rock that led him to a kind of anarchist-punk politics. One day, the roommate pointed to the adornments on Richard's clothes—a Soviet hammer and sickle and an anarchist image of snakes eating a cross—and suggested he learn what the symbols meant.

"I didn't understand the ideas of Karl Marx, Friedrich Engels, or even read anything on Prudhon or Bakunin or any of the anarchists," Richard says of this time. "I didn't have a grasp of socialism or what had gone on in history." So he took out student loans, spent two years at San Francisco State, then transferred to the Arts Center College of Design in Pasadena, where he was working toward a degree when, in the summer of 1997, word went out to graffiti artists about painting the Venice Pavilion.

---

The Paint-Out was intended to restore the Pavilion's beauty and to celebrate the visual richness of the city, but SPARC had an additional motive: to establish some rare common ground for the kids and police. Graffiti is illegal in Los Angeles, as in most American cities, and with California's three-strikes-and-you're-out law, punishment can be severe. Risk seems to be part of the thrill, but the danger is not just of getting arrested. Writers fall from bridges, get maimed in accidents, get shot by rivals or police. Richard tells of the death of a boy called Skate, who had started the CBS crew: "He was killed painting freight trains. He got hit by an Amtrak train. His girlfriend found him dismembered." He wasn't yet twenty.

An urban phenomenon, graffiti evokes all the fears of the city: crime, decay, anonymity, corruption—what families move to the suburbs to avoid. Its advocates praise its strong work ethic and argue that it is better for kids to work out antagonisms with paint cans than with guns, but even its fans probably wouldn't welcome unsolicited painting on the side of their houses. "The difference between graffiti and art is permission,"[10] proclaims an antigraffiti Web site in another oversimplification about what art is and isn't. Whether you enjoy graffiti, ignore it, outlaw it, or exhibit it depends on whether you think it is art or vandalism, but the official response for the past two decades has all the earmarks of a moral panic: social uneasiness over marginalized expression that leads to scapegoating, political grandstanding, journalistic hand-wringing, and an overzealous crackdown that vilifies and further alienates kids thought to be at risk.

Richard contends that repressive laws don't abolish graffiti; instead, they undermine good graffiti. "How can you pursue beautiful graffiti art when you're doing it in the middle of the night and you're scared you're going to get shot, arrested, whatever?" he asks. It seems disingenuous to claim that legalizing graffiti will solve anything, though, when the goal of graffitists is to draw outside the law. "Bandit art," Richard calls it, and when banditry loses its stigma, what's left but not-so-radical chic?

"Obviously a certain lawlessness goes with adolescence, but there does not need to be the degree of endangerment on both sides," insists Judy Baca, cofounder and artistic director of SPARC and a noted muralist who teaches at UCLA. "We're talking about young people going to prison for life for making art. And as adults we're acting irresponsibly if we don't understand that the creation of these new art forms comes primarily out of the ghettos and inner cities across the country. It's in those places where some of the most interesting innovation occurs." If those who enforce the laws could recognize that, she continues, "if the cops could begin to see these kids as other than gang members, then they would be less apt to perceive them as useless and expendable."

As preparation for the Paint-Out, SPARC held four meetings where organizers explained that the murals should address the theme "City of Angels" and laid down rules: no violence or obscenity in the pieces, "no drugs, no booze, no BS" from the writers. They also convinced the kids that this wasn't a sting operation, no mean feat, since graffitists treasure their anonymity. SPARC has a good reputation among writers, particularly those who think of themselves as muralists, as Richard does, but since it discourages illegal graffiti, an outlaw faction was skeptical. They particularly disliked having to go through the approval process SPARC had negotiated with the city. Ultimately, though, all participants agreed to let representatives of the Recreation and Parks Department review their sketches at the last of the SPARC meetings. Richard's sketch and another weren't available that night, but SPARC and the department agreed in a videotaped conversation that these two murals would be reviewed as they were being painted.

---

On August 16, 1997, Paint-Out Day, ninety-seven writers, boys between sixteen and twenty-five, who usually resisted anything that smacked of authority, painted two thousand feet of eye-popping, lapel-grabbing, pulsating mural. Rival crews worked side by side, talking and joking with police officers, city officials, corporate sponsors, journalists, and passersby, as images ranging from biblical scenes to political statements like Richard's emerged from the whitewashed walls.

Richard's mural, *Time for Slaughter,* was a diptych. On one side, an oversized kid hunched over a book that emitted orbs of light, a look of astonishment on his face; opposite, a blue-uniformed figure with a pig's face raised a billy club over a cowering tagger who looked like a dark-skinned Richard. It was clearly a picture of official aggression, but not necessarily, he insists, police brutality; he left the identity vague on purpose. SPARC was later to call the image "trite," but the mural is skillfully executed, and, Richard maintains, well balanced. "It had the yin and the yang. It was not just nihilistic and negative." He knew the piece was going to "push buttons," but, like every artist I spoke to, he insists that shock was not his aim. Instead, he cites Picasso, that all-purpose reference point, and political cartoonist Thomas Nast and talks about "spark[ing] people's interest in the relations of power" and throwing a metaphorical "brick through the limousine window." As he worked, police officers stopped to talk. "They came up to me and they said, 'Oh, that's cold, man, that's cold.' I'm like, well look, there's a lot of things that are cold that go on. This is just a piece of art."

One Recreation Department employee saw Richard's piece as he was putting it up and made no comment, though he recommended a change to an adjacent mural. A second employee saw the piece near completion and also said nothing. Given their previous agreement, SPARC assumed the silence constituted approval.

Richard had a great time at the Paint-Out, calling it "a peaceful day of painting and a productive day of painting." The press raved, the community glowed, and Judy too thought it "a pretty amazing event." So it was a sharp disappointment when, nearly two weeks later, a woman call-

ing herself Boston Dawna held a press conference to denounce Richard's
piece. A self-styled defender of the LAPD ("I have a big mouth and I'm
100 percent pro police," she told the *New York Times*),[11] she decided
that the pig-faced image insulted them. She claimed the police were going
to walk off the job in protest, and though SPARC never found any evidence of this, the charge was enough for the story to lead all the major
newscasts that night.

Slow news day, Judy figures, though the media frenzy probably had
something to do with the attention focused on police behavior after six
New York City policemen brutalized a Haitian immigrant earlier that
month. Richard was in the Bay Area when the controversy broke and
first heard about it from his sister, whom the press had tracked down.
Angry at how the media misrepresented him and his work, he was particularly unhappy with a local TV station that described his mural as kids
of color being beaten by a cop, adding, as if it were a damning revelation, that the muralist was a white kid from the suburbs.

Judy too was in San Francisco, which is where journalists besieged her
as she received an award. When the story turned up on national talk
shows, strangers called to accuse her of being a gang leader, apparently
unable to conceive of a responsible adult finding value in the expression
of disgruntled kids, or of teenagers joining together in anything other
than a gang. Still angry when we meet a year later, she says, "It was an
excellent opportunity for the police and the graffiti artists to meet and
have an exchange. I think the media usurped that capacity by whipping
people up against what we were doing in a way that made no sense."

The pressure to back down was fierce, but SPARC and Richard stood
their ground. Early in September, the Recreation Department, insisting
that it had not approved Richard's mural, asked the city council for permission to remove it. SPARC wasn't invited to the meeting but showed
up in protest, citing a federal law that requires ninety days' notice before
a work of art on a public building can be altered or removed. The council voted to cover up Richard's mural anyway, the first time the city had
prevented viewing of a public mural since 1932, when federal agents defaced David Siquieros's *American Tropical*. (In an irony Richard relishes,
the Getty Trust was trying to restore the Siquieros mural as his was being
destroyed.)

After the vote, the city covered Richard's mural with a heavy tarp.
Someone removed it. The city replaced the tarp and someone removed
it again. Next, the city tried wood planks, but these were torn down too.

Finally, someone—Judy says the police—spray-painted over part of Richard's image, and the piece was essentially ruined. In an attempt to turn down the heat, SPARC apologized publicly to the police. "Apologizing is no big deal," Judy says simply. "If they were offended, we were sorry."

SPARC proposed that Richard and another artist whose image the city also criticized be allowed to paint alternative murals. Don't change your ideas, Judy counseled Richard, change the way you present them to make them more acceptable. Richard has nothing but praise for Judy and SPARC, but other kids from the Paint-Out argued, why bother when the city already lied to us? It's worth seeing if adults can be trusted to let you make legal sites, Judy argued back. Let's try.

The objections to Richard's mural centered on the usual complaints about adolescent expression—bad taste, inappropriateness, mockery, insult—but he understood that more than good manners was at stake, so he set to work on a new sketch to present for the city's approval. The single figure became a family, probably immigrants, fleeing a threat, which now came from a large boar lurking around the corner. And because getting even is the artist's prerogative, vultures hovering overhead represented the news media.

At a meeting that November, two sketches were submitted to the Recreation and Parks Commission. The other artist's sketch, devoid of political content, was approved; Richard's was turned down. It is not a matter of censorship, but of permission, said the commissioners, and this is not a story we want to tell on our wall. Wait a minute, Richard and SPARC argued, it's not your wall, it's a public wall. And where does it say you get to decide? What makes one sketch okay and the other not? What about parks being public spaces? What about neutrality on the content of expression? What about the First Amendment?

"They did it all on record," says Judy. "And Richard Taylor sued them."

It wasn't such a big leap. Lawyers from SPARC and the ACLU were already involved, and the constitutional issues crystallized the next day at a meeting of the city's Cultural Affairs Commission. When that commission agreed to help Richard find another wall to paint on, the discrepancy between the responses highlighted the subjectivity of the Recreation Commission's decision and the flimsiness of its argument.

Public art has legal protection, but, as Judy points out, it suffers from its historical association with people of color. Think of the roiling, muscular murals of the WPA with their Mexican influences. Think about the collaborative, community-based nature of public art with its challenge to ideas of authorship and property. Those associations—WPA, dark-skinned, foreign, communist—cast suspicion on public murals in the United States and made them seem a lesser form of art. So too with graffiti. "Graffiti is a frontline attack in a battle for the privatization of all public space," Judy proclaims, citing the billboards that graffiti rivals for public attention. "The kids make very powerful statements to say, why is it that you get your name and your ideas up there big if you are a corporation and you have money? What about me?" She concludes, "Public art is the creation of civic space . . . civil discussion . . . public memory."

By banning Richard's mural, the city asserted its dominion over the civic space Richard and his fellow writers also laid claim to, over the civil discussion they wanted to take part in, and over the freedom they thought was theirs. To police and city officials, the issue was disrespect for authority. To Judy, it is the brutality police use to control public images and the kids who make them. To Richard, it is how kids learn to be productive citizens. "The visions of artists such as myself do not become positive through negative reinforcement and censorship," he wrote as the controversy wore on.[12]

When it came time to face the city, Steve Rohde, the lawyer who took Richard's case for the ACLU, cited the artist-friendly ruling in *Finley v NEA* (see Chapter 5). This was before the Supreme Court overturned that decision and sanctioned some subjective criteria in awarding government benefits, and Rohde argued that both the federal and the California constitutions barred the city from refusing Richard's new sketch because it disliked the message. By now, everyone, including the police, was sick of the whole thing, and when Richard and I talk, the city has just agreed to enact new rules to protect the rights of artists and to find a good public site for him to paint his revised mural. Though it is too late to save his first mural, this is a sweet victory. All that remains is to decide where the new mural will go.

That was in August 1998. Richard has since finished his college degree and now does some commercial artwork and teaching and lots of experimenting in his own art. He still paints an occasional wall, just to keep his hand in, and reports proudly that one of his murals is being documented in a friend's thesis. Meanwhile, I've been e-mailing Steve Rohde regularly since the settlement came through. Every holiday, it seems, I send off the same question: Is Richard Taylor's case resolved? And back comes the reply: Happy Easter, Fourth of July, Thanksgiving, New Year. . . . Not yet.

## TELEPHONE CONVERSATION TO NEW HAVEN, CONNECTICUT, SEPTEMBER 2000

While place was a defining element in Mike's and Richard's stories, for Paul Kim, it was time: the year 1994, when a nascent Internet was taking hold in the popular imagination as an unsettled and unsettling frontier where techno-cowboys, cyberbandits, and adolescent boys roamed free, uninhibited by rules or social niceties. News stories from that time painstakingly explain what the World Wide Web is and put quotation marks around "home page," but since relatively few people actually were online, misperception reigned.

At the time, Paul was a seventeen-year-old senior at Newport High School in Bellevue, Washington. A teacher had arranged an internship for him and two of his friends with the University of Washington's Astrophysics Group, where they learned HTML, the language of the Web, built educational sites, and fooled around. "One of the things that I thought would be fun to do," he says, "was to create a Web site for my high school because at the time there were only maybe a dozen or so. So like wow, you know? They've done it, let's do it." Using university computers and later his own at home, Paul created and hosted The Unofficial Site of Newport High School.

The site, he admits more or less readily, depending on his mood, was silly. It made fun of the school's physical plan and championship football team and included links to other pages about subjects he figured would interest his visitors, including sex. Under the heading "Favorite Topics of Newport High School Students," he created links to *Playboy* and articles about masturbation. "Pretty juvenile, really," he says, laughing. "But then I was a juvenile. So there!" Six years later, Paul and I talk. He is starting his second year at Yale Law School and shoehorns our phone conversation amid efforts to finish an overdue paper. Paul has e-mailed me a photo of himself taken at Yosemite that shows a slender young man in a white T-shirt with short, dark hair cresting over a high forehead. He stares sternly at the camera through round glasses, though on the phone, he is anything but stern. He laughs often in a low-pitched giggle, as if unsure whether to be amused, amazed, or outraged at the tale he's telling. At times, his voice curls up at the end of sentences like a kid's;

at others, he weigh his words carefully, sounding like the lawyer he is to become.

"Obviously when I chose to put provocative material on there—and it's there in the word, there has to be an object to provoke—there was the thought that if somebody [discovered the site], it would be fun in that way. . . . I weighed whether I could get in trouble and I decided, no, I could not. I guess being that, I don't know, thorn in someone's side, being in a situation where somebody is trying to shut you up and they can't because we have free speech in this country, being in that position wasn't going to bother me."

Bellevue is a prosperous suburb of Seattle, more conservative than the city but not outstandingly so. Paul moved there with his family—he is the youngest of three children by several years—when he started high school. Before that, they lived in Chicago, and before that, in Korea, where he was born. His parents are divorced. He lived with his mother, who spends a lot of time in Korea. His father was once a Catholic priest. "Is that funny or what?" he asks, not particularly amused. "I grew up Catholic. Catholics are always the incredibly naughty ones." His high school was, he says, "very white," then adds, almost as an afterthought, "There were Asian students, but very few black or Hispanic students. I stood out because I was one of a group of students who were, you know, academically talented, but I didn't stand out socially."

In fact, Paul was a stellar student and somewhat of a leader, and the mockery on his home page came from high spirits, not resentment, as with Mike, or resistance, as with Richard. At worst, it was irreverent or puerile, but before long, more alarming material started showing up on the Web. In February 1995, Jake Baker, a sophomore at the University of Michigan, was arrested for writing and posting a rape-murder fantasy in which he named a female classmate. He spent twenty-nine days in prison before charges were dismissed. The following fall, Richard Machado e-mailed death threats to fifty-nine Asian students at the University of California at Irvine, where he had been enrolled, and became the first person convicted of a hate crime on the Internet. The Web is an ideal milieu for extreme and antisocial viewpoints, but what appears there is speech, most of which is protected, and convictions for online hate crimes remained relatively rare.

Then, on April 20, 1999, at Columbine High School in Littleton, Colorado, two students killed twelve classmates, a teacher, and themselves, creating a fault line in the national psyche between fear for our children and fear of our children. "[Children] deserve, they demand, special protection, not just for their protection, but for the rest of our protection,"[13] said James Garbarino, a psychologist, on *Meet the Press* soon after.

The claim is sometimes made that we are a child-centered society, but our social and economic policies give the lie to that. What we are is child-anxious, and that anxiety is particularly prominent among the striving, achievement-oriented middle class, who were now confronted with white kids killing other white kids in communities where they had thought themselves shielded from this brand of horror. Schools are generally safe places. According to government figures, fatalities, fights, injuries, and weapon seizures fell steadily between 1991 and 1999, as did all other rates of teenage violence.[14] At the end of the decade, the chance of getting killed in an American school was about one in two million.[15] But security is part reality, part perception: 70 percent of respondents to a poll taken at that time believed that a shooting in their local school was likely.[16]

In the ongoing national discussion about how to bring kids to adulthood safely, talk turned frequently to the decline of manners, the customs we use to address and interact with each other. It is a well-worn lament, centuries old, but not an irrelevant one. Even Columbine involved manners to some extent. The rest seems to have been a complex web of anger, bravado, and despair that we can't understand—how can we?—and so we supply whatever devil suits our politics, fears, and fashion statements: guns, jocks, Marilyn Manson, trenchcoats. At the time of the Columbine killings, three-quarters of school districts nationwide already had character education programs planned or in place.[17] After Columbine, anxious parents, adamant experts, and edgy school officials seized on manners like a swarm of exorcists waving a crucifix before a vampire. Under "zero tolerance" policies, they regulated student speech, dress, music, and artwork and punished violations with suspensions and expulsions mounting to more than three million incidents in 1999.[18] This overreaction would be funny—a Florida middle school went so far as to prescribe acceptable colors for shoelaces—if the consequences weren't so serious.

Much of the uneasiness has focused on the Internet and what students find there—as if pubescent boys didn't thumb through *Playboy* long before they clicked on it, or bad guys weren't as gorily dead in cowboy movies as in video game bloodbaths, or teenagers wouldn't think about sex if it weren't for computers. As soon as the Internet became commonplace, the government tried to restrict it. The Communications Decency Act (CDA) of 1996 criminalized the transmission of "indecent" messages to minors over the Internet, but it was ruled unconstitutional. In 1998, Congress enacted the Children's Online Protection Act (COPA), a variation of the CDA, but a court blocked enforcement, and when the Supreme Court reviewed it in 2002, the justices voiced doubts about its constitutionality, remanded it to a lower court, and kept it from taking effect until the issue was settled. In 2000, Congress slipped through the Children's Internet Protection Act (CIPA), which mandated that schools and libraries benefiting from federal subsidies or a federal discount on technology called the E-rate install filtering software, known in some circles as censorware. As usual, poor communities would be hardest hit because they depend most heavily on the E-rate, and, as usual, when the law was reviewed in court—the case applied only to filtering in libraries—it was struck down by a panel of judges who called the filters "blunt instruments." The Supreme Court will hear the case, *U.S. v American Library Association,* in its 2002–2003 term.

About 17 percent of libraries and a large majority of schools already use filters to limit what their students can read online, though the software is notoriously clumsy and ineffective. It is unlikely that the government could get away with legislation that blocks as much and as capriciously as these programs do, sites covering everything from safe sex to Oprah Winfrey, Amnesty International to Massachusetts Congressman Ed Markey, the Southern Poverty Law Center to the Traditional Values Coalition, and literary giants from Aristophanes to Voltaire.[19] As Daniel Silverman, a student who set up a system to bypass the blocking system in his high school, notes, "The idea that a handful of employees at InterGate [his school's filter] have been able to read through millions upon millions of Web sites and determine what is 'objectionable' is laughable."[20] Two far-reaching reports, one by the federally appointed COPA Commission[21] (itself frequently blocked) and another by the National Research Council,[22] more or less agreed, rejecting overreliance on techno-fixes and recommending education as a better idea.

Paul's case was the first of its kind to get widespread attention, but it soon became common for schools to crack down on students' Web sites.[23] When we talked, two such incidents had recently unfolded near Seattle. One involved an off-campus site mocking an assistant principal; the student was expelled for a year but eventually won $10,000 in damages.[24] The other, in which a student was suspended for posting a hit list on his Web site, had caught Paul's attention. "Obviously this was such a major threat in this post-Columbine era that the student had to be immediately punished," he says, his voice dripping with irony, since the "hit list" turned out to be a spoof stemming from a class assignment to write obituaries.

I counter with a story of three teachers in a suburban Indianapolis high school who took the unusual step of suing a student over a Web site that mocked them as "Satan-worshiping demons."[25] The teachers claimed emotional distress and defamation; the student, predictably, said it was a joke. "At least they sued him," Paul responds. "This seems to be, from one perspective, a more valid way to attack a problem. Because in a school setting, the students do not have as much protection." It didn't take Paul long to learn that firsthand.

---

It had never occurred to him to ask permission for his home page. To his mind, there was nothing that needed permitting, and according to the Student Press Law Center, case law largely exempts the off-campus speech of public school students from school control.[26] Paul doesn't think school officials would have understood what he was talking about anyway, since he doubts the school had Internet access when he unveiled his site. That was October 1994; he remembers because it was when he met his boyfriend. It was also around the time he was coming out as gay, but he mentions this in passing, no big deal. The page sat obscurely on the Internet for a few months until a teacher at another high school in the district came across it, printed it and its links, and faxed the packet to Paul's principal, Karin Cathey, with a note asking if she knew what her students were up to. The implication was that she didn't and at her own peril. Paul's was the only name on the site, so he was held responsible.

Adolescent behavior is full of pushes and pulls, testing limits while seeking adult approval. Paul was, by his own lights, "a good kid." He didn't get into trouble or think of adults as the enemy, so when the assistant principal called him to a meeting in March, he wasn't alarmed. Since she apparently knew nothing about the Web, he explained that he hadn't created the sexy stuff, that you had to make an effort to jump to *Playboy* and the like, that no one would confuse his site with a school-sanctioned one since a banner headline proclaimed it unofficial. He recognizes that bureaucrats tend to be overly cautious but says, "I think even then—especially then—people probably realized that not all content on the Web is official and verified."

The assistant principal listened, then asked Paul how he'd feel about being suspended. "I was pretty shocked," he tells me. "Maybe I wasn't that shocked, but I was still bothered that they would threaten me with a suspension." He agreed to remove the page from Yahoo's listings and eventually took it down completely, but the site itself seemed to be less of a problem than his perceived disobedience. On March 28, 1995, Principal Cathey called him into her office and, with little preamble, announced that she had written to revoke the school's endorsement of him for a National Merit Scholarship.

"The things she did were so bizarre," he says, stretching the word till it snaps. "And this was possibly the most bizarre thing that she did." National Merit scholars are selected from a pool of semifinalists who have earned a certain score on their PSATs. Semifinalists complete a mostly factual form, not a recommendation, which requires their principal's signature, and since National Merit scholars redound to their school's credit, the signature is routine. "So she had me demoted from finalist to semifinalist status"—he laughs in disbelief—"and thereby ineligible for the actual award. I like to think that I have a pretty keen sense of justice and I knew this was so unfair. And it was $2,000 for that matter!"

Paul had had little to do with his principal until then. In his outrage and disbelief, he didn't bother to figure out why she did what she did, nor did she explain, but it appears that Cathey, like many adults at the time, felt threatened by technology that was foreign to her. Did she also think he was doing something immoral? I ask. "That's what she made it sound like," he says.

Late March, when college acceptance letters are imminent, is an anxious time for college-bound high school seniors, so when Paul got a phone call from an admissions officer at Columbia University, he paid attention. The officer reported that he had received, in Paul's words, "this very strange letter" from Cathey and wondered what it was all about. The letter indicated that Paul had gotten a copy, but this was the first he had heard of it. Contemplating the ruin of his academic career, he immediately drove to school to read the letter, which is when he found out that there was not one letter, but two, sent by Cathey to all the schools he had applied to. The first letter, citing no specifics, announced that he was no longer a National Merit finalist and that the school rescinded any recommendations on his behalf but offered no details or explanation. The second letter, sent a few days later, stated that the earlier letter was not intended to have any adverse effect on admission decisions. By this point in his narrative, Paul is snorting with laughter. "She was just covering her ass. . . . Even she must have realized what a horrible thing she had done." The principal had a copy of the second, backtracking letter with its FedEx receipts, but she claimed not to be able to find a copy of the first one. Still not knowing what it said, Paul wrote the schools with his version of events.

Then he wrote the ACLU, who agreed to take his case.

Schools violate kids' civil rights all the time and usually get away with it.[27] Educators have considerable legal backing when they argue that they have the authority to restrict students' speech that interferes with the educational environment, and even victimless pranks like Paul's have been punished using that rationale. Newport High was split on the issue— some teachers signed a letter in support of Paul, others backed the principal—while local and national news media took up Paul as a poster child for both free speech and adolescent obnoxiousness. When schools do get a legal challenge, it is in their interest to settle, rather than to run up big legal bills, and with good sense prevailing at Newport, settlement talks soon got under way.

Paul sat in on these meetings, finding the legal exchanges intriguing and the accusations against him disturbing. Still, his take is judicious. "On one hand, I realize that the power of speech is tremendous and that's one of the reasons we have it be free. On the other hand, I think there's a break somewhere between the weightiness of [adolescent] speech and the weightiness with which it is handled. It amazes me that just because somehow it suggests the person in authority has a lack of control, it gets dealt with very severely."

That fall, Paul went east to Columbia University. He had been turned down by most of the schools he applied to, though he doesn't know if the letters made a difference. Cathey's correspondence led Columbia to withhold a planned offer of a prestigious research fellowship, but that decision was reviewed and the scholarship restored. Meanwhile, negotiations with his high school continued. As he sees it, "There wasn't that much room to give. They either admitted they did something wrong or they didn't. And eventually, they did." In December 1995, the settlement was made public: the school district issued an apology, paid Paul the $2,000 he would have gotten from a National Merit Scholarship, and agreed to correct his records at the universities where he had applied.

---

As with many battles with teenagers, Paul's story reads like so much fuss over so little of consequence. Had he published a newspaper with the same content as his home page, school administrators would have been barred from interfering or punishing him, but because his medium was the Internet, everything seemed up for grabs.

Technological innovations from the printing press on have exacerbated cultural anxiety, as Cassandras warn of stolen souls, machines run amok, tyranny by a technical elite, privacy undermined, human interaction devalued, and social restraints weakened. The fears are not without basis: the medium does affect our relationship to the material and to each other, and each new technology tends to pull its users progressively away from the public sphere. Before the telephone, we spoke face to face; before television, we shared cultural experiences in theaters, grange halls, and parlors. Now, with computers, we can call up culture or converse at home on a screen large enough for only one. Our interaction with the world is increasingly private and disembodied, and where we once relied on physical communities to absorb rambunctious behavior, we now are asked to put our faith in virtual ones. The Internet can be a disruptive medium, a place where impatient kids with minimal social sophistication leapfrog over their parents and teachers in technical sophistication and dexterity.[28] It is also an ideal place for adolescents to test-drive their burgeoning autonomy. Yet for kids who, like Mike, feel trapped in a geographic place, it offers alternative communities and outlets for the fantasies that are central to their development.

Telecommunications expert Eli Noam has likened the Internet to a Rorschach blot onto which we project our hopes and fears,[29] and public opinion polls bear this out. One recent poll found that a majority of parents in "computer households" support the Internet as an educational tool, but 49 percent believe Internet use could interfere with their ability to teach values and beliefs. (The poll also found that in a year's worth of reporting about the Internet in mainstream newspapers, one of every four stories concerned sex crimes with children,[30] which is way out of proportion to the phenomenon.) In another survey, large majorities of respondents wanted pornography and hate speech blocked on school computers,[31] and a third survey found that kids themselves—67 percent of fifteen- to twenty-four-year-olds—supported legislation tying the E-rate to filtering, though many also reported being blocked from sites where they had sought health information.[32]

"I think that you have an irrational response these days, if it's on the Internet it's somehow ten times more threatening," says Paul. And later, "I don't have children yet and so I don't know how I'll feel about it when I'm a parent, but if a kid accidentally sees a nude image, for example, is it really going to warp their minds forever?"

Children, we are told repeatedly, are innocent—meaning, I suppose, that they lack knowledge of themselves and awareness of what they don't yet know. But adolescents are quickly introduced to knowingness, if not understanding, and forbidden knowledge, when discovered, looms larger for having been hushed up. "Innocence is a state in which we try to maintain our children; dignity is a state we claim for ourselves," writes J. M. Coetzee,[33] which may be why a lot of child rearing seems aimed at breaking the anarchistic back of childhood. Well, fair enough. The charms of adolescent anarchy pall quickly, and somebody has to be in control while kids come to terms with societal rules and norms. But why do adults—including baby boomer parents who were once served their own set of dire predictions about the things that entertained them—seem destined to repeat this ritual of speaking bitterness about kids and their culture? Embarrassment at having been young? Mistaking the erosion of one's cultural authority for cultural decline? Sticking a finger in the dike, not because it will keep back the sea of adolescent confusion, but because that is what adults are supposed to do? Is it amnesia? Or is it remembering too well how difficult it is to be young and unformed and wishing to spare kids that pain?

Popular culture, with its idealizing of adolescent rebellion and its endless capacity to irritate and strut—Combs' Bad Boy Records, Eminem's Anger Management Tour—isn't much help. Kids naturally reject their parents' cultural touchstones to seek out their own, just as parents, in turn, seem destined to rail against those choices. Even the vocabulary changes little. In the 1930s, Cardinal O'Connell denounced crooning as "a man whining a degenerate song, which is unworthy of any American man."[34] In the 1950s, Frank Sinatra wrote that rock 'n' roll was "the most brutal, ugly, desperate, vicious form of expression it has been my misfortune to hear"[35] (to which Elvis replied, "You can't knock success"). Today, the *New York Times* describes Eminem as "a white rapper who has successfully burrowed his way to the nauseating depths of degradation and self-loathing."[36]

But it's not the same, cry parents: the culture has become so much more coarse, explicit, menacing. The Beatles may have sung, "Why don't we do it in the road," but Eminem raps, "Bleed bitch bleed" about his wife. As it gets harder to shock, images get more shocking, and kids supposedly grow numb. There is a difference between the Beatles and Eminem, just as there is between *Mad Magazine*'s silly sex jokes and Mike's raped babies. What remains constant about provocative images is that their creators are playacting, indulging in fantasies of power and abandon. The Beatles probably preferred "doing it" in bed, Eminem's wife is alive and apparently fed up enough with his misogyny to have considered divorce, and most Alfred E. Newman fans graduate to more sophisticated fare, learning to worry along the way.

The rub for those distressed about kids and words is probably less what the creators of vexing images say and do, or even that their audiences won't be able to make the distinction, than that somebody is losing control. Senator Orrin Hatch poignantly told a congressional committee, "The knowledge of our children's lives—without which we cannot hope to fulfill our responsibilities as parents—seems increasingly out of our grasp."[37] Typically, the response to losing control is to push for more control, and so we get "zero tolerance" policies, which ignore that democracy is predicated on tolerance and maturity on the capacity to make distinctions. And we get situations like Mike's, Richard's, and Paul's, which involved, not parents' disciplining their children, but people in authority Teaching These Kids a Lesson.

I've noticed a strange dynamic in conversations about kids and speech: what begins as discussion about expression, such as what movies kids get to watch, turns at some point into questions about actions, like how old they should be to have sex or to go on a school trip to Costa Rica. I don't know the right age for sexual activity or visiting Costa Rica, though I'd guess it depends on the child. The same goes for movies and books and other forms of expression, which is why overarching regulation by the government or its stand-ins seems so wrongheaded. Much of popular entertainment is repugnant, and kids are susceptible to its messages, but young people have always had to make their way through the words, images, and ideas they encounter. They need guidance in figuring out how to respond to those they dislike or fear, and until they can protect themselves, they need some kinds of protection. Among the necessary protections are their civil rights. The lessons and responsibilities of free expression are not learned in a vacuum; they must be lived with and practiced. Denying those rights to kids, even in the name of safeguarding them, is a real harm to minors.

part three

# BALANCING ACTS

TRY AS WE MIGHT to draw lines when speech challenges an orthodoxy or institution, contemporary word wars are a riot of smudged distinctions. In 1958, in "Two Concepts of Liberty," Isaiah Berlin examined what should be done when the rights of reasonable people collide and suggested, "When ends are agreed, the only questions left are those of means." We agreed long ago in America that the First Amendment is a means to liberty, only now to find ourselves at odds over the ends to which that liberty should be put. Though few people champion censorship outright, we all can probably make a list of words or images that cross some line, and lately we have been trained by vivid object lessons to test what we say or think according to someone else's acceptability scale. This caution and its backlash are particularly apparent in arenas like the workplace, where First Amendment law is evolving, and in fields of knowledge, such as science, which has expanded vastly beyond what the framers of the Bill of Rights could have anticipated.

These are the settings for the stories of Steve Johnson and David Kern, which make up this final section. Steve was a firefighter with the Los Angeles County Fire Department when he sued his employer over a sexual harassment policy that banned *Playboy* from all fire stations. David was a doctor specializing in occupational medicine in Pawtucket, Rhode Island, when the owners of a textile factory where he had uncovered a dangerous new lung disease threatened to sue him if he reported his findings and the hospital and university where he worked declined to back him up.

Though both sought to defend the principle of free speech, it would be hard to find two people less alike in manner or circumstance. Steve initiated his fight to make a point; David reacted to an attack on his professional integrity. Steve thrived on the resulting publicity; David preferred anonymity. Steve put his faith in the legal system; David doubted that a court should determine medical policy. Steve's struggle concerned the freedom to read what he wanted; David's potentially concerned life and death. Finally, in an arena where outcomes are seldom clear-cut, Steve won and David lost. What the two men shared, and share with everyone in this book, was a refusal to shut up and go away, and at their most high-minded, these were struggles against giving into someone else's view of the world. Acquiescing would have been easier, but when a person is separated from his or her truth, something ruptures and integrity is lost.

Despite our radical beginnings, Americans are not a particularly revolutionary people. We tend to turn our anger inward, preferring Prozac to Marx and counting political misdeeds as the cost of stability. We are avid reformers, but only up to a point. We have a soft spot for troublemakers up to a point, too. Beyond that point, we distance ourselves, fearing the taint of their stubborn or noisy refusal. When David and Steve insisted their rights were being trammeled, they were denounced and snubbed—Steve as a "troublemaker," David as a "renegade physician"—and because their would-be censors were people they knew and had worked and cooperated with, the sense of betrayal was bitter on both sides.

Those who wanted to limit these men's speech painted themselves as voices of reason: the fire department claimed to be responding to the context, not content, of the magazines; the textile company, rather than challenging the accuracy of David's findings, argued that disclosure was premature. David and Steve understood the need to weigh purposes and values or aims that might compete—David recognized the potential for abuse in scientific research, Steve the injury from sexual harassment—but they also knew that the attempts to restrict what they could read or report, that is, to restrict information and knowledge, were neither necessary nor balanced.

Knowledge is frequently unwelcome. From bad news to images of cruelty to scary science: Who at some point hasn't wanted not to know? (Or is it that we want it both ways: to want to know everything and to want what we know to be nice?) Sometimes we need to push the boundaries of knowing—for safety, judgment, social cohesion, the historical record. Sometimes we simply desire to know. But curiosity is not an unalloyed good. There is hubris in pursuing risky knowledge, arrogance in insisting on knowing more than we have a purpose for, and the relentless thrum of information that engulfs us is surely more than we can possibly use.

In *Forbidden Knowledge,* literary scholar Roger Shattuck lists six categories of knowledge that have, in various times and places, been off limits. Under knowledge that is dangerous, destructive, or undesirable, he includes technology, sexual cruelty, and violence, and he recommends that such material be labeled and restricted. The walls erected to keep knowledge out also keep ignorance in, though—as women find when they are shielded from information (usually about their bodies) that someone (usually a man) thinks will harm them. Also, such barriers seldom withstand the test of time, as scientists throughout history have demonstrated. So from carnal knowledge to scientific discovery, the pressing issue, as David and Steve learned, is how we will deal with the consequences of knowing.

In 1633, Galileo Galilei was called before the Inquisition in Rome to disavow what his judges believed to be heresy and he believed to be truth: that the Earth rotates on its axis. Nearly seventy years old, sentenced to house arrest, and banned from publishing his work for the rest of his life, Galileo knelt before his censors and recanted.

"And yet," he is said to have whispered as he rose slowly from his knees, "it turns."

chapter eleven

# WHAT DO YOU MEAN I CAN'T READ *PLAYBOY?*

Steve Johnson

*Newport Beach, California, December 1996*

Captain Steve Johnson of the Los Angeles County Fire Department likes to repeat himself, and one of the assertions he repeats often is that affirmative action gives preference to minorities and women only when all other things are equal. He seems to like this perspective because it lets him be in favor of affirmative action and against it at the same time. "I really think that there's room for that philosophy in our society," he says, but adds that too often the policy is misapplied. When his fire department issued a sweeping, new sexual harassment policy that prohibited anyone from reading *Playboy* at a fire station, even in off-duty hours, it seemed a gross misapplication to him. Steve is no feminist, but he wasn't opposed to efforts to prevent discrimination in the department. He just didn't think a magazine could harass, nor did he want anyone telling him what he could and could not do in his nonworking hours. So, in 1994, he took Los Angeles County to court over the right to read *Playboy*.

Since the term *sexual harassment* was first used a quarter-century ago,[1] employers and employees, lawyers, judges and juries, politicians and theorists have tried to figure out what it is and what should be done about it. In 1975, the feminist group Working Women United described sexual harassment as "the treatment of women workers as sexual objects."[2] In 1993, Supreme Court Justice Ruth Bader Ginsburg wrote that it revolved around "whether members of one sex are exposed to disadvantageous terms or conditions of employment to which members of the other sex are not exposed."[3] In 2001, Women in the Fire Service deemed it "a power play that is degrading, humiliating and intimidating to its vic-tim."[4] And the Equal Employment Opportunity Commission, whose guidelines form the basis for most sexual harassment policies, defines sexual harassment as "unwelcome sexual advances, requests for sexual favors and other verbal or physical conduct of a sexual nature" that are terms or conditions of employment.[5]

High-profile incidents, such as Paula Jones's accusations against Bill Clinton, Anita Hill's testimony against Clarence Thomas, and the group grope at the Navy's Tailhook convention, have dramatized the problem, but it is the ambiguous middle ground where most conflicts over sexu-ality at work occur. As the definitions suggest, part of the confusion is semantic, since that pesky little "sex" means more than one thing: sex-ual behavior used to bully, threaten, or abuse women at work; sexism, in which a woman is persecuted because she is a woman; and sexual ex-pression that supposedly makes a work situation unbearable for women. While the first two are clearly discriminatory, the last category, which comes under the rubric of "hostile environment," puts much sexual ha-rassment policy on a collision course with the First Amendment.

Sexual harassment is a serious problem with significant psychological, societal, political, and economic consequences,[6] and the women in L.A. County Fire Department couldn't have had an easy time of it. When Steve challenged his employer's policy, there were all of eleven female firefighters in a department of nearly 2,400, and one of them was un-dergoing a sex change procedure. These women had breached a citadel of "men's work," where sexual harassment appears to be common; by one reckoning, as many as 85 percent of paid and volunteer female fire-fighters have experienced it.[7] But women don't benefit when sexual ha-rassment is reduced to an all-purpose retort to boorish behavior, and Steve is adamant that no one wins when speech is curtailed. His story has all the trappings of a classic—sympathetic "victims," high-minded rhet-oric about dirty pictures, the clash of civil rights with civil liberties—but because his case rested solely on the ostensible offensiveness of words and pictures, it has a purity rare in the messy world of sexual harassment complaints.

---

To someone who has left Boston in a northeaster, southern California is a David Hockney watercolor, all starched blues and whites. In Newport Beach, where Steve lives, birds-of-paradise bloom brazenly and Christ-mas lights wrap around palm trees, turning them into chubby candelabra. It's one of those days that makes me think God must like the First Amendment. As that law's advance man, Steve has apparently been busy. When I try to track him down from the airport, everyone I speak to knows why I'm there: the dispatcher says she wants a copy of the book, the guy who answers the phone at the station near Mount Baldy where Steve now works tells me, "He's in the other room reading *Playboy*." I've gotten up before dawn, flown six hours, and spent the last forty-five minutes feeding quarters into a pay phone because Steve hasn't given me the right number. "Tell him to come to the telephone," I say.

Steve is a solid chunk of a man, barrel-chested, dimpled, walrus-mustached, and double-chinned. He walks on the balls of his feet with surprising agility for someone many pounds overweight (when he says, "You get less fit as you get older," his wife, Cathy, laughs and agrees, "*You* sure do"). He likes to drive fast and wear cherry-red suspenders and talk. His speech is Southern Cal–casual, with dropped g's at the end of words and reiterated phrases that create a comfortable cadence. His stories have back-stories and his back-stories have cross-references with footnotes, so that listening to him is like watching a home movie in reverse with a voluble narrator popping up from time to time to point a finger and promise that he'll soon get to the point.

Most of Steve's stories are about how he stirred things up at work. Battle clearly energizes him, particularly when he's sure that he is right. His lawyer described him to me as the kind of person employers call a troublemaker because he holds others to their stated policies. "With the fire department, yeah, I'm a professional pain in the ass," Steve acknowledges, "only because I would refuse to submit to the career intimidation."

He has been a firefighter for thirty years—he's fifty-two when we meet—and, except for a three-year stint in the Navy, has spent his whole life around Los Angeles. He trained as a Linotype operator, but one night, hot lead spurted into his shoe and convinced him that his days in that trade were numbered. His mother suggested firefighting instead, but jobs weren't easy to come by, so he felt lucky when he was hired by the small city of Signal Hill. His first marriage fell apart when his wife didn't want to be married to a firefighter, but that doesn't seem to bother his current wife of many years. Cathy Johnson matches her husband with her short, graying hair, stocky build, good humor, and inability to understand why women would insist on working where they aren't wanted. She doesn't worry about Steve, she tells me, though he did fall through a roof on the eve of their wedding.

Within a year of his training, he had moved to Huntington Park and then to Los Angeles County, a huge fire department that covers 2,278 square miles, an area bigger than Delaware or Rhode Island, and encompasses mountain ranges, high deserts, forests, and beaches, as well as fifty-seven cities. Steve has worked at more than one-fifth of the department's 157 stations, attending to plane crashes, urban riots, and massive blazes that required round-the-clock battles, courage, and strong nerves. He took to firefighting from the start, and he's proud of his career. "Every time the bell goes off it's a new challenge. As a rule the people you work with are really top-caliber people. We have our pranks, we have our fights, but when the chips are down, we're a team." More to the point, as he's fond of saying, "Our Band-Aids stick and our fires go out. What more do you want?"

---

In 1983, Steve made captain, the first-level supervisory rank. Three years later, spurred on by a perceived injustice to a young firefighter seeking a promotion, he became active in his union. "I heard his story and I saw nothing but red and decided that it's time somebody starts standing up for the rank and file," he says. Steve ran in the next union election and won handily, quickly earning a reputation for being aggressive, honest, and independent. "Clearly by then I had established myself as no one's going to own me, I'm here for the guys. I became the Robin Hood, if you will, of the union." He won the firefighter's case when it came before the civil service commission and boasts of winning 90 percent of the cases he took up as a union rep.

The union had an operating budget of approximately $1 million, though many times that amount passed through its books from a health insurance plan it managed. "Our union's internal financial system, I thought, was very vulnerable to a cheater. Guys could spend almost without being questioned," Steve says. He had long been curious about why the officials in his local wanted so badly to stay in office, and now that he was in a position to find out, his suspicions lit on the treasurer, a captain and a popular veteran of the department, who was making $60,000 but seemed to live far beyond his means.

It took Steve a year and a half to come up with anything concrete, and he did only when he chanced upon a bill from an American Express account that the treasurer had left behind in a copy machine at the union hall. Steve carefully analyzed the expenses the treasurer claimed, and, convinced that he was double- and triple-dipping, became a man with a mission. None of the other union officers would listen to him, though, and not until he took the highly unusual step of hiring an attorney at his own expense did they look into his charges. What they found was alarming. According to the *Los Angeles Times,* in his ten years in office, the treasurer had embezzled $300,000.[8] He was convicted and spent two and a half years in prison.

Steve says, "They"—union and fire department officials—"thought I was some kind of a crazy guy coming after this guy. They watched all this, but they didn't do anything about it till right at the end when it was obvious that I was right all along." Adding insult to injury, department officials denied him release time to work with the district attorney, and when Steve broke the chain of command to get permission to spend time on the case, they slapped him with a letter of reprimand. The letter wasn't a big deal, but it could provide an excuse not to promote him, and besides, he insists indignantly, he didn't deserve it. He fought to have it overturned and eventually succeeded.

"I made up my mind then," he tells me, promising that this will all come round to his lawsuit soon. "Now understand, I'm like you. I had a passion for the First Amendment too and I'm not a vindictive person as a rule, unless somebody really gets me. The department made me jump through hoops for two and a half years to get rid of a lousy letter of reprimand when, in my own mind, I was the hero. The fire department is a big family. We depend on each other with our lives. Any time the bell goes off, we might be counting on each other to get us out. Sounds melodramatic, but that happens on a daily basis in this department. So I made up my mind that if they ever stumbled again on a policy or anything, I was going to make *them* jump through hoops for a couple of years."

Opportunity presented itself sooner than expected. Or, as Steve puts it, "Six weeks after the final arbitration settlement on removing the letter of reprimand from my files, my Christmas came in July." Specifically, July 15, 1992, when the department issued a new policy against sexual harassment. In addition to prohibiting quid pro quo bargains and unwelcome physical contact, it banned vulgar or obscene comments or jokes, jeers, whistles, leering, and profanities meant to embarrass coworkers. Nude calendars or "pinups" were also banned, but they hadn't been allowed in fire stations for some time. What caught Steve's attention, however, was Section III-C, which read: "The following types of sexual material are prohibited in all work locations, including dormitories, rest rooms and lockers: . . . Sexually-oriented magazines, particularly those containing nude pictures, such as *Playboy, Penthouse* and *Playgirl.*"

"When they came out with that policy, I looked at it and I laughed. I read it a second time and I thought, Holy Toledo! They can't do this." His voice drips with scorn. "I know enough about the First Amendment. *Playboy*'s a legal magazine that's sold on the newsstands. They could have cited *Mechanics Illustrated, Snowmobile Magazine,* and *Bicycling Magazine.* When they came out with examples of legal materials and said we couldn't read this in the fire station, they were wrong. They were wrong."

There had been no complaint filed about the magazines. According to Patricia Vaughan, Senior Departmental Employee Relations Representative, as of June 2001, the L.A. County Fire Department (LACoFD) hadn't had a complaint that rose to the level of sexual harassment. The policy was meant to be "proactive," she tells me, part of an effort to make the department more welcoming to women. That apparently was a priority of the man at the top, Fire Chief P. Michael Freeman, who had come to L.A. County in 1989 from Dallas, where he had once served as an affirmative action officer. In an affidavit filed in Steve's case, he stated, "I would like our employees to feel good about coming to work each shift. I believe the policy is an important element of our broader effort to promote a more cohesive workforce."

For firefighters, cohesion is essential for effectiveness and safety. Theirs is a dangerous and stressful occupation, where disaster and death are ever-present.[9] "No work is good work," Steve says. As a defense, they create a distinct culture, dividing the world into themselves and the "civilians" who depend on them, as communities have ever since the Roman emperor Augustus organized the first firefighting brigade of *vigiles,* or watchmen, in about 21 B.C. Benjamin Franklin and George Washington were volunteer firemen (Washington is said to have imported the country's first fire engine), and our faith in firefighters remains justifiably strong.

Firefighter positions are sought after because they offer job security, flexible schedules, good pay, and generous benefits: starting salary at LACoFD in 1997 was $36,000.[10] When Steve began, a high school diploma was sufficient, but now a college degree is preferred. For one thing, the type of work has shifted; as a result of improved building codes and fire prevention, about 80 percent of the calls for southern California fire departments are now medical or emergency.[11] "When we started taking the defibrillators into the street and started IVs and drug therapy, that was the turning point," he says. LACoFD set up the second firefighter-paramedic program in the country, and Steve was the first paramedic in his department to be promoted.

Until quite recently, fire departments, whether paid, volunteer, municipal, or private, were made up of men. Though an 1818 account mentions the firefighting efforts of a female slave owned by a member of an engine company in New York City, no woman held a career (i.e., paid) position with an American fire department until 1974.[12] In some cities— New York, San Francisco, and San Diego among them—it took court orders to open the fire department to women, and nearly three decades later, their number remains very small.[13] In 2000, only about five thousand, or 1.9 percent, of the country's career firefighters were female.[14] The culture is now elastic enough to include women who are "one of the guys," in the words of Steve and other firemen he introduces me to, but it's not hard to imagine that it would be less than generous to anyone who can't or chooses not to fit in.

The change in the kind of work that firefighters do coincided with the start of affirmative action, so that by the time Steve and I talk, only slightly over half of the firefighters in L.A. County are white men, and seventeen African Americans and Latinos hold management positions.[15] A diversified workforce brought fresh perspectives and changes. For years, firefighters had to be at least five feet, eight inches tall, apparently not for any reason beyond perpetuating the image of a he-man to the rescue. That ended when Asians in the department pointed out that firefighters in Tokyo averaged five-foot-six and put out fires just fine. Similarly, female firefighters got rid of the required mannish haircuts by proving that long hair is not a safety hazard. "Those things were long overdue," Steve says. "They should have gone out the window."

He's less sanguine about challenges to the physical qualifications. Applicants take a rigorous physical exam, those who pass are ranked according to their score in an oral interview, and recruits are selected from the top of the list to enter a training academy. Women and men undergo the same tests and training, but at the time the new sexual harassment policy came down, only 20 percent of the relatively few women who took the physical exam passed it, in contrast to nearly half of the hundreds of men.[16] Steve, like many veteran firemen, thinks the advent of women in fire departments has brought a decline in safety. "If they're truly qualified, that's one thing, but they've stretched that to where there's women who've been hired that can't lift a ladder like they're supposed to be able to do. We're throwing out the biological differences, and you can't do that with certain occupations." When physical standards are altered, who suffers? he asks rhetorically. "The public does, first of all. We do secondly because we rely on each other."

For all his griping, he doesn't cite any incidents in which women put others at risk, and at times he can sound almost supportive. He is proud that, as union rep, he maneuvered to get a woman promoted to captain, a first for the department, and he thinks that the women who do join have been accepted as well as can be expected in a male-dominated profession. "They've been chided and poked and teased like we do to *all* new firefighters when they came on and probably more so because it's a girl, it's a female. But nothing they couldn't survive."

Firefighters like to pull "crams," or pranks of the summer camp or fraternity variety: short-sheeting beds, hanging a guy upside down in the hose tower tied to a backboard. Steve insists that most of it is friendly teasing, a way to let off steam, though it's a good idea to prove that you can take it. No, there haven't been any crams aimed at women because they were women, he tells me, then recalls hearing something about a Tampax sign. That seems to be a story the first woman to join the department told a reporter about someone throwing a Tampax dispenser at her feet, not, apparently, in the spirit of play.[17] Still, Steve claims, the "minor sexual harassment incidents" at work are just inconsiderate behavior. For instance, when a female firefighter wanted to go to bed and a male firefighter watching the Playboy channel refused to turn off the TV, she filed a complaint. "Legitimately so, in my opinion," Steve says. "The standards of decency were being violated, but because it was the Playboy channel, it was called sexual harassment. . . . The guys are afraid anything they do out of the norm that they've done to each other for years and years and years will be construed as sexual harassment. So the women are treated different. Truth be known, the guys don't want the women in the fire stations."

---

L.A. County firefighters work ten twenty-four-hour shifts a month and may spend as long as seventy-two hours straight at the station, making it a home away from home. A busy station can get up to forty calls a day, while quieter ones, like the one where Steve was working when he challenged the policy, go out maybe twice a day. During the day, firefighters also maintain equipment, conduct drills, and do fire prevention work.

After work hours, they prepare and eat meals and sleep, which leaves a lot of downtime—and boredom—that they fill with the stuff of restricted leisure: exercise, card games, studying for promotional exams, shooting the breeze, watching TV, reading.

Steve isn't much of a reader, but he knows his *Playboy*. He has subscribed off and on for years and claims, as in the threadbare joke, to read it primarily for the interviews. "The first thing you do is check out the centerfold, take about fifteen seconds. It gets less the older you get. Fold it back up and go on to other issues in the magazine that are important to you." He claims to have read the magazine quietly in his off-duty, or "personal," hours and shared it only with coworkers he knew would be interested, but more important, he recognized that, in singling out constitutionally protected publications, the policy was vulnerable to a First Amendment challenge. "Here's the ticket," he thought gleefully, as he contemplated getting back at his superiors. "It's going to be their turn."

Less than two weeks after the policy was issued, he filed a grievance. Steve has filed perhaps a dozen grievances over the years and won nearly all of them, which makes him unusual on both counts, since most firefighters never file any. ("The masses are pretty complacent," he says.) The grievance was little more than a nod to internal procedures, though. His real focus from the beginning was the constitutional issue, which he turned to soon after.

"I called 411 and said, give me the number for the Playboy Mansion in West Los Angeles. I said, I want to talk to the top person there. I said, I'm a fire captain on duty in a fire station, and we've got a First Amendment rights issue that can potentially cost a lot of us our freedoms and you guys maybe a million dollars a month [if the policy spread]." A few phone calls later, Steve connected with Burt Joseph, whom he likes to call "Hugh Hefner's attorney." Joseph is a prominent First Amendment lawyer in Chicago, chairman of the Playboy Foundation, and special counsel to Playboy Enterprises. He agreed that Steve's case had merit, but except for a lot of faxing back and forth, not much happened until the following May, when the *Fort Lauderdale Sun-Sentinel* ran a front-page article about Steve's grievance. With an apt metaphor, he says, "The fire was lit by this article in Florida." That December, Joseph flew out to Los Angeles for the grievance hearing. Steve thinks his bosses were impressed that he had such a high-powered attorney, but, as he expected, his claim was denied.

In December 1993, Steve filed a lawsuit in federal district court, asking that the department be barred from prohibiting the private possession, reading, and consensual sharing of *Playboy* at fire stations. (*Penthouse* had declined to join the suit, and no one read *Playgirl;* Steve thinks it was included to make the policy sound gender-neutral.) "From day one, losing was never a thought," he says more than once. He and his lawyers—Joseph had been joined by four other attorneys, including someone from the ACLU, who led the team—were encouraged by the wealth of case law on their side and the absence of a Supreme Court decision finding that sexually oriented material in itself constituted a hostile work environment. "I knew that we were going to win this thing," Steve repeats. "It's just horse sense, I guess. Somebody tells you in America what you can and can't read and that *Playboy,* that's in the Library of Congress, that's printed in how many languages, that's printed in a Braille edition, if you can believe that! How do you make centerfolds in Braille? Kind of like the old scratch-and-sniff days."

When explaining his motives, Steve vacillates between principle and revenge. "One of the two [women firefighters] that were pushing this thing, she needed to be put in her place a little bit. She believed she was speaking for all the females," he says in one breath, then, in the next, "It needed to be won because it was right. How many gallons of American blood have soaked into foreign beachheads because of the Bill of Rights?" And later, "We're not individuals any longer if we can't express ourselves without fear of reprisal." And still later, "I told the fire chief later on, I says, 'Chief, this is a win-win for everybody.' " The department could find a better way to combat sexual harassment, he reasoned, and all firefighters, women included, would still have their civil rights. Then he finishes in a scathing voice, "Some fire chief who thinks he's beyond the Constitution is going to tell me what I can and can't read? Never."

---

Only a small portion of the impediments women contend with at work result in formal sexual harassment charges, and those that do are usually mediated or dismissed.[18] Complaints filed with the Equal Employment Opportunity Commission (EEOC), nearly all by women,[19] peaked in 1997 at 15,889, which was about half again as many as in 1992, when the LACoFD policy came down. These numbers don't include cases that went to court,[20] but the percentage of EEOC complaints found to have reasonable cause and the percentage of "unsuccessful conciliations" both increased proportionally much faster than the number of complaints,[21] indicating growing antagonism. That combativeness got the attention of employers, and some, like the LACoFD, recognizing that, increasingly, they would be held accountable, took preemptive steps. Others took out insurance: by 1998, indemnification against sexual harassment claims was a $200 million business.[22]

The politics and legalities of sexual harassment have developed remarkably in the relatively short time since radical feminists broached the idea that it is a form of discrimination. Title VII of the Civil Rights Act of 1964, which outlawed sex-based discrimination in the workplace, was enacted as women began joining the workforce in unprecedented numbers. For men who felt that this undermined them in their role as breadwinner and paterfamilias, the dare of crotch shots and centerfolds was a handy way to let it be known who belonged in their workplace and who didn't, but these were just two of many weapons used to thwart female coworkers. In 1980, the EEOC issued guidelines that drew on Catharine MacKinnon's influential book *Sexual Harassment of Working Women*, published the year before. These guidelines, which are still in place, recognized two types of sexual harassment. "Quid pro quo" covers such clearly illegal acts as sexual assaults and threats, unwanted touching, and bargains for sex, as in "Sleep with me or lose your job." The other type, "hostile environment," involves the presence of sexuality in the workplace, which frequently includes crude talk and lewd pictures said to create an environment so harsh as to constitute discrimination.

The hostile environment theory gained credibility in 1986, when MacKinnon used it in *Meritor Savings Bank v Vinson* to argue that the injury didn't have to be economic to be in violation of Title VII. In this, its first sexual harassment ruling, the Supreme Court agreed, deciding that if sexual harassment was "sufficiently severe or pervasive" to impinge on the victim's employment, it could amount to an abusive work environment. (*Vinson*, which included charges of fondling, sexual coercion, and rape, turned on the voluntariness of the behavior.) In 1993, in *Harris v Forklift Systems* (a case that didn't involve speech issues), the Court refined the concept of hostile work environment and established a lesser burden of proof in which the victim didn't have to demonstrate psychological damage or impairment to job performance. The justices, though unanimous, were unable to come up with definitive criteria for hostile environment. Instead, they stressed the need to weigh factors such as the presence of physical threat, humiliation, or interference with the victim's work.

No court at any level has ruled that a hostile environment complaint based on legal speech alone trumps the First Amendment.[23] Nonetheless, many employers have come to define sexual harassment so expansively as to cover nearly anything related to sex, an idea that has swept in its wake everything from a waitress in California objecting to serving a customer who was reading *Playboy* (a journalist—this is too good to make up—reading an article on the Bill of Rights) to a female professor in Pennsylvania insisting that a print of the Goya painting *Nude Maja* be removed from the wall of a classroom in which she taught. As if to prove that intolerance rebounds, two men subsequently charged the professor with sexual harassment over a book about representations of the female figure that she used in her teaching.

Not all feminists share this pornophobia, and some—Nadine Strossen, Marcia Pally, Nan Hunter, and Ellen Willis prominent among them—have long argued that defining sexual harassment to include sexual expression does not serve women well. According to this critique, such speech-limiting policies are based on fuzzy thinking (equating words, images, and fantasies with actions), oversimplification (casting women as benighted, asexual wimps and men as out-of-control beasts and bypassing all the ridiculous and demeaning images of women in mainstream culture), and bad social science (insisting that dirty pictures cause discrimination when no such link has been proven). As Katha Pollitt writes, "Social science is one part science and nine parts social."[24] In 1998, legal scholar Vicki Schultz published an influential article in the *Yale Law Review* in which she contended that by concentrating on the "sexual desire-dominance paradigm" (basically, a man hitting on a woman who works in a subordinate position), current sexual harassment law reinforces the impression that naughty pictures, nasty talk, and loutish behavior are more detrimental than the nonsexual, gender-based discrimination that nearly every woman who has worked for any length of time has encountered.

It is probably impossible and not necessarily preferable to purge the workplace of sexual expression (Why can't women be sexual *and* professional, as men are?), but sexual expression can rise to the level of harassment when it is abusive, insistent, directed at a specific person, and demonstrably a hindrance to her in her work. Moreover, as theorists in critical legal studies have argued, the law isn't as neutral as it claims to be because it is premised on a set of power relationships, which, in this case, put women at a disadvantage. Regardless of where one stands, simple decency argues for some control, voluntary or imposed, on the behavior of people working closely, as firefighters do. No one should be humiliated at work, and though that happens in nonsexual ways too, many

people believe that sexual pictures and innuendo are especially humiliating, threatening even, to the "reasonable woman" the law proposes as
a barometer. Then too, sexual harassment takes place within a context,
and the context that Steve operated in was an entrenched male preserve
in which women were so rare that many stations never saw one. "It's still
a men's club," a female firefighter told a journalist after Steve went to
court, "or, as I like to call it, a boys' club, because some of them aren't
that mature."[25]

Yet tempting as it may be to think that by banning a picture we are
fighting inequality, if the purpose of sexual harassment policies is to ensure that women can earn a living without unfair interference, it is hard
to see how getting rid of *Playboy* will help. More often, this shrinking-
violet standard hinders women. Clumsy, overreaching policies encourage
paternalism, discourage collegiality and mentor relationships, and reinforce a double standard (often class-based, as Schultz notes)[26] that pun-
ishes the "bad" girls who supposedly get what they deserve because they
talk dirty or, in a pernicious Catch-22, act like they "can take it." Throughout America's history, women have been barred from jobs, prevented
from signing contracts or serving on juries, excluded from trade and professional schools, and denied information crucial to their well-being—all
in the name of shielding them from morally or physically "hostile environments." Conflating sexual abuse and sexual expression underplays the
harm of the abuse and overestimates the danger of the expression and the
need for restriction—precisely what happened in this case.

———

One evening, Steve takes me to visit Fire Station 30 in Cerritos. Station
30 is a nondescript, two-story building with a fake fire pole. On its first
floor is a public office and the garage, where I linger, never having out-
grown my childhood crush on those shiny, hulking fire engines. Lined up
alongside the trucks are pairs of rubber boots, different ones for different kinds of fires, with pants tucked inside and suspenders opened out-
ward to be pulled on at a run. Behind the office are the personal areas:
a narrow, barrackslike dormitory with beds tucked behind lockers that
provide a modicum of privacy, a communal kitchen, and a lounge with
a TV that, like other recreational equipment, was bought with firehouse
dues. Phones and speakers everywhere are reminders that firefighters are
always on call.

Upstairs is a well-equipped exercise room and the office of Battalion
Chief Richard Meyer. Here Meyer shows me a prize possession, an old

fire hat from Holyoke, Massachusetts, and Steve shows me a lifesize cardboard cutout of John Wayne. A story had appeared that day in the L.A. *Times* about recent arguments at fire stations between black and white firefighters over displaying posters or cutouts of Wayne, whom some saw as a symbol of racism[27] and others as the embodiment of rugged individualism. A black battalion chief was quoted as asking, "How would you like it if I had a picture of Farrakhan in my office?"[28] "There is no comparison," Steve replies indignantly. "A true American legend and hero and a damn anarchist!" Often, when whites say "blacks" in public, they lower their voices, as if it were an epithet. Steve does that too the next day when we are in a restaurant and he tells me about his shock when he first encountered racism while he was in Florida with the Navy, but he doesn't do it here at the station, where resentment between whites and blacks seems more stubborn even than between men and women.

Meyer, the father of two daughters, tells me that when word came down that women would be joining the force, the men went nuts.

What did they imagine would happen? I ask.

That they couldn't walk around naked and would have to mind their language, he answers, adding that the only ones who like change are wet babies and people playing the slot machines. But women joining the department turned out to be "just a blip on the screen." At the Cerritos station, the changes were minor: the lockers added between the beds and a small sign on the bathroom door to indicate if a man or woman is inside. The girlie magazines, "a firehouse tradition," as a female firefighter in San Diego put it,[29] had always been whisked out of sight when schoolchildren or families visited.

Earlier, I had asked Steve if his wife works, curious if she had run into sexual harassment. She's a part-time bookkeeper, he said, then, as if in reply to my second question, told me that he had been attracted to her because she's kind of tomboyish, one of the guys, not a feminist. (When I meet Cathy, she makes a reference to "firemen." "Firefighters," Steve corrects her. "Firemen," she insists.) "I'm a feminist," I had told him, not for the first time, but he just apologized for me by explaining that he sees a difference between feminism and femininity.

So if Steve is less adamant this evening about the deficiencies of women workers, it is probably out of courtesy or deference to my feelings. I appreciate that, but relying on good intentions falls short as a plan for fostering a workplace that is acceptable, safe, and hospitable to all employees. Civility—voluntary or enforced—along with sensitivity training, consciousness raising, and use of nonsexist language, may change people's ideas about gender and competence over time, but in the short run, it is more useful to work at changing their behavior. That is what most of the fire department's new sexual harassment policy set out to do, but the stipulation Steve challenged went a step further by trying to change hypothetical thoughts, or, as Steve's lawyers argued, by attempting "mind control."

---

As the trial date approached, the two sides set out their positions in legal briefs. Steve's lawyers condemned the policy as overbroad, content-based, and not the least restrictive means of fighting gender-based discrimination, a problem because, as the Supreme Court ruled long ago, "Broad prophylactic rules in the area of free expression are suspect."[30] They pointed out that public employees have clear First Amendment protection (private-sector employees do not) and argued that the peril to Steve's rights to read and receive information was concrete and immediate, while the danger of sexual harassment arising from someone reading *Playboy* was conjectural.

The fire department's lawyers countered that sexual images have no place at work. They also emphasized the department's responsibility as a public employer, arguing that people working at fire stations are a captive audience and that the public would be shocked to find firefighters reading *Playboy* at work, even in their personal time. (This last makes Steve mad. "The department maintained that because they paid me, they could dictate what I did for twenty-four hours. See, it's like they own you. They don't own me, damn it!")

Thus, the positions were set: the expressive rights of the individual against the communal right to a nondiscriminatory workplace. Ultimately, though, the case turned on whether erotica harms women, and, as nearly always when that is the issue (see Chapters 6 and 7), the debate turned angry and divisive. In January 1994, several members of the department gave affidavits, including two women firefighters who testified in support of the ban. One stated that there was "a constant barrage of abusive and suggestive sexual remarks made by male colleagues while they were looking at such magazines."[31] Another, the first woman to join the department, added that sexually explicit material (the term preferred over *pornography* by witnesses, who were also fond of repeating "Playboy, Entertainment for Men") is degrading to women. Because firefighters work in a "situation of forced intimacy," the magazines and the re-

marks they occasioned created "an offensive, unprofessional and intimidating atmosphere." It wasn't necessary to read them, she said; just having to look at the covers was a burden, but since the new policy was in
place, she had noticed a "significant and dramatic improvement."[32]
(*Playboy* has no nudity on its covers, but its cover art can be suggestive,
which puts it in good company. At the airport newsstand, I find bal-
looning, barely clothed breasts on the covers of *US* and *Spy*, models with
major cleavage in come-hither poses on *New Woman, Vogue, In Style,*
and *Cosmopolitan,* and Sharon Stone about to unbutton her blouse on
*Allure.* In comparison, Marilyn Monroe holding her dress together and
apart on the cover of *Playboy* looks positively demure.)

The policy was part of a larger effort to curb sexual harassment,
which included training sessions for all recruits, according to Pat
Vaughan, the employee relations representative who had drafted it. She
testified that a primary reason for including Section III-C was her concern that male readers of sex magazines would have negative feelings
about their female coworkers. A stack of *Playboy*s on the back of the toi-
let at a station she had visited suggested to her "that women are viewed
as sexual objects rather than competent, professional workers."[33] This
idea was reinforced by Daniel Linz, a professor of communications at
the University of California at Santa Barbara, who had done extensive
research on the psychological effects of mass media, sexual aggression,
and the law. According to Marcia Pally in a review of the literature on
the subject, Linz had stated on several occasions that his research had
not established a conclusive causal link between pornography and aggression,[34] but in his affidavit for L.A. County, he suggested that "at-
tractiveness of women in nonviolent pornography" and sexual education materials makes "real-life" women appear less attractive and less
competent.

Among those testifying in support of Steve's challenge to the policy
were two other female firefighters, one of whom was the department's
sole woman captain at the time. Also weighing in were Christie Hefner,
CEO of Playboy Enterprises, who cited some of the fine journalism the
magazine had published. (She didn't bother to mention "Some Like It
Hot," a photo spread featuring female firefighters and their equipment.)
She noted *Playboy*'s policy against violence, degradation, or subjugation
of women in pictures, proclaimed herself a feminist, and declared,
"Erotic is beautiful." A woman from *Playboy*'s market research office
filled in the details: only about 15 percent of the magazine consisted of

nude photos, over half of *Playboy* employees were women, and nearly two million women read the magazine monthly.

This side had its experts too, notably Neil Malamuth, a UCLA professor of communications and psychology, who studied sexual aggression against women and testified that the connection between *Playboy* and "sexual stereotyping" was speculative at best. The contradictory testimony of expert witnesses was not surprising. As with theories about other kinds of harm caused by pornography, research about sexual imagery and discrimination suggests that there may or may not be a connection, that the connection may or may not be causal, and that access to sexually oriented material may or may not affect the degree of prejudice against women in a given situation. Human nature is complex, sexual influences particularly so, and research linking expression and conduct is limited because acceptable methodology can only simulate, not replicate, real-life situations.

Both sides also had feminist organizations filing friends-of-the-court briefs: NOW, which had formed in 1966 to push for the enforcement of Title VII, continued its fight for equality by supporting the fire department; Feminists for Free Expression, a much smaller, New York–based organization, supported Steve. In an amicus brief, FFE argued that while gender-based harassment was of great concern, policies aimed at curtailing it did not benefit women unless they were reconciled with free speech concerns. Characterizing the L.A. County regulations as the country's most sweeping at that time, the brief pointed up the irony that "just as women are finally making inroads into such male-exclusive venues as handling a skyscraper construction crane, a hostile corporate takeover attempt, and an Air Force fighter plane, we are being told we cannot handle dirty pictures, and certainly that we would never enjoy them."

When I tell Steve I'm a member of FFE, he's pleased. "That tells me for sure that you're not a feminist," he says.

"But I am a feminist," I repeat.

"I don't mean it that way. Let's put it this way: you're a feminist that hasn't lost sight of what's important." Not like NOW, he says. "That's the feminist movement in my opinion. It's them against us."

---

The trial took place on June 7, 1994. Steve took the stand for about twenty minutes, and though he had appeared in court before for his work, this felt different. "It was really an exciting thing to walk into court the day the trial happened. We all see it on TV, but to be involved in a high-profile case and sit in the room, watch this bank of attorneys put their skills to work, that was a learning process." His attorneys had coached him, warning that the case wasn't as cut and dried as he thought, but still he says, "I suppose I would have been totally disillusioned in the system had I lost."

Two days later, U.S. District Judge Stephen V. Wilson issued his ruling. He explained that, because the policy banned only "sexually oriented" nudity, it was clearly content-based, which the First Amendment disallows. As for the "secondary effects" of the magazines, he reaffirmed that it is impermissible to regulate "the emotive impact of speech" or to try to mold employees' thoughts by limiting their reading. Finally, he found that the defendants had failed to convince him that the presence of the magazines constituted a hostile work environment. (In an interesting aside, he suggested that if they had offered evidence that the sight of the *Playboy* logo could be as shocking to a woman as a swastika to a Jew, they would have had a stronger argument.) "Defendants' desire to eliminate sexual harassment in the fire station is laudable," he concluded. "Defendants must, however, do so in a constitutionally permissible manner."[35]

It was a vindication of the First Amendment and victory for Steve, who, in gratitude to his lawyers, became a member of the ACLU, though he disagrees with several of its positions. Sounding every inch the newly minted civil libertarian, he says, "I felt in my heart that I was taking the right stand for something that's precious to every person in this country. Whether they agreed with my case or not, I protected their right to disagree with people like me." As a clear statement from a federal court on the issue of speech as workplace harassment, it was big news, and Steve was inundated with requests from as far away as Philadelphia to appear on radio talk shows. All the activity and attention was exhilarating, and he would willingly have ridden it longer, but four days later, in awful confirmation of the real dangers women face, Nicole Simpson was murdered, and Steve's story was bumped off the front page.

LACoFD appealed the decision, but it also set up a committee to hammer out a sexual harassment policy that would pass legal muster. Steve agreed to serve on the committee for strategic reasons—to find out where the department stood on its appeal—but also because he hoped to find a reasonable response to targeted harassment. He thinks the committee accomplished that goal with revised regulations now in place that permit sexually oriented material to be viewed privately and quietly and shared on a consensual basis. At the end of the year, the department dropped its appeal.

Still, some bad feeling lingered. One of the female firefighters who had testified in support of the ban gave a department-sanctioned interview to the *Los Angeles Times* in which she said some less-than-complimentary things about her coworkers and talked candidly about salaries and other internal matters. Steve saw that as breaking rank, so he and a former president of the union wrote letters to the editor rebutting her claims. Before mailing the letters—as a courtesy, Steve notes—they ran them by the department, which ordered that they not be sent. "There goes the mentality again," he says in disgust. "This is a free country. We can't write a letter to respond to an article in the paper?" At his urging, the other man sent his letter in his union capacity, which irritated department officials further.

Shortly after, Steve requested a meeting with Fire Chief Freeman. "I told him it was time for us to try to have a meeting of the minds because we're costing the taxpayers a lot of money"—he estimates at least $150,000 in court costs—"and I'm getting worn out." Steve describes the meeting as one of "adversaries, not enemies." Freeman even encouraged him to position himself for promotion to a management job, though Steve reads that as an attempt to get him out of the department's hair. Still, he gives Freeman grudging respect—"You know it's an awesome job that the man is in charge of"—and the respect appears to be mutual. At a recent luncheon where Steve was given an Overachiever Award, Freeman sat with him and his wife and sent a follow-up letter of congratulations. Steve, seldom sentimental, was touched.

---

When I ask Steve what sexual harassment means to him, he is dismissive—"It means that people who would consider something like [*Playboy*] threatening are very insecure"—but also practical, since firefighters enter into people's private lives all the time in their work. "Let's say that you're this female firefighter that's making these allegations. You know that I get that magazine out and I go in and sit down on the can and I'm reading this magazine and then I come out and put it back in my locker. If that's a threat to you, then how are you going to respond when the bell goes off and you go into John Doe Citizen's house and on his coffee table he's got his *Playboy*? Are you going to tell me you can't perform CPR or do your job as a firefighter?"

As for the childish behavior that may accompany the magazines, there are already rules on the books against incivility. The LACoFD Manual of Operations runs to ten volumes. "If Joe Fireman over here is throwing open the centerfold in Susie Fireman's face and saying, 'Yours like that?' that's out of line. Deal with it with the rules under Standards of Behavior. Let's don't throw the Constitution of the United States out because somebody can't live by appropriate standards of propriety. Ten declarations of freedom. The first one, the most important, is the freedom of speech and the correlated interest in the freedom to read and write what you want. And if we break that down, we haven't got anything." Besides, he adds, "There's no constitutional guarantee against being offended."

I suggest that women might bring some useful traits to firefighting. Like what? he challenges.

Cooperation, organization, compassion . . .

"We're not in the compassion business," he answers firmly, though he has talked earlier about losing sleep over the suffering he's witnessed in his work, and firefighters do provide succor, sometimes under horrific conditions. The fireground is like a battleground, he says, and if he had a daughter, he wouldn't want her put in such danger—a danger he accepts for himself as a matter of course. "I know I sound sexist," he has told me the night before, "but when you work with it . . ." Women in firefighting simply doesn't work, he repeats now, and neither does "forced desensitizing of the male's feelings for women as tender creatures."

"And what about the women who don't think of themselves as tender creatures?"

"Obviously, a very small minority of women don't."

I'm weary of this argument, as I imagine Steve is too, but it returns us to a central problem with prevailing ideas about sexual harassment: All the emphasis on sexually oriented expression distracts us from the more invidious obstacles—the sexism—that women meet at work. The causes of gender injustice in the workplace and beyond are complex, but most have to do with imbalances of economic, social, and political power for which there are concrete solutions. To begin with, employers concerned about sexual harassment could hire more women, since being present in sufficient number—having critical mass—is one of the best remedies.

In news stories about women firefighters elsewhere, old-timers are often dismissed as "dinosaurs," with the implication that they will soon be extinct. Steve is too nimble to be a dinosaur, too ready to stir things up, and troublemakers like him are part of social progress, along with reformers and policy makers. The number of women in the Los Angeles County Fire Department still isn't large—twenty-four in 2001, or thirteen more than when Steve went to court—but they're moving up in rank, with four firefighter specialists and five captains. And they have outlasted Steve. He retired in 1998 with some work compensation and misconduct actions still pending against the department. He expects, of course, to win them all.

chapter twelve

# THE PUBLIC TRUST

David Kern

*Pawtucket, Rhode Island, October 1997*

When it comes to speech and money, the debate usually centers on how much speech money should be allowed to buy. The question figures in attempts to reform political campaign financing, in concerns about advertising aimed at kids, in complaints about concentration of media ownership, and in A. J. Liebling's dictum that freedom of the press is guaranteed only to those who own one.[1] But money is also used to buy silence. The market shuts out voices and messages regularly—Liebling again—while fear of losing funding, employment, or prestige can keep researchers from challenging orthodoxies, even in pursuits, such as science, that we don't generally think of as market driven. The dynamic is seldom so crass as a bribe, but more often suggestions—to delay publication, to tone down a conclusion, not to ask certain questions in the first place—and promises, which hold as long as everyone agrees to be "reasonable."

David Kern was a physician at Memorial Hospital in Pawtucket, Rhode Island, and an associate professor at Brown University Medical School, when he uncovered a serious new lung disease at a textile factory in town. Like other elite groups, scientists sometimes choose to keep information among themselves, trusting in the peer review process to determine when it is ready for disclosure. As a doctor, however, David was committed to getting information about the disease out so it could be treated and prevented, but when he tried to publish his findings, the company where the outbreak occurred told him to keep quiet. It is no great mystery why a business would prefer to suppress bad news, but hospital and university officials also "urged" David not to report his research and, when he did, closed his program in occupational medicine and relieved him of his duties in that field. That institutions supposedly dedicated to promoting the public good and the expansion of knowledge ended up trying to restrict the speech they are meant to guard suggests disturbing truths about the effect of money on scientific integrity, doctor-patient relationships, and academic freedom.

---

David first encountered what came to be called "flock worker's lung" in October 1994, when a thirty-six-year-old man suffering from worsening shortness of breath was referred to him by a lung specialist. The specialist believed the illness was work related, and David directed Rhode Island's only program that combined occupational research and clinical care.

Occupational medicine has a long history, which enlightened European doctors built on during the Industrial Revolution when they began to pay attention to workers' safety. In the United States, it gained ground early in the twentieth century but remained focused on treating injuries until after World War II, when it shifted to include prevention. By the mid-1950s, it had become a distinct specialty. Funding for training became available with the passage of the Occupational Safety and Health Act of 1970. Though it is still somewhat of a medical stepchild, today, there are thirty-seven residency programs, sixty clinics, and many unofficial programs (David's was one) that teach occupational health.[2]

David's program was unusual in offering a variety of learning experiences to Brown's medical students and doctors-in-training. These included regularly scheduled teaching tours of work sites, and after examining his new patient, David arranged a visit to the man's workplace for that purpose. So a couple of weeks later, he visited the Rhode Island plant of Microfibres, Inc., with a few students and Kate Durand, his industrial hygienist, whose role was to assess and recommend ways to enhance the health and safety of work environments.

Microfibres, a privately held company, was established in Rhode Island in 1926. It is among the world's largest manufacturers of fabric made from flock: nylon filaments, twice as fine as silk, that are attached to cotton and polyester to make a velourlike material. David shows me plastic baggies of the stuff. It's brown and white and shiny and forms into clumps that look like balled-up stockings. The strip inside a car door that brushes the window as it opens can be made from flock, as are toys, clothing, and upholstery, which is Microfibres' specialty. Microfibres employs about 175 people in its Rhode Island plant and another 800 or so at factories in Canada, North Carolina, Georgia, and Belgium.[3] It prides itself on providing good employment opportunities and on its recent growth at a time when the textile industry as a whole declined.[4]

When David and his cohort arrived at Microfibres, they were met at the door by the personnel director, who required them to sign Agreements of Secrecy and Confidentiality before they entered. Such nondisclosure agreements, aimed at keeping visitors from divulging trade secrets, are common in occupational health, and since he viewed the visit as primarily educational, David signed, thinking of it as a one-day pass.

They viewed a production process and collected air samples but found nothing to support the diagnosis of pneumonia that the patient had received, which led David to suspect that the problem was a different kind of interstitial lung disease, or ILD. ILD is a collective term covering as many as two hundred lung diseases, some occupationally or environmentally related, that occur when interstitia (the space in the lungs between the air sacs and the blood vessels that exchange oxygen and carbon dioxide) become inflamed. If inflammation persists, scar tissue forms, inhibiting the flow of oxygen and sometimes damaging the lungs irreversibly. Symptoms are similar for all ILDs—in the early stages, a dry cough and breathlessness, maybe fatigue or fever—and distinguishing among them is important because some are fatal.

With treatment, David's patient's health improved, so it wasn't until January 1996, when a second doctor referred a twenty-eight-year-old man, another Microfibres employee with the same symptoms, that David became concerned. ILD is unusual in young men, and estimated rates for *all* kinds of ILD per year are less than 1 percent in the general population.[5] Here were two patients out of a concentrated workforce of about 170.

David called Dr. John Parker, a friend and colleague, at the National Institute for Occupational Safety and Health (NIOSH), the arm of the Centers for Disease Control that researches the prevention of work-related illnesses and injuries. David calls it the brains behind the brawn of its sister agency, the Occupational Safety and Health Administration (OSHA), which is based in the Labor Department and acts as an enforcer of occupational safety standards. Each year, NIOSH conducts about three hundred Health Hazard Evaluations (HHEs), field investigations into new, unusual, or unaccounted-for occupational health problems. NIOSH makes recommendations based on its findings, but, according to

Dr. Philip Landrigan, a former director of NIOSH's Division of Surveillance, Hazard Evaluations and Field Studies, it follows up on these only occasionally.[6]

"Was this an official call or an advice call?" I ask David." This was a working-out-a-strategy call," he answers. He wanted to inform Microfibres of his concerns about their employees and to recommend that they ask NIOSH to undertake an HHE, but he knew that NIOSH, still recovering from the labor-unfriendly Reagan years, had limited resources,[7] so he wanted to make sure that they would accept such a request. Parker said they would. David then asked for guidance on whom to approach about making the request, since an evaluation can be sparked by an employer, employees, or a labor group. Parker advised that the company might be more cooperative if the investigation was their initiative, but, just in case, David might want to alert the union. Finally, they agreed that the research would be enhanced by close collaboration between NIOSH and David's program.

David called the union's business agent, who agreed to the plan. Then he wrote to Microfibres to alert them to the life-threatening situation at their plant and to urge them to request an HHE. He also proposed that they contract with his program to diagnose and treat affected workers and to help find the cause of the disease. "As a health practitioner, it was important to me to make sure that they did something," he says, quick to defend his actions by the time we meet. "I didn't care how they did it, but they needed to have help."

Helping employers do something to help their employees had been at the heart of David's work since 1988, when he came to Memorial Hospital. He had grown up in Pawtucket, a city known to baseball fans as home to the principal farm team of the Boston Red Sox. Its history is that of a mill town, though, with textiles and unions playing central roles. Typical of such cities, factories and workers' housing line the riverbanks, and grander houses for the factory owners cap the hills that rise above. Memorial Hospital sits on one of those hills in an old residential neighborhood not far from downtown. The original building, turreted and girdled by porches, looks like a Victorian lying-in hospital, but the complex has been much expanded in a mishmash of architectural styles.

David's office is in a newer building where everything is painted institutional white, which he sabotages with books and paper piled everywhere and photos, art prints, and kids' drawings gracing the walls. David is in his late forties, trim, tallish, and dressed in khakis, a dusty pink, button-down shirt, and a blue tie with pink dots. With his long jaw and eyebrows that arch up to emphasize, question, and mock, he looks like a young Dick Van Dyke in aviator glasses. He talks fast, leaving sentences dangling when he switches to a new thought, and adds an "r" at the end of some words, swallowing the final one on others in a classic Boston accent, though apparently a Rhode Island one too. David comes across as smart, gentle, good-humored, and compassionate, also conscientious and firm: all in all, a good bedside manner.

We stand in line at the hospital's cafeteria, chatting easily, until someone he no longer trusts passes by and he hushes me. Rhode Island is a small state—people go to the same schools, sit on committees together, run into each other at the grocery store—and David has learned to be careful about what he says. Then we get some candy to take with us to his office, this being Halloween, a holiday David clearly takes seriously. He expects a quiet evening this year, what with his youngest kid refusing to trick or treat and his older two doing it elsewhere. When his daughter calls, he asks what she's going to dress up as, then talks to her in that sweet, corny way parents use with teenagers: "Don't wear black and walk on the white stripe in the highway."

---

While David awaited a response to his letter to Microfibres, he and Kate, the industrial hygienist, happened across a recent article describing what sounded like an identical disease at a flocking plant in Ontario, Canada. The outbreak had occurred in 1990–91, with five cases among eighty-eight workers: one had spent weeks on a breathing machine and nearly died, two remained dependent on supplemental oxygen, none could return to work. The cause was thought to be mold, and the article reported no new cases since the plant had been cleaned up. But a few weeks later, when David and Kate met with Microfibres officials, they were handed volumes of information about the Canadian plant, which, it turned out, Microfibres had owned since 1972. Two new cases had just been diagnosed, well after the problem was supposedly solved, and Microfibres seemed eager to pinpoint their genesis. They decided to hire David's occupational medicine program at Memorial to investigate and simultaneously to make a formal request to NIOSH for an evaluation.

This is where the paper trail should begin, but Microfibres balked at putting anything in writing. Rick Dietz, Memorial's Assistant Vice President for Marketing and Development (and, incidentally, a son of the hospital's president), tried to negotiate a contract but never succeeded in getting one. Money wasn't the problem: Microfibres ended up paying the hospital about $100,000 ("a significant reduction from the standard commercial rate" for David's time, according to an early proposal). Microfibres just seemed reluctant to be pinned down, happier with an oral agreement and a handshake.

The company also stalled on signing the operating principles David provided. These twelve points, derived from the Code of Conduct of the American College of Occupational and Environmental Medicine, were standard in the field, including the stipulation that David might need to make his research public. He felt it essential that the employees trust him, so he urged the company to endorse and post these principles for all workers to see. But the company dragged its feet, consulting lawyers, requesting changes, and, in the end, neither signing nor posting the principles, despite David's requests at nearly every meeting. Throughout these negotiations, no mention was made of the nondisclosure agreement he had signed fifteen months earlier.

In March, David and Kate began their investigation and almost immediately got ensnared in the complicated relationship between Microfibres and the local of UNITE, the Union of Needletrades, Industrial and Textile Employees. David is firmly prounion; Microfibres, considerably less so, accused him of making trouble. After initial employee education sessions where he explained that his team considered the company, the employees, and the union all their clients, company officials called him in to express their displeasure. When he met alone with union officers who worked at the plant, the company objected. After he gave the union a copy of his first progress report, the company demanded that he sever all ties with UNITE. At each confrontation, he told himself that the most important thing was to complete the investigation and find the source of the disease, so, though unhappy with the terms—*irked* is the word he uses—he talked to the union and then agreed to Microfibres' demands.

In March, patients 3 and 4 were diagnosed; by the end of April, two more had been identified. The accumulated pathological material pointed to a nonspecific interstitial pneumonia, and David was eager for the company to provide data he needed, specifically chronologies of materials they used and details of production processes at their two plants. He was looking forward to what the NIOSH team would find.

The medical surveillance part of NIOSH's investigation—questionnaires, chest X rays, and breathing tests—was set to begin in May. NIOSH reported the results of its tests to the workers but otherwise held them in confidence, meaning that David could see the medical data only for workers who authorized NIOSH to share them with him. Experience had made NIOSH sensitive to confidentiality issues, so the agency insisted that the release forms had to be signed in the presence of its field investigators—only the investigators couldn't distribute the forms or remind employees to sign them, nor could anyone from the company or David's team stand within a hundred feet of the testing trailer and do so. So on the Friday afternoon before the Monday testing, David met workers on each shift to hand them the form and to tell them to bring it, unsigned, to their tests. He also arranged for someone from company management to stand at the appropriate distance and remind workers about the form as they arrived for testing.

Amazingly, it all got done, though David's team didn't have long to congratulate themselves. "Monday morning comes," he reports, "and I'm called by the union rep, who says, 'NIOSH just began their thing, and within two hours we shut it down.' " Microfibres, it seems, was giving out two consent forms: David's and another that would let the company see test results and thereby get medical clearance, free of charge, for their employees to wear respirators. NIOSH, which sets standards for respirators, was counseling the workers not to sign the second form, but the union assumed that David had something to do with slipping it in and felt betrayed.

"So I called the company, furious. Not furious," he corrects himself, though he certainly sounds exasperated. When he asked how they thought they would get away with slipping in an extra form, he was told that NIOSH had cleared it. They couldn't have, he insisted, because it's illegal and unethical to release medical information to nonmedical people. "They couldn't have," he repeats, his voice growing more insistent, and indeed the head of the NIOSH medical team later confirmed that she had not approved the form. Though worried that the workers would blame him for the attempted sleight-of-hand, David continued to cover for the company, saying that the second form was merely a mistake. It was withdrawn, screening proceeded, and David followed up with letters to the over one hundred employees who had authorized him to see their results.

It may be in the interest of employers to foster safe and healthy workplaces, but their relationships with occupational health workers are adversarial almost by definition. When businesses open themselves to outside scrutiny, their reputations may suffer, insurance costs may rise, or sick workers may take legal action against them, and fixing a problem can be expensive, sometimes enough to force an operation to lay off workers or close down. Recognizing this, David says, "The things that companies do in these investigations are understandable. They've never been in them before. It's like being a parent: you make mistakes, you don't get practice." He claims that at one point, Jim Fulks, the Microfibres vice president overseeing the research, threw up his hands and said, "I can't stand this! I'm losing control of this investigation."

"Had I known that control meant keeping everyone apart and secrets and so forth, then I agree," David adds dryly. "He was doing pretty well at botching it."

"Did you know all this at the time?" I ask.

"We just knew that they were taking an awful long time to give us things," he replies.

Finally, in September, six months into their consultancy, David and Kate received significant data: Microfibres gave them the information about materials and processes; NIOSH furnished air-sampling results; and a pilot study provided preliminary findings about the capacity of tiny particles of fiber to enter the lungs. By this time, David's team had diagnosed nine cases of ILD at the plant, including one with life-threatening complications that he thinks could have been prevented had the company been more cooperative. But Microfibres was worried about losing its workers' compensation insurance, and when David recommended that another patient be provided with a respirator, Fulks accused him of coddling the employees, whom any other doctor would send back to work. "No ethical doctor would suggest so," David replied.

---

David had cochaired a faculty committee reviewing Brown's investments in South Africa for about three weeks in 1989, until a university official lectured them that faculty were indebted to corporations and he resigned in protest. The official had a point, though. Universities and their affiliated hospitals increasingly court corporate support, a trend particularly prominent in medical research. To encourage the availability of new technology, Congress passed the Bayh-Dole Act in 1980, which permits universities to benefit from patents for their scientific inventions. Other policies to promote cooperation between government and industry followed, and business funding of health-related research took off. Colleges and universities spent nearly $30 billion on research in 2000, with life sciences taking by far the largest share.[8] The budget of the National Institutes of Health, the primary federal funder of biomedical research, ballooned from just over $3 billion in 1980 to nearly $18 billion in 2000, but industry funding grew even faster: drug companies spent $1.5 billion on research in 1980, over $22 billion in 2000.[9]

By the end of the twentieth century, academia and industry were heavily entangled. A survey of leading research universities found that 43 percent of faculty researchers in the life sciences had recently received a corporate gift;[10] approximately 60 percent of medical experiments on people under way in the United States were conducted by for-profit entities;[11] and large biomedical companies were carrying out about a fifth of their research at universities,[12] with major research institutions, such as MIT, receiving as much as a quarter of their funding from industry.[13] (Brown's research operation is relatively small, and only 5 percent of its sponsored research in medicine in 1999–2000 came from corporate sources.)[14] The potential benefits from these relationships are substantial. For scientists, industry offers a rich, new source of funding and access to the sophisticated research instruments they increasingly require. For businesses, universities provide broad expertise and prestige, and teaching hospitals provide patients for testing drugs and other treatment. And for everyone involved, there is money to be made, reputations to enhance, and public policy to influence.

The Biotechnology Industry Organization hails a "synergy" in which the NIH sponsors basic research and industry funds applied research, but academic and business cultures are very different, and their goals can clash. Scientists are supposed to pursue a disinterested search for truth by trial and error, while businesses aim for efficiency and for successful, marketable outcomes that create profits for their investors. Scientists are committed to reporting their findings in a timely manner, while businesses guard proprietary information against competitors. In science, knowledge is valued in itself; in business, it is a commodity, valued when it can be exploited as intellectual property. In practical terms, this means that industry supports research into treating disease, but not into preventing it or examining its environmental causes, and that health care in the United States focuses more on curing sickness than on keeping us well.

Profit-oriented funding can also lead to unethical activities, such as doctors accepting payment for enrolling their patients in experiments or researchers signing articles that have been ghostwritten by drug company employees. Such obvious breaches aren't widespread, but other, accepted practices may do more to undermine reliable research. Industries gravitate toward researchers who have done work favorable to their interests, and researchers tend to absorb the values and biases of those who employ or sponsor them. Positive results of drug trials often get published faster than negative ones[15] (which may not get published at all), and having a monetary stake in the outcome of research can influence findings or give the appearance of doing so. What, for instance, should we make of federal guidelines for cholesterol levels when nearly one-quarter of the panel of specialists who set them report having received funding at some point from companies making cholesterol-lowering drugs?[16] And how much should we trust assessments of calcium-channel blockers used to treat high blood pressure and heart disease when 96 percent of the authors of favorable articles have gotten financial support from the drugs' manufacturers?[17] To address the problem, a dozen of the world's most prestigious and influential medical journals issued a new policy in 2001 requiring researchers to guarantee their scientific independence in writing. But because corporate funding is so pervasive, it can be difficult to find disinterested and knowledgeable people to do the peer review that underpins medical research. So in June 2002, the prestigious *New England Journal of Medicine* altered its policy to say that it expected only that authors of articles reviewing medical studies would not have *significant* financial interest in the companies under discussion.[18]

For all that, academic-industrial partnerships don't lead inexorably to tainted research, fraud, or other misconduct, nor are they likely to go away, so the question for scientists and health workers is what the terms of the relationships should be. Most medical schools and professional associations have policies to govern extramural funding of research, though these vary widely. At Brown, rules have long barred faculty from engaging in classified research and encourage careful scrutiny of "explicit or implicit financial commitments" concerning external funding of research.[19] David held a joint appointment at Brown and an affiliated hospital, but the university's research guidelines and procedures had little to do with the kind of field consultation and patient care he was providing at Microfibres, so its grants office was not involved.

---

Different as David's investigation was from most industry-sponsored research, he encountered many of the same tensions, plus a baffling recalcitrance on the part of NIOSH to share its data. As a policy, the agency releases interim information only to the employer and employees' representative involved in an HHE, unless asked to do otherwise, but David was Microfibres' consultant, and the idea that Microfibres was muzzling NIOSH was, for him, simply "too mind-boggling to register." He and Kate plodded on until the end of October, when the principals in the investigation met at Microfibres for two days of scientific meetings. During a coffee break on the first morning, one of the NIOSH team told David that Microfibres had explicitly stopped them from sharing air-sampling data with him. (Much later he saw an internal memo from August 1996, in which the company's environmental director offered, as she had told Kate she would, to write NIOSH to request sampling results, but a note written in the margin said, "This will not be done.")

"It was so offensive," David says, shifting slightly in his chair. "All along they had been saying, 'Oh those bad NIOSH people, they won't give you this. But then again, they're your friends, you asked them to come in.'"

With a blend of hurt and incredulity, he tells about going out to dinner that evening with all the investigators. By this time, he knows he has been lied to and he is seated next to Jim Fulks, who is currently making his life miserable, but he's still trying to make this thing work, so he chats amicably as if nothing were wrong. "I sit next to this vice president and he talks about being a Boy Scout troop leader and his kids are Scouts. I was a Boy Scout in my day, and I go home and bring out these badges, these things I had gotten twenty-five years ago that are now probably incredibly valuable. I thought his kids would like them. And I leave them for him the next day, and by the end of that day, we're making our ultimatum. I never hear from him again. I'm surprised he hasn't charged me with bribery or something like that."

The ultimatum was that David and Kate could not continue as consultants unless they were assured of unencumbered communication among everyone involved in the investigation. The participants had spent the meeting dividing up tasks, but this seemed pointless if they could not collaborate freely. Microfibres said it would consider the matter, and the meeting drew to a close.

David then gave company officials a draft of a scientific abstract about flock worker's lung that he planned to present at a "poster session" at a conference of the American Thoracic Society the following May. The abstract was a single page of text, accompanied by eight smallish posters showing pathology tissue and x-rays. This presentation would be propped up on easels, one of a thousand such presentations in a huge auditorium where ten thousand people would be milling about. He hoped that by making the findings known, he would alert health professionals to this new disease and also hear of related research that might identify its cause.

To a layperson, this reporting sounds like what any responsible scientist would do, since research findings have little use until they are made public. But Microfibres maintained that the abstract contained proprietary information whose disclosure would jeopardize their business interests and asked David not to submit it. In a written statement to *Science* in April 1997, the company insisted, "To date, no definitive cause for the cases at the Pawtucket plant has been confirmed. Microfibres believes it is premature to release the information."[20]

Cutting the company's managers no slack, David countercharges, "They clearly did not want a cause to be found. They acknowledged that they didn't care about whether the public health was improved by finding the cause and then applying that elsewhere." As for his disclosing business secrets, "The last sentence is the only place where [the abstract] talks about anything, and it's already mentioned in the Canadian article and it's generic in the industry, so this had nothing to do with trade secrets." A company spokesman was later to concede to a journalist that managers worried that if their European competitors, who used natural fibers, learned about the disease, they would exploit it by arguing that synthetic flock was a health hazard.[21] Finally, in response to Microfibres' argument that NIOSH's HHE report would take care of alerting doctors to the disease, David argues back that NIOSH had none of the clinical material his team had and that HHE reports are unwieldy, technical documents, not easily available, and read by a limited number of people.

Microfibres showed no interest in negotiating. Instead, they pulled out the nondisclosure agreement David had signed nearly two years earlier and threatened to sue if he went forward with the presentation. Still trying to salvage his investigation, he rewrote the abstract to eliminate identifying details, including the name and location of the Canadian plant, a specific description of the product, even the word *flock*. He also offered to delay the presentation for one year if the company agreed to the open communication policy he had demanded. The next day, Halloween 1996, Microfibres refused all of his terms. "In light of the above," he tells me exactly one year later, "we terminated our consulting relationship with the company."

———

David went ahead and submitted the abstract, knowing he had until mid-January to withdraw it. In retrospect, he doubts Microfibres intended to sue—it would have been bad public relations—but at the time he was less sure, so he consulted colleagues about what to do. Those in other fields often recommended that he give in to the company's demand and then appeal to the university for support of his academic freedom, but those in occupational health were adamant that he had a responsibility to report. He also sought guidance from Brown's grants office but was disappointed in the response. Peter Shank, Associate Dean of Medicine for research, reviewed the documents and wrote David that, given the nondisclosure agreement, "I see no way in which you can publish the results of your studies at the company without their written approval."[22] He advised David to withdraw the abstract immediately. He also sent copies of the letter to the hospital's administrators, who apparently took it as support for their position.

Those administrators, including hospital president Frank Dietz, his son Rick, a hospital vice president, and Dr. Denman Scott, Chief of Medicine and David's boss, were trying to smooth things over with Microfibres. At first, David deferred to their wishes, eliminating background information from a letter in which he formally severed ties with the company and agreeing to postpone addressing the union. He had taken advantage of the lull in activity to draft a letter to the Microfibres employees whose respiratory problems put them at risk to recommend that they get flu shots and to tell them he was no longer consulting with the company, but Scott wanted the hospital's lawyer to review the letter, so that too was put on hold.

By early December, the consultancy was moribund, but hospital officials still tried to placate Microfibres. When David ran into Frank Dietz at a Christmas luncheon, Dietz pressed him to withdraw the abstract, insisting that there was no public health hazard and no other company that made flock. David corrected him on both counts, but Dietz's angry response—that David was trying to destroy the company—convinced him that the matter had already been settled and not in his favor. David is a man of finely honed integrity, but in asserting his principles or justifying his actions, he can flirt with self-righteousness. In a synopsis of events, he writes, "As an internist, an occupational medicine physician, and a public health practitioner, I had professional responsibilities I could no longer defer." When the hospital continued to stall on approving his letter to the workers, he sent it anyway, a move Dietz later called "preemptive notification."[23]

David and Frank Dietz had never gotten along. In David's first year at Memorial, they had had a run-in over slipshod removal of asbestos in the industrial hygienist's office, an operation that came under the jurisdiction of another of Dietz's sons, who also worked at the hospital. "I spoke to his father and said, it was uncomfortable to do this," he reports, his voice getting softer, as it does when he talks about controversy, "but I think it's important for him to know that his son was violating the law and also imposing a public health hazard. I got screamed at: 'Now I know why my son calls you a troublemaker. What do you do, work for OSHA?' " For a while, the chief of medicine acted as a buffer between Dietz senior and David, but when he left and Denny Scott took the job, David reported on morale problems that Scott apparently didn't want to hear about, and they got off on the wrong foot too.

When the relationship with Microfibres collapsed, Scott blamed David, charging that he had squandered the confidence of the company's management and forfeited his academic freedom by signing the nondisclosure agreement. In answer, David "explained that there were three mutually exclusive ways one could characterize what had happened. First, I was a well-intentioned, but bumbling scientist. Second, I was a scientist who intentionally had attempted to harm the company. Third, I was a well-intentioned scientist, who had been as accommodating to the company as was reasonably possible and who had fifteen years of experience successfully investigating suspected outbreaks of occupational and environmental disease, a full awareness of the nonscientific pitfalls inherent in such investigations, and the knowledge that a fair number of my occupational health colleagues had at one time or another suffered similar threats during their careers. I stated that the third scenario was in fact the truth."

David was summoned to a meeting on December 18, where Dietz scolded him for sending the letter, instructed him to have nothing more to do with Microfibres' employees, and formally recommended that he withdraw the abstract. He also announced that Memorial would no longer be in the occupational health business, a particular blow to David because it meant that his program was being closed down. He could continue his teaching and clinical activities in internal medicine, but he was told to cease all investigations in occupational medicine.

Two days before Christmas, when faculty and students were dispersed for the winter break and unavailable to object, Dietz sent David a memo, reiterating the gist of their meeting. Three weeks later, on the last day of his extension, David announced that he would not withdraw the abstract. Soon afterward, the Rhode Island Department of Health recommended that his findings be published in the Centers for Disease Control's influential publication, *Mortality and Morbidity Weekly Report*, an indication of his work's significance.

In January 1997, when the spring semester began, David turned to the university as his last hope. About this time, he began his meticulous documentation, recounting events and answering each charge in exact, increasingly testy language. ("Seeing the kind of people I see, I cringe when people come in with the notebooks full of. . . . And so, I find I'm one of those people," he admits.) Before we meet, a fat packet of reports, letters, chronologies, charges, and countercharges arrives in the mail. I make my own chronology that grows obscure with arrows and cross-outs. I start a list of key players to keep score; the deans and committee heads alone fill a page.

"Microfibres was not funding Brown research or research at all," a university spokesman tells me three years later, still smarting from the earlier bad press. "We support our faculty. We support their right to publish."[24] But, like it or not, Brown was becoming involved. David appealed first to Dr. Donald Marsh, dean of the medical school, who replied that, given the university's "risk-averse stance" and the independence of its affiliated hospitals, his hands were pretty much tied. In March, six professors in various disciplines sent the Faculty Executive Committee a strongly worded statement of concern "about coercive attempts . . . to prevent publication concerning an important public health problem."[25] David's situation outraged that committee's vice chairman, who brought it up with Brown's president, Vartan Gregorian, and also met with Dean Marsh on the matter. Soon after, Marsh named a Committee of Inquiry to look into the academic freedom issues.

Academic freedom is an easy target, given the absurd-sounding research and tortuous titles that get trotted out when we want to make fun of intellectuals, which is often, but in theory, at least, its benefits are substantial. Academic freedom licenses scholars to think, teach, research, and publish independently. It offers students robust debate and exposure to a range of ideas, and it provides the public with an educated citizenry and a healthy flow of information and opinion. In practical terms, the guarantee of academic freedom insulates professors from political or other pressure to conform to the orthodoxies of the day: in the 1950s, it was invoked to protect those with communist sympathies; in our day, those accused of racism or sexual harassment. Over time, this amounts to a balancing of sorts, and since intellectual fashion will surely take yet another turn soon, this is one more argument in academic freedom's favor.

In the United States, academic freedom is buttressed by tenure, a concept first codified in 1915 and cherished by those who have it and impugned by those who don't ever since. Difficult to get, it is harder to lose, and from the outside, it can seem like a scam, since tenured faculty can get away with doing almost anything, or doing almost nothing. This makes governance of universities notoriously cumbersome, but, as philosopher Richard Rorty writes, "The one thing that has proved worse than letting the university order its own affairs . . . is letting somebody else order those affairs."[26]

David didn't have tenure, but with his promotion to associate professor in 1994, he could count on automatic, renewable, five-year contracts. Brown has had its share of free speech battles—in 1990, it was the first college to expel a student for violating a speech code; in 2001, students upset over an ad they considered racist burned copies of the campus newspaper—but the university is proud of its tradition of intellectual freedom, and David trusted that its officials would "do the right thing," a phrase he repeats often. "The medical school administration was acting horribly, but we figured Vartan Gregorian would do the right thing when he heard," he says. So when his faculty supporters advised against going public with the controversy, he agreed.

By the end of April, though, a friend prominent in occupational health persuaded David to let him organize a letter-writing campaign. Soon, some eighty doctors and researchers from around the world wrote to insist on David's duty to publicize his findings, and, in time, these were joined by statements of support from all the major organizations in his field. Meanwhile, a colleague at Harvard was so disturbed by David's situation that he faxed details to *Science* magazine. David consulted his supporters at Brown, then agreed to an interview. The day after it was published, newspapers picked up the story and kept it going through the summer. So much for keeping the conflict in-house, he notes.

Articulate, precise, and eager to explain, David interviews well, and for the most part the press portrayed him sympathetically. "I'm not someone who enjoys this," he says of the interviews, the publicity, the battle. "I have colleagues who would give their eyeteeth to be in this situation and colleagues who have said, 'I'm putting up my own money to arrange for CNN to be on your doorstep.' I said, 'I don't want that.'"

Like most people in a public controversy, David has complaints about how it was reported. Why are certain questions asked and others not? he demands. Who benefits? "I keep saying [to journalists], instead of rehashing the same old stuff, will you please do just a little investigative reporting? What is the financial relationship?"

That implies that there was one, which is open to interpretation.

Memorial Hospital's 1996 Annual Report notes support from 983 individuals and businesses and $6.2 million in research grants. Though a breakdown of these figures is not available for previous years, in 2001, approximately one-third of research funding came from industry.[27] Microfibres, as a private company, is not required to report its finances, but a plaque in the hospital's histology laboratory lists it as one of eight benefactors, and the annual report shows three McCullochs, the family that founded and owns Microfibres, as members of the hospital corporation. David charges that around the time Rick Dietz was negotiating with Microfibres over the fate of the investigation, he was also part of a team soliciting the company for a contribution to a capital campaign. Memorial has always maintained that the activities did not overlap.

So is Microfibres a good corporate citizen or a bad corporate bully? Hospital officials insisted, predictably, that money, power, and retaliation had nothing to do with their decision to close David's program. He doesn't suggest that the terms were as flagrant as a donation in exchange for his silence. "I don't think it was that specific," he says of the Memorial-Microfibres relationship. "I just think it was the broader issue of this [being] a safe haven for monies from benefactors, not necessarily this one company." In other words, research institutions worry that if they get a reputation as unfriendly to industrial research, corporations will take their projects—and money—elsewhere.

Blatant suppression of research findings is rare, and some scientists argue that industry needs academics more than the other way around, but many businesses keep secrets by reflex, and researchers who don't go along can run into trouble. The most obvious response is to withdraw or threaten to withdraw funding, but corporations bent on preventing disclosure also employ a host of other tactics. They can try to get researchers fired or attack their findings, reputations, and characters;[28] deny them the data or materials they need to do their work; hobble them with demands for information; threaten litigation and insist on gag orders in settlement agreements; confuse the issue in the media and courtroom; demand prepublication review or veto power; and pressure researchers to play down risks or play up favorable findings when they do report.

In an early instance of medical progress hidden in the interest of profit, the Chamberlen brothers kept secret their obstetrical forceps, a device they developed in seventeenth-century Europe to make childbirth easier and safer, so for generations, Chamberlens grew rich while women and children died.[29] Around the time of David's struggle, two disputes pitting scientific inquiry against industrial reticence were much in the news, and the three cases were frequently used to comment on each other. In 1987, Betty Dong, a pharmacologist at the University of California at San Francisco (UCSF), was hired by Boots, the British drug company, to compare Synthroid, their hypothyroidism drug, with three cheaper, rival drugs. When Dong found no difference, Boots cited a confidentiality agreement she had signed and threatened to sue. They also prevented the *Journal of American Medicine* from publishing an article about her findings, and only after the *Wall Street Journal* broke the story ten years later did Knoll, the company that had bought Boots, back down and allow publication to go forward.

In the second instance, Dr. Nancy Olivieri, an expert on blood disorders at the University of Toronto, received funding from the Canadian drug company Apotex for research on thalassemia, a genetic blood disease that causes anemia. In 1996, when she found life-threatening side effects from the medication she was studying, the relationship soured. Again, her contract included a nonpublishing clause, and again lawsuits were threatened. Olivieri informed her patients anyway and consequently lost her position at a hospital affiliated with the university. (She was reinstated after colleagues protested.) Meanwhile, the drug proceeded for licensing in Europe.

Charges of interference with research and reporting continue to surface.[30] Says Dr. Drummond Rennie of UCSF in a condemnation of universities and scientists who acquiesce to corporate pressure, "They are seduced by industry funding and frightened that if they don't go along with these gag orders, the money will go to less rigorous institutions. It's a race to the ethical bottom."[31]

---

As spring wore on, a quick succession of events changed David's faith that the university would do the right thing into disdain for what he calls its moral illiteracy. Clearly, Brown, along with Memorial and Microfibres, wished the controversy would go away, and maybe David with it, but instead it swirled on, pulling everyone deeper in. At the end of April, the dean of the medical school, who had been telling David, his supporters, and the press that the decision to end Memorial's Occupational Medicine program was made solely by the hospital, publicly acknowledged that he now remembered he had attended the meeting where it had been decided. Stung, David wrote a heartfelt appeal to President Gregorian: "Having grown up in this state, having taught at the University for now 14 years, and having lived the ideal that little is more important than the truth, I find the ongoing silence of the University disturbing. . . . Given that there is no longer any recognizable moral authority within the current medical school administration, I turn to you for a final hearing."

David and his wife, Robin, met with Gregorian, who is by all accounts a charming and cultivated man. He reiterated that the university could not control the hospital's actions, but he listened to their concerns and then gave them what David calls "a mission": make a list of what it would take to resolve the controversy. So, in a letter to the provost, David asked for, among other things, official apologies to Microfibres employees and the creation of a fund, using the company's payment for his services, to investigate the health problems at the plant.

Meanwhile, the Committee of Inquiry had issued its report, which is full of the bureaucratese that passes for balance: expressing concern about the public health issues and the hospital's violation of David's academic freedom on one hand, concluding that the company had a right to protect its economic position and avoid bad publicity by firing him on the other. Angry that the committee sidestepped the issues of censorship and intrusion on the doctor-patient relationship, David dismisses the report as "wishy-washy."

Two weeks later, he flew to San Francisco to present his findings about flock worker's lung to the American Thoracic Society. The university sent along an associate dean and a public relations representative, who stood beside him as he spoke. Of David's presentation, a doctor wrote to Gregorian, "Lives may be saved by his action."[32]

The semester ended and the campus was again quiet when David received letters from presidents Dietz and Gregorian, informing him that his position at the hospital would not be renewed when his contract expired two years hence. Gregorian had apparently brokered a compromise, giving him extra time to find employment elsewhere, but it was clear that the sooner he left, the better.

For David, losing his appointment at Memorial meant losing it at Brown as well, though the question of whether one institution could fire him without the other's consent is another bone of contention. It was never clear who was calling the shots for the university. David guesses administrators made some bad initial decisions, then dug their heels in, which put Gregorian in an awkward position. Gregorian was and continues to be a champion of free speech, and these were his final months at Brown before he left to become president of the Carnegie Corporation, a major charitable foundation. Given the fuzzy relationship between Brown and Memorial and the university's reliance on its affiliated hospitals for clinical revenue, he probably could have done little to change the outcome for David or his investigation. But he and other university officials could have come out strongly in support of David and academic freedom, thus reassuring other researchers that they didn't have to avoid controversial work to keep their jobs.

As usual in free speech clashes, this one is chock full of arguments over legal and organizational fine points. Did the nondisclosure agreement apply to the consultancy? Was David at fault for failing to get Microfibres to endorse the operating principles? Did his Occupational Medicine center at Memorial bring in or cost money? Had occupational medicine ever been an official program at Brown? Was David's academic freedom really compromised if he got to present his abstract? All of these questions figured in the controversy, but the central issues are clear: a private company tried to suppress information important to public health, a hospital interfered with attentive care for patients, and a doctor was punished for doing his job.

"Why [were] they so blatant about it?" David asks of the hospital officials. "They could have waited three months and said I had a bad attitude or something." I tell him about Penny Culliton, the English teacher charged with insubordination (see Chapter 9), and he replies, "It's funny, because the hospital president and chief of medicine were quoted in the local papers saying they were, I'm not sure what the word was, upset or frazzled or befuddled by the media attention and may have to terminate me before my contract ends. They made reference to the well-delineated language in our contracts that would allow for this. Well, let's look at the contract."

This takes some doing among all the stacks of papers in his office, but he eventually locates the document, and we parse it as if it were a holy text. He can be let go "upon a due process determination by the hospital trustees, only after consultation with the appropriate officers of Brown University . . . that you have not properly carried out your duties." Those duties are research, teaching, and patient care. Well, he says, uncovering a new disease was important research, and he has just been named Teacher of the Year, and his capabilities as a doctor have never been questioned. He could also be fired if his department were eliminated, but his contract is with the division of General Internal Medicine, which shows no signs of demise. "So we're back to attitude or insubordination," he says. "Insubordinate about what?"

Unlike Penny, David didn't disobey a direct order. It was suggested, urged, advised, and requested, but never demanded, that he withdraw the abstract, and though this is drawing a fine line, it still leaves the nagging problems of scientific responsibility and academic freedom. "Even when they try to say, we didn't tell him he couldn't, we said he should delay, all these organizations are saying, delay is tantamount to not reporting and it is egregious and inconsistent with public health and medical practice." In short, officials at the university and the hospital had the opportunity to act honorably, and they didn't.

---

"There are just some real core values that are pretty intransigent," David says about finding himself in the middle of the controversy.

"Like what?"

"Like truth, like justice, as I see it. I'm not someone to stand on the barricades, but there are certain things that I'm not going to budge from, whether it's patient care, whether it's being honest with patients, whether it's issues of public health like this. I like to say that these players here didn't realize that it's one thing to push other academics around, but you don't mess with a group of half-crazed public health ideologues, which is what people in this field are. These are people who, because they confront these issues, have already decided how they'll stand."

His moral instincts come from his parents, whom he describes as traditional liberals. "We were raised as goody-goods," he says, illustrating with a story about not being allowed to say "oy vey" or "lousy" because his father had written his college thesis on swearing. "But things like caring for other people and honesty were, I think, the two most important things."

Honesty, decency, candor, fairness are by now familiar refrains in this book—along with the sickening realization that they will not necessarily be honored. Are Americans naive to expect that they will be, or just lucky that the First Amendment can shield us against what most of the world learns in childhood? I'm not crazy, David and the others here insist in various ways, but in that missing beat, you, and maybe they, wonder. There is craziness in refusing to go along, as most people do most of the time, but also these fights make you crazy. They haunt your thoughts and use up your time and leave you little peace, and they're hard to let go of because, at some point, you become the fight. More, that fight is exciting, as doomed struggles so often are.

"I've always been this armchair person. I'm even an armchair fisherman," David says to explain why he has read a lot of political theory, in-

cluding a surprising amount about free speech for someone not directly
involved. When we first talk, he's attracted to Owen Fiss's argument in
*The Irony of Free Speech* that, in the interest of maximizing democratic
public discourse, the government may be justified at times in limiting the
speech of some people. "It's one perspective. I'm not saying it's the right
one, but it gives me for the moment a way of dealing with what's otherwise an uncomfortable situation," he says. "I've always had trouble with
the ACLU. It's not that I think they shouldn't be supporting the Nazis as
they walk through Skokie, but I'd rather spend my time doing something
else. I'd like to think that they would too."

David went to Harvard in the thick of 1960s student activism and
took part in the requisite rebellion of the era: got arrested in the takeover
of University Hall, met Robin at a Eugene McCarthy rally, moved to Ver-
mont after graduation in 1971. But theirs was the resistance of middle-
class kids, and they realized early on that they weren't going to be revolutionaries. "We see ourselves as political people, but not really
organization-type people," he says, using the first-person plural as he
tends to when he talks about things that matter in his adult life. Robin
became a lawyer, the kind, David says proudly, who defended down-
trodden workers and got a fish in exchange. He went to Boston University Medical School, but now that he wouldn't be a revolutionary, he
struggled to figure out what kind of doctor he would be. He imagined
leading the fight for universal health coverage but knew he wasn't an organizer, pictured himself working at United Mine Workers' clinics in the
South but didn't finish med school until after they had closed down. So
he did another year of training at a V.A. hospital, which is where he discovered occupational medicine.

He returned to Rhode Island in 1984 to join the Brown faculty and
take a position at Roger Williams Hospital with the understanding that
he would develop an occupational health service there. Four years later,
he moved to Memorial, where he was able to expand his research and
teach without having to worry about generating money. Training physicians brought in substantial government funding, but, in time, the hospital bowed to the fiscal realities of health care in America and began
pushing faculty to bring in additional income.

David understood the economic pressures but felt that firing him was
not a reasonable response. So, as the letters about not renewing his contract reached David, Frank Dietz was receiving a letter from OSHA, informing him that David had brought charges under Section 11(c) of the
Occupational Safety and Health Act, which protects workers from re-

taliation for raising health or safety issues. David hadn't seen much come of 11(c) claims over the years,[33] but Robin, who had left the law to become a singer, dusted off her legal skills and found that an 11(c) could involve any class of employer or employee. This meant that David had a basis for action against the hospital, the company, and the university. The OSHA officer they met with early in May felt their case had merit and could perhaps break new ground, so they were encouraged to try.

This was the only legal action they pursued. "I really don't ascribe to the notion that suing makes the world a better place and would rather focus energies on trying to expand rights," David says—for instance, stretching what Section 11(c) covers. When we meet in 1997, OSHA has just recommended that the Labor Department begin prosecution against all three parties, and he praises the agency for having taken it this far. In the end, though, Labor Department lawyers decided that his case wasn't strong enough to prove in court, and his claim was dismissed.

---

NIOSH published its HHE report in April 1998. (It continues to point to the investigation with pride on its Web site.) The investigators had detected fragments of nylon in the air small enough to get into the lungs and had found evidence of severe inflammation in lung tissue exposed to dust from the Microfibres plants. They determined that a health hazard existed and that "epidemiologic findings suggest a much wider presence of occupational lung disease than the physician-diagnosed cases."[34] A panel of prominent pulmonary pathologists confirmed the findings of David's team, and NIOSH credited him with making the initial connection. By this time, Microfibres claimed to have complied with all of NIOSH's recommendations and to have spent some $5 million investigating and improving the air quality at its factories,[35] yet the cause of the disease remained unknown.

When we catch up by phone a month later, David tells me unhappily that he knows very little about what's happening with the Microfibres employees. The doctors brought on to replace him were, for a variety of reasons, not in a position to offer the same kind of clinical care he had, and David's team had identified a new case just the week before, a man who had developed symptoms at a time when the company said it had done everything NIOSH requested. "I don't know if there are more cases appearing even now. The company says no, but who's looking?" he asks.

He had been set to leave Rhode Island: the defeat was too bitter, the reminders everywhere. At a particularly low point, he says, "I realized it's not a question of winning or losing, but rather, we're just going to go away and nothing's going to have changed here, that this was all for naught." Then things started to shift. Brown's newspapers covered the story, medical students planned some action on the issues, the Rhode Island Medical Society and the AFL-CIO issued statements of support, and the union also endorsed the creation of a state center for occupational health. So lately, he and Robin have been thinking that maybe they should stick around and try to make sure that something similar doesn't happen again.

But in time, they go. Sometimes, he had told me, they pictured themselves living in the country, far from others, and that's what ultimately happened. In August 1999, David left research and academic medicine and took a job on the Maine coast as a community-based internist with time devoted to occupational health. On a clear day, he writes in an upbeat e-mail, a short climb from their house earns a panorama of the White Mountains, Mount Desert Island, and the Atlantic Ocean. There is good news too about his patients. "The affected Rhode Island workers are all well tucked in with other physicians," he writes the next month. The count is then twenty-three cases of flock worker's lung: twenty at Microfibres plants, three at other factories in Massachusetts.

---

In our first conversation, David describes a meeting of the American Association for the Advancement of Science's Committee on Scientific Freedom and Responsibility, where a representative of the Biotechnology Industry Organization (BIO) said that businesses seek to conceal information about their failures as well as their successes. David didn't find the desire to delay reporting on successful research hard to fathom: it gave a head start on the competition, extra time to woo customers. But when the man explained why they also quashed useful but negative information, David says, "I don't think any of us listened beyond his first reason. We just kind of froze. He said, 'Number one, we want to sabotage our competitors. By that, I mean, if a company spent two million dollars on a failed effort, they want to make sure that their competitor does the same.' "

A prominent oncologist interrupted to ask, if the company found that a particular agent killed people and knew that a competitor was about to launch a comparable study, the first company still wouldn't tell? According to David, the BIO man replied, "I know why you and the others here find this hard to accept. You are physicians and scientists, there's an ethical mandate, but you have to realize that our only mandate is to our venture capitalists and to the shareholders."

David gives the man points for honesty and acknowledges that scientists can be cutthroat too, but he also knows from firsthand experience that many companies behave ethically and try to balance the drive for profit with other concerns. The benefit of the BIO representative's candor, however, is a benefit of free speech. "If you accept this reality," David says, amused at the imagined conversation, "then you can say, okay, we got a problem here, and we can now figure out how to respond."

I remind him that he had once said he didn't agree with me on some First Amendment issues. Does that mean that he would suppress any scientific inquiry or information? He considers this with his usual diligence. "I don't think that there are issues that shouldn't be investigated. I don't think there should be information that should not be conveyed. There are issues of timing to make sure that people are prepared to receive information. We have to come to grips with the rights of companies to make profits versus the rights of patients, the rights of media to publish, and so forth. So I acknowledge that there are these competing rights. But I'd be very hard pressed to find situations that shouldn't be reported eventually to everybody."

In March 1999, David is a featured speaker at a conference on secrecy in science that the American Association for the Advancement of Science is hosting at MIT. Secrecy and its abuse are where this book began, and some people who figured in that first story appear here too. Daniel Patrick Moynihan, then still a senator, talks of fearing "secrecy that is not functional, but symbolic." Ex-CIA chief John Deutsch says secrecy isn't always bad but is certainly overused. Then David takes the podium and, with quiet, careful anger, corrects what has been said about his case and the choices it posed.

It was not a moral conundrum, as one commentator framed it, not a question of scientists who report findings versus scientists who honor legal agreements with sponsors. Monetary profit and public health are not morally commensurate, he reminds his listeners, and life forces us to make choices. Then he quotes from Benjamin DeMott's essay "Seduced by Civility." "Democracy can coexist with the belief that all humans are sinners but not with the belief that all sins are equal. Democracy has within each of its camps, not excluding the civilitarian camp, thugs in number. And when you're in an argument with a thug, there are things much more important than civility."[36]

"I do not like incivility," David concludes, "yet I like thugs even less."

# EPILOGUE

*In Other Words*

I began this book as a First Amendment absolutist and finish it as something less comfortable. I still think free speech is a good idea, certainly better than alternatives I've come across, but how can I not be bothered by its limitations? That the freer our speech becomes, the less difference it seems to make, particularly in the political realm. That it seems disingenuous to seek to shock, then get upset when someone objects. That on all sides of these fights, it is too easy to fall into melodrama and self-righteousness. That real change comes more often from confrontation than civility. That the law resolves legal tensions more effectively than human ones.

Early on, I talked with Dr. Jonathan Mann, then director of the François-Xavier Bagnoud Center for Health and Human Rights at Harvard and, before that, founding director of WHO's Global Program on AIDS. As winter gave way to spring, I visited him in his office, sat in on a class he taught, ran into him at a bookstore. We talked about the connection between health and human rights, principally the right to information, and always he spoke with a lucid urgency because he had seen firsthand what was at stake and had committed himself to helping heal the world. "We're trying to link together our hearts and our heads," he said about himself and his students. "We're trying to find the balance for ourselves that we think is best."

He was particularly concerned with the costs of silence to those who live on the margins of any society and are therefore most vulnerable, but lately, he said, he had come to appreciate the limits to the power of information to change behavior. He had been thinking about this in relation to health and to people who know that an activity exposes them to danger and engage in it anyway. Often they had good reasons, he said, but he was aware too that "when people are coerced or stigmatized or afraid, they aren't in a good position to do the right thing."

On September 2, 1998, Jonathan Mann was on his way to Geneva to talk with the United Nations about resuming his work against AIDS when he was killed in the crash of Swissair flight 111. The last time we talked, I had thanked him. He was a busy man who had little interest in courting publicity. "You were generous with your time," I said, "and for no particular reason."

He answered, "There was a reason. You listened."

In part because I've been listening for so long to the strife words can create, I enter this chapter admitting defeat. Yes, censors may triumph only temporarily, and eventually truth (and falsehood) will out, bad words will be said, sex will happen, orthodoxies will be questioned, hierarchies will be challenged, and dark corners will be investigated. Yes, there is common sense to speak, and there are other actions to propose. The government, for instance, could refrain from using public anxieties as a backdoor to censorship, reformers could stop pretending that when they scapegoat speech they're engaged in political action, and everyone could agree that civic life is a balancing act that, not infrequently, requires talking things over. But censorship won't go away. Neither will the pain and anger words and images can cause or the desire to get rid of expression we hate. People will be punished for doing their jobs, thinking their thoughts, heeding their consciences, speaking their minds, and insisting that others be allowed to do so too, as the stories in this book illustrate.

But the stories also suggest better ways to deal with objectionable speech. Fortunately, most people don't get embroiled in full-fledged speech fights. More often, we encounter expression that bothers us and try to figure out how to deal with it. What follows, then, is not a blueprint for action but alternatives to consider.

First, only when we listen to what is being said (and to what isn't) can we respond accurately and effectively. A corollary is to try to hold conflicting ideas in our heads at the same time: to listen *and* disagree, to find words offensive *and* necessary to tolerate, to think an idea is wrong *and* yet not dangerous, to dislike an image *and* allow it to exist. This last suggests a collateral response: Ignore expression you don't like. If it is true that ideas rise and fall in the marketplace like commodities, then, to survive, speakers need listeners and speech needs buyers. Even if denying an audience to speakers who aggrieve you makes no difference in their marketing plan, you'll at least have removed an irritant from your life.

Next, the old chestnut that the antidote for bad speech is more and better speech happens to be true. More speech is the noise of democracy at work: informing, arguing, criticizing and mediating, holding public forums, challenging what is being said while championing the right to say it, and encouraging people to speak for themselves, then letting them have their say. (It can be remarkably salutary to hear directly from kids and others who are supposedly being protected from bad speech.) More speech also involves shining light on abuses of power: autocrats dislike publicity, especially bad publicity. It may entail appealing to people's morality or sense of fairness, since the impulse to protect speech arises from our better nature. And it can include shaming those who speak shamefully because, if words are powerful enough to hurt us, they ought to be powerful enough to goad us into better behavior as well.

This implies that those made to feel ashamed of their words are connected to the community doing the shaming. When people don't care how they're perceived, what you get instead is humiliation, which is counterproductive. One can sometimes bring offensive speakers into a community by humanizing their targets or showing them the consequences of their words. As a student explained, he and others in an after-school program had painted a "Hate Speech Mural" because "We as Latinos felt an urge to do something to show people how hate hurts." Another added, "We also learned about our own prejudices and that will help us. We can't get rid of them but we can work around them and on them."[1]

Those who must struggle to be heard need to create places where they will be heard. If press freedom belongs to press owners, then people with muffled voices, and their allies, must find ways to get their hands on their own presses or whatever technology works best for them. They can start with the Internet by shifting the focus from how to limit it to how to use it productively.

Then, all people concerned with free and fair speech can, must, use their presses to object whenever censorship is attempted—of others as well as of themselves. In a good example, Dance USA, a service organization for nonprofit, professional dance, recognized that laws banning erotic dancing challenged the expressive rights of all dancers and filed a legal brief against such prohibitions when the Supreme Court considered the issue.[2] On a local level, Denise Marika, one of the artists in Chapter 7, called to object when a photo lab she had used in the past handed over to the police photographs another artist had taken of her son naked. She explained, "I think that's part of our economic ability to try to get people together and make it very clear that we're not just putting the work out there. We're also going to back it up."

Parents and others who are worried about the influence of various expression on children have alternatives to retreating into fear or ceding responsibility to the government or its stand-ins. As a nation, we know of specific practices and policies that would make this a safer, healthier, and more congenial place for children—and adults—but we lack the political will to put them in place, turning instead to symbolic arguments. Many of these conflicts are intergenerational, and kids have always needed to be taught, by lesson and example, how to use language and other tools of communication. Meanwhile, the cultural industry can be brought into the discussion about making ethical choices, and schools can teach literacy in new media so that their students approach these tools, not as victims, but as participants in the culture.

A crucial element in responding to word-blame is to identify the real concerns underlying the attack and to focus discussion on actual choices people face in their lives. Once this happens, refreshingly creative possibilities present themselves. Take, for instance, a governor of Missouri, who, after the Ku Klux Klan enrolled in an adopt-a-highway program near St. Louis and the courts upheld their right to do so, renamed that stretch of road, leaving the Klan to pick up trash on Rosa Parks Highway.[3] Or the citizens of Boyertown, Pennsylvania, and Coeur D'Alene, Idaho, who put their money where the Klan's mouth was by pledging funds to antihate efforts for each minute the KKK marched or leafleted in their cities. The fund-raising was so successful in Boyertown that the Klan threatened to sue for a share of the proceeds.[4] Or the city council of Charlottesville, Virginia, which gave its city an unusual monument when it approved plans for the Thomas Jefferson Center for the Protection of Free Expression to erect a giant chalkboard across from City Hall, where people will be able to write whatever they want. Council members were apprehensive about what that might be, but they ultimately decided it was a risk worth taking.[5]

In the end, after the stories and examples and object lessons, the state of free expression in America today is, as perhaps it has always been, our glory and our shame. That means that sometimes there is nothing to do, or rather that the argument itself is the thing to do. This may be the hardest lesson to learn about free speech, and it has to be learned again and again and again.

# NOTES

## INTRODUCTION

A version of this introduction appeared as a paper in the Andy Warhol Foundation for the Visual Arts Series on Arts, Culture, and Society in August 1997.

1. John Stuart Mill, *On Liberty and Utilitarianism* (New York: Bantam, 1993), 17.

2. Harry Kalven, Jr., *A Worthy Tradition: Freedom of Speech in America* (New York: Harper and Row, 1988).

3. This definition from *Brandenburg v Ohio,* 395 U.S. 444 (1969), supplanted *Chaplinsky v New Hampshire,* 315 U.S. 568 (1942), where fighting words were defined more broadly as words that "by their very utterance inflict injury or tend to incite an immediate breach of the peace."

4. For a work to be legally obscene, it must be taken as a whole and, according to community standards, appeal to prurient interest; depict sex in a patently offensive way; and lack serious literary, artistic, political, or scientific value. *Miller v California,* 413 U.S. 15 (1973).

5. *Falwell v Hustler,* 485 U.S. 46 (1988).

6. Richard Chacon, "Tonics with Titillating Titles Test Limits of Good Taste," *Boston Globe,* February 28, 1997.

7. Transcript of press briefing by Ari Fleischer, September 26, 2001, retrieved December 12, 2002, from White House Web site: www.whitehouse.gov/news/briefings.

8. The broken windows theory, proposed by James Q. Wilson and George Kelling in 1982, gained visibility after it was embraced by the New York City Police Department as a rationale for cracking down on "quality of life" crimes. See James Q. Wilson and George Kelling, "Broken Windows: The Police and Neighborhood Safety," *Atlantic Monthly,* March 1982, 29–38.

9. Statement regarding FY 1997 appropriations by Thomas A. Constantine, Administrator, Drug Enforcement Agency, before House Appropriations Committee Subcommittee on Commerce, Justice, State, the Judiciary and Related Agencies, 104th Cong., 2d sess., May 1, 1996.

10. Jim Impoco et al., "TV's Frisky Family Values," *U.S. News and World Report,* April 15, 1996.

11. Henry J. Kaiser Family Foundation, *Generation Rx.com: How Young People Use the Internet for Health Information* (Menlo Park, CA: Henry J. Kaiser Family Foundation, December 2001). The survey also found that of fifteen- to seventeen-year-olds who had gone online, 70 percent had stumbled across porn, but 55 percent of that group were not particularly upset by it.

12. "Rap Attack Back on Track," *Newsletter on Intellectual Freedom* (American Library Association), September 1996, 147.

13. SafeSurf, "Proposal for the Online Cooperative Publishing Act," presented at White House working meeting, July 16, 1997, retrieved July 20, 1997, from www.safesurf.com.

14. *Ginzburg v U.S.,* 383 U.S. 463 (1966).

15. Catharine A. MacKinnon, *Only Words* (Cambridge, MA: Harvard University Press, 1993), 67.

16. Mari J. Matsuda, "Public Response to Racist Speech: Considering the Victim's Story," in Mari J. Matsuda et al., *Words That Wound: Critical Race Theory, Assaultive Speech, and the First Amendment* (Boulder, CO: Westview Press, 1993), 35.

17. The phrase comes from Oliver Wendell Holmes, Jr., who wrote in *Abrams v United States,* 250 U.S. 616 (1919), "that the ultimate good desired is better reached by free trade in ideas—that the best test of truth is the power of the thought to get itself accepted in the competition of the market." Holmes was in the minority here; the majority of the Supreme Court upheld harsh punishment for a group of antiwar activists whose thought didn't stand a chance in the market of World War I jingoism.

18. Thomas I. Emerson, *Toward a General Theory of the First Amendment* (New York: Random House, 1966), 23–25.

19. When the United States began bombing Afghanistan in October 2001, access of journalists to the fighting was limited, but three months later, the Pentagon officially disbanded its press pool system and permitted open coverage.

20. In response to the events of September 11, 2001, a provision in the USA Patriot Act again permitted federal agents to gather information from the reading records of library users.

21. See Richard Bolton, *Culture Wars: Documents from the Recent Controversies in the Arts* (New York: New Press, 1992).

22. Daniel Hackett, "Ricci Moves to Close Show of Erotic Art," *Providence Evening Bulletin,* May 16, 1978.

23. Edward J. Sozanski, "Crowd Shows up for Peek after Unfavorable 'Review,' " *Providence Journal-Bulletin,* May 16, 1978.

24. Before it stopped counting in 1996, People for the American Way documented record highs of 137 challenges to artistic freedom in 1995 and 475 challenges to educational material in the 1995–96 school year.

25. In 1991, 39 percent agreed; in 2000, 22 percent agreed. First Amendment Center, *State of the First Amendment 2001* (Nashville, TN: First Amendment Center, 2001), 11.

26. *R.A.V. v St. Paul,* 505 U.S. 377 (1992).

27. Louis Menand, "Illiberalisms," *New Yorker,* May 20, 1991, 104.

28. U.S. Department of Education, "Getting There: A Report for National College Week," November 1999, retrieved December 11, 2002, from U.S. Department of Education Web site: www.ed.gov/pubs/CollegeWeek. Statistics are for 1997.

29. Higher Education Research Institute, "The American College Teacher: National Norms for 1998–99 HERI Survey," Executive Summary retrieved December 16, 2002, from www.gseis.ucla.edu/heri/press_faculty.htm.

30. Daphne Patai, "There Ought to Be a Law," *William Mitchell Law Review* 22, no. 2 (1996): 124.

31. According to a 1992 review of hate speech laws worldwide conducted by the free speech organization called Article 19, such laws had little connection to lessening ethnic or racial violence or tension. See Sandra Coliver, "Hate Speech Laws: Do They Work?" in *Striking a Balance: Hate Speech, Freedom of Expression and Non-Discrimination,* ed. Sandra Coliver (Essex, England: Article 19 and Human Rights Centre, University of Essex, 1992).

32. Grace Paley, "Midrash on Happiness," *Index on Censorship,* March 1990, 19.

## CHAPTER ONE. I PLEDGE ALLEGIANCE

1. Tim Weiner and Sam Dillon, "In Guatemala's Dark Heart, C.I.A. Lent Succor to Death," *New York Times,* April 2, 1995.

2. This historical review draws on Senate Select Committee on Intelligence, *Guatemala: Hearing before the Senate Select Committee on Intelligence,* 104th Cong., 1st sess., April 5, 1995, testimony of Alexander F. Watson; and Brian E. Klunk, "Jennifer Harbury's Hunger Strike: The U.S. in Guatemala," unpublished case study, 1995, retrieved March 8, 1999, from University of the Pacific Web site: www.uop.edu/sis/tf/klunk2.html.

3. Tom Barry, *Inside Guatemala* (Albuquerque, NM: Inter-Hemispheric Education Resource Center, 1992), 272.

4. Allan Nairn, "CIA Death Squad," *Nation,* August 17, 1995.

5. Tim Weiner, "Tale of Evasion of Ban on Aid for Guatemala," *New York Times,* March 30, 1995.

6. In 1995, Ortiz and eight Guatemalans won a landmark lawsuit in a Boston court against Hector Gramajo, Guatemala's defense minister at the time of her abduction. Though he made it clear back in Guatemala that he had no intention of paying his victims a penny, the State Department eventually revoked his visa. See "*Ortiz v Gramajo,*" *Center for Constitutional Rights Docket,* Fall 1995, 15–16.

7. A junior army officer was found guilty of the murder in 1993, but it was not until 2002 that an army colonel was convicted of ordering the murder. He was the highest-ranking military officer to be convicted of murder in Guatemala.

Marion Lloyd, "Long Fight Brings Guatemalan Officer to Justice," *Boston Globe*, October 5, 2002.

8. David Corn, "Strongman on Campus," *Nation*, April 17, 1995.

9. Weiner and Dillon, "In Guatemala's Dark Heart."

10. These statistics come from several sources, including Amendment 94 to H.R. 1561, by Mrs. Morella, "Regarding the Guatemala Peace Process," *Congressional Record*, May 24, 1995; Amnesty International, *Guatemala: State of Impunity* (London: Amnesty International, April 1997); Archdiocese of Guatemala, *Never Again* (Maryknoll, NY: Orbis Books, 1999); and U.N. Commission for Historical Clarification, *Memory of Silence: U.N. Report on Human Rights in Guatemala (Summary)*, February 25, 1999, retrieved March 1, 1999, from American Association for the Advancement of Science Web site: http://shr.aaas.org/guatemala/ceh/report/english.

11. Richard A. Nuccio, *What's Wrong, Who's Right in Central America* (New York: Facts on File, 1986), 64.

12. Barry, *Inside Guatemala*, 272.

13. Ibid., 273.

14. Victor Perera, *Unfinished Conquest: The Guatemalan Tragedy* (Berkeley: University of California Press, 1993), 49.

15. Guatemala is a signatory to the Geneva Conventions and the International Convention Against Torture; both outlaw torture and other cruel treatment.

16. M. Lee McClenny, spokesperson for the Bureau of Latin American Affairs, "Harbury Press Release and CIA Documents," memorandum to Peg M. Willingham, Guatemala desk officer, November 30, 1994. Obtained by Jennifer Harbury through Freedom of Information Act request. Retrieved October 28, 2002, from Electrical Engineering and Computer Science, University of Michigan Web site: www.eecs.umich.edu/~paur/harbury/archive.

17. The only statutory basis for classification is the Atomic Energy Act, which classifies all atomic energy data at birth. These "born secret" documents accounted for about 1.5 percent of all secrets in 1997. Daniel Patrick Moynihan, "The Science of Secrecy," talk given at MIT, March 29, 1999.

18. From 1990 to 1995, the CIA accounted for 30 percent of all classification activity. Commission on Protecting and Reducing Government Secrecy, *Report of the Commission on Protecting and Reducing Government Secrecy* (Washington, DC: Government Printing Office, 1997), 31.

19. Brian McGrory, " 'Top Secret' Open to Interpretation," *Boston Globe*, November 8, 1997.

20. Commission on Protecting and Reducing Government Secrecy, *Report of the Commission*, xxxix.

21. Tim Weiner, "Guatemalan Agent of C.I.A. Tied to Killing of an American," *New York Times*, March 23, 1995.

22. Weiner and Dillon, "In Guatemala's Dark Heart"; Tim Weiner, "C.I.A.'s Workaday Cloak," *New York Times*, April 5, 1995; Corn, "Strongman on Campus."

23. Weiner, "Guatemalan Agent." The CIA eventually released two hundred documents after Harbury filed an FOIA suit in 1995, but she still doesn't know

where her husband is buried. "*Harbury v CIA, Harbury v Deutch,*" *Center for Constitutional Rights Docket,* Fall 1998, 21–22. In 2000, the Inter-American Court on Human Rights found the Guatemalan military guilty of the kidnapping, torture, and murder of Bámaca.

24. Four years later, the CIA honored the highest-ranking of the officers for "exceptional achievements" in his career. Vernon Loeb, "CIA Giving Fired Agent Top Award," *Washington Post,* March 10, 2000.

25. Documents Rick obtained through FOIA and information that *60 Minutes* verified elsewhere point to others high up in the administration as the probable sources, but that was never confirmed, and no one came forward to challenge Seikaly's version during the investigation.

26. Quoted in Tim Weiner, "For the U.S., a Bad Bedfellow in Guatemala," *New York Times,* May 12, 1996.

27. Weiner, "Tale of Evasion"; Weiner and Dillon, "In Guatemala's Dark Heart."

28. A study by the Pew Research Center for the People and the Press in 1998 found that only 13 percent of the presidential appointees and 14 percent of the executive civil servants interviewed believed that Americans knew enough to make good policy decisions. Pew Research Center, "Washington Leaders Wary of Public Opinion," April 17, 1998, retrieved April 18, 1998, from http://people-press.org/reports.

29. L. Britt Snider, "How Intelligence-Sharing with Congress Has Evolved," unpublished monograph, CIA Center for the Study of Intelligence, 1996–97, note 8.

30. Title IV, Intelligence Authorization Act for Fiscal Year 1981, 50 U.S.C. 501 [a][1].

31. National Security Act of 1947, as amended, 50 U.S.C. 403(d)(3).

32. Daniel Seikaly investigated for the Justice Department, but the report was classified, so Ortiz has not seen it. Mary McGrory, "A Nun's Story Brings Tears," *Boston Globe,* June 29, 1998.

33. Harbury took the unusual step of arguing her own case before the Supreme Court. She argued that the government, in lying to her, had deprived her of her constitutional right of access to the courts at a time that seeking injunctive relief might have saved Bámaca's life. According to the *New York Times,* the Supreme Court justices "appeared uneasy" when faced with Harbury's passionate accusations and their implications. Linda Greenhouse, "Widow Argues for Right to Sue Officials," *New York Times,* March 19, 2002.

34. After he left office, Deutsch was stripped of his security clearances when he was found to have kept highly classified files on an unsecured home computer.

35. Al Cooper, quoted in "Online Sex Addiction on Rise, Specialists Say," *St. Louis Post-Dispatch,* May 6, 2000.

36. U.N. Commission for Historical Clarification, *Memory of Silence.*

37. Richard Chacón, "Clinton Cites Guatemala Errors," *Boston Globe,* March 11, 1999.

38. Sergio de Leon, "4 Get New Trial in Slaying of Guatemalan Bishop," *Boston Globe,* October 9, 2002. The first conviction of troops involved in mas-

sacres during the civil war came in August 1999 (Laura Wides, "25 Soldiers Convicted of Massacre," *Boston Globe,* August 14, 1999), the first investigation of any of the country's leaders during that time in 2001 (Ricardo Miranda, "2 Dictators Face Probe of Deaths in Guatemala," *Boston Globe,* September 14, 2001).

## CHAPTER TWO. A MATTER OF CONSCIENCE

1. Pentagon figures show a 64 percent increase in CO applications filed over the previous year and an 18 percent decrease in the number approved. Phone interviews with Air National Guard Lt. Col. Doug Hart, Defense Department spokesman, August 8, 1991, and September 20, 1991.

2. *West Virginia State Board of Education v Barnette,* 319 U.S. 624 (1943).

3. Among the findings, 19 percent, or nearly five times as many blacks as whites, believed they had gotten an unfair evaluation because of race, and 62 percent of blacks, compared to 17 percent of whites, thought the military paid too little attention to racial discrimination and harassment. Jacquelyn Scarville et al., *Armed Forces Equal Opportunity Survey,* Report No. 97–027, Executive Summary (Arlington, VA: Defense Manpower Data Center, 1999).

4. David Freedman, "People of Color Make Up Large Percentage of Enlisted Military," *The Objector,* Central Committee for Conscientious Objection, January–February 1991, 14–15, using figures obtained from the Department of Defense.

5. Phone interview with Defense Department spokesman, December 2, 1999.

6. Ron Kampeas, "Black Recruits Say Bigotry Forcing Them Out," *Boston Globe,* April 2, 2002.

7. This includes 239,187 reservists who were called up and 26,135 who volunteered. Phone interview with Lt. Col. Mike Milord, Defense Department, December 6, 1999.

8. "The Right Not to Fight," resource packet from Amnesty International USA, January 1991.

9. See *United States v Seeger,* 380 U.S. 163 (1965), and *Welsh v United States* 398 U.S. 333 (1970).

10. According to a *Wall Street Journal*/NBC News poll taken in January 1991, 48 percent of African Americans supported the war, compared to 81 percent of whites. Jonathan Confino, "The Gulf War: Race Split Feared as U.S. Blacks Oppose War," *Daily Telegraph,* January 26, 1991. Other polls found similar disparities.

11. W. E. B. Du Bois, *The Souls of Black Folks* (New York: Penguin, 1996).

12. Hart interview, August 8, 1991.

13. This review of conscientious objection comes primarily from Stephen M. Kohn's *Jailed for Peace: The History of American Draft Law Violators, 1658–1985* (Westport, CT: Greenwood Press, 1986).

14. Laurie Goodstein, "Hearings of Gulf War Objectors Begin at Camp Lejeune," *Washington Post,* April 16, 1991.

15. In 1973, a new policy, under which reserve and National Guard units would be used to reinforce active-duty units, replaced the draft, but after the Gulf

War, military leaders determined that these part-time troops were unprepared for rapid deployment into combat. John Cushman, Jr., "Limit Seen on Reserve Combat Role," *New York Times,* March 15, 1991. By 1999, the Army had more reservists and National Guards than active-duty soldiers. "Cohen to Keep Reserve Forces at Current Level," *Boston Globe,* December 21, 1999.

16. Dale Van Atta, "The Mother of All Injustices," *Oakland Tribune,* August 14, 1991.

17. The first brief stated that though "Larsen's public pronouncements could possibly be punishable as statements disloyal to the US," First Amendment considerations made it advisable to do nothing unless he broke the law. Fact Briefs summarizing phone conversations between Capt. Kohlmann, Office of the Judge Advocate at Marine Corps Headquarters, and Capt. Lassiter, Office of Staff Judge Advocate, 4th Marine Air Wing, September 19, 1990, and October 9, 1990 (author's files).

## CHAPTER THREE. BEYOND MERE DISSENT

1. Decision of INS District Director A. H. Guigni, October 2, 1985. Reprinted in *Randall v Meese,* 854 F.2d 472, 486–87 (D.C. Cir. 1988).

2. Mark Shapiro, "The Excludables," in *Freedom at Risk: Secrecy, Censorship, and Repression in the 1980's,* ed. Richard O. Curry (Philadelphia: Temple University Press, 1988), 163.

3. *Afroyim v Rusk,* 387 U.S. 253 (1967).

4. The massacre was never accurately reported. An official investigation did not begin until 1999, and millions of documents remained classified until 2002, so the number remains uncertain.

5. Paul McMasters, "Analysis," in First Amendment Center, *State of the First Amendment 1999* (Nashville, TN: First Amendment Center, 1999), 3.

6. In 1997, about 10.4 percent of the U.S. population was foreign born, and approximately one-fifth was of foreign stock. Diane A. Schmidley, *Profile of the Foreign-Born Population,* U.S. Bureau of the Census, Current Population Reports, Series P23–206 (Washington, DC: Government Printing Office, 2000).

7. *Mathews v Diaz,* 426 U.S. 67 (1976), and *Plyler v Doe,* 457 U.S. 202 (1982).

8. McCarran-Walter Act, 8 U.S.C. 1182 (a) (27) and (28) (1982).

9. Curry, *Freedom at Risk,* 166.

10. INS Appeal Brief, May 29, 1987, quoted in David Cole, "What's a Metaphor? The Deportation of a Poet," *Yale Journal of Law and Liberation* 1 (Fall 1989): 13.

11. Decision of the Board of Immigration Appeals, Dissenting Opinion of Fred W. Vacca, July 27, 1989. File: A11 644 708 El Paso. Obtained through Freedom of Information Act request.

12. This standard, which had never been used before to argue for deportation, appears, not in McCarran-Walter, but in a section permanently barring people from becoming citizens. Cole, "What's a Metaphor?" 11n.

13. Margaret Randall, *Coming Home: Peace without Complacency* (Albuquerque, NM: West End Press, 1990), 18.

14. Thomas Jefferson, *Notes on the State of Virginia,* 1781–85, Query 17, reprinted in *Thomas Jefferson: Writings* (New York: Library of America, 1984), 286.

15. Cole, "What's a Metaphor?" 14. The language is from the McCarran-Walter Act, 8 U.S.C. 1101(e)(3).

16. Decision of Martin F. Spiegel, Immigration Judge, El Paso, Texas, August 28, 1986, File No. A11 644 708. Obtained through Freedom of Information Act request.

17. Board of Immigration Appeals, Oral Argument Transcript, October 20, 1987, 18, quoted in Cole, "What's a Metaphor?" 13.

18. In 1999, the State Department designated twenty-eight groups foreign terrorist organizations; over half were Islamic or Arabic groups. U.S. State Department, "Patterns of Global Terrorism: 1999," April 2000, retrieved September 2000 from www.state.gov/www/global/terrorism/1999report. After September 11, 2001, the list was expanded multiple times.

19. David Cole, "A Legal Breakthrough for Immigrants," *Boston Globe,* July 1, 2001.

20. In this lengthy, multifaceted case, *Reno v American-Arab Anti-Discrimination Committee,* the "L.A. Eight"—seven Palestinians and one Kenyan—were originally targeted for deportation in 1987 under McCarran-Walter for their affiliation with the Popular Front for the Liberation of Palestine. When McCarran-Walter was repealed, the INS charged six of them with technical violations of their visas. The defendants argued that they were being singled out because of their beliefs, but in 1999, the Supreme Court dismissed their First Amendment claims to such protections. Kit Gage, "Other Secret Evidence Cases," *The Link* 23, no. 3 (1999): 8–9, and *"Reno v American-Arab Anti-Discimination Committee," Center for Constitutional Rights Docket,* Fall 2000, 15–16. In the wake of 9/11, the government maintained that several U.S.-based charitable organizations had links to terrorist groups.

21. *Reno v American-Arab Anti-Discrimination Committee* (No. 94-55404), 9th Circuit Court of Appeals, November 8, 1995.

22. *Reno v American-Arab Anti-Discrimination Committee,* 525 U.S. 471 (1999).

23. The judge ordered the release of Hany Kiareldeen, a Palestinian who had been held for nineteen months. Susan Sachs, "Due Process, but How Much Is Due?" *New York Times,* December 5, 1999.

24. David Cole, "No More Secret Evidence," *Washington Post,* December 3, 1999.

25. Betty Molchany, "Using 'Secret Evidence' Based on Translation, Transcription Errors, U.S. Orders Two Iraqi Kurds Deported," *Washington Report on Middle East Affairs,* September 1999, 17–18.

26. Mary Leonard, "Lawyer Presses Fight over Secret Evidence," *Boston Globe,* March 9, 2001.

27. *INS v St. Cyr* (No. 00–767, decided June 25, 2001, cert. U.S. Ct. App., 2d Cir.) established that immigrants convicted of a range of crimes are entitled to court hearings before being deported, and *Zadvydas v Davis* (No. 99–7791, decided June 28, 2001, cert. U.S. Ct. App., 5th Cir.) barred the indefinite im-

prisonment of immigrants convicted of crimes when their home country would not accept them. Cole, "Legal Breakthrough for Immigrants."

28. *New Jersey Media Group Inc. v Ashcroft,* No. 02–2524 (3d. Cir.), 7.

29. *Detroit Free Press v Ashcroft,* No. 02–1437 (6th Cir.), 4.

30. Randall, *Coming Home,* 21.

## CHAPTER FOUR. LA MORDAZA

Original interview translated from the Spanish by Emilio Vilella, Maria Skufka, and the author.

1. Ronald Fernandez, *Los Macheteros: The Wells Fargo Robbery and the Violent Struggle for Puerto Rican Independence* (New York: Prentice Hall, 1987), 132.

2. See, e.g., *Balzac v People of Puerto Rico,* 258 U.S. 298 (1922).

3. Fernandez, *Los Macheteros,* 159.

4. Ralph Ranalli, "Bill Planned to Revamp Federal Grand Jury System," *Boston Globe,* January 4, 2000.

5. In December 1998, when Puerto Ricans voted on their status, independence got 2.5 percent of the vote; in 1993, it was around 4 percent.

6. Brian Glick, *War at Home: Covert Action against U.S. Activists and What We Can Do about It* (Boston: South End Press, 1989), 12.

7. Senate Select Committee on Intelligence, *Hearing on Global Threats and Challenges: The Decades Ahead,* January 28, 1998, testimony of Louis Freeh, FBI Director, "Statement on Threats to U.S. National Security."

8. Ibid.

9. Efforts to find an acceptable definition of terrorism date back to the League of Nations. In 2001, the United Nations put off negotiations on a Comprehensive Convention on International Terrorism, perhaps forever, because it could not agree on a definition. Joe Lauria, "Definition of Terrorism Eludes Negotiators," *Boston Globe,* November 22, 2001.

10. Fernandez, *Los Macheteros,* 66.

11. In a 1996 poll conducted by *El Nuevo Día,* 62 percent of respondents said they considered Puerto Rico, not the United States, their nation. Cited by Mireya Navarro, "Marking a Puerto Rican Anniversary," *New York Times,* July 26, 1998.

12. Reporters Committee for Freedom of the Press, "Agents of Discovery," 2001, retrieved December 6, 2001, from www.rcfp.org/agents. In another accounting, the Justice Department wrote Senator Charles Grassley that it had authorized eighty-eight subpoenas of the news media from 1991 to September 2001. Reporters Committee for Freedom of the Press, "News Media Update," December 6, 2001, retrieved December 10, 2001, from www.rcfp.org/news/2001/1206grassl.html.

13. Reporters Committee for Freedom of the Press, "Paying the Price," n.d., retrieved November 5, 2002, from www.rcfp.org/jail.

14. Thirty-eight percent of those polled by the Pew Research Center for the People and the Press believed journalists hurt democracy; see Pew Research Center, "Public Votes for Continuity and Change in 2000," February 25, 1999, re-

trieved December 13, 2002, from http://people-press.org/reports. In 2002, Freedom Forum's First Amendment Center found that 42 percent of respondents believed the press in America has too much freedom to do what it wants, although 69 percent agreed that newspapers should be allowed to publish a story without government approval. This last number dropped considerably from previous similar polls. First Amendment Center, *State of the First Amendment,* 2002 (Nashville, TN: First Amendment Center, 2002).

15. In a survey conducted in 2000 by the Pew Research Center and the *Columbia Journalism Review,* journalists who acknowledged succumbing to self-censorship occasionally or more often gave the following reasons, in descending order of frequency, for avoiding stories: concern that audiences would find them dull or too complex, desire to protect sources, careerism, and need to avoid offending the news organization's ownership and advertisers. Pew Research Center, "Self Censorship: How Often and Why," April 30, 2000, retrieved May 23, 2000, from http://people-press.org/reports.

16. In its annual ranking of countries on a corruption scale, Transparency International, a Berlin-based monitoring group, compared its Corruption Perceptions Index with Freedom House's index of newspapers per capita and found that countries with higher newspaper circulations seemed to tolerate less corruption. "Dr. Peter Eigen, Chairman, Transparency International," in International Institute for Democracy and Electoral Assistance, *Democracy Forum Report,* July 1997, chap. 11, retrieved December 13, 2002, from www.idea.int/publications/1997forumreport/chapter11/eigen.html.

17. José A. Delgado, "El privilegio de pueblo," *Nuevo Día,* September 25, 1991.

18. Thomas Jefferson, letter to Colonel Edward Carrington, January 16, 1787, in *Papers of Thomas Jefferson,* vol. 11, ed. Julian P. Boyd (Princeton, NJ: Princeton University Press, 1950), 49.

19. *New York Times v United States,* 403 U.S. 713 (1971).

20. *Gonzales v National Broadcasting Co., Inc.,* 155 F.3d 618 (2d Cir. 1998).

21. Daisy Sánchez, *Cita con la injusticia* (Puerto Rico: Editorial DG, 1996), 87.

## CHAPTER FIVE. POINT OF VIEW

1. Agreement for Facilitating the Educational Circulation of Visual and Auditory Materials of an Education, Scientific and Cultural Character (Beirut Agreement), ratified by the United States, May 26, 1960 (22 C.F.R. 61). Retrieved December 13, 2002, from UNESCO Web site: www.unesco.org/human_rights/hraa.htm.

2. 22 C.F.R. 502.6 (a) (3), as of 1985. The regulations have since been changed.

3. 22 C.F.R. 502.6 (b) (5), as of 1985.

4. Christopher Borelli, "Case Closed!" *Independent,* July 1995, 7–8.

5. John S. Gibson, "Public Diplomacy: Public-Private Cooperation to Represent the United States to the World," *International Educator* 7, nos. 2–3 (1998): 55.

6. John W. Mendenhall, USIA, letter to Steve Jarrett, Bullfrog Films, August 5, 1982.

7. Molly Ivins, "100 Navajo Families Sue on Radioactive Waste Spill," *New York Times,* August 15, 1989.

8. Doug Brugge, Timothy Benaly, and Phil Harrison, *Memories Come to Us in the Rain and the Wind: Oral Histories and Photographs of Navajo Uranium Miners and Their Families* (Boston: Navajo Uranium Miner Oral History and Photography Project, 1997).

9. Robert Gehrke, "Bush Seeks to Delay Payments to Sick Uranium Workers," *Boston Globe,* August 29, 2001.

10. Ward Sinclair, "Radioactive Dam Break Described as Preventable," *Washington Post,* October 23, 1979.

11. Mendenhall, letter to Jarrett.

12. Joel Brinkley, "In Focus: The U.S. Movie Reviewer," *New York Times,* March 19, 1984.

13. USIA Decision Regarding Certification—"In Our Own Backyards: Uranium Mining in the United States," February 22, 1985, 3–4.

14. With the implementation of NAFTA in 1994, all duty was suspended, and Bullfrog no longer applies for certificates.

15. Industry-sponsored films, such as Edison Electric Institute's *To Catch a Cloud: A Thoughtful Look at Acid Rain* and the Atomic Industrial Forum's *Radiation . . . Naturally,* were certified. So was *The Family: God's Pattern for Living,* which, according to the accompanying program notes, includes "God's Pattern for Wives" that "illustrates the need for wives to submit to their husbands."

16. USIA Decision Regarding Certification—"Save the Planet," November 21, 1984, 3.

17. John W. Mendenhall, USIA, letter to Churchill Films, October 17, 1984.

18. USIA Review Board, letter to Charles Light, Green Mountain Post Films, March 29, 1984.

19. *Bullfrog Films, Inc. v Wick,* 646 F. Supp. 492 (C.D. Cal. 1986).

20. USIA Decision of Reconsideration Regarding Certification—"In Our Own Backyards," January 15, 1988, 4.

21. National Campaign for Freedom of Expression, "NEA Four Win Settlement," *NCFE Bulletin,* summer 1993, 1.

22. President George H. Bush, letter to John Frohnmayer, NEA, June 19, 1990.

23. Holly Hughes, "Now Playing at the Supreme Court: Environmental Theater," *NCFE Bulletin,* Special Supplement, July 1998, 53.

24. Susanna Styron, "Risk Management," *New York Times Magazine,* April 3, 1994.

## CHAPTER SIX. THAT SPECIAL SHIMMER

1. "To the NEA's partisans, this is ancient history. They swear that the Annie Sprinkle days are over." Jeff Jacoby, "Despite Promises, the NEA Hasn't Changed," *Boston Globe,* August 21, 1998.

2. "Performance Pick of the Week," *LA Weekly,* March 21–27, 1997.

3. The Arizona theater owner was acquitted, but *Deep Throat* was found obscene by a Georgia court in a ruling affirmed by the Supreme Court in 1976. *Sanders v Georgia,* 424 U.S. 931 (1976).

4. This trend holds for live performance too. According to a 1998 White Paper by the Free Speech Coalition, *The Truth about California's Adult Entertainment Industry* (Canoga Park, CA: Free Speech Coalition, 1998), female erotic dancers make three to four times as much money as men. Don Waitt of *Erotic Dancer Magazine* estimates that there are 350,000 "house dancers" in the United States (phone conversation, September 2000). Men, however, make much more money on the business end of pornography.

5. Walter Kendrick, *The Secret Museum: Pornography in Modern Culture* (Berkeley: University of California Press, 1987), 11.

6. Angela Carter, *The Sadeian Woman and the Ideology of Pornography* (New York: Harper and Row, 1978), 18.

7. Kendrick, *The Secret Museum,* 126.

8. Reprinted in *Ulysses* (New York: Modern Library, 1942), xiv.

9. The effect of this ruling, *United States v One Book Entitled Ulysses,* 72 F.2d 705, 708 (2d Cir. 1934), was limited because a federal court decision, even one upheld by the Supreme Court, does not control legal determinations in other states.

10. Edward deGrazia, *Girls Lean Back Everywhere: The Law of Obscenity and the Assault on Genius* (New York: Random House, 1992), 8.

11. Jonathan Green, *The Encyclopedia of Censorship* (New York: Facts on File, 1990), 320.

12. *Roth v U.S.,* 354 U.S. 476 (1957).

13. deGrazia, *Girls Lean Back Everywhere,* 290.

14. Ibid., 310.

15. "Text of Statement Rejecting the Report of Obscenity," *New York Times,* October 25, 1970.

16. *Miller v California* 413 U.S. 15 (1973).

17. For high-end estimates, see, e.g., Edward Q. McKenzie, "I'm Ready for My Dildo Mr. DeMille," *Hartford Advocate,* June 27, 2000. The low-end figure comes from calculations by Forbes.com columnist Dan Ackman, who charged that the study by Forrester Research on which the oft-quoted figure of $10 billion is based does not exist. Dan Ackman, "How Big Is Porn?" May 25, 2001, retrieved July 3, 2002, from www.Forbes.com.

18. Free Speech Coalition White Paper, 1999. Phone interviews with Jeffrey Douglas, Legal Counsel, Free Speech Coalition, and Mark Kerns, Senior Editor, *Adult Video News,* August 2000.

19. Frank Rich, "Naked Capitalists," *New York Times Magazine,* May 20, 2001, 51.

20. Gary Webb, "Sex and the Internet," *Y-Life,* April 2001, retrieved April 5, 2001, from www.zdnet.com/yil.

21. Robert Jackson, Jr., "The Dirty Business of Internet Porn," *AlterNet,* November 17, 2000, retrieved November 22, 2000, from www.alternet.org.

22. Jennifer A. Peter and Louis M. Crosier, *The Cultural Battlefield: Art Censorship and Public Funding* (Gilsum, NH: Avocus Publishing, 1995), 40.

23. Annie Sprinkle, *Post-Porn Modernist: My 25 Years as Multimedia Whore* (San Francisco: Cleis Press, 1988), 166.

24. Women Against Pornography, which formed in New York in 1979, explicitly disavowed censorship. Chronology of antiporn feminism from Lisa Duggan and Nan D. Hunter, *Sex Wars: Sexual Dissent and Political Culture* (New York: Routledge, 1995), 18–23.

25. Catharine MacKinnon, "Not a Moral Issue," *Yale Law and Policy Review* 2 (1984): 325.

26. When MacKinnon was asked why only those who agreed with her were allowed to testify at a public hearing in Minneapolis, she replied, "Saying a body of research is open to interpretation to which it is not open is not professional." Quoted in Christopher M. Finan, *Catharine A. MacKinnon: The Rise of a Feminist Censor, 1983–1993* (New York: Media Coalition, 1993), 13.

27. Sprinkle, *Post-Porn Modernist,* 152.

28. A woman reviewing an academic conference where Annie's films were shown writes, "Watching her work leaves me feeling awe-struck and inexperienced. Although Sprinkle's films may show her as an empowered woman working within the sex industry, I would question how much they empower a female audience." Rosie Gunn, "On-Scenities," *body politic* 2 (1996), retrieved June 26, 1998, from www.bodypolitic.co/uk/body2/onScenities.html.

29. In a survey of members of COYOTE, a prostitutes' rights organization, Wendy McElroy found that 51 percent had college degrees. Wendy McElroy, *XXX: A Woman's Right to Pornography* (New York: St. Martin's Press, 1995). For sex workers' writing, see Frédérique Delacoste and Priscilla Alexander, eds., *Sex Work: Writings by Women in the Sex Industry* (San Francisco: Cleis Press, 1968), and Erika Langley, *The Lusty Lady* (New York: Scalo, 1997).

30. C. Carr, "This Witch-Hunt's for You," *Village Voice,* February 20, 1990.

31. Kendrick, *The Secret Museum,* 16.

32. Willard M. Gaylin, "Obscenity Is More Than a Four-Letter Word," in *Censorship and Freedom of Expression,* ed. Harry M. Clor (Chicago: Rand McNally, 1971), 170–71.

33. "Lieberman Skips Panel on Media Censorship," *Boston Globe,* August 17, 2000.

34. This idea is developed in detail in Baruch D. Kirschenbaum's "Private Parts and Public Considerations," *Exposure Magazine,* Fall 1984, 5–21.

## CHAPTER SEVEN. SOMETHING TO OFFEND NEARLY EVERYBODY

1. Joanne Wypijewsky, ed, *Painting by Numbers: Komar and Melamid's Scientific Guide to Art* (Berkeley: University of California Press, 1999).

2. Center for Cultural Conservatism, "A Short History of Cultural Conservatism," January 20, 2001, retrieved January 20, 2001, from the Free Congress Foundation Web site: www.freecongress.org/centers/conservatism.

3. House Committee on Appropriations, Subcommittee on Interior, *Hearing on Arts and Humanities,* 102d Cong., 1st sess April 18, 1991, testimony of Louis Sheldon.

4. Quoted in Michael Brenson, *Visionaries and Outcasts: The NEA, Con-*

*gress, and the Place of the Visual Artist in America* (New York: New Press, 2001), 17.

5. Timothy Healy, "Government—A Good Patron but Bad Censor," *New York Times,* September 15, 1989.

6. Robert M. Andrews, "25% in Survey Back Limits on Artistic Freedom," *Boston Globe,* September 15, 1990.

7. J. M. Coetzee, *Giving Offense: Essays on Censorship* (Chicago: University of Chicago Press, 1996), vii.

8. Doreen Carvajal, "Photography Meets Paranoia," *New York Times,* February 19, 1995.

9. Phone conversation with Ansin Kaye, Middlesex District Attorney's Office, June 12, 2000.

10. In "The Trade in Child Pornography," Jan Schuijer and Benjamin Rossen trace the gestation of this statistic. It began with a guess made by a journalist in 1976 about the extent of boy prostitution, which was picked up by a drug counselor, who, on a hunch, doubled it to include girls, then doubled it again to compensate for what the journalist couldn't validate statistically. This number was adopted by John Conyers, then heading a congressional investigating committee. He doubled it again to conclude, "So we have somewhere possibly in the neighborhood of 2 million kids who form a ready market for sexual exploitation from pornographers and the like." *Issues in Child Abuse Accusations* 4, spring 1992, retrieved November 11, 2002, from the Web site of the Institute for Psychological Therapies: www.ipt-forensics.com/journal/issues92.html.

11. *Ginsberg v New York,* 390 U.S. (1968).

12. *New York v Ferber,* 458 U.S. 757 (1982). The court wrote that "the evil to be restricted so overwhelmingly outweighs the expressive interests, if any, at stake, that no process of case-by-case adjudication is required."

13. *Osborne v Ohio,* 495 U.S. 103 (1990).

14. Child Pornography Prevention Act of 1996, 18 U.S.C. 2256(8)(2).

15. Psychologist Michael Bader suggests, "Perhaps the reason that sexual abuse is the form of damage that we deem most heinous—despite other childhood experiences that might contend for this distinction—is that such abuse is easiest to identify and involves impulses that are the most forbidden." Michael Bader, "Priests, Sexual Abuse and Illusions of Innocence," *AlterNet,* March 14, 2002, retrieved March 15, 2002, from www.alternet.org.

16. Nathaniel Hawthorne, "Fancy's Show Box," in *Twice-Told Tales and Other Short Stories* (New York: Washington Square Press, 1960), 164.

17. Paul J. Kelly, letter to *Cambridge Chronicle,* October 20, 1994.

18. According to the American Library Association, it was the second most challenged book for all of the 1990s.

19. People for the American Way, *Artistic Freedom under Attack,* 4th ed. (Washington, DC: 1996), 8.

20. Janet Parshall, "Time Out for Moms," *Family Voice* (Concerned Women for America), June 1993, 17.

21. *Newsletter on Intellectual Freedom,* American Library Association. July 1993, 123.

22. Ibid., 125.

23. *CFV Report* (Colorado for Family Values), May 1993, reprinted from the *Lambda Report* of the Citizens' Rights Foundation.

24. Jamie Jamieson, "Village Exposed to Art," *Brookline Tab,* May 31, 1994.

25. A study of creative and performing artists in Los Angeles, Minneapolis, New York, and San Francisco found that 60 percent earned less than $7,000 from their art in 1996, while only 8 percent earned more than $40,000. Joan Jeffri, *Information on Artists, Abstract 2* (New York: Research Center for Arts and Culture, Columbia University, 1998). According to the Department of Labor, in 2000, actors, directors, and producers earned an average of $25,920; dancers and choreographers, $22,470; musicians, $36,740; and visual artists, $31,190. Bureau of Labor Statistics, *Occupational Outlook Handbook* (Washington, DC: U.S. Department of Labor, 2000).

26. Eric S. Bassin and Jeffery N. Gell, "Walsh Is Tried for Tearing Dildoes," *Harvard Crimson,* April 8, 1995.

27. Pamela Ferdinand, "Partitions Shield Cambridge Exhibit," *Boston Globe,* October 6, 1994.

28. Nadine Gordimer, *Writing and Being* (Cambridge, MA: Harvard University Press, 1995), 9.

29. People for the American Way, *Artistic Freedom under Attack,* 14.

30. Hans Evers, letter to *Cambridge Chronicle,* October 20, 1994.

31. Sandy Coleman, "Show Is Canceled over Artist's Work," *Boston Globe,* May 12, 1996.

32. "Give Just One Good Reason," *Pilot,* November 25, 1994, 12.

33. J. A. Kashmann, "Faude Admits He Stuck His Foot in His Mouth," *Hartford News,* March 20–27, 1991.

34. Bill Rodrigues, "The Language of Hate," *Providence Phoenix,* February 4, 1994.

## CHAPTER EIGHT. THE SEDUCTION OF ABSOLUTES

1. Bertrand Russell, "An Outline of Intellectual Rubbish," in *Unpopular Essays* (New York: Simon and Schuster, 1951), 104.

2. "Survey Shows Intolerance among Christian Activists," *Freedom Writer,* September/October 1997, 1.

3. Bruce Bawer, *Stealing Jesus: How Fundamentalism Betrays Christianity* (New York: Crown, 1997), 127.

4. Ibid., 68.

5. Sidney Blumenthal, "Christian Soldiers," *New Yorker,* July 18, 1994, 34.

6. D. James Kennedy, Coral Ridge Ministries, general fund-raising letter, May 1999.

7. Pew Research Center, "Religion and Politics: The Ambivalent Majority," September 20, 2000, retrieved October 2, 2000, from www.people-press.org/reports.

8. The divorce rate for self-described born-again Christians is 27 percent, for "non-Christians," 24 percent. Barna Research Group, "The Year's Most Intriguing Findings from Barna Research Studies," December 12, 2000, retrieved February 5, 2001, from www.barna.org.

9. "Robertson Advocates Stoning," *Freedom Writer*, July/August 1997, 15.

10. Skipp Porteous, *Jesus Doesn't Live Here Anymore: From Fundamentalist to Freedom Writer* (Buffalo, NY: Prometheus Books, 1991), 195.

11. *Field Manual of the Free Militia* (Great Barrington, MA: Riverwalk Press, 1996), 34.

12. Ibid., 3.

13. Ibid., 28.

14. Porteous, *Jesus Doesn't Live Here Anymore*, 212.

15. Michael Kranish, "For the Christian Coalition, Signs of a Growing Influence," *Boston Globe*, September 8, 1995.

16. Barna Research Online, "Evangelical Christians," 2002, retrieved November 12, 2002, from www.barna.org.

17. Pew Research Center, "Religion and Politics."

18. Flannery O'Connor, *Mystery and Manners* (New York: Farrar, Straus and Giroux, 1957), 91.

19. J. M. Coetzee, *Giving Offense: Essays on Censorship* (Chicago: University of Chicago Press, 1996), 15–19.

20. Rutherford Institute, "Free Speech," retrieved December 13, 2002, from www.rutherford.org/issues/free_speech.asp.

21. *West Virginia Board of Education v Barnette*, 319 U.S. 624 (1943).

22. Jeffrey Rosen, "Is Nothing Secular?" *New York Times Magazine*, January 30, 2000, 42.

23. In *Everson v Board of Education*, 330 U.S. 1 (1947) USCC, the Supreme Court ruled against a local government paying transportation costs to religious schools, thus establishing the principle that no tax money can be used to support religious activities or institutions.

24. American Family Association, "School Prayer and the Decline of America," *Christians and Society Today*, February 1994, 1.

25. *Newdow v U.S. Congress*, 292 F.3d 597 (9th Cir. 2002).

26. Public Agenda, "For Goodness' Sake: Why So Many Americans Want Religion to Play a Greater Role in Public Life," November 2000, retrieved January 14, 2001, from www.publicagenda.org.

27. National Association of Evangelicals, "Evangelical Political Views," unpublished survey, March 9, 2000.

28. Shelley Murphy, "Removal of Bricks Brings Suit," *Boston Globe*, January 24, 2001.

29. Anne Fowler et al., "Talking with the Enemy," *Boston Globe*, January 28, 2001.

30. Jonathan Wallace, "The First Amendment Protects the 'Nuremberg Files' Web Site," *Ethical Spectacle*, March 1999, retrieved April 4, 1999, from www.spectacle.org.

31. Pew Research Center, "Religion and Politics"; Public Agenda, "For Goodness' Sake."

32. Pew Research Center, "Religion and Politics."

33. "Religious Affiliations of Federal Prisoners," *Freethought Today* 17 (June/July 2000): 5.

## CHAPTER NINE. INSUBORDINATE

1. Paul Bush, "Fighting the Good Fight," *Boston Globe,* January 17, 1999.

2. In 1999, salaries ranged from $21,388 for a first-year teacher to $36,751 for a long-term teacher at the highest pay level. Bush, "Fighting the Good Fight." In 2000–2001, New Hampshire ranked twenty-seventh among the states in teacher salaries, which were about $5,000 below the national average. National Education Association, "Table 1. Average Salaries ($) of Public School Teachers, 2001–2 and 2000–2001 (Revised)," in "Rankings and Estimates: A Report of School Statistics, Update Fall 2002," retrieved December 13, 2002, from www. nea.org/edstats/reupdate02.html.

3. According to the New Hampshire Board of Education, the state's average per pupil funding was $5,390. According to the National Center for Educational Statistics, which calculates state spending differently, New Hampshire's expenditure, at $5,740, was slightly higher than the national average that year.

4. Studies repeatedly show homosexual students to be at greater risk than their straight counterparts. The Gay, Lesbian, Straight Education Network (GLSEN) found that 63 percent of gay, lesbian, bisexual, and transgender students had experienced some harassment and 27 percent some physical harassment. Joseph G. Kosciw and M. K. Cullen, *The 2001 National Climate Survey* (Washington, DC: GLSEN, 2001). A Harvard Medical School study determined that gay and bisexual students are more likely to try suicide and take sexual risks. "Gay Youths Face Risks, Study Says," *Boston Globe,* May 5, 1998. Human Rights Watch found that harassment at school undermines the health and education of gay and lesbian students. Michael Bochenek and A. Widney Brown, *Hatred in the Hallways* (New York: Human Rights Watch, 2001).

5. "Voices of New England," interview with Penny Culliton, *Boston Globe,* April 16, 1996.

6. Dana McKenney, "Memo Re: Meeting to Discuss Parent Concerns," December 29, 1993.

7. Quoted in "Arbitration Decision: Mascenic Education Association and Mascenic Regional School District [Grievant: Penny Culliton]," 5.

8. Ibid., 6.

9. Quoted in "Arbitration Decision," 7.

10. Elizabeth Shogren and Douglas Frantz, "Schools Boards Become the Religious Right's Pulpit," *Los Angeles Times,* October 12, 1993. In other interviews, CEE's president, Robert Simonds, cited different numbers but generally declined to give specifics.

11. Edward Sharp, letter to Sue Teluigator, Chair, Chicago Local, National Writers Union, November 3, 1994.

12. "Arbitration Decision," 19.

13. Corriveau testified that the school board hadn't required approval of any book in his decade as English department chair. People for the American Way, *Attacks on the Freedom to Learn: 1996 Report* (Washington, DC: PFAW, 1996), 196.

14. Francine Fullam, Acting Superintendent, letter to Penny Culliton, May 15, 1995.

15. Jesse Salisbury, "Board to Appeal Culliton Ruling," *Telegraph* (Nashua, NH), April 16, 1996.

16. Ibid.

17. Jane Eklund, "NH Teacher Fired for Using Gay-Themed Books," *Bay Windows,* September 28–October 4, 1995, 1.

18. Bush, "Fighting the Good Fight."

19. Steve Farkas, Jean Johnson, and Ann Duffett, *Playing Their Parts: Parents and Teachers Talk about Parental Involvement in Public Schools* (New York: Public Agenda, 1999).

20. "Rights Group Reports Increase in Books Banned," *New York Times,* August 31, 1995.

21. "Culliton Is Confused," *Union Leader,* October 12, 1995.

22. New Hampshire Senate Bill 653-FN, April 9, 1996.

23. The year after Penny's dismissal, the Mascenic school board rejected a proposal to include sexual orientation in its antidiscrimination policy. "Mascenic Says No to Bias-Wording Change," *Union Leader,* April 15, 1996.

24. *Romer v Evans,* 517 U.S. 620 (1996).

## CHAPTER TEN. BLAME THAT TUNE

1. Ad for Parents Television Council, *Boston Globe,* November 12, 2000. Such an ad costs about $31,000 for a nonprofit group.

2. Kenneth Thompson, *Moral Panics* (New York: Routledge, 1998), 2.

3. Quoted in Mike Diana, "Zero Tolerance," *Request,* May 1995, 23.

4. Amy Kiste Nyberg, *Seal of Approval: The History of the Comics Code* (Jackson: University Press of Mississippi, 1998), 5.

5. Ibid., 47.

6. Fredric Wertham, *Seduction of the Innocent* (New York: Rinehart, 1954), 155.

7. Ibid., 167.

8. Comics Magazine Association of America Comics Code, 1954, cited in Nyberg, *Seal of Approval,* 166–69.

9. Norman Mailer, *The Faith of Graffiti* (New York: Praeger, 1974), unpaginated.

10. "An Anti-Graffiti Web Page," 1996, retrieved September 5, 2000, from DougWeb Online Web site: www.dougweb.com/faq.

11. Don Terry, "Where Life Is Sideshow, Street Art Passes Limit," *New York Times,* September 19, 1997.

12. Richard Taylor, "Silence Is the Fool," *National Campaign for Freedom of Expression Quarterly,* summer 1998, 5.

13. James Garbarino on *Meet the Press,* April 25, 1999.

14. In 2001, the violent death rate for American teenagers was the lowest in fifty years, though it was forty times higher for the poorest kids than for the wealthiest. Mike Males, "The Culture War against Kids," May 22, 2001, retrieved May 23, 2001, from AlterNet Web site: www.alternet.org.

15. Tamara Strauss, "Super Predators No More," December 19, 2000, retrieved December 20, 2000, from AlterNet Web site: www.alternet.org.

16. Ibid., citing *Wall Street Journal* poll.

17. Martha Groves, "Making Common Courtesy," *Los Angeles Times,* March 18, 2001.

18. Strauss, "Super Predators."

19. Marjorie Heins and Christina Cho, *Internet Filters: A Public Policy Report* (New York: Free Expression Policy Project, 2001), 55–68.

20. Daniel Silverman, "Censorship High," June 19, 2001, retrieved June 23, 2001, from Salon Web site: www.salon.com.

21. Commission on Child Online Protection, "Final Report of the COPA Commission," October 20, 2000, retrieved January 8, 2001, from www.copacommission.org.

22. Dick Thornburgh and Herbert S. Lin, eds., *Youth, Pornography, and the Internet* (Washington, DC: National Academy Press, 2002).

23. As of May 2001, five censorship cases about independent student speech had gone to court; in only one did the court side with school officials. Student Press Law Center, "SPLC CyberGuide: A Legal Manual for Online Publishers of Independent Student Web Sites," 2001, retrieved July 8, 2001, from www.splc.org.

24. Joshua Robin, "Judge Upholds Student Who Posted Web Parody," *Seattle Times,* July 19, 2000. Also, "Ex-Student Suspended over Web Site Will Get $10,000," *Seattle Times,* February 21, 2001.

25. "Indiana Teachers Sue over Web Site," August 9, 1999, retrieved August 8, 2000, from Freedom Forum Web site: www.freedomforum.org.

26. Student Press Law Center, "SPLC CyberGuide."

27. The Student Press Law Center, which deals primarily with high school publications, noted a 31 percent increase in requests for help from 1999 to 2000. "High School Censorship Calls Soar in 2000," *SPLC Report* 22, no. 3 (2001): 3.

28. In 2000, one-fifth of Internet users worldwide were under fifteen. "Remarks by Henry Jenkins," *Newsletter on Intellectual Freedom* (American Library Association), September 2000, 171. In 2001, 90 percent of fifteen- to twenty-four-year-olds in the United States had gone online. Victoria Rideout, *Generation Rx.com: How Young People Use the Internet for Health Information* (Menlo Park, CA: Kaiser Family Foundation, 2001), 2.

29. Eli Noam, "An Unfettered Internet? Keep Dreaming," *New York Times,* July 11, 1997.

30. Annenberg Public Policy Center, "National Survey Shows Parents Deeply Fearful about the Internet's Influence on Their Children," press release, May 4, 1999.

31. John Schwartz, "Support Is Growing in Congress for Internet Filters in Schools," *New York Times,* October 20, 2000.

32. Rideout, *Generation Rx.com.*

33. J. M. Coetzee, *Giving Offense: Essays on Censorship* (Chicago: University of Chicago Press, 1996), 14.

34. Gary Giddens, *Bing Crosby: A Pocketful of Dreams* (Boston: Little, Brown, 2001), 202–3.

35. Quoted in "What Did Frank Think about Rock and Roll?" retrieved

May 8, 2001, from the Sinatra Archive Web site: www.sinatraarchive.com/tis/opinion.html.

36. Bob Herbert, "In America: A Musical Betrayal," *New York Times,* January 29, 2001.

37. Senate Committee on the Judiciary, *Hearing on Hate Crime on the Internet,* 106th Cong., 1st sess., September 14, 1999.

## CHAPTER ELEVEN. WHAT DO YOU MEAN I CAN'T READ *PLAYBOY?*

1. The setting was a speak-out for working women in Ithaca, New York. Vickie Schultz, "Reconceptualizing Sexual Harassment," *Yale Law Journal* 107 (April 1998): 1699.

2. Dierdre Silverman, "Sexual Harassment: Working Women's Dilemma," *Quest,* winter 1976–77, 15, as quoted in Schultz, "Reconceptualizing Sexual Harassment," 1699.

3. *Harris v Forklift Systems,* 510 U.S. 17 (1993).

4. Women in the Fire Service, "Sexual Harassment in the Fire Service," 2001, retrieved June 30, 2001, from www.wfsi.org.

5. Equal Employment Opportunity Commission, "EEOC Guidelines on Discrimination Because of Sex," 29 C.F.R. 1604.11(a) (1997).

6. According to a former investigator for the EEOC, America's 500 largest companies were losing about $6.7 million per year in absenteeism, low productivity, and turnover resulting from sexual harassment. *Facts on File World News,* November 15, 1995, retrieved June 30, 2001, from www.facts.com/cd/i00007.htm.

7. Women in the Fire Service, unpublished survey, 1995, cited in "Sexual Harassment in the Fire Service," 2001, retrieved June 30, 2001, from www.wfsi.org.

8. Bob Baker, "True Detective," *Los Angeles Times,* January 12, 1992.

9. On average, about one hundred firefighters die on the job and tens of thousands are injured each year. U.S. Fire Administration, "Heart Attack Leading Cause of Death for Firefighters," Press Release No. 02–193, October 23, 2002, retrieved December 13, 2002, from http://www.usfa.fema.gov/dhtml/media/02-193.cfm. In 2001, 343 firefighters died while responding to the World Trade Center collapse on September 11.

10. Ken Ellingwood and Solomon Moore, "All Fired Up," *Los Angeles Times,* April 11, 1997. This was the first year since 1990 that LACoFD accepted applications.

11. Phone conversation with LACoFD media relations officer, June 12, 2001.

12. Terese M. Floren, "Women in Firefighting: A History," 2002, retrieved November 17, 2002, from Women in the Fire Service Web site: www.wfsi.org.

13. Exceptions include San Francisco, Minneapolis, and Miami-Dade County, where women constitute 13 to 16 percent of their fire departments. Douglas Belkin, "Fire Department to Boost Number of Women on Force," *Boston Globe,* March 9, 2002.

14. Rebecca Richardson, "Closing the Gender Gap in Emergency Services, January 18, 2001, retrieved June 30, 2001, from http://firefighting.com. See also

U.S. Department of Labor, "Firefighting Occupations," in *Occupational Outlook Handbook 2002–03* (Washington, DC: U.S. Department of Labor, 2002), 342.

15. Frank B. Williams, " 'Duke' Wayne Fuels Firefighters' Tensions," *Los Angeles Times,* August 1, 1994.

16. Tracey Kaplan, "Female Firefighters Still Face Obstacles," *Los Angeles Times,* August 1, 1994.

17. Ibid.

18. About three-quarters of sexual harassment charges filed with the EEOC between 1992 and 2000 went nowhere, either because of administrative problems or because they were found to be without merit. EEOC, "Sexual Harassment Charges EEOC and FEPAs Combined: FY 1992–FY 2000," retrieved June 3, 2001, from www.eeoc.gov/stats/harass/html.

19. Men lodged 9.1 percent of complaints in 1992 and 13.6 percent in 2000. The EEOC doesn't record the sex of the accused, but in 1998, the Supreme Court ruled in *Oncale v Sundowner Offshore Services,* 523 U.S. 75 (1998), that sexual harassment could involve people of the same sex.

20. The number of sexual harassment lawsuits filed by the EEOC peaked in 1992 at 242. The settlement total peaked in 1997 at $112.3 million. EEOC, "Trends in Harassment Charges Filed with the EEOC during the 1980s and 1990s," retrieved June 3, 2001, from www.eeoc.gov/stats/harass/html.

21. Between 1992 and 2000, while the number of complaints increased 1.5 times, the portion found to have reasonable cause increased 2.6 times and the portion of "unsuccessful conciliations" increased 3.8 times. Ibid.

22. "More Companies Seeking Sexual Harassment Insurance," July 8, 1998, retrieved June 3, 2001, from Feminist Daily News Wire Web site: www.feminist.org/news.

23. In *Robinson v Jacksonville Shipyards,* 760 F. Supp. 1486 (M.D. Fl. 1991), probably the most significant lower court ruling to touch on the subject, a federal court in Florida found in favor of a female welder because she had been singled out as the target of extensive harassment, which included actions as well as speech. The court imposed a remedial policy that prohibited the possession and display of photos of nude women at the shipyard. Ironically, a male coworker who had severely berated the welder denied that he was harassing her because he had not propositioned her for sexual favors.

24. Katha Pollitt, *Reasonable Creatures: Essays on Women and Feminism* (New York: Knopf, 1994), 49.

25. Kaplan, "Female Firefighters."

26. Schultz, "Reconceptualizing Sexual Harassment," 1729–33.

27. The objections stemmed from a 1971 *Playboy* interview with Wayne. Williams, " 'Duke' Wayne."

28. Ibid.

29. Joseph P. Kahn, "Under Fire," *Boston Globe Magazine,* December 7, 1997.

30. *NAACP v Button,* 371 U.S. 415, 438 (1963).

31. *Johnson v County of Los Angeles Fire Department,* 865 F. Supp. 1430 (C.D. Cal. 1994), Declaration of Janet Babcock, January 1994.

32. *Johnson v County of Los Angeles Fire Department,* Declaration of Cynthia Fralick, January 1994.

33. *Johnson v County of Los Angeles Fire Department*, Declaration of Patricia Vaughan, January 1994.

34. Marcia Pally, *Sex and Sensibility: Reflections on Forbidden Mirrors and the Will to Censor* (Metuchen, NJ: Ecco, 1994), 36–39.

35. *Johnson v County of Los Angeles Fire Department*, Opinion by Stephen V. Wilson, U.S. District Court for the Central District of California, October 25, 1994.

## CHAPTER TWELVE. THE PUBLIC TRUST

1. A. J. Liebling, *The Press* (New York: Ballantine, 1961), 30.

2. Home page, Association of Occupational and Environmental Clinics, retrieved November 18, 2002, from www.aoec.org; and "Preventive Medicine Residency Programs," retrieved November 18, 2002, from American College of Preventive Medicine Web site: www.acpm.org.

3. Felice J. Freyer, "Doctor: Hospital Tried to Silence Health-Risk Findings," *Providence Journal*, April 25, 1997.

4. "Embraces TQM," 2002, retrieved November 18, 2002, from Microfibres Web site: www.microfibres.com.

5. Rita Washko, Joe Burkhart, and Chris Piacitelli, *Health Hazard Evaluation Report 96–0093* (Cincinnati, OH: National Institute for Occupational Safety and Health, April 1998), 28.

6. Phone conversation with Dr. Philip J. Landrigan, Chairman, Department of Community and Preventive Medicine, Mt. Sinai Medical Center, August 28, 2001.

7. Adjusted for inflation, NIOSH's total budget was smaller in FY 2000 than in 1980. NIOSH, "Performance Highlights of the National Institute for Occupational Safety and Health 1995–1999," March 31, 2000, retrieved August 21, 2000, from www.cdc.gov/niosh/ooo–134.html.

8. National Science Foundation, "National Expenditures for R&D, by Performing Sector and Sources of Funding: 1993–2001," retrieved July 18, 2001, from www.nsf.gov.

9. PhRMA, "Pharmaceutical Industry Profile 2001," retrieved January 4, 2002, from www.phrma.org/publications.

10. Richard Saltus, "Corporate Gifts Raise Issue of Objectivity," *Boston Globe*, April 1, 1998.

11. Alice Dembner, "Research Integrity Declines," *Boston Globe*, August 22, 2000.

12. Liz Kowalczyk, "New Steps Urged on University Research Bias," *Boston Globe*, February 21, 2001.

13. Lita L. Nelsen, Director, Technology Licensing Office, Massachusetts Institute of Technology, "Now That the Cold War Is Over? Part I: Industry and University Relations" (panel presented at the Secrecy in Science Conference, Cambridge, MA, March 29, 1999).

14. "Research Funding Reaches Record Level," *George Street Journal* 25 (October 27–November 2, 2000): 1.

15. Larry Tye, "Researchers Say Good News Travels Faster," *Boston Globe,* January 28, 1998.

16. Naomi Aoki, "Drug Makers' Influence Pondered," *Boston Globe,* May 31, 2001.

17. In contrast, only 37 percent of authors of critical articles had been funded by the drug's manufacturers. Richard A. Knox, "Study Finds Conflicts in Medical Reports," *Boston Globe,* January 8, 1998.

18. Jeffrey M. Drazen and Gregory D. Curfman, "Financial Associations of Authors," *New England Journal of Medicine* 346 (June 13, 2002): 1901–2.

19. Brown University Faculty Rules and Regulations, Section 10, Part 4, F, October 13, 2000.

20. Eliot Marshall, "Publishing Sensitive Data: Who Calls the Shots?" *Science* 276 (April 25, 1997).

21. Miriam Shuchman, "Secrecy in Science: The Flock," *Annals of Internal Medicine* 129 (August 15, 1998): 341–44.

22. Peter R. Shank, letter to David Kern, November 18, 1996.

23. Francis R. Dietz, memo to constituents of Memorial Hospital, July 10, 1997.

24. Phone conversation with Mark Nickel, Brown University News Service, August 6, 2001.

25. Kim Boekelheide et al., letter to the Faculty Executive Committee, April 21, 1997.

26. Richard Rorty, "Does Academic Freedom Have Philosophical Presuppositions?" *Academe,* November–December 1994, 56.

27. Phone conversation with Janice Vaillancourt, Memorial Hospital grants accountant, August 12, 2001.

28. See, e.g., Richard Deyo et al., "The Messenger under Attack: Intimidation of Researchers by Special-Interest Groups," *New England Journal of Medicine* 335 (April 17, 1997): 1176–80.

29. Steven A. Rosenberg, "Secrecy in Medical Research," *New England Journal of Medicine* 334 (February 8, 1996): 392–94.

30. These incidents include a study of a high blood pressure medicine manufactured by Sandoz, an AIDS drug trial sponsored by Immune Response, and a review of Pharmacia's arthritis drug Celebrex.

31. Drummond Rennie, introducing David Kern, "A Recent Case Study" (paper presented at the Secrecy in Science Conference, Cambridge, MA, March 29, 1999).

32. William S. Beckett, M.D., M.P.H., letter to Vartan Gregorian, May 27, 1997 (author's files).

33. OSHA's Boston office reports that Section 11(c) claimants prevail in about one-quarter of the 230 cases it investigates yearly. Jody McPhillips, "Fired Doctor Files Complaint," *Providence Journal-Bulletin,* July 9, 1997.

34. Washko et al., *Health Hazard Evaluation Report,* iv.

35. Dolores Kong, "Three New Cases Reported of Lung Disease Linked to Textile Mill Work," *Boston Globe,* August 15, 1998.

36. Benjamin DeMott, "Seduced by Civility," *Nation,* December 9, 1996.

## EPILOGUE

1. "Off the Cuff: Q&A with Children Who Have an Artistic Message against Hate," *Boston Globe,* May 18, 1997.

2. Judith Lynne Hanna, "Wrapping Nudity in a Cloak of Law," *New York Times,* July 29, 2001.

3. "Klan Road Named for Rosa Parks," *Detroit Free Press,* May 24, 2000.

4. Douglas Belkin, " 'Lemonade' Puts Squeeze on Pa. Klan," *Boston Globe,* February 1, 1998; Carol Ostrom, "Town Hates Idea of March," *Seattle Times,* July 17, 1998.

5. Carol Morello, "In Va. Town, Free Speech Hits a Wall," *Washington Post,* February 11, 2001; also Carol Morello, "Va. City Allows Test of Free Speech with Giant Chalkboard," *Boston Globe,* March 22, 2001.

# BIBLIOGRAPHY

Amar, Akhil Reed. *The Bill of Rights*. New Haven, CT: Yale University Press, 1998.

Barry, Tom. *Inside Guatemala*. Albuquerque, NM: Inter-Hemispheric Education Resource Center, 1992.

Bawer, Bruce. *Stealing Jesus: How Fundamentalism Betrays Christianity*. New York: Crown, 1997.

Berlin, Isaiah. *Two Concepts of Liberty*. Oxford, England: Clarendon Press, 1958.

Bok, Sissela. *Secrets: On the Ethics of Concealment and Revelation*. New York: Oxford University Press, 1984.

Bolton, Richard, ed. *Culture Wars: Documents from the Recent Controversies in the Arts*. New York: New Press, 1992.

Bork, Robert H. *Slouching towards Gomorrah: Modern Liberalism and American Decline*. New York: Regan, 1996.

Brenson, Michael. *Visionaries and Outcasts: The NEA, Congress, and the Place of the Visual Artist in America*. New York: New Press, 2001.

Brown, David Jay, and Rebecca McCles Novick. *Voices from the Edge*. Freedom, CA: Crossing Press, 1995.

Brugge, Doug, Timothy Benaly, and Phil Harrison. *Memories Come to Us in the Rain and the Wind: Oral Histories and Photographs of Navajo Uranium Miners and Their Families*. Boston: Navajo Uranium Miner Oral History and Photography Project, 1997.

Carr, C. *On Edge: Performance at the End of the Twentieth Century*. Hanover, NH: Wesleyan University Press, 1993.

Carter, Angela. *The Sadeian Woman and the Ideology of Pornography*. New York: Harper and Row, 1978.

Coetzee, J. M. *Giving Offense: Essays on Censorship*. Chicago: University of Chicago Press, 1996.

Commission on Protecting and Reducing Government Secrecy. *Report of the Commission on Protecting and Reducing Government Secrecy*. Washington, DC: Government Printing Office, 1997.

Curry, Richard O., ed. *Freedom at Risk: Secrecy, Censorship, and Repression in the 1980's*. Philadelphia: Temple University Press, 1988.

D, Chuck. *Fight the Power*. New York: Delta, 1997.

deGrazia, Edward. *Girls Lean Back Everywhere: The Law of Obscenity and the Assault on Genius*. New York: Random House, 1992.

Delacoste, Frédérique, and Priscilla Alexander, eds. *Sex Work: Writings by Women in the Sex Industry*. San Francisco: Cleis Press, 1968.

Demac, Donna. *State of the First Amendment*. Arlington, VA: Freedom Forum, 1997.

Douglas, Lawrence. "The Force of Words: Fish, Matsuda, MacKinnon and the Theory of Discursive Violence." *Law and Society Review* 29, no. 1 (1995): 169–90.

Duggan, Lisa, and Nan D. Hunter. *Sex Wars: Sexual Dissent and Political Culture*. New York: Routledge, 1995.

Dworkin, Ronald. *Freedom's Law: The Moral Reading of the American Constitution*. Cambridge, MA: Harvard University Press, 1996.

Emerson, Thomas I. *Toward a General Theory of the First Amendment*. New York: Random House, 1966.

Fernandez, Ronald. *The Disenchanted Island: Puerto Rico and the United States in the Twentieth Century*. 2d ed. Westport, CT: Praeger, 1996.

———. *Los Macheteros: The Wells Fargo Robbery and the Violent Struggle for Puerto Rican Independence*. New York: Prentice Hall, 1987.

*Field Manual of the Free Militia*. Great Barrington, MA: Riverwalk Press, 1996.

First Amendment Center. *State of the First Amendment 2001*. Nashville, TN: FAC, 2001. Also available online from Freedom Forum Web site: www. freedomforum.org/templates/document.asp?documentID=14295.

———. *State of the First Amendment 2002*. Nashville, TN: FAC, 2002. Also available online from Freedom Forum Web site: www.freedomforum.org/templates/document.asp?documentID=16840.

Fiss, Owen. *The Irony of Free Speech*. Cambridge, MA: Harvard University Press, 1996.

Gates, Henry Louis, Jr., et al. *Speaking of Race, Speaking of Sex: Hate Speech, Civil Rights and Civil Liberties*. New York: NYU Press, 1994.

Glick, Brian. *War at Home: Covert Action against U.S. Activists and What We Can Do about It*. Boston: South End Press, 1989.

Godwin, Mike. *Cyber Rights: Defending Free Speech in the Digital Age*. New York: Times Books, 1998.

Gordimer, Nadine. *Writing and Being*. Cambridge, MA: Harvard University Press, 1995.

Green, Jonathan. *The Encyclopedia of Censorship*. New York: Facts on File, 1990.

Harbury, Jennifer K. *Searching for Everardo*. New York: Warner, 1997.

Heidenry, John. *What Wild Ecstasy: The Rise and Fall of the Sexual Revolution.* New York: Simon and Schuster, 1997.

Heins, Marjorie. *Not in Front of the Children.* New York: Hill and Wang, 2001.

———. *Sex, Sin, and Blasphemy.* New York: New Press, 1993.

Hentoff, Nat. *Free Speech for Me—But Not for Thee: How the American Left and Right Relentlessly Censor Each Other.* New York: HarperCollins, 1992.

Kalven, Harry, Jr. *A Worthy Tradition: Freedom of Speech in America.* New York: Harper and Row, 1988.

Kaminer, Wendy. *Free for All: Defending Liberty in America Today.* Boston: Beacon Press, 2002.

Kendrick, Walter. *The Secret Museum: Pornography in Modern Culture.* Berkeley: University of California Press, 1987.

Kohn, Stephen M. *Jailed for Peace: The History of American Draft Law Violators, 1658–1985.* Westport, CT: Greenwood Press, 1986.

Kovach, Bill, and Tom Rosensteil. *The Elements of Journalism.* New York: Crown, 2001.

Langley, Erika. *The Lusty Lady.* New York: Scalo, 1997.

Liebling, A. J. *The Press.* New York: Ballantine, 1961.

Linfield, Michael. *Freedom under Fire: U.S. Civil Liberties in Times of War.* Boston: South End Press, 1990.

MacKinnon, Catharine A. *Only Words.* Cambridge, MA: Harvard University Press, 1993.

MacKinnon, Catharine A., and Andrea Dworkin. *In Harm's Way: The Pornography Civil Rights Hearings.* Cambridge, MA: Harvard University Press, 1997.

Matsuda, Mari J., et al. *Words That Wound: Critical Race Theory, Assaultive Speech, and the First Amendment.* Boulder, CO: Westview Press, 1993.

McElroy, Wendy. *XXX: A Woman's Right to Pornography.* New York: St. Martin's Press, 1995.

Menchú, Rigoberta. *I, Rigoberta Menchú.* Edited by Elisabeth Burgos-Debray and translated by Ann Wright. London: Verso, 1983.

Mill, John Stuart. *On Liberty and Utilitarianism.* New York: Bantam, 1993.

Nuccio, Richard A. *What's Wrong, Who's Right in Central America.* New York: Facts on File, 1986.

Nyberg, Amy Kiste. *Seal of Approval: The History of the Comics Code.* Jackson: University Press of Mississippi, 1998.

Pally, Marcia. *Sex and Sensibility: Reflections on Forbidden Mirrors and the Will to Censor.* Metuchen, NJ: Ecco, 1994.

Patai, Daphne. "There Ought to Be a Law." *William Mitchell Law Review* 22, no. 2 (1996): 491–516.

People for the American Way. *Artistic Freedom under Attack.* 3d ed. Washington, DC: PFAW, 1995.

———. *Artistic Freedom under Attack.* 4th ed. Washington, DC: PFAW, 1996.

———. *Attacks on the Freedom to Learn: 1993–1994.* Washington, DC: PFAW, 1994.

———. *Attacks on the Freedom to Learn: 1994–1995.* Washington, DC: PFAW, 1995.

————. *Attacks on the Freedom to Learn: 1996 Report*. Washington, DC: PFAW, 1996.

Perera, Victor. *Unfinished Conquest: The Guatemalan Tragedy*. Berkeley: University of California Press, 1993.

Peter, Jennifer A., and Louis M. Crosier. *The Cultural Battlefield: Art Censorship and Public Funding*. Gilsum, NH: Avocus Publishing, 1995.

Phillips, Susan A. *Wallbangin': Graffiti and Gangs in L.A.* Chicago: University of Chicago Press, 1999.

Pollitt, Katha. *Reasonable Creatures: Essays on Women and Feminism*. New York: Knopf, 1994.

Porteous, Skipp. *Jesus Doesn't Live Here Anymore: From Fundamentalist to Freedom Writer*. Buffalo, NY: Prometheus Books, 1991.

Randall, Margaret. *Coming Home: Peace without Complacency*. Albuquerque, NM: West End Press, 1990.

Rembar, Charles. *The End of Obscenity*. New York: Random House, 1968.

Sánchez, Daisy. *Cita con la injusticia*. Puerto Rico: Editorial DG, 1996.

Schultz, Vicki. "Reconceptualizing Sexual Harassment." *Yale Law Journal* 107 (1998): 1683, 1774–89.

Shattuck, Roger. *Forbidden Knowledge: From Prometheus to Pornography*. New York: St. Martin's Press, 1996.

Sprinkle, Annie. *Post-Porn Modernist: My 25 Years as Multimedia Whore*. San Francisco: Cleis Press, 1988.

Steiner, Wendy. *The Scandal of Pleasure: Art in an Age of Fundamentalism*. Chicago: University of Chicago Press, 1995.

Strossen, Nadine. *Defending Pornography: Free Speech, Sex, and the Fight for Women's Rights*. New York: Scribner, 1995.

Sunderland, Lane V. *Obscenity: The Court, the Congress and the President's Commission*. Washington, DC: American Enterprise Institute, 1975.

Tax, Meredith, et al. *The Power of the Word: Culture, Censorship, and Voice*. New York: Women's WORLD, 1995.

Thompson, Kenneth. *Moral Panics*. New York: Routledge, 1998.

Trudeau, Robert H. *Guatemalan Politics: The Popular Struggle for Democracy*. Boulder, CO: Lynne Rienner Publishers, 1993.

Vaculík, Ludvik. *A Cup of Coffee with My Interrogator*. Translated by George Theiner. London: Reader International, 1987.

Vance, Carol, ed. *Pleasure and Danger: Exploring Female Sexuality*. London: Pandora, 1992.

Wagman, Robert J. *The First Amendment Book*. New York: Pharos, 1991.

Wertham, Fredric. *Seduction of the Innocent*. New York: Rinehart, 1954.

Williams, Linda. *Hard Core: Power, Pleasure and the Frenzy of the Visible*. Berkeley: University of California Press, 1989.

Wypijewski, Joanne, ed. *Painting by Numbers: Komar and Melamid's Scientific Guide to Art*. Berkeley: University of California Press, 1999.

# INDEX

Text:        10/13 Sabon
Display:     Sabon
Indexer:     Andrew Christenson
Compositor:  Binghamton Valley Composition, LLC
Printer:     Maple-Vail Manufacturing Group